Gittings

REUBEN

FLEET

and

The Story of CONSOLIDATED AIRCRAFT

To HAZEL - and to all the other wives, especially Gladys (Ryan) and Eve (Fleet) - who for decades have tolerated the devotion of their husbands to a second love - Aviation.

REUBEN FLEET

FLEET

and The Story of
CONSOLIDATED AIRCRAFT

By William Wagner

AERO PUBLISHERS, INC.
329 West Aviation Road, Fallbrook, CA 92028

Library of Congress Cataloging in Publication Data

Wagner, William, 1909-
    Reuben Fleet : and the story of Consolidated Aircraft.

    Includes indexes.
    1. Fleet, Reuben Hollis. 2. Consolidated Aircraft
Corporation.   3. Aeronautics—United
States—History.
TL540.F53W33   629.13'092'4 [B]   75-32727
ISBN 0-8168-7950-8

Printed and Published in the United States by Aero Publishers, Inc.

CONTENTS

CONSOLIDATED INDEX

GENERAL INDEX

PREVIEW

A̲T NINE O'CLOCK ONE MORNING recently, Major Reuben Hollis Fleet pulled on his swim trunks and strode determinedly from his bedroom down to the heated swimming pool just below his huge Spanish home on a hilltop overlooking San Diego Bay.

As he had almost every morning for the past quarter century, he was about to swim 36 lengths of the pool—a third of a mile. And he was about to time himself as he did it. The time was important to him.

In recent years his time for the distance had almost always been about 25 minutes. But in the past few weeks it had been 30 or 31 minutes because of a shoulder bruise from which he was recovering. This morning he was determined to speed up the time.

Major Fleet seldom fails to accomplish a goal he sets for himself. He swam his 36 laps in less than 29 minutes. Having thus satisfactorily begun his day, he took a quick shower and hurried on to confront the other goals on his agenda for that day. At the age of 87, he considered that he had little time to waste.

Attired in harmonious but sober brown slacks and sweater, he breakfasted leisurely, to be joined briefly by his vivacious wife Eve, whom he married when he was 60. Having finished the morning paper, he then marched into his double-sized office just beyond the large living room. He assumed that telephone messages must have been accumulating there during the past hour.

One end of the office was occupied by his desk and appurtenances. The morning's mail and customary stack of phone-message slips awaited him. At the other end of the room, his long-time financial assistant, Russ Stanberry, and his secretary, Martha Green, were at their desks. The Major greeted them jovially and got to work.

His posture at the desk became curiously hunched for a man with the erect bearing acquired in boyhood at a private military school—and fixed even more stiffly during six years as an Air Service officer. He was bent over because he was reading the mail, for he still refuses to wear eyeglasses, considering them undignified and unsoldierly.

Reuben and Eve Fleet, Fall 1974, on the terrace of their 'Spanish castle' overlooking his beloved San Diego where he learned to fly in 1917 and to which he brought his Consolidated Aircraft Corporation in 1935.

Photo by Ted Lau

Having ascertained that the mail contained nothing requiring instant action, and that the long distance phone messages likewise did not seem crucial, the Major picked up his phone and soon was talking authoritatively. His first-priority objective on this particular morning was to arrange for round-the-clock nursing care for a former business associate whose life seemed to be nearing its end.

Rather than a once or twice a week drive at the wheel of his Cadillac to downtown San Diego where he meets business friends or perhaps joins an old Air Force comrade for lunch, this would be a full day of "office" routine.

While his week is varied to include occasional out of town trips, perhaps to Los Angeles for an evening of camaraderie and reminiscense with pioneering fliers, the priorities have now been directed to "advanced planning" much like any other business executive.

Now, with mail, phone calls, daily stock market reports and decisions out of the way, the pioneer aircraft industrialist settles down after lunch to the serious study of current economic and political matters.

These are affairs he likes to share with others, an interest that in this case prompts him to include Martha. "Step over here, Martha, and let me show you on this map what I've just learned," he gestures, his index finger tracing a snake-like path southward on a map of Canada.

"Now, you can see, the pipeline is going to follow this valley for nearly a hundred miles. This natural gas project ought to work to the company's advantage," he reasons aloud, noting that some additional stock for one of the trusts might be advisable.

"Let's get Phil Neary [his stockbroker] on the phone," adds the Major, a crisp note of conclusion punctuating the request.

Reuben's arms now rest on the desk top and he leans forward heavily, a steady gaze falling on the neat stacks of charts and statistics compiled for him and to which he turns constantly as a source of references. Each project studied is part of a larger plan, demanding comprehensive knowledge and familiarity. Only when armed with all the facts does the Major make his financial and political decisions.

All his life Reuben Fleet has been an unabashed patriot. He believes in the basic virtues which made his beloved country great—self reliance, personal integrity, respect for truth, devotion to duty, thrift, belief in God, living within one's means, love of country. Too, the Major has always been a staunch advocate of free enterprise, coupled with minimum government interference and less burdensome taxation.

His most intimate friends and associates well know the Major's unquenchable drive for business facts and his not infrequent outbursts of a temper, now somewhat subdued by the passing of the years. Nothing, they know, arises his wrath to quite the extent as does income tax.

One typical outburst attended a visit from an Internal Revenue Service agent checking a recent tax return. After lengthy discussion, the mood of patient indulgence the Major had displayed changed swiftly once an incorrect conclusion on the agent's part was exposed.

A huge, tightly clenched fist smashed down on the table top as a stabbing finger directed the agent's route of departure with the admonition to recheck his figures and confront his adversary another day.

During the foregoing negotiations Major Fleet was quite aware of comporting himself like a four-star general—as usual. "I am an autocrat . . . and guess I always have been," allows Reuben Fleet, a tiny smile tugging at the corner of his mouth as he raises his hands locked together behind a thin thatch of now white hair.

Fleet's career would seem to indicate that he also possesses other attributes of the better generals. For example, generals usually are aware that whom they know can be as important as what they know. Reuben Fleet found ways from early manhood on to cultivate the friendship of bankers, captains of industry, government bigwigs, Wall Street operators and military chieftains.

Those in the latter categories were particularly important to him when he determined to become an aircraft manufacturer in the years shortly after the end of the first World War.

Military budgets were shrinking at that time toward the vanishing point. It was not an auspicious period in which to build military aircraft or start a new company. Nevertheless, instead of digging in prudently, Major Fleet advanced, with boldness worthy of Caesar or Napoleon.

In 1923 he acquired the most useful assets of not one but two aircraft builders, both of whom were on their last legs financially. Swollen, wartime demands had shrunk in peacetime to virtually nothing.

Consolidating the remnants of the Dayton-Wright Company (which had been the largest wartime plane manufacturer) and Gallaudet Aircraft Corporation (which had been one of the smallest) he gave his new enterprise the logical, if perhaps colorless, name of Consolidated Aircraft Corporation.

Its technical and financial feats during the next two decades were considered monumental. And, "Reub" Fleet became a legendary figure among aircraft manufacturers. Repeatedly, he startled his peers with unconventional solutions to problems that seemed likely to engulf him in red ink.

One such problem arose when he won a design competition for a new military plane, only to see someone else underbid him on producing his own design, so that he was left holding the bag for half a million dollars in development costs. It occurred to him that a civilian version of his plane might sell to commercial customers.

Failing to find any interested customers, he created one. He started an airline which would use the planes. This enabled him to build and sell two million dollars worth of planes at a profit, and then trade his interest in the airline for enough stock in a rival line to finance all of his charitable gifts for a decade!

Eventually Consolidated became the world leader in training planes, built seaplanes in larger numbers than all other flying boats combined and produced more bombers for World War II than any other American aircraft manufacturer.

In 1941, six years after moving his plant from Buffalo to San Diego—in one of the largest industrial relocations in history—Fleet sold his interest in the corporation he had founded 18 years earlier for ten million dollars.

Instead of subsiding at the age of 54 into a life of peaceful affluence—which would not have fit the character of Reuben Fleet—he plunged into myriad community projects, government matters and long neglected personal tasks. Among his early endeavors was San Diego's metropolitan sewer system, and service as an advisor on aviation matters to President Roosevelt and the Defense Department. He also continued to speak out often and forcefully on national issues involving defense, free enterprise, fiscal responsibility and labor unions.

And beyond all of these involvements, there was a third family to raise, a responsibility that further nourished his self-appointed role as investment counsellor to supervise trusts and funds he had established for his children and grandchildren, as well as for his former wives.

Patriarch of the Fleet clan, Reuben is the father of two sons and six daughters—offspring of his three wives, all of whom are living. There are also ten grandchildren and five great-grandchildren.

By sheer strength of character, the Major has served through the years and still prevails as the nucleus around which all the Fleet family orbits. Despite their different heritages, all share a common, almost awesome respect for the strong, venerable and now gentle man.

From October to May each year, Reuben and Eve lived in their Palm Springs winter home that also doubled as a second office. There, at a desk opposite his, Eve resumed the role with which she became so familiar as his secretary for years.

Phone lines between the desert and the Spanish hillside home in San Diego stayed busy daily with continuing contacts with Martha and Russ, who kept the base office moving with usual competence.

Not unlike many businessmen, the Major prefers the company of family members or a small group of friends to large social gatherings or civic events, though the social prominence of Reuben Fleet in San Diego life is kept alive by occasions appropriate for his and Eve's participation.

Typically, an evening out might include an International Aerospace Hall of Fame banquet where new inductees will join Major Fleet in the ranks of the venerated. Among those selected on a recent occasion were now deceased Admiral John Towers, an old friend, and in the audience were his fellow Hall of Fame pioneers and friends, Grover C. Loening and T. Claude Ryan, another San Diegan.

Seated at two tables in the front of the banquet hall were members of the Fleet family from the three marriages, ample testimony to Fleet's great love for his family as well as his regard for community involvement.

There always has been a first-contact quality about Reuben Fleet that drills the impression into memory. Tall, erect, proud, he is obviously self-confident. Blue eyes sparkling, his very presence dominates the room. Without uttering a word, his magnetism energizes the atmosphere with a quality of compelling charm.

Those who have known him most intimately in business and personal life draw on a score of contradictory adjectives to describe a man who has long been a legend in his own time. He is in turn abrasive...considerate...egocentric...compassionate...domineering...thoughtful...hot-tempered.

The list goes on and on—impatient...sensitive...blunt ...irascible...sentimental...stubborn...boring...emotional...shrewd...self-righteous ...courtly.

Major Reuben Hollis Fleet was and is all of these, and more, though he looms less awesome than in his younger years. Yet the gripping respect his presence commands is always there. The fierce pride still glints from his clear gaze and the qualities of leadership exemplified in his career continue to mark his life with distinction.

The personality is complex, but two characteristics stand out—absolute integrity, and love of country.

Nor does he ever forget the heritage of the English ancestry which from childhood he was expected to emulate. His upbringing brought out the best traits of his positive, can-do approach to life and business. In industry, he expected of others the same devotion to duty and principle which have been the hallmarks of his own career.

One of those most knowledgeable had this observation: "Fleet is a dynamic person; one never forgets him. He is restless, untiring; one whose nature demands activity; a man made for accomplishment and success. Failure is a word he does not recognize; a fight cannot last long enough to exhaust him; he is victorious a goodly portion of the time because of his will to win. He overpowers his adversary by his sheer force of will, and wears him out with his insistence."

That evaluation of the then 42-year-old head of Consolidated Aircraft was offered six years after he entered the aircraft manufacturing industry.

It could just as well have been offered 46 years later, in early 1975. The description still fits the man.

WILLIAM WAGNER

March 1975
San Diego, California

Like the good soldier he was, Major Reuben Hollis Fleet stood proud, erect and active to the end of a long and distinguished career. The pioneer airman passed away October 29, 1975, at the age of 88 years.

xi

BOOK I

"TESTING MYSELF AGAINST THE BEST"

1922 - 1928

General Dynamics/Convair

NEW COMPANY, New Plane. *Consolidated unveils PT-1 tandem trainer. From left, George Newman, factory manager; Ray Whitman, chief inspector; Thomas Kenny, treasurer; Col. V. E. Clark, chief engineer;* *Wolfe (later commanding general Air Materiel Command); Lieut. Carl A. Cover (later chief test pilot-vice president Douglas Aircraft Company); and Major Ralph Royce, commanding officer Brooks Field (later WW II*

"TESTING MYSELF
AGAINST THE BEST"

IT WAS NOVEMBER 30, 1922 when 35-year-old Major Reuben Hollis Fleet, having completed nearly four years as Contracting Officer and business manager of the Air Service Engineering Division at McCook Field, Dayton, Ohio, decided on a third career—a return to business, this time as an aircraft manufacturer.

When Major Gen. Charles T. Menoher, Director of the Army Air Service, had asked Fleet to stay on after the Armistice of November 1918 the Major had done so with the understanding he would be given the task of developing a new training plane for the Army. It was a task for which he felt particularly suited and in which he had a great interest. But conditions at McCook Field were so bad that Reuben spent nearly his entire assignment there straightening out its contracts and placing Army procurement at the 2300-man facility on a sound business basis.

Because of his long association with major aircraft builders, Fleet was not lacking for offers once his decision to leave the service became known.

"Along with Col. Thurman H. Bane, Commanding Officer of McCook Field, and Major George E. A. Hallett, Chief of the power plant section," Fleet recalls, "I resigned the Air Service on Thanksgiving Day. I was immediately offered three jobs.

"Clement M. Keys was president of Curtiss Aeroplane and Motor Co. and he offered me $15,000 a year just to advise him on aviation matters. Born in Canada, he was a New York financial writer and editor turned investment banker who had risen to the top of the highly regarded Curtiss organization. He said I wouldn't have to run a factory or anything like that, just be his advisor.

"Boeing Airplane Company out in Seattle—I'd lived nearby until I was thirty—offered me $10,000 a year to become Vice President and General Manager. I'd known William E. (Bill) Boeing earlier when he was in the lumber business, as I was, around Grays Harbor, Washington, and it was hard to turn the offer down as it would have brought me back to the area where I grew up and started in business.

"The third offer, which I accepted, came from Gallaudet Aircraft Corporation. It's a name which is hardly known today, but was well regarded in 1922 for the many engineering innovations of its founder, Edson Fessenden Gallaudet."

A fellow officer recalls an informal farewell dinner at McCook Field for Major Fleet at which Reuben said he was going out and make a million dollars.

"He even offered to make bets on it," the now retired Air Force General told us. "I never saw a man who got greater pleasure out of business activities than Reuben. Striving for success was not just a matter of dollars with him; rather it was the feeling of accomplishment which the dollars came to represent.

"He was dynamic in everything he did. Reuben had a great mind and terrific energy. Time meant nothing. His most inspired ideas often came in the middle of the night. And always he would act immediately to bring his ideas to fruition."

This is the story of how Reuben Fleet drove himself to the top of the aircraft industry—and how others came to follow his dynamic leadership.

As a young Yale physics professor, Edson Gallaudet was a very creative engineer with concepts which, for that day, were very advanced and so 'far out' as to be considered impractical. Before the turn of the century he was working with model kites to demonstrate his then radical theory of warping an airplane wing to achieve lateral control. In this he was ahead of the Wright Brothers, but did not follow through.

By 1908 Gallaudet had opened an engineering office in Norwich, Connecticut, and incorporated the Gallaudet Engineering Company in 1910 to build airplanes. Two years later he learned to fly at the Wright School where he secured Aero Club of America pilot's license No. 32, then went overseas where he obtained pilot's license No. 706 from the Aero Club of France.

With his brother Denison as a partner, he began to build planes and in 1912 they exhibited the A-1 'Bullet', a stubby low-wing monoplane, at New York City's first Aero Show. Gallaudet claimed a speed of 130 m.p.h. for his new plane, well above that achieved several years later even by World War I combat planes.

While piloting the 'Bullet'—which had a rotary engine in the nose to drive the pusher propeller behind the tail—Gallaudet had an accident which ended his flying career but did not stem his enthusiasm and creative design ideas.

His 1916 twin-engine Navy seaplane, the D-1, used another unique propulsion arrangement, the 'Gallaudet Drive.' Its radical feature was a four-bladed propeller mounted in the center of the fuselage aft of

the wings and forward of the tail. The propeller hub section was enclosed in a metal ring the same diameter as the circular fuselage, allowing only the most efficient portion of each blade to revolve in the airstream.

Navy acceptance tests of the D-1 were performed at Pensacola, Florida, in January 1917, with Lt. (j.g.) Marc A. Mitscher as one of the Board of Inspection. Performance of the plane was unsatisfactory but the 'Gallaudet Drive' mid-fuselage pusher propeller concept was accepted. Other D-series planes followed, all on an experimental basis.

The D-1 project, for which the company had a $15,000 Navy contract, actually cost over $40,000 and resulted in reorganization as the Gallaudet Aircraft Corporation with stock control passing from the founders' hands. Under tutelage of George M. Pynchon of the New York brokerage firm of Raymond, Pynchon & Co., railroad executives W. A. Harriman and Frederick F. Brewster, and other prominent New York business men, joined the board of directors. One of these was John Kelly Robinson, Jr., president of the Ox Fibre Brush Company, who took over day-to-day management of Gallaudet. His father was the inventor of the sulphur match and had organized the Diamond Match Company.

When the United States entered World War I in April 1917, only five American firms had produced ten or more aircraft in their history. Gallaudet was not one of them but private capital saw the potential for military plane orders and additional backing was obtained from Wall Street interests headed by Harry Payne Whitney.

A large new factory was opened in May in East Greenwich, Rhode Island. A single box car moved all the factory equipment from Norwich.

Smithsonian Institution

MID-FUSELAGE propeller of "Gallaudet Drive" power system was tested in early seaplane.

POTENTIAL for military orders led Gallaudet management to open new factory in East Greenwich, Rhode Island in 1917.

Small orders for Gallaudet experimental planes and radical power plants followed, but it was not until a contract was received in January 1918 from the Navy for 60 Curtiss HS-2 pontoon-equipped biplanes that production reached any significant quantity.

After the war Gallaudet tried unsuccessfully to market several private plane designs including the two-place 'Flyabout' sport monoplane and the five-place Liberty Tourist. On the drawing boards was the 16-passenger D-14 twin engine Liberty Passenger and Express Monoplane. But conversion of wartime DeHavilland DH-4 biplanes were about the only contracts available for any of the aircraft companies and Gallaudet got a share of this work.

The company's design ideas were often revolutionary but seldom successful. Among them were all-metal fighter and bomber planes, and a multi-engined power unit of three 400 h.p. Liberty engines driving a single propeller. The nacelle was so large space could be provided aft of the engines for a mechanic to make repairs in flight. Three units—a total of nine engines—were to be used in a huge Navy triplane flying boat, the 'Pacific.'

Three Army Air Service contracts, each for only experimental quantities of new designs were obtained by Gallaudet from 1920 to 1922 and had been negotiated with McCook Field while Major Fleet was Contracting Officer.

The CO-1 corps observation plane was the first all-metal plane in the United States. Covered with corrugated aluminum alloy it was a high-wing monoplane of 56-foot span, designed in 1921 by the Engineering Division's principal designer, Isaac Machlin Laddon. Power was supplied by a single 420 h.p. Liberty water-cooled engine.

Three Gallaudet PW-4 (pursuit, water cooled) metal biplanes were ordered in 1921. Of 30-foot span, and powered by a 350 h.p. Packard engine, the plane featured steel wing spars covered by dural skin and a fuselage of dural sheet stock riveted over metal structure.

Largest of the new Gallaudet military planes, with a 67-foot span, was the DB-1 day bomber contracted for in December 1920. It had this country's first welded fuselage. Designed for 140 m.p.h. speed, the low-wing monoplane had the Engineering Division's own 700 h.p. "W" engine as its power plant. Design of the internally-braced full-cantilever monoplane had been influenced by similar German aircraft.

NEW DESIGNS built by Gallaudet included CO-1 observation (above), DB-1 bomber (center) and PW-4 pursuit (below).

By late 1922, the company was not only in serious financial straits but also in technical difficulty with all three of its Air Service military plane contracts. The company's founder and somewhat impractical design genius, Edson Gallaudet, resigned and went into business for himself—making waterproof tennis racquet strings. The situation was critical.

At McCook Field, Major Fleet had come to know the situation at Gallaudet through the contracts he administered. Under the circumstances, Gallaudet Aircraft hardly seemed the vehicle for Major Fleet to launch a new career in aviation, but, as always, Reuben saw more than meets the eye.

"Kelly Robinson, president, and Harry Payne Whitney, the New York multi-millionaire investment banker who was helping out on financing, contacted me and asked me to join the Gallaudet company as Vice President and General Manager," Fleet related.

"They asked what salary I wanted, and I said I thought $10,000 a year would be enough.

" 'How long a contract?' they asked.

" 'I don't want a contract,' was my reply. 'If I'm not the right man you don't want to be saddled with me. And if I'm the right man, I won't need a contract to hold my job.'

"So, of the three offers, I selected the one from Gallaudet.

"I looked forward to testing myself against the best business brains on the east coast, for among the stockholders were reportedly 300 prominent Wall Streeters. I wanted to make the acquaintance of the men who embraced the wealth of the country; to see if I could hold my own in business with them because they were the top business figures in New York and, many thought, really ran the United States.

"I'd told Whitney and Robinson that I wanted three months to study the company and its future potential. It didn't take long to find out in what deep trouble they were. When I got into it I discovered, to my surprise and to my chagrin, that they had lost over $3 million. They still didn't have anything worthy of perpetuity and they expected me as their manager to pay their debts out of earnings. That just wasn't possible.

"In making my report I said that except for two small commercial products they manufactured, which were then accounting for half the sales volume, the rest of the company—the aircraft business, including buildings—was, in my opinion, hardly worth $100,000. That is, if they could get it.

"Whitney, who was presiding, said, 'Major Fleet, isn't that if-you-can-get-it reference just a slang expression?'

" 'No, I don't think so,' I replied. 'If I had said "try and get it" that would have been a slang expression. What I said was "it's worth $100,000 if you can get it."

I can't see anything slang about it. You know that without asking.'

"Thoroughly startled, Whitney turned to the others saying, 'Gentlemen, this is the first honest report we have ever had. We might just as well have put the three million dollars that we invested in this company in the toilet and pulled the chain as far as any accomplishment is concerned.'"

Fleet went on to explain. "Edson Gallaudet was a fine but impractical man. As a graduate of Yale and stroke of the crew, he was very popular with these gentlemen, most of whom were also from Yale, though some had graduated from Harvard and other Ivy League schools.

*Edson
Fessenden
Gallaudet*

Yale University

"He would tackle any job offered him by the Air Force—jobs that no one else would do—jobs with so many unknowns that if any one went wrong it would spoil the whole effort. The man doesn't live who can hit it right all the time. He had several such contracts and his business partners were anxious to get somebody they thought could manage them to completion. So they offered me the job.

"Gallaudet and his backers had parted company before I ever got there because he was hopeless and in a sense helpless. When I took over I quickly put as many of Gallaudet's contracts to sleep as I could, at the same time negotiating two or three new deals.

"The all-metal DB-1 day bomber was a good example of a bad design decision. At that time the game hadn't gotten to the point where an internally braced full cantilever low wing could make a go of it, although Edson and Joseph M. (Joe) Gwinn, Jr., his assistant, approached it to a certain extent in their design.

"Nobody had yet invented a steel trussed wing covered with fabric, and I had no confidence in it. We finished one plane up, sent it to the Engineering Division for flight tests, which finally came off in August 1923, and got the Government to cancel the balance of the contract because the DB-1's flight characteristics made it extremely dangerous.

"Lieut. James H. (Jimmy) Doolittle flew the DB-1 day bomber but had no confidence in it, nor did the Engineering Division. I told Major Gen. Mason M.

Patrick, then Chief of the Army Air Service, to fly it a few times and then put it in a museum."

Similarly two of the three PW-4s were cancelled. Later Mac Laddon also conceded that the all-metal CO-1 he designed "was not a good airplane because I had messed up the air flow over the fuselage so that the plane had very poor performance."

One of the first new jobs Fleet took as manager of Gallaudet was to convert 50 DHs into a version that didn't have the fuel tank between the pilot and the observer. That was the way these "flying coffins" had been built by the Dayton-Wright Company, and the Air Service had hundreds of them stored in Texas in overseas shipping crates. They offered nearly every company in the post-war aircraft industry 50 airplanes each to convert, and distributed the work around among the various companies the government wanted to keep alive.

"Because the other companies had known me through the Contracting Office at McCook," Reuben explained, "I more or less planned the DH operation for all of us.

"I hired a ship to leave Houston with all of the crated planes that were to come to the eastern seaboard. When it docked in New York harbor we distributed the 350 DHs to the seven companies that were going to modify the fuselages to meet the Army requirement, which was principally to relocate the fuel tank. There was the Aeromarine Plane and Motor Corporation headed by Inglis M. Uppercu, the Cadillac dealer in New York City. There was the Witteman Lewis Aircraft Company, mostly owned by Lorillard Spencer, and there was the Curtiss Company at

PW-4 Pursuit being assembled in Gallaudet factory. Major Fleet 'put the contract to sleep.'

Garden City and L.W.F. Engineering at College Point, L.I. and a number of others.

"We saved an immense amount in freight charges by having these planes all come together to New York City in a consolidated shipment. We had all the wings shipped to Dayton. There was no change in the wings anyway and we had them sent to Al Johnson who was running the Johnson Supply Mfg. Company in Dayton. When we finished the fuselages we shipped them to him. He assembled the planes and the Army took over. Since there were so many of these DHs down in Texas the Army loaded an extra one or two for every contractor—so that if he found on opening the original crate that a particular plane had been damaged and wasn't worth repairing he would still have his 50."

Seeing nothing really promising in the way of plane designs at Gallaudet, yet wanting to get into production of aircraft, Major Fleet looked around for other opportunities, particularly in the training plane field in which he had long been interested.

The automobile companies which helped produce planes in wartime were finding things quite different in peacetime. Perhaps there would be an opportunity to pick up something of value from one of the companies about to retire from the aircraft industry.

Fleet was already familiar with the Dayton-Wright Airplane Company because it had been a neighbor during his days at McCook Field. Its $31.5 million in sales made it the largest U.S. manufacturer of military planes during the recent world war. The company had produced 3506 planes, including 3098 British-designed DeHavilland DH-4 reconnaissance bombers, out of a total of 13,511 aircraft built by more than two dozen firms between April 7, 1917 and November 1, 1919.

The Dayton-Wright organization had gotten its start in 1916, as explained by Harold E. Talbott, Jr., its president, who 37 years later became the second Secretary of the Air Force:

"My father, Colonel H. E. Talbott, who was an industrialist, together with Charles F. Kettering, the inventor, and E. A. Deeds decided to form the Dayton-Wright Company with Orville Wright (as consulting engineer) to rehabilitate him and to give him the facilities to carry on some development. I was made President of this small company.

"We built a wind tunnel and laboratory for Orville Wright, two hangars, a small machine shop, and a woodworking shop on Deeds Field near Mr. Deeds' home in Dayton.

"We built a couple of planes and had an organization of perhaps 100 people when the war broke out in 1917."

Three days later, April 9, 1917, the enterprise, now

Aircraft Year Book

TOP BRASS of Dayton-Wright. From top, Colonel H. E. Talbott, inventor Charles F. Kettering, and Harold E. Talbott, Jr.

backed by Detroit auto interests, was reincorporated as the Dayton-Wright Airplane Company.

Deeds, later head of the National Cash Register Company, withdrew from Dayton-Wright to serve on the Aircraft Production Board and was commissioned an Army colonel as chief of the equipment division of the Signal Corps Aviation Section.

In July 1917 Col. Deeds sent the first DH-4 to arrive from England to Dayton-Wright for study and modification to accept the new American Liberty engine and American machine guns. It was test flown in late October by Howard M. Rinehart, Dayton-Wright test pilot, who had learned to fly with Orville Wright.

"We took over the new Frigidaire building near the field," Talbott continued, "and were eventually given contracts to construct 400 Standard training planes and 5000 DeHavilland-4 battle planes. We employed nearly 10,000 people and the operation was very successful."

At the cost of just over a million dollars, General Motors bought the company in 1919 and merged it into the automotive giant. The word 'airplane' was dropped from the Dayton-Wright name after the war, and still later Alfred P. Sloan, Jr. went on the board of directors.

DAYTON WRIGHT COMPANY
DAYTON, OHIO.

THE BIRTHPLACE OF THE AIRPLANE.

Several new designs were introduced, notably the "R. B. Racer," a high-wing, full-cantilever wood veneer racing monoplane of advanced design. It incorporated a variable-camber wing, enclosed cockpit and the first retractable landing gear. It had been built to compete in the 1920 Gordon Bennett Cup Race in France. Flown by Rinehart, the plane developed mechanical trouble and withdrew from the race.

Another Dayton-Wright design was the F.P.2 Forest Patrol twin-float seaplane. Like Gallaudet and most other aircraft companies of that day, Dayton-Wright also conducted a school for training pilots.

Most significant to Reuben Fleet, however, were the training plane designs Col. Virginius Evans Clark, the chief engineer, had developed in 1921 for the U. S. Army Air Service. Like Fleet, Col. Clark had been an officer at McCook Field, leaving in 1920 as the Chief Aeronautical Engineer, U. S. Army, to join the General Motors aircraft subsidiary.

FAMED DH-4 Bomber was being mass produced in August 1918 at Dayton-Wright Airplane Company factory.

FIRST DH-4 DeHavilland bomber came from England for installation of American "Liberty" engine. Test pilot Howard M. Rinehart (right) with pioneer Orville Wright.

R. B. RACER supports a dozen Dayton-Wright notables including its test pilot, Howard M. Rinehart, far left; Charles F. Kettering, far right; and president Harold E. Talbott, third from right.

"CHUMMY" Trainer designed by Col. V. E. Clark for Dayton-Wright featured single cockpit with side-by-side seating, carried over into TW-3 military version (below).

Air Force Museum Photos

MOCK-UP of 'Aerial Coupe' which General Motors hoped would find postwar commercial market.

The airframes for Col. Clark's TA-3 'Chummy' and TW-3 trainers were identical. The TA-3 (trainer, air-cooled) primary version was powered with a LeRhone rotary engine of 80 or 110 h.p., and 13 were purchased by the Army. The TW-3 (trainer, water-cooled) advanced trainer was powered by the 180 h.p. Wright model E war-surplus version of the French Hispano-Suiza vee-type engine. Two TW-3s had been sold to the Army.

Pilot and instructor in the 'Chummy' trainers were seated side-by-side, theoretically facilitating student instruction. As the Dayton-Wright school told prospective students, "the arrangement of our training machines, in which the seats and dual control systems are side-by-side, permits constant communication and mutual observation between student and instructor." They described it as the "Improved Gosport System," a reference to the British wartime training method.

Design of the biplane trainers had been simplified so that upper and lower wings were interchangeable. The same tail surface could be used for rudder or for left or right hand elevators. For the first time extensive use was made of commercial grade low-carbon steel tubing for the fuselage structure, tail surface framework, struts and landing gear members. Only the fabric covered wings were of wooden construction. All these features appealed to Fleet who saw the need for a new trainer as a replacement for the OX-5-powered Curtiss JN-4D Jenny which had been withdrawn from service as unsuitable for primary training by postwar standards.

In its three Dayton-area plants, the company had employed thousands of workers at the peak of war production. Like others, its efforts to build commercial and private planes like the 'Aerial Coupe' and 'Honeymoon Express' after the war came to naught, and employment dwindled. Too, there were unpleasant investigations of wartime production contracts involving Col. Deeds and his relations with the Dayton-Wright company. Particularly telling were the charges that Deeds, while in uniform, had continued to act as confidential adviser to the elder H. E. Talbott.

"While visiting with President Woodrow Wilson and Secretary of War Newton D. Baker in May 1918," Fleet remembers, "the President told us he had requested Chief Justice Charles E. Hughes to investigate with the Attorney General the very serious charges of dishonesty and skullduggery connected with the production of aircraft. A few days later, Secretary Baker detached Deeds and two other colonels from their duties and directed them to report to and cooperate with the Attorney General in the investigation."

Despite some orders for modifying DH-4s, for Clark-designed trainers and for night observation planes, the Dayton-Wright company was in such poor shape by

1923 that General Motors was ready to dissolve it so as to use the plants for automobile production. "Harold Talbott," Fleet recalls, "was the leading spirit at Dayton-Wright but the General Motors people felt he was a Chrysler proponent and didn't like him, and wanted to get out of the aircraft business." It was a fortuitous opportunity for Reuben Fleet.

Preliminary negotiations were begun by the Major to acquire rights to Dayton-Wright designs.

"We desire," he wrote on April 13, 1923, "to confirm our offer to purchase your airplane projects upon the basis of a royalty of $200 for each Training Airplane (TW-3) sold, $300 for each 'Alert' PS-1 Army pursuit version of the 'R. B. Racer' monoplane and $500 for each Amphibian (Navy W-A float-equipped observation biplane) with $10,000 for your good will and all drawings, data, tools, design rights and patents.

"Our plan would be to employ Colonel V. E. Clark, with a small engineering force, to improve these airplanes and make and keep them superior to any competitor's product and worthy of adoption by our Army and Navy Services; to exploit other governmental prospects and to commercialize the Training Plane and develop a market for it with the general public—this policy to continue to the extent that resultant business in our opinion justifies.

"Clark and I were trained in the Air Service and know its aircraft needs; both of us are pilots and are acquainted with most of our aviation officers; our Gallaudet Factory Manager, George Newman, held a similar position with Curtiss on JN and other airplane construction during and since the War.

"We feel that we enjoy the thorough confidence of the officials of our Government with whom we would propose to deal; we know how and where to improve the product and believe we can make more out of it for all parties concerned than anyone else. Our company's (Gallaudet's) side-line business permits our operation with a low overhead, and we have no fear but that our prices will insure customers. Your prospects for future royalties should be excellent. In fact we anticipate an order for 20 or 25 Training Airplanes very shortly.

"We are not in the engine business and hold no brief for any particular power plant, but would propose to give each Service that most adaptable to its specific need in each instance."

"General Motors," Reuben recalls, "wanted me to buy their company and thus put them out of business. I looked it over but couldn't even afford the buildings, which were very good. They had contracts which were losers and I didn't care to take them over from Harold Talbott. I preferred to let him finish his own contracts. I didn't want anything but the trainer design and patent rights."

PS-1 'ALERT' Pursuit, below, military version of R. B. Racer which flew in French air race.

Air Force Museum Photos

Musing over the future and the possibility of forming his own company, Reuben began to conjure up a possible name that would emphasize his determination to build only first class aircraft. First Class! The words had the same initials as Fleet and Clark. Perhaps FC Aircraft Corporation. Or should it be United, Continental, Reliance, Acme, or Consolidated? The possibilities seemed endless.

FLEET CLARK Aircraft
FIRST CLASS

Then, while jotting down some preliminary costs estimates on producing 20 or 25 trainers of the TW-3 type, the Major also tried to express his basic business philosophy—the credo for a company of his own—in these words:

* Values and hopes to merit the good will of the public, the government and the aircraft industry
* Conceives, creates and flies its own designs; confines its efforts thereto, and specializes in one type of aircraft
* Does not bid against others to manufacture their designs
* In aviation, safety is ever first; in aircraft manufacture, honesty is ever paramount.

11

HAVING COMPLETED ARRANGEMENTS to acquire the Dayton-Wright trainer designs and the services of Col. V. E. (Ginny) Clark, Major Fleet went back to the Gallaudet management with a proposition. As he didn't care to run a company that had a $3.5 million debt to be repaid, he offered to organize a new company, lease Gallaudet factory facilities and employ their workers while phasing out the Gallaudet business.

"I felt I could do Gallaudet as well as myself a service, but made it clear I wanted to retain 51% of the new company. If they wanted me to manufacture the trainers in the plant we could split the overhead and there would be a contract to which Gallaudet workers could turn while the Gallaudet business was being terminated. I felt labor wouldn't lag, for the 400 workers would be cutting off their meal ticket if they did. They'd not only be finishing the Gallaudet contracts but also working on my job.

"I proposed to help Gallaudet further by using as much material from their stockroom as was sufficiently tested to be reliable, buying it as cost plus ten percent. For rent I would pay ten percent of my profits, if any—and payment of my salary would be split 50-50 between the new company and Gallaudet. 'Thus,' I told Gallaudet owners, 'I will kill off your company to your best advantage, while establishing my own.' However, if Gallaudet didn't want to fiddle with me I'd resign the management, let them close down their company and I'd take the trainers elsewhere to manufacture.

"I offered the Gallaudet people a 40% interest but frankly I didn't like the attitude of some of the Wall Streeters. All they were after was making dollars and they didn't seem to care whether the airplane was satisfactory or not, just so they could make money out of it. I told Kelly Robinson and George Pynchon that 'I'd just as soon have you gentlemen with me but there are these others who don't seem to give a damn whether the airplanes are safe or not.' All they cared about was the almighty dollar.

"I didn't want to be associated with them because safety was the first thing that I considered, nor did I want them associated with me. Pynchon said, 'Well we can't very well say to our associates we'll let you, you and you in but we won't let the rest of you in.' They would say, 'here we've got a chance to back a new horse who is going to make a go of things and we think that if you get in we should get in also.'

"So I told them, I'll run it myself, keep it myself and won't have any stock for sale."

Thus Consolidated Aircraft Corporation came into being—got off the ground—only 20 years after the Wright Brothers' first heavier-than-air flight. It was May 29, 1923, when Fleet signed an agreement with Kelly Robinson of Gallaudet for use of the East Greenwich, Rhode Island, aircraft production facilities and employment of its workers.

The lease was to expire the end of 1923 or "until Consolidated completes its performance of contract for training planes which it expects to receive from the United States Government." However, the lease would not be binding unless and until Consolidated received the expected training plane order.

The new company began with an authorized capital of $60,000 divided into 600 shares of $100 each, but not before Reuben had made a trip home to Montesano, Washington. His sister, Lillian Fleet Bishop, and her lumberman husband, Edward K. (Ned) Bishop, agreed to put up $10,000. To this Reuben added $15,000 of his own so that the new company started out on an investment of $25,000 and with 250 shares outstanding.

Eleven days after Consolidated was formed the new company signed a contract with Dayton-Wright, giving Major Fleet's new firm one TA-3 side-by-side training plane plus design and manufacturing rights and production equipment. The consideration had been increased from $10,000 to $25,000 in order to meet an offer which Wright Aeronautical, the engine company, was ready to make. In addition there was an informal agreement that General Motors would assign all its Dayton-Wright aviation patents to Fleet's new venture.

Just two weeks before the Army's aircraft production funds for that fiscal year would have reverted to the Treasury Department, the Air Service signed a $200,000 contract with Fleet's Consolidated Aircraft Corp. for 20 model TW-3 trainers—with the equivalent of three more planes as spares.

Consolidated was in business, with Fleet's promise to the Government that "we propose to keep this always 'the best training airplane in the world.' "

Form 52   D.W.Co.3m-10-13-22

DAYTON WRIGHT CO.
DAYTON, OHIO

SOLD TO **Consolidated Aircraft Corp.,**   Invoice No. **7138**

Address **East Greenwich, R. I1**   Date **7/24/23**

Shipped to   Your Order **Agreement**
June 9, 1923

Address   Our Order **16238**
Del.Slip **#5307,**

Via   Car Initial   Car No.

QUANTITY	DESCRIPTION	PRICE
One (1)	Item #1 Type TA-3 Side by Side Training plane, complete Delivered at our plant to J.W.Pattison, July 3rd, 1923, Union Central Life Insurance Bldg., Cincinnati,O Item #2 All the original data, plans, designs, specifications, sketches, drawings, blueprints, dies, jigs, patterns, machinery and equipment relating to and especially adapted for the designing or manufacture of airplanes. Delivered according to lists attached marked Exh.A,B & C,in cars PRR #500611,via CCC&STLRR on 7/2/23 and Car B&A #38931 via C on June 23 (2) Or	

HAVING MOVED THE TW-3 TRAINER project and its designer, Ginny Clark, from Ohio to Rhode Island, Fleet was anxious to push forward on production and further sales to the Army and Navy. So, as soon as several planes had been completed, Reuben flew back to Dayton and McCook Field to show the new model to the Air Service. There on June 10, 1924, official performance tests were flown by Lieut. Eugene Barksdale.

Later, Fleet recalls, "I was flying the first TW from Dayton back to East Greenwich. The airplane was slightly tail-heavy, and I had my thumb against the stick control to keep the nose approximately on the horizon. All of a sudden the stick jumped out of my hand and hit me on the left leg just above the knee; I grabbed it, brought it back to neutral and glanced out over the right wing. The upper aileron had let go from its inboard hinge and had pivoted on the outboard hinge almost down to the lower wing. I landed the airplane in a cornfield in Ohio and got a step ladder from a farmer and crawled up to the upper wing to examine the break.

"I found that the hinges, both male and female, were almost like knife blades. They were entirely too thin for durability. The hinge-pin had cut through. It was just as if the top hinge on a door, held by just two hinges, had broken. Everything went akimbo. So I carefully prepared a long telegram to the factory directing that all seven moveable surfaces (four ailerons, two elevators and the rudder) be redesigned with three hinges for each instead of two so that if one broke the other two would hold the control surface in line; also that the hinges be trebled in width, and that the hinge-pin be changed."

Reuben put down the pencil with which he had been sketching, then went on.

"The weather looked like it might delay me for several days as I didn't want to fly over the clouds so I felt I had better wire the factory. In those days there was no radio and besides there were no ground services for pilots.

"After making repairs I had to fly through Erie, Pennsylvania, also to Buffalo and then down the Mohawk Valley to avoid both the Adirondacks and Appalachian mountains.

"When I reached our factory in Rhode Island, George Newman said my order to make all surfaces with three hinges was going to cost us a lot of money because it necessitated making the trailing edge that supported the hinges stiff enough to cover all three points of attachment like a rifle with three sights.

"I explained to my associates that the Services would never condone only two hinges for their trainers because of accidents just like the one that had happened to me. Obviously if one hinge of three broke, the moveable surface would still be operable and no disaster would occur.

"It was essential to get the 'bugs' out of the design at the earliest possible moment if we were going to survive as a supplier of military training airplanes. My accident was really a God-send as it enabled us to make our airplanes as fool-proof as we could early in their manufacture."

Fleet believed that service after sale was an essential part of business success, as he explained.

"By the end of the year Consolidated delivered its 20 airplanes to the Army at Brooks Field in San Antonio, Texas. After loading the Gallaudet plant up with machine shop work so as to hold the best of the employees on the job, Newman, Clark and I went to Texas to see how the first few TW-3s satisfied the customer.

"We flew with the various pilots who were instructing others and found to our dismay the Army didn't like the side-by-side seating. With this arrangement you couldn't see the near-ground on the opposite side of the cockpit. If you were sitting on the left you couldn't see the ground on the right very well, and if you were sitting on the right you couldn't see the ground on the left. A clear view in landing is especially important in training. So the side-by-side feature was no good.

FIRST Consolidated Planes were TW-3 side-by-side trainers built in Gallaudet factory.

General Dynamics/Convair

"With the Army's cooperation we took one of the planes, narrowed the fuselage by bringing the longerons in and placed the seating for instructor and pupil in tandem. The fore-and-aft plane made an immense hit with the boys because it greatly improved visibility. They called it the Consolidated Camel because of a hump between the two cockpits, and in order to have a descriptive designation for the modified trainer.

"It was the best trainer they had and the Army recommended adoption of a similar design in the future with an air-cooled radial engine, which was just coming onto the market at the time.

"In the meantime we were 'stuck' with the in-line water-cooled Hisso vee engine which was a hard engine to design around and the source of some problems because it was so broad and very difficult to cowl.

"This aggravated the visibility problem for instructor and student because the many-louvered top-cowling obliterated considerable vision—you can't see through aluminum—and you need all the visual reference you can get when the student is trying to hold the plane level. So the Army literally threw away the cowling. But doing so reduced some blind spots while flying since it permitted peeking around the engine, and it also helped cool the engine in those high Texas temperatures."

A faint smile came over the Major's face as he anticipated what followed.

"Colonel Jacob E. Fickel, the Air Service contracting officer, docked us $50 per airplane and instructed us not to manufacture any more top-cowls for the Hisso-powered trainers.

"Then there was the matter of the radiator. It was a real headache.

"Clark had designed an elaborate 12-sided radiator core for the TW-3. It had to be built of hexagonal brass cartridge tubing, all fitted and dip-soldered. Total cost of the first core was $564, and it leaked under pressure of only one pound (it was required to withstand more than three).

"I stayed at the plant one night and worked out a simple rectangular radiator of my own design, using a wood packing box for size. We cut a series of holes to let the box fit over the propeller shaft in various positions. I studied the best positioning for visibility from the cockpit, while my 13-year-old son, David, stood on a ladder and moved the box."

The shop was ordered to build a simple core to fit Fleet's pattern. This was quickly done. Under test, the core withstood five pounds' pressure without leaking but there was still the question of whether or not it would cool properly. Fleet proposed that they put this rectangular radiator core underneath the prop so the pilots could see right over it. While this was going on,

General Dynamics/Convair

INSTRUCTOR and student had trouble seeing past bulky radiator and cowl of TW-3.

Clark and the Army inspector at the plant complained to the Air Service that Fleet was cheapening the product and spoiling the appearance of his airplane design. I. M. Laddon, at that time chief of Design Branch 2 in the Air Service's Engineering Division, was sent by Colonel Bane to investigate the complaint.

"Clark said he didn't know whether or not the new radiator would cool," Fleet recalls. "I asked Laddon about it and he didn't know either. So I said, 'My God, give me an engineer who knows! It's a sad commentary on the engineering profession that you gentlemen, supposedly two of the country's best aeronautical engineers, can't predict whether this will cool or not. You can tell the Engineering Division, Mac, that I'll guarantee it will cool and we'll just make it that way.' We did. It cooled, and was out of the pilot's line of vision. It was just exactly right.

"And it cheapened the ship—in price. I told Laddon that if the government wanted to go on paying the ridiculously high figure of $12,500 each for trainers ad infinitum, it could. But this was only an experimental order for 20 planes, so why not see if we could improve things and reduce cost?

"So Mac went back and reported to the Division that what I was doing was reducing the cost of the ship. In his opinion it was the proper thing because if the radiator cooled properly in San Antonio, Texas where they were going to use them why the radiator would be alright anywhere. So he made a fair, honest report and it enabled us to carry on and finish the job, and it all panned out fine."

It was the first of many confrontations between Reuben Fleet and his engineers but Mac Laddon also recalls "it was the beginning of an era of mutual respect between Fleet and myself." Often engineers were so close to their work they failed to comprehend simple, basic approaches to problems they made unduly complex. Fleet's instinct was always to simplify design and production and make safety paramount above all else.

Walking through the plant one day, Fleet noticed a workman scribing neat circles on a length of duralumin stock. After stopping to talk, Fleet said: "Finish what you're doing and keep track of how long it takes. Then bring me the work, with all the washers you make when you cut out those circles."

The workman was making "lightening holes" while building a fuel tank header. The finished job of fabrication took 4 hours and 40 minutes. Fleet put the cutouts in an envelope and placed it on a postal scale; the weight saving amounted to 5½ ounces. He noticed that the stock was "bastard" gage—.042 thousandths of an inch. Inquiring further, he learned that the tank header was the only item in the aircraft for which this thickness was specified. The company had been required by the mill to place an order for 1,200 pounds, although only 200 would be needed.

"I called in the acting chief engineer," Fleet has related. "He was a nice young fellow, and immediately got out his slide rule and began fiddling. I said, 'Never mind, let's see what happens if we take some standard .035 stock and bend it up on a sheet-metal brake.'

"He was back in 20 minutes with the new header. We weighed both items on the scale in the laboratory; the one without holes was two-hundredths of a pound lighter. And it was certainly strong enough. So I said, 'My boy, go all over the plant and take down your signs, "Save Weight." We're only building trainers. A little weight doesn't mean a damn thing.'"

Fleet and Ginny Clark, his chief engineer, clashed so often that Ginny's threats to resign came with almost clocklike regularity. And of Joseph M. Gwinn Jr., whom he inherited from Gallaudet, Fleet wrote that "he was a very brainy engineer but one who had a screw loose always unless you could, figuratively speaking, hold him by the hand."

Col. Virginius E. Clark was a fine but eccentric engineer who had run into some personal problems while serving at McCook Field as the Army's chief aeronautical engineer. A graduate of the U. S. Naval Academy in 1907, Clark switched to the Army and learned to fly in 1913 at North Island, San Diego.

The next year he was assigned to study at the Massachusetts Institute of Technology. There he won the first doctor's degree in aeronautical engineering conferred by M.I.T.

After serving in Europe in mid-summer 1917 as a member of the Bolling Commission which was studying military aircraft design of the Allies, Clark went to the Air Service Engineering Division at Dayton.

On leaving the Air Service in 1920, Colonel Clark became chief engineer for aeronautics of General Motors' Dayton-Wright Company. He was the originator of the famous Clark 'Y' airfoil and many other technical advancements in aeronautics. His design of airframe structures of mild steel tubing contributed greatly to the trend away from early wood-and-fabric aircraft construction methods.

R EUBEN FLEET'S SENSE of timing could hardly have been improved upon when, in summer 1924, the Army conducted a competition for new primary training airplanes to replace the wartime Jennies.

Consolidated was ready with a new airplane—the improved version of the tandem 'Camel' trainer. The fly-off was held at Brooks Field, San Antonio, home of the Air Service primary school. Against competitors which included Cox-Klemin, Huff-Daland, Fokker, Thomas-Morse and Vought, the Consolidated trainer won the award which was to be for an initial quantity of 50 aircraft.

Designated the PT-1 'Trusty,' the Consolidated trainer was the first of a new series in the Air Service and was destined to be the country's principal primary training plane for many years. As with the earlier TW-3 model, the Government furnished the war-surplus American-built Hispano-Suiza 180 h.p. water cooled V-eight engines.

With its engine completely uncowled and everything else exposed as much as possible for ease of maintenance, the PT-1 was no beauty, but did win praise for its functional simplicity. As aviation historian Joseph P. Juptner wrote, "It was a lean, stark and rather ugly airplane; surely no thing of beauty in the general sense but none will deny that it was just about perfect for the job intended. It was quite amiable and extremely rugged in nature, and it took a pretty sloppy 'dodo' using extra effort to hurt himself or one of these airplanes."

If ever there was a consummate artist at the 'hard sell' it was Reuben Fleet. He was never accused of underplaying the capabilities of either himself or his company and was equally effective in personal contacts, on the phone, by letter or by telegram.

July 11, 1924

Subject: Consolidated Tandem Training Airplanes.

To: The Chief, Supply Division, A. S., Munitions Bldg.,
        Washington, D.C.

Referring to your letter of the 1st instant opening negotiations with me towards procuring some of our tandem training airplanes, we have just built and delivered to you twenty of our TW-3's at a unit price from you of $8145.71 (unit cost to us of $8629.41) manufacturing them to drawings which had been checked by the construction, during a development period of two and a half years, of eighteen training airplanes.

In order to be able to serve you more effectively, we propose, upon receipt of your order for one hundred of our tandem training airplanes, to move to San Antonio, Texas, and there construct and deliver to you within the next two years, these airplanes, building them in lots of ten, delivering each lot to be put immediately into actual training service while we are working on the next lot. We will incorporate in the third lot, all changes which your service tests of the first ten prove desirable, repeating this procedure for each lot throughout the entire one hundred, whereupon we will have developed a training airplane along lines indicated continuously by your operating and maintenance personnel at Brooks Field. We will stand all losses due to changes, provided the type of airplane remains fundamentally the same, at the basic unit price of $11,000.

When the airplane is developed to your satisfaction, so that we can manufacture thenceforth without changes and on a production basis, the unit price will drop $2500 on all remaining airplanes and we will receive 25% of your $2500 saving as a bonus, thus establishing a pecuniary incentive for both of us to accomplish the desired result at the earliest possible moment.

This proposition contemplates airplanes in accordance with your Handbook and your Specifications, requiring our use of Air Service standard parts throughout and with every detail and assembly passed under your inspection. We estimate these requirements add about 18% to what would otherwise be our cost. If you wish to allow us to regard your Handbook and Specifications as general guides only, and to rely solely upon our inspection, we will guarantee our product against latent defects or weaknesses, as do automobile manufacturers, and reduce our price accordingly. This will save also the cost of maintaining your inspection force at our factory.

We consider that by establishing our factory in the immediate vicinity of your field operations you will receive each airplane about one month earlier than otherwise, will save the cost of packing, handling, freight, and possible damage enroute; and the cost of, and time required for, unpacking and setting-up each airplane.

At the same time we will be in a position to keep in constant touch with your problems, so that we may solve them promptly and to the satisfaction of your operating officers, whose cooperation will be very valuable. Shall we not profit by the experience which has taught us that we cannot over-estimate the benefit that will accrue to us both when we, who are responsible, can see the effect in order to determine intelligently and quickly the cause and the remedy? Never before have your operating officers had, under their very eyes, a factory, designing and building airplanes for their use and willing and anxious to cooperate with them in striving to develop the ultimate training airplane.

CONSOLIDATED AIRCRAFT CORPORATION

R. H. Fleet
General Manager

PT-1 'TRUSTY' Tandem Trainer sports Consolidated Aircraft name on tail and ungainly but functional installation of its uncowled water-cooled engine.

WHILE CONSOLIDATED did not get the 100-plane order which Major Fleet went after, he did sign a half-million dollar contract for the initial 50 aircraft, plus spares, as provided in the competition. Nor did Consolidated establish the proposed factory in San Antonio.

In May 1924, a year after forming Consolidated, and 18 months after having gone to work for Gallaudet, Fleet gave up his dual role as general manager of both companies and resigned from the Gallaudet firm.

With the prospect of an immediate 50-plane order from the Army and the probability that contracts for additional quantities would follow from both the Army and Navy, Fleet began to look for a new production facility.

A second consideration was the labor market available in New England.

"By the time we got up to 450 employees in the Rhode Island plant," Fleet has related, "we were having to import workers from New York City, Boston, New Haven or some place like that.

"Getting people to work on the new, potentially large contracts was a problem even though the aircraft companies on Long Island were running out of work. We figured some of these plants would be glad to farm their employees out to us with the prospect of getting them back when they obtained new contracts; still this plan wasn't successful.

"In many cases, to get people we had to pay the imported labor more than the men already on the payroll were getting and that created new problems we didn't want to have to live with. For example, Grover Loening called me about a crackerjack mechanic for whom he had no work but would like to farm out to work for Gallaudet and/or Consolidated. He came up to Rhode Island and the first thing he asked about was the pay, which was 65 cents an hour as a tinsmith. 'Well,' he said, "Loening has been paying me $1 an hour.' So we met that rate, but doing so upset the applecart.

"That taught me a lesson instantly and I said to myself, 'Hell, I can't afford to continue here. I can only get 450 people from this vicinity and will be unable to expand, or I'll have to go to some location where there are all kinds of trained people—a pool of skilled workmen.

"In Rhode Island we were in the district where handwork done by silversmiths and coppersmiths was probably better than any other place in the country. Now Detroit was pretty much the opposite. Everything in the automobile industry was done by machinery with precision jobs. Buffalo was about halfway between in geography and techniques and had the largest trained labor pool at that time, outside of the auto industry. Buffalo was the home of large wartime production by the Curtiss Aeroplane and Motor Co. and by Elias Brothers. We needed that pool so we went there, where Newman knew many of the mechanics.

"We leased the largest and newest aircraft factory in the country, a modern, one-story plant which the government had built for Curtiss' wartime production. The huge North Elmwood Avenue plant, which had been bought by American Radiator Company and called American Terminal Warehouse Corp., was taken over by Consolidated Aircraft under a 10-year 'accordian lease' on September 22, 1924. With the accordian arrangement, Consolidated could expand or shrink the square footage under lease as production requirements fluctuated from contract to contract. It was an ideal arrangement for an expanding company and one which did not tie up needed working capital in 'brick and mortar' plant facilities."

Not long after signing the lease Major Fleet drove in from Rhode Island in his Model T Ford Coupe. He was met in Buffalo by Lieut. James L. Kelley, the new Air Service representative. "I remember the Model T so well," Kelley said, "because it wasn't long until the Major was driving a Stutz Bearcat."

Fleet at once set a crew to work unloading the three freight cars that brought all of Consolidated's equipment, stock and records from the East Greenwich, Rhode Island plant. With expanding production it wasn't too many months before the Consolidated payroll exceeded a thousand workers.

As a pioneer aircraft manufacturer, Reuben's patriotic rhetoric—often overblown—had a way of cropping up in his pleading with procurement officials. Take this example in a letter to Major General Mason M. Patrick imploring the Air Service Chief to purchase the experimental TW-3 'Camel' prototype of the tandem seating PT-1 trainer:

General Dynamics/Convair Photos

MAJOR FLEET was proud to fly American flag at his new plant, above and below, formerly used by Curtiss at Buffalo, New York.

Your $5000 offer for this machine discourages us terribly. We need the $15,000 invested in it - we need it to carry on - for the Air Service.

We have presented aeronautics with something that bids fair to mean much to it in future years, in our five new Clark wing sections - the Government has not borne the cost. Without remuneration to us, our Clark Y was used against us in eleven designs in competitions.

We have proved faithful to our trust, often giving more than we bargained. But how long can we carry on, and what is the incentive, if we cannot receive back even cost, upon successful experiments!

Earnestly and calmly, yours

R. H. Fleet

ONE UNIQUE IDEA in Major Fleet's proposal of July 11 to the Army was accepted and did much to establish Consolidated's excellent reputation for quality with the Air Service as related by Reuben:

"We took the development contract for 50 airplanes for half a million dollars and agreed to build them in five units of ten planes each. The Army could have us make all changes that the Air Service training people wanted without any extra charge. Consolidated would deliver them four airplanes of each batch of ten, while I made the remaining six of that batch, to incorporate any changes that the customer wanted.

"This contract was very successful, because after our delivery of the 34th airplane, the Army announced it didn't want any more changes; that the airplane was entirely satisfactory and suited them fine.

"The test board which came to Buffalo for the evaluation of the final lot of planes consisted of Major Ralph Royce, the commanding officer at Brooks Field, and two very capable young Lieutenants, Carl A. Cover and Fred I. Patrick, all good friends from my earlier visits to Brooks Field. The board flew the latest PT-1 off the production line for three days, then certified the design as acceptable without further changes.

"Ours was a unique contract in that it was the first time the Army permitted the builder rather than the Engineering Division to be the boss of all changes. And it was a change in philosophy for me, too.

"As long as I was at McCook Field in the Air Service I was imbued with the fact that the Engineering Division was supreme in everything. When I got out in industry and had personal experience with the TW-3 and PT-1 contracts I found the opposite position had more merit.

"My visits to Brooks Field convinced me that the needs of the customer—the user—should be foremost. While the Division did talk with the ultimate user during the four years I was at McCook Field, the customer did not have final say so.

"When, as a contractor to the Army, I got out into the field I concluded that was the wrong procedure. I talked it over with General Patrick and his staff and told them in my opinion the customer should be the person to control the design. The Engineering Division should be consulted all the time on strength, safety factors and everything of a technical nature, but should not be the deciding factor. That should always be with the customer who was going to use the product.

"So that concept was approved by the Army; General Patrick decided he'd try it out. He asked me to draw up a contract that would embrace that philosophy and we did this on the PT-3 which was the follow-on to the PT-1.

"The PT-1 had excellent flying characteristics. Because of the 34-inch stagger of the upper wing, placing its center section ahead of the leading edge of the lower wing, the nose of the airplane always went down when the occupant put the airplane into a spin. If the pilot did nothing to reverse the controls, our airplane would pull out of the spin automatically in a turn and a

TRAINING BOARD at Brooks Field, 1923, included Lieutenants Hez McClellan (right, rear row), Fred I. Patrick (left, second row), and Carl A. Cover (right, front row). Commanding officer was Major Ralph Royce, second from right, front row.

Brooks Field/U.S. Air Force

David G. Fleet

GENERAL Officers are hosted by Major Ralph Royce at PT-1 inspection. Note spurs and cavalry boots of non-fliers.

General Dynamics/Convair

FIRST PT-1 appeared with its Hisso engine cowled in until new radiator designed by Reuben Fleet, and uncowled engine installation, made possible simpler approach *(below)*. It was, said historians, **lean, stark and rather ugly, but perfect for the job.**

Air Force Museum

half. By reversing the controls, the pilot could accelerate coming out of the spin, or if the pilot did nothing it would automatically come out of the spin.

"About this time the Navy had acquired its first radial air-cooled engine—the 200 h.p. Lawrance J-1—and had awarded the Boeing Airplane Company a contract for 50 trainers for a bid price of half a million dollars. Of these, 37 spun into the ground, so the Navy had to restrict the Boeing NB-1 trainers from doing any spins or acrobatics, greatly reducing their effectiveness for instruction. Later we were asked for an explanation of how we had overcome this design problem in the PT-1."

WITHIN A YEAR after Consolidated won the competition for the 50-plane PT-1 order, the Air Service had appropriations approved for 150 trainers. What disturbed Reuben Fleet was that the Army asked him to arrange so other companies could bid to build to Consolidated's design. It was against everything in which he believed.

"We cannot but regard such an arrangement," he wrote the Army, "as disadvantageous, if not disastrous, to both the Government and ourselves, and unnecessary in peace time.

"You would propose to contract with our competitors to produce our airplanes, and to pay us for our proprietory design rights—an expense which seems unjustified to the United States so long as we are a source of supply, satisfactory in price and producing ability.

"The originator takes great pains with its product, attaches its name proudly to it, and stands firmly behind it, assuming full responsibility for its merits and demerits."

The letter, and another three weeks later, went on in like vein for eight pages: "Our quotation is based upon

GENERAL PATRICK and Brooks Field C. O., Major Royce, discuss the merits—and possible faults—of the PT-1.

an estimated profit of 15% and, since the aeronautical business is such a hazardous one, we feel that we cannot accept any orders at a smaller prospective profit. In this regard, we consider that the United States is in a very fortunate position when it can go to an industry and purchase for only 15% above actual cost, an article custom-made to its own specifications and under its own inspection, with the manufacturer taking all the risk."

At the time, Consolidated was working on the 50-plane order, but funds were available for 100 more. Finally Major Fleet fired off another salvo:

AVID SPORTSMAN and skilled trap shooter, Reuben Fleet (second from left with Brooks Field officers) prepares to 'fire off another salvo.'

July 14, 1925

Major General Mason M. Patrick,
Chief of Air Service,
Washington, D.C.

Dear General Patrick:

You are now spending more than half the cost of a **Consolidated** PT-1 in making fit to fly each old war-time JN-6. Its maintenance thereafter is terrific. If it crashes, the remnants are like kindling wood and the occupants may be killed or maimed for life. You should look at the photographs of the wrecks of Jennies during the past two years at Brooks! Furthermore, your boys can't use parachutes with Jennies and we ought not to continue to require our young men to train without them. You and I wouldn't want our sons to go through their first 75 hours of flying training without them. You won't permit your finished fliers to go up ever without a parachute, and yet the student is not nearly so safe in the air.

. . . . So why defer buying 100 planes now? You recognized the need for them two years ago (Major Ralph Royce requires 144 continuously) and asked for the money. Congress gave it to you. You announced on February 5th that you would buy 158 training planes. Ever since, we have planned to furnish you at least 100 this year, and everyone in the industry has expected us to do so. They all have had a chance at the business. With your order for 100 we would not have as much business in our plant as Curtiss, Wright, Boeing, Martin or Douglas, and yet we have as good equipment and as trained an organization as anyone in the business and we can add our profit and sell below actual cost to any other firm in the United States.

Moreover, with 100 planes we can tool up almost twice as much as with 50, and parts will be interchangeable. This means a tremendous money saving to you. In buying material too, it is an awful waste of money to ask a supplier to manufacture specially, half one's requirements, and then repeat the order after he has gone on to other work. It's hard enough now to get steel strip, tubing, screw machine parts, special alloy castings, etc., in the small quantities we require. Sometimes five times the quantity would not increase the price more than 20%.

So why delay ordering 100 planes from us. You have the engine, the instruments and the standard parts required—that is almost half the cost. We can make the planes for you now at a lower figure than later, for right now we have a trained organization just the right size to take care of an order for 100 — Why? Because for six months we have been expecting it under your own announcement sounding the warning to be prepared. This is the reason we can offer you one hundred of the best training planes in the world—your own people all concede this—for only $8,625 each, under conditions where they will more than pay for themselves in the first year's service in money return, not to consider probable life saving, for our **Consolidated** training airplanes will reduce the hazard of flying training to a point where either of us, I dare say, would be willing to have our only sons learn the game in one of them.

Yours faithfully,

R. H. Fleet

P.S. Morning paper reports two boys killed in flying training yesterday. They fell in a spin and burst into flames. Of course, they must have had a Jenny. Should you continue the use of this old relic any longer than absolutely necessary?

FIRST PT-1s are assembled in new Buffalo plant formerly used by Curtiss for WW I plane production.

TWO DAYS LATER in a memorandum for Colonel William E. Gillmore, head of his Supply Section, General Patrick indicated a willingness to place the order for 50 trainers at $8600 with a three-month option on 100 more at $8500 each, but with a profit limitation.

"The contract," wrote General Patrick, "will contain a provision that the contractor's profit shall not exceed 15%. The cost of the work will be determined by an Air Force auditor and the contractor's books and records will be available for his inspection at any time."

In the course of negotiations, the profit ceiling was never agreed upon because of Fleet's insistence that such a provision should be two-edged; that is, if he accepted the profit limitation, the government should in turn guarantee the 15% profit margin.

The same day General Patrick was writing Colonel Gillmore, so also was Major Fleet, continuing his plea for the order for the additional 100 PT-1s:

"Improved performance in fighting aircraft is ever necessary, and competition will obtain it. Not so with training aircraft. Constant improvement in performance is not necessary; birds learn to fly the same way they always did. With training planes your problem is to develop a plane to serve you safely with the least possible expenditure for maintenance, and to reduce the initial cost, which can be done only by concentrating production in one source of supply that has earned your confidence and that you think will continue in business to serve you."

"Despite all the points I raised," Fleet recalls, "General Patrick thought somebody else might underbid us. He would not promise us the other orders, although we pointed out to him the enormous savings that could be made by purchasing materials for the entire quantity. So we decided to take the risk ourselves, firming believing no other company could compete successfully with us.

"General Patrick had given us the order for 50; then 63 days later another order for 50, and 60 days later still another order for 50. The last two orders totaled over $900,000. So in the long run we were right to have ordered materials for at least the 150 airplanes and let the Army have the benefit of the savings.

"Meantime, we bid for the Navy's trainer requirements and were judged to have the best airplane for the lowest price of 14 potential competitors. The Navy's price was the same as the Army's price, excepting an addition of $400 for the single main landing float and the two wing-tip floats for those to be operated as seaplane trainers.

"We immediately purchased steel tubing for fuselage members, spruce for the wing spars, and other materials for 220 airplanes, even though at that time we didn't have an order for the two last 50s from the Army. I knew nobody had a better trainer, and nobody could design a better one."

The initial Navy order was for 16 Model NY-1 (N for Navy; Y for Consolidated) trainers at about $10,000 each. Within a few months the Navy ordered 40 additional NY-1 'Husky' trainers, then 10 more—all with spares. Each time the Navy needed trainers it held a new competition. Each time Consolidated entered, and each time Consolidated won.

ONE TW-3 TRAINER built by Dayton-Wright was tested as seaplane by Navy at Washington, D.C.

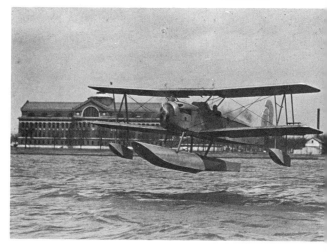

WITH RADIAL ENGINE installed in Navy NY-1 trainer, popular name for trainer became 'Husky.'

As 'sponsor' of the air-cooled radial engine, the Navy had already specified this new type power plant, designed by Charles L. Lawrance of Wright Aeronautical Corp., for the Boeing trainers. Because of the success of the basic Army PT-1 model in the Navy competition, the Navy decided to try the same Wright J-4 nine-cylinder 200 h.p. engine used in the Boeing trainers in its first Consolidated trainers, later switching to the J-5 version of 220 h.p.

With its modern radial engine, the 'lines' of the Navy NY-1 were far more graceful than the Army PT-1 with its naked, uncowled appearance and exposed engine. Provision was made for removal of the wheeled landing gear and the installation of a main central float and small floats outboard for lateral stability on the water. This also required redesign of the tail group with a bit more area.

Engineering acceptance trials of the NY-1 were flown in December and January near Washington, D. C. prior to shipment of the first production planes to the Naval Air Station at Pensacola, Florida.

As was typical of Consolidated's flying president, Major Fleet, accompanied by George Newman, flew to Pensacola in June 1926 for the Navy demonstration flights. Supervised by the Consolidated officials, two of the planes were assembled and Reuben made the first flights in each plane himself.

Except for unexpected overheating and related loss of power in the Wright J-4A engine due to the warmer Florida climate, the demonstration flights went well.

Flying one of his Consolidated trainers, Reuben Fleet was to make many trips to Pensacola, and to the Army's Brooks Field in Texas. As a basic tenet, Consolidated always maintained close personal contact with operating personnel of both services, primarily to see that difficulties were corrected as soon as they arose.

"The way to stay in business with the Army and Navy," Fleet told his associates, "is to give them your best without any holding back. Sometimes we gave them what was best before they knew it themselves.

"I probably had more experience in flying trainers than anyone I knew of in our Service, including those who were training students every day. I had graduated from the Gosport advanced school for flying instructors in England in 1918 and gave a course in accuracy flying at McCook Field when I first reported for duty there. This training course had included such top students as Lieutenants John A. Macready and Oakley G. Kelly, who were to make the first non-stop transcontinental flight in May 1923.

"As a pilot who had been responsible for the wartime primary training program I wanted, in my new role as a businessman, to be sure that the product we built was safe and would produce good pilots. The only way to assure that was to get in as much flying time as possible myself in Consolidated trainers.

"Wherever I went in those days I piloted my own plane if at all possible. As a result I got caught in bad weather, had forced landings and all of the vicissitudes that any flier over years of flying is bound to have, and especially in the early days when there weren't any parachutes."

GRACEFUL APPEARANCE of NY-1 was emphasized in this seaplane version.

In the meantime, the Army followed its initial purchase of three batches of 50 trainers each with orders in 1926 for 70 more Hisso-powered PT-1s, followed by another 20 planes plus spares order. The new contracts were tangible evidence of the superiority of the PT-1 design and Major Fleet's determination to make it the safest trainer in the air. During the first year of operation of PT-1s at Brooks Field, the Air Corps Primary Flying School had trained 531 students without a single serious injury or casualty.

In 1924, its first year, Fleet's new company did $210,975 in sales; the next year $593,695 and over a million dollars in each of the next two years. By then Consolidated was well established as the leading training plane manufacturer, and was moving up fast in total business volume. In all it had sold 326 planes: 260 to the Army; 66 to the Navy. Although unit prices for the trainers continued to come down, Consolidated operated at a healthy profit.

"WHEREVER I WENT in those days I piloted my own plane (a PT-1) if at all possible." —Reuben Fleet

REUBEN FLEET ALWAYS wanted those who worked with him to feel the same loyalty to the company and pride in its accomplishments that he did. One way to assure this was to give his key executives an opportunity to have a proprietary interest—a share of ownership in its successes and failures.

"When the company was 25 months old," Fleet related, "I proposed to my sister Lillian that she sell me half of her stock for the $10,000 she had paid for her 100 shares plus 8% interest for the 25 months she had had the money invested. Thus, from there on she would be playing on velvet with the other half of her stock, and I would be able to take in as partners influential people who worked for us at the same price that she had sold it to me. If anyone to whom I offered a chance to buy stock later left the company he was to surrender his holdings at what was then the book value.

"As a rule I had to stand these people off because they didn't have the money to pay cash for their shares. Ginny Clark agreed to pay me $3500 for seven

percent of the outstanding shares and when he later resigned and I concluded to accept his seventh resignation (he having 'resigned' six times prior to that), I paid him $125,000 for the stock that he had 'bought' from me for $3500 and on which he had never paid me a dime.

"George Newman, who was factory manager, got six percent. Joe Gwinn, assistant chief engineer, came in for one percent as did Ray P. Whitman, vice president, who had been a McCook Field project engineer; Thomas Kenny, secretary and treasurer, and, as I recall, Felix Rossoll, one of the original Gallaudet crew who came over to Consolidated along with Newman and Gwinn. All were key people who had come to Buffalo with us from Rhode Island, as also had George Newman, Jr."

It was about this time that an old Grays Harbor, Washington, business partner of Reuben's, Charles T. Leigh, joined the company as assistant factory manager.

Not long after this, Reuben Fleet was visiting in his

home town of Montesano, Washington. The townspeople were always anxious to hear from Fleet as he was to some extent a celebrity—a local boy who had made good.

Interest was running high in planned trans-Atlantic flights as Comdr. Richard E. Byrd, Clarence Chamberlin, and Lt. Comdr. Noel Davis were poised for take-off at Roosevelt Field, New York; and at Paris, the French ace, Captain Charles Nungesser, was completing preparations for a west-bound crossing.

Then a new name appeared among the starters, a young airmail pilot from St. Louis, Charles A. Lindbergh, who soon would fly from San Diego to St. Louis to New York and, eventually, on to Paris in his new Ryan monoplane.

How did Reuben Fleet evaluate their chances?

"In my opinion," he told his audience, "of those attempting the flight or have it in mind, perhaps Lindbergh is most likely to make it. First, I like the airplane he has selected. Second, I like the way he has gotten into every detail of the plane and the flight. Third, he is an airmail pilot who has pushed through on many occasions when others would have landed. And he has great tenacity, courage and savvy."

It was a sound judgment.

AUTOROTATION—flat spinning—was a problem not only in the Boeing NB-1 and NB-2 Navy trainers, but also in the Douglas O-2 observation biplane. Lieut. Eugene Barksdale spun in and had been killed in August 1926 when flying the Douglas job as he couldn't even get over the side to bail out because of the centrifugal force. The Boeing trainers had been designed to permit spinning as required by the Navy training curriculum but in so doing went into flat spins from which they could not recover. Even the Navy's great test pilots Al Williams and Marc Mitscher could not solve the riddle.

"Not until recently," Fleet said in an interview 40 years later, "have I revealed why the Boeing trainers and the Douglas biplane that killed Barksdale suffered autorotation.

"The Army had asked Col. Clark, 'Have you any theory that will stop autorotation?'

"Clark brought the letter in to me. I said, 'Have you, Ginny?' and he said, 'No.'

"'Well,' I said, 'tell them that you haven't.'

"He did, but also told them 'Fleet has a theory and he's a better pilot than I am. He feels confident he has the answer.' Clark came to me and said, 'They want to know what it is. What is your theory?'

"I said, 'I'm not revealing it. It's one of the secrets of our business.'

"Well, the Army practically ordered me down to Dayton and they said they would give us no more business unless we did reveal it.

"So I said, 'All right. I have taken my life into my own hands a good many times to find out. We will take the flat spin out of this Douglas airplane for $50,000. If you can tell how we did it, that's fine. You'll then have the secret. If you can't, that's my business.'

"They said, 'Well, how do we know that you're going to take it out?'

"'Well,' I said, 'after I've done it I'll go up with any pilot that is agreed upon, kick it into a spin and if I can't take it out repeatedly—say a half a dozen or a dozen times—and in a turn and a half, I don't get my $50,000.'

"They wouldn't do it. They wanted to know what I was going to do. So they put reverse camber in the Douglas airplane because Clark had reverse camber on the stabilizer of the TW-3. That didn't cure it, of course.

"My $50,000 offer wasn't a bad deal for the Army either, because I would have had to put stagger into the wings of that ship and change all the wing fittings of every kind. It would be virtually a redesign of the ship, you might say. So I wouldn't tell them what I'd do, and they refused to give me the contract. So I didn't care and we kept on our own way, and our ships didn't flat spin. Ours always came out. Therefore, I had it nailed to the cross as far as the answer was concerned. I knew. It was a trade secret which I wasn't going to give away for nothing.

"Autorotation cost Boeing the training plane business as I told Claire Egtvedt who had designed the NB-1. Egtvedt, who had been Vice President and Chief Engineer of Boeing at the time, lived across the street from me in Palm Springs many years later and I told him why his planes had the problem they couldn't solve but Consolidated had.

"The thing that caused autorotation I can now reveal because I am out of the business and the secret is no longer a secret. It was the centrifugal force of the fuel in the gas tanks. We had 28 inches of stagger between the top and bottom wing in our airplane. The upper wing center-section carried the fuel tanks and they were so far ahead of the lower wing that when the ship went into a spin the stagger was such that the nose automatically went down.

"One could always pull the ship out in a turn and a half or, if you let go of it and didn't do anything, it would swing out of the spin of its own accord.

"Now Boeing and Douglas used the cheaper way of building because their between-wing struts were at right angles with no stagger of the wings. It was the fatal way to do it because any ship built like that was bound to spin flat.

"For a long time I planned to write a technical article on 'Discovery of the Cause and Cure of Autorotation in a Biplane' but never seemed to have the time to get it done.

"Because I didn't have any college engineering training some of the officers at McCook Field were skeptical of the practical approach I often used.

"I didn't find the answer to autorotation from something any college taught because they didn't know it. They didn't take their lives in their hands like I did to find out. And they wouldn't believe you even if you told them. The great Ernest W. Dichman, a brother-in-law of Col. Thurman Bane, was one of the dumbbell engineers of the Air Service. So was Major Clinton W. Howard, brother-in-law of then Major H. H. (Hap) Arnold.

"Howard, Chief Engineer of the Army Air Service after Ginny Clark left, had learned to fly with me at North Island, San Diego, in 1917. One day he asked me, 'How much education have you had?'

" 'Well,' I said, 'not too much, but I am a graduate of Culver Military Academy, which at the time I graduated included two years of college work. That's all I've had in the way of formal education.'

" 'I'm a graduate of West Point,' he replied, 'and also have finished two years at Harvard.'

" 'Well, then, I guess if education is any criteria you ought to be a whiz banger when you graduate from the Air Service.'

"To which he responded, 'That's what I figure.' "

BUILDING GOOD TRAINERS and occasionally scrapping with the Army about claimed excess profits were not the only matters on Major Fleet's mind. Just below the surface always loomed Reuben's concern with flying safety.

Two years after severing all connection with Gallaudet Aircraft the Major felt it necessary to warn the Engineering Division at McCook Field that they should discontinue flights of the Gallaudet DB-1 day bomber they were still testing.

"I feel I should put myself on record," he wrote, "as advising extreme caution in further flying of this plane, if not an entire cessation of such tests. Three years of experimentation with the DB-1, coupled with corrosion perhaps, possibly may have rendered it unsafe for flight."

The matter of aviation patents which Fleet had expected to get from Dayton-Wright when General Motors sold him rights to three plane designs continued to be a matter of controversy. After paying $15,000 of the $25,000 agreed upon with General Motors, Fleet held up further payment until the patents were received. There the disagreement rested for several years.

SAFETY-CONSCIOUS Reuben Fleet advised "extreme caution in further flight tests with the Gallaudet DB-1 day bomber."

"The ownership of these patents," Fleet wrote General Motors, "is immaterial from the standpoint of our products. For the good of aviation, however, any that have promise should not be forced to lay dormant undeveloped. In many, the patent applicants are now our employees. We would not bind ourselves to develop any, but if we owned them we might deem experimentation with several worthwhile. Since you elected to retire from the aeronautical business we submit that it is in your interest to transfer these aircraft patents to us.

"Of the three types of airplanes mentioned in our June 9, 1923 agreement, we were able to sell twenty TW-3s only, our Air Service being the purchaser on June 14, 1923. The government gave them a thorough test (in the side-by-side configuration) and concluded they were not satisfactory. Thereupon it circularized the entire aeronautical industry announcing a competition for new training airplanes.

"We were compelled to design a complete airplane from the ground up and were forced to abandon the training plane design we had purchased from you, whereupon your opportunity to collect royalties on it ceased. We had to employ an entire Engineering Department to design completely our present plane."

Fleet had been particularly interested in rights to a wing molding process which Col. Clark had perfected while with Dayton-Wright. General Motors decided that they wanted to retain the patents—that one in particular.

By this time Harold Talbott was an officer of Chrysler Corporation and more or less persona non grata at General Motors.

"Finally," Fleet recalls, "Charles E. Wilson, head of General Motors, asked me whether or not Talbott had promised me this particular patent. He took my word for it that Talbott had struck such a bargain and that since General Motors wanted to retain this patent I need never pay the $10,000 balance due under our agreement with General Motors. They kept the patent, of course, but it expired long ago."

ALONG WITH SUCCESS came problems. Ginny Clark was one of them.

His seventh resignation hit Reuben Fleet's desk on June 12, 1927, right in the middle of a controversy with the Army over "excess profits" on trainer contracts.

Major Fleet:

Will you please tell Newman, Leigh, Whitman, Kenny and Gwinn that I am resigning—convey to them my best regards and tell them that I am genuinely sorry that I will not be able to continue what has been a very pleasant association with them.

Having in mind the custom of giving notice—I should be glad to undertake any definite tasks you might have for me before I leave Buffalo.

In the meantime I should appreciate the privilege of using Consolidated's technical books and files—I want to write a book.

No one connected with the Government Service has any idea of any intention on my part of resigning—and I shall not tell them until after the present deal is closed. Please let me know immediately when the deal is closed.

(Signed)

Clark

Despite his all-business facade and reputation as a tough man with whom to deal, Reuben revealed his very human and compassionate side in his reply:

June 14, 1927

Dear Ginny:

For a long time I have been aware of the fact that you are not happy in your work and with me—and, after all, I guess happiness is what is most desirable in life. At times you have been almost a brother to me and I have really loved you. I have trusted you always. At times I have felt the corporation ought to have someone of a more stable temperament in its engineering—for while I realize that stability of temperament is not kin to genius (I almost believe the opposite is the case)—I could not help having the fear that you might anytime want to quit, which would be terribly bad, say if we were midstream on a new design.

I know you'd never treat me unfairly, but a company should guard against occasions when, perhaps, its creators—its geniuses—try to function but have not—cannot get under the circumstances of unhappiness—the necessary inspiration. I therefore abide by your decision to resign and suggest you come back and carry on with your regular tasks in engineering until I can get the present Government controversy settled as I see the right. Then, say your resignation would take effect, with $1000 pay (one month's leave) to be paid you also. Either the company or I will buy your stock at book value, when we see how much we have to give back.

There is a position where you would be in your element and happy, I am sure—counsellor and advisor to the three Air Departments—each paying one-third of your salary $15,000 to $18,000. You would save them millions of dollars and pick up what the country and the world is doing in the art—in two years you should stand without a peer in aeronautical engineering. Then if you should be dissatisfied, we will by that time, I hope, be ready and in a position to tackle fundamental research and could offer you a problem to solve for us under an arrangement whereby you would profit by your success.

As a prelude to connection with the Government, I suggest you establish yourself in New York City, and take a trip to Europe shortly thereafter (perhaps with Lester Gardner) getting what you can there. Meantime you might start your book—of course using anything you want here, including space and stenographer—and if you feel so disposed, I would appreciate number one—of the first edition, autographed.

As time proceeds, I hope you will look back on your trials and tribulations with me and with Consolidated with fond memories—such trials always make us better men. And I hope what you have earned in salary and dividends will afford you the means toward the end of your rainbow of dreams—to do that for your chosen art that will mean much for posterity. I cannot but feel regretful, Ginny, that you should leave us but we all wish you God-speed, success and happiness.

Faithfully, your friend,

(Signed)

Fleet

General Dynamics/Convair

PARTING OF THE WAYS between Reuben Fleet (left) and Ginny Clark (right) took place after static tests of PT-3 trainer in summer 1927.

Years later Fleet was to reminisce about his relations with Col. Clark:

"We kept at the business specializing on training airplanes and declining to build any other type for so long that our engineers got to the point they were not interested in working for us, and some of them resigned.

"Ginny Clark resigned several times in the first four years he was with us. When he resigned the seventh time, in part because we were not yet ready to tackle fundamental research, I accepted his resignation.

"Ginny was never really happy because he had been Class B'd out of the Army and had fought it bitterly. Class B was, of course, conduct unbecoming an officer and a gentleman. It was more or less his personal habits that got him in bad. Marriage, and lack of marriage, but I don't really know. Mac Laddon said he had a drinking problem. In any case he hired an attorney and fought the Class B action strongly but lost."

Had Fleet and Laddon been mistaken about Clark's character? A search of Air Force historical files more than supports their mild comments:

"Clark's ostensibly amorous bent created marital problems, and in 1920 he was convicted by both a court martial and by a civilian court on forty counts of bigamy. Our staff judge advocate assured me that that was a matter which could not have been taken lightly although it did provoke uproarious laughter among the legal staff. Clark was dismissed as a Class B officer under less than honorable conditions. He attempted unsuccessfully to have the blot removed from his record which was reviewed, left unchanged, and probably unequaled."

Continuing his recollections of Ginny Clark, Major Fleet said, "When he tried to make me give back more to the Army on profitable contracts than we should it appeared he'd have been willing to give the whole company back to get himself restored to the Army, but I overlooked that.

"After we finally accepted his resignation I gave him a five months trip to Europe at my personal expense with his wife, accompanied by Lester D. Gardner, then editor of 'Aviation' magazine, and his wife.

"Of course we bought out his stock interest in Consolidated, paying him $125,000 on a $3500 investment, the money for which we had advanced him. Then because he was being washed out of the [stock] market I gave him $10,000 as he came down to see me off when I later went overseas myself."

In a year Clark's book 'Elements of Aviation' came off the press and later he autographed a copy for Major Fleet:

"Courage, Imagination, Initiative, Perseverence—and again, Courage!
"The rare and perhaps inborn capacity to hold friends through complete trust and respect is something for which Reuben must always be thankful.
                    Ginny"

Clark's resignation of course brought other problems.

"When Ginny resigned," Fleet related, "Major Leslie MacDill, who was Chief Engineer of the Army, asked me who I was going to put in Clark's place and I told him I had not yet decided, that in the meantime I would personally be responsible for everything that we do.

"This of course gets back to a basic philosophy of mine. Much of our success had been that we never let the engineering end dominate the business. With Consolidated, engineering was always a service organization.

"While I was reluctant ever to overrule any engineering recommendation, I did so on occasion and lucky for us I did. It was a sad commentary, at least on the engineering profession of those days, that they were not businessmen as well as engineers.

"With us the business end always ran the business and the engineering end was treated the same as the flying end, or inspection or sales—that is, they were service agencies. That was the secret of our success. The Engineering Division of the Air Service, where I learned the folly of that corps running the thing, taught me that lesson."

Air Force Museum

THE CONSOLIDATED 'HUSKY' trainer for the Navy, with the Wright J-5 air-cooled radial engine, was a logical evolution and an improvement on the original Hisso-powered PT-1 'Trusty' with its clumsy V-eight water-cooled engine.

When the Army opened negotiations for its trainer requirements to be delivered in 1928 it specified the radial-engine version which was given the new PT-3 designation. A total of 310 'Husky' trainers were delivered in 1928 of which 177 model PT-3s went to the Army Air Corps and 133 model NY-2s to the Navy.

There was an earlier version of the improved trainer, a single XPT-2 model which was a PT-1 type powered for the first time with the Wright air-cooled engine. This aircraft was also equipped with new wing panels incorporating the Clark Y airfoil and it then became the XPT-3.

When the Air Corps began taking delivery of PT-3 trainers, the earlier PT-1 models began to be transferred to National Guard units throughout the country. The PT-3, in turn, was succeeded by the PT-3A version with minor modifications.

The Navy's NY-2 model was basically an up-dated and slightly larger NY-1, both versions being used as primary trainers in both landplane and seaplane configuration. The new NY-2 was also used as a secondary trainer in teaching aerial observation work and aerial gunnery. There was also a small quantity designated by the Navy as NY-3 because of an up-dated engine installation.

NY-2 SEAPLANE, up-dated version of NY-1, was in turn followed by NY-3 model.

CONSOLIDATED PT-3 became standard trainer of Army Air Corps between WW I and II.

Air Force Museum

"BEST, STRONGEST, flying-est trainer in the world" was Reuben Fleet's own
description of the rugged, safe PT-3 in which thousands of Army and Navy pilots
learned to fly.

CRESCENT of 74 Consolidated trainers on Brooks
Field, Texas, flight line 1926 (left). Thirteen years
later 34 PT-3s were flying at Spartan WW II military
school at Tulsa, Oklahoma.

THROUGH VOLUME PURCHASING of supplies and relatively uninterrupted assembly on the production line, Fleet had managed, with each succeeding contract, to reduce Army and Navy costs for the PT-1 and NY-1 trainers. Consolidated was, in fact, too efficient and in the view of Maj. Gen. Mason M. Patrick, too profitable in its operation. Fleet had gambled on future orders and had won but was now about to lose because of his success.

After four years in business Consolidated had earned some $800,000 and General Patrick insisted that the company should refund $300,000 of what he considered to be excess profits on Army and Navy contracts, all of which had been won in competitive bidding.

The General appears to have forgotten that the 15% profit limitation he had proposed two years earlier was never made a part of the contracts; still the Army insisted that Consolidated reveal its audited costs.

"General Patrick," Fleet had related, "proposed that we agree to give the Services 50 airplanes at no cost to the government." This would be the means of refunding the $300,000 which, if paid the Services in cash, would go into the general fund of the U. S. Treasury where even the Army would not likely get it back for its own use.

Fleet and the company directors felt there was no viable alternative but to accede since the military services were Consolidated's sole customer. Not one to give up easily, Reuben went to Washington to confront General Patrick, but saw him only briefly. A few days later a blistering telegram reached the General's desk:

I went to Washington, waited three days and was granted a six minute conference with you. I offered to remain over Saturday if you could see me but you stated you would be too busy. I request a conference of at least one hour at your convenience next week.

R. H. Fleet

Maj. Gen. Mason M. Patrick

Maj. Reuben H. Fleet

In a conciliatory response, the Chief of Air Corps wrote that he was indeed busy and that "When you did appear without advance warning I found my time entirely occupied." A new appointment was set.

Major Fleet was ushered into General Patrick's office by his assistant executive officer, Capt. Ira C. Eaker. "Reuben," Eaker later said, "protested violently that he shouldn't be required to return the $300,000 nor, he told General Patrick, would he build the Army 50 airplanes for nothing.

"The argument went on vigorously for quite some time and was obviously very heated. When Major Fleet left, General Patrick walked him to the door. Somehow all the animosity had vanished. They parted on obviously good terms. Fleet had made his point. He had sold the Services 50 airplanes—for $1 each."

General Patrick had requested the Navy to join the Army in seeking return of alleged excess profits which he had unilaterally decided amounted to an overcharge by Consolidated.

The Navy, which had bought about one-fourth as many of the trainers as the Army, had a vastly different viewpoint. Rear Admiral W. A. Moffett, Chief of the Bureau of Aeronautics, must have been an ardent believer in free enterprise for on August 3, 1927, he wrote General Patrick:

NY-2 SEAPLANE Trainers. Hampton Roads, Virginia.

"The question is whether or not the Navy Department will join with the War Department in an endeavor to secure, without cost to the United States, certain airplanes from the Consolidated Aircraft Corporation, as a result of the excessive profits alleged to have been made in connection with contracts for furnishing airplanes to the United States.

"The records of the Navy Department covering its transactions with Consolidated show that all procurements from it have been subjected to competition in accordance with law. Whatever the profits made by Consolidated, it is evident that potential competitors put forth their best efforts to obtain this business.

"It is the opinion of this office that, having procured aircraft from the Consolidated Aircraft Corporation after due competition, the Navy Department is not in a position to question the profits that the company may have made."

"Because 26% of Consolidated's total trainer business was Navy," explained Reuben, "we expected to be relieved of the 13 airplanes which were their share. But General Patrick went it alone against us, also taking the Navy's 13 'one-dollar' airplanes."

The $300,000 "fifty planes for fifty dollars" settlement was a bitter pill for Fleet to take for he felt it took no account whatever of risk he had assumed to gain the enormous savings from buying materials in advance of receiving orders.

"It was," Fleet said, "distinctly unfair but typical of the Army's penuriousness and unfairness. We took the gamble; the government did not. We should therefore have been entitled to the resultant savings. Our profit certainly would not have been large considering the fact that we guaranteed our airplanes against the phenomenon of 'auto-rotation' which was imperiling the lives of student fliers in competing airplanes. As a result of the excess profits' refund, Consolidated was unable to pay a dividend to its stockholders for nine and a half years."

ADMIRAL MOFFETT, right, didn't agree with General Patrick, center. At left, Major Dargue.

The Major decided he would submit individual statements of $1 each for every airplane and frame the 50 government checks as a reminder. The Army even did him out of that by paying for the 50 planes with a single $50 check!

Although he had fought bitterly with General Patrick, Reuben Fleet was not one to carry a grudge. At the end of the year, General Patrick retired and Fleet sent him a warm personal wire of congratulations on "a most enviable record of over forty-five years Army service crowned by the remarkable success you have made as Chief of its newest and most difficult branch."

In a hand-written response Patrick said,"I want you to know that the friendship you have always shown has meant a great deal to me. My retirement must not end it. I shall watch what you do in the future and I wish for you a full measure of success in your chosen field."

Two men of strong and determined character, each convinced that he was right, had shown the basic warm and generous nature of their personal relationship.

On a later occasion, Brig. Gen. William E. Gillmore, Chief, Air Corps Materiel Division, Wright Field, simply could not understand why Reuben Fleet failed to respond to any Army invitation to Consolidated to bid on a new two-seater pursuit airplane.

"I am interested to know," the General wrote, "whether this construction could not have been undertaken by your company."

It was an open invitation to free-enterpriser Fleet to take a strong stand on a proposition in which he deeply believed—that efficient companies should be rewarded, not penalized. His reply to General Gillmore:

"We do not care to undertake the design and development of a new type of aircraft, which, to be superior, must absorb our brain power and facilities for quite a length of time, unless we are to receive a fair and ample remuneration thereon in the future.

"You realize that the 'raison d'etre' of business is to make money, and at the same time to win and hold customers, through superiority of product in perhaps performance and certainly in safety, durability and cheapness of maintenance. Your buying officers seem to feel that a contractor's profit should be limited to 15% on cost as determined by government audit, which chops off costs the day delivery has been effected, whereas certain costs continue while the contractor stands by to render service and rectify things that require rectification due to his inability to foresee them.

"Fifteen percent may be sufficient for a firm possessing inferior ability, or lacking in application, hard work and perseverence, but we have found that if we make more through hard work, superior methods and good management, we are liable to be condemned under this audit system, as profiteers. We believe the audit system is unfortunate in that it places a premium on careless management, inefficiency and extravagance; or upon crookedness, in attempting to charge into costs, items that do not belong there.

"We have worked diligently to make our product as satisfactory as we could, at a cost as low as possible, and are now returning the part of a profit which the Chief of Air Corps regarded as too great. We have yet to furnish twenty more PT-3As at a dollar each, and when we have finished we may find we have worked quite a while for nothing; it is very hard to have passed any period without financial progress."

A CONSOLIDATED NY-2, because of its low landing speed and robust construction, was selected for the first demonstration of 'blind flying' as part of the project called "Solving the Problem of Fog Flying."

Lieut. James H. Doolittle, on loan from the Army Air Corps to the Daniel Guggenheim Fund for the Promotion of Aeronautics, made the historic flight in a hooded cockpit on September 24, 1929, at Mitchel Field, Long Island.

Three instruments had been developed to make instrument flight possible. An artificial horizon indicated the longitudinal and lateral attitude of the airplane with relation to the ground. A direction-finding radio cast a beam picked up by a visual radio receiver.

The sensitive altimeter showed the pilot his altitude to within a few feet of the ground.

In 1928 the Navy made available the NY-2 for the test program. The plane was modified at Buffalo for Doolittle, "and, boy," as he said, "did the Guggenheims scream about the bill!"

In a humorous vein Jimmy also complained about the cruising speed for "on one occasion, while we were flying low over a road and into a head wind, a green automobile overtook and passed us. Hurt my pride no end."

While the first official demonstration, with Harry Guggenheim present, was made with Lieut. Ben Kelsey as safety pilot in the front cockpit accom-

JIMMY DOOLITTLE, flying NY-2 trainer, made first fully instrumented blind flight in 1929.

PT-3 TRAINER with hooded cockpit was used by Army to simulate flight under zero-zero visibility.

panying Jimmy Doolittle, the actual first instrument flight had been made by Doolittle flying solo an hour earlier.

"We had waited several months," Doolittle related, "for a zero-zero fog and finally one morning, just at dawn, it came. The mammoth heater [to dispel the fog] was turned on but the fog was moving slowly across the airport and as soon as some was dispersed more took its place.

"The [heating] experiment was not successful but we had been making practice blind landings for a year and here was the chance to try our system out under actual operating conditions. Our airplane was rolled out and I got aboard. Bill Brown manned the radio equipment on the ground and a successful flight was accomplished as I flew up through the fog, and came back and landed."

Thus, in such laconic terms did the famed pilot describe the historic 15-minute solo flight. Although Doolittle flew and landed by instrument alone, as a safety measure he was not flying under the hood and could see out if necessary. In a zero-zero fog, however, that would have been of scant help. Doolittle then went on to describe the official demonstration which followed. It was, he said, "the first instrument flight on record, but, the real first flight was made alone in the fog."

For this first fully blind instrument flight, Doolittle won the Harmon Trophy in 1930.

Based in part on Jimmy Doolittle's work for the Guggenheim Fund, the Army Air Corps was also working on the problem of blind flight training.

At Brooks and Kelly Fields in Texas, Major William C. Ocker and civilian Carl J. Crane developed an in-

David G. Fleet

O-17 'COURIER' was used by Army National Guard units.

strument training system in 1930 which Gen. Frank P. Lahm of the Air Corps Training Center directed be included in the advanced training program. They knew from long experience that when a pilot is flying through clouds or fog, his reliance needed to be placed on a good set of instruments rather than on any 'seat of the pants' instinct and that this would require a formal training program under conditions which would simulate zero-zero visibility.

Again the Consolidated trainer, the Army's PT-3, was selected for blind flight training and equipped with the necessary instruments and an adjustable canvas hood over the rear student cockpit.

SPECIFICATIONS FOR A NEW advanced training plane were issued by the Army in late 1926 and the following spring Reuben Fleet and his designers were ready with the Whirlwind-powered 'Courier' to meet Air Corps needs for flight training, gunnery practice, photo missions and general cross-country flying. Basically it was a more streamlined, more refined version of the PT-3/NY-2 'Husky.'

Fleet entered the 'Courier'—a PT-3 modified as the XO-17—in a competition held at McCook Field on April 4, then got off a strong sales letter to Brig. Gen. James E. Fechet, Assistant Chief of the Air Corps.

"I flew our Consolidated 'Courier,'" he wrote, "from Buffalo to Dayton one week ago yesterday to have it there on the eve of the competition. It performs every stunt equally as well as any service plane you have and is far and away the best airplane our company has ever produced. We hope you will investigate it thoroughly with a view to its adoption by the National Guard and

by our Regular Service for all cross-country hops where it is too expensive to use fighting aircraft.

"It performs the functions of an advanced training plane having the advantage of being a two-seater and yet costing several thousands of dollars under the [Curtiss] AT-4. Ninety-six percent of its parts are the same as those you carry for the PT so your supply and storage problems are very simple.

"Consolidated airplanes are now located in more than 25 different stations in the United States so that one can hardly travel more than 500 miles without running into them—important from the standpoint of maintenance and standardization.

"In one man-hour, at an added expense of $100, it can be made ready for gunnery training from the rear cockpit and in the same length of time, at an added expense of $150, it will accommodate a front gun syncronized with the propeller. Its wonderful vision makes it very satisfactory for observation missions. It is powered with the Wright Whirlwind, the gasoline consumption of which is about half that of the service engines such as the Liberty, Curtiss D-12, etc.

"In 20 minutes the landing gear can be removed and in 1½ hours a flotation gear can be substituted, thus making the airplane available for land or water use—a very important thing from the standpoint of such National Guard units as are located on the seaboard.

"We will guarantee it in service against anything, excepting a crash, for one year's time. This is the greatest and best guarantee that has ever been offered by any airplane company and is four times that offered by any automobile company in America."

In 1928 Consolidated delivered 28 of the advanced O-17 models to the Army, for use by the National Guard

The O-17 'Courier' also seemed a good prospect for export business, particularly in Canada. Major Fleet contacted the Army asking permission for Lieut. Jimmy Doolittle to demonstrate the plane to Canadian prospects but General Fechet replied that "the Chief disapproves this application and says he will not permit any Air Corps officer to engage in this work."

Well, no harm trying, reflected Reuben, who then proceeded to Canada himself in July to demonstrate the plane to the Royal Canadian Air Force. As a result, three 'Couriers' were sold.

During 1928 there were also eight PT-3 type sold to Cuba. In order to capitalize on the growing foreign market, Fleet sent Lieut. Leigh Wade, his new sales manager, who had recently resigned from the Army, on a South American demonstration tour in a PT-3. There Wade often encountered Lieut. Jimmy Doolittle, who had traveled with him to South America on a similar mission for Curtiss. [Somewhere along the line, the Army had reversed its policy about Army pilots demonstrating planes for manufacturers abroad, but Doolittle, too, resigned his commission and went to work for Shell Petroleum]. As a result of his South American trip, Wade sold one PT-3 each to Brazil and Peru. Four of the earlier PT-1 trainers had been sold to Siam.

Sales of the ever-popular Consolidated primary trainers continued into 1929 with purchase by the Navy of 60 NY-1s and 25 NY-2s, while the Army Air Corps purchased an additional 73 PT-3s. One O-17 went to the Army and one PT-3 to Argentina.

With delivery in 1930 of 20 more NY-2s, another NY-1 to the Navy, and PT-3s to Cuba and Argentina, an era of concentration by Consolidated Aircraft on primary trainers was coming to a close.

In seven years, Reuben Fleet, who had the single-minded goal of building the country's best training airplane, had accomplished his objective by producing

LIEUT. LEIGH WADE who became Consolidated sales manager in 1929.

865 trainers. In all he had worked 12 years specializing on trainers, and had made aviation training as safe as training in any other Army or Navy branch.

His success in his chosen field had actually been assured several years earlier for he was already the largest volume manufacturer of planes in the United States. It was time to look ahead to new challenges. The ever-impatient Reuben Fleet was ready to tackle the multi-engined military aircraft field.

But to get a better perspective on Fleet's compelling interest in aviation it is useful to first go back to 1917 and pick up the story of his five and a half years in the Signal Corps Aviation Section and Army Air Service.

FOUR of the earlier PT-1 trainers in Siam.

BOOK II

"WE ARE ENTITLED TO NO CREDIT FOR DOING OUR DUTY"

1917-1922

U. S. AIR MAIL SERVICE became a reality May 15, 1918 when Major Reuben H.
Fleet was placed in charge of its initial operation.

"WE ARE ENTITLED TO NO CREDIT FOR DOING OUR DUTY"

IN SPRING OF 1917 it was clear to Reuben H. Fleet, successful businessman and Captain in Company G of the Washington National Guard, that America's entry into the war in Europe was only a matter of weeks away. As an early aviation enthusiast, Fleet felt the Aviation Section of the Signal Corps was not only the service where he should do his duty as a patriotic American but perhaps offered an entree into what might prove to be a dynamic new technology.

Just 73 planes were operational in the Signal Corps and 30 of them were in San Diego, to which Fleet had been posted for pilot training at North Island. In all the Aviation Section there were only 131 officers; in all the country only one real aircraft factory, that of Curtiss.

"I got the appointment," Fleet reminisced, "through service with the National Guard in which I became an officer soon after graduating from Culver Military Academy in 1906. I was already 30 years of age and had a successful real estate and timber business in my home town of Montesano, Washington.

"I was sure we were going to get into the war and I wanted to be in aviation. So, I closed my office on March 22, 1917, left Mrs. Fleet and the two children behind temporarily and took the train for San Diego.

"Six years earlier I had been in San Diego on special duty with the National Guard on the Mexican border and had learned to appreciate the area for its mild winter climate, its sunny beaches, its magnificent harbor and its scenic back country.

"It was not difficult to understand why the War Department had selected San Diego for the Aviation Section's pilot training school.

"On April fifth I reported for duty; that is, took my first flight from North Island. The next day war was declared. I held up my right hand to be sworn into the military service of the United States by Major Frank P. Lahm as a National Guard Captain attached to the Signal Corps Aviation School (SCAS) of which Major Lahm was Secretary."

San Diego's decades-long role as a center of aviation had gotten off to a notable start the same year Reuben Fleet was patrolling the Mexican Border, although he was not then aware that Glenn H. Curtiss had made the first successful seaplane flight in history from Spanish Bight between North Island and Coronado on January 26, 1911.

Earlier that month Curtiss had obtained a three-year use permit to conduct the Curtiss Aviation School and Experimental Station on North Island, which he described as "a flat, sandy island about four miles long and two miles wide with a number of good fields for land flights. The beaches . . . necessary for the water experiments I wished to make . . . are good, affording level stretches for starting or landing an airplane."

"But North Island," Curtiss noted, "is uninhabited except by hundreds of jackrabbits,

General Dynamics/Convair

*REUBEN FLEET: "I was older and slower to teach,
but once I caught on . . . "*

cottontails, snipe and quail."

In November 1912, at the invitation of Glenn Curtiss, the Army Signal Corps sent a detachment to San Diego to establish an aviation camp at North Island. Promoter as well as inventor, Curtiss no doubt saw the possibility of having the Army as well as the Navy as a customer for Curtiss planes.

Army aviation activity at North Island the next few years was sporadic but it did bring forth two civilian employees of the Signal Corps who were later to make their mark—Grover C. Loening, aeronautical engineer, and George E. A. Hallett, aircraft engine specialist. Loening had left the original Wright company in 1914 to take a $3600 per year job as the Signal Corps' first aeronautical engineer. Loening in turn was succeeded by Capt. V. E. Clark.

In July 1915, Lieut. Col. Samuel Reber, Officer-in-Charge of the Signal Corps Aviation Section, inspected the San Diego area with the objective of finding a suitable location for a permanent Signal Corps aviation school. The corps of officers at the school the following year included Colonel W. A. Glassford, commanding officer; Captain Lahm (the first Army officer to learn to fly), secretary; Lieut. H. A. Dargue, officer in charge of training; Lieut. B. Q. Jones, erection and repair; and Capt. H. H. Arnold, supply officer. Arnold was soon detached to Panama and shortly thereafter reported to Signal Corps headquarters in Washington.

Thirty-year-old Captain Fleet was somewhat more mature than the other student pilots both in age and experience. "I was older," Reuben said, "and therefore slower to teach, but once I caught on to it I

progressed rapidly. Along with Lieut. Frederick Eglin, of Indiana, I graduated one week ahead of the class, which had included nine other National Guard representatives.

"But at first, things were slow and difficult. A fellow by the name of Robbins was my first instructor. When he started me out, I was slow to learn. He said, 'Fleet, you are too tense. You should go to an osteopath and get him to loosen you up a bit.'

"So I went and had a treatment from an osteopath in San Diego. On my way back to catch the ferry for North Island I took the street car. When I jumped off at the end of the line I was so loose that I severely twisted my back. That confined me to bed for a week and could do nothing but lie there and rest to get the crick out of my back. It was then I decided I'd like to change instructors.

"When I returned to the flight line I asked Lieut. Dargue to give me another instructor. I figured that Robbins didn't trust me and I knew I didn't trust him because I was having trouble learning under him. Dargue assigned me to Sergeant Krull and he and I hit it off like a million dollars. So well, in fact, that although I was knocked out for a week I finished a week ahead of the others. Of course I'd had help, too, from Oscar Brindley who had been taught by and instructed for Orville Wright, and from Lieut. A. D. Smith, my instructor in acrobatics.

*LIEUT. A. D. SMITH (above). Oscar Brindley, left
(below) with Lieut. Leslie MacDill.*

Erickson/National Archives

"WE WERE FLYING JENNIES (left) *and a few Martin TT trainers."* (right).

"In those days, the training syllabus for Junior Military Aviators was pretty detailed. For example:

Climb 3000 feet, kill motor, spiral down, change direction of spiral and land within 150 feet of a previously designated mark.

Cross-country triangular flight without landing, of approximately 60 miles, passing over the following points: Starting from North Island over Del Mar, La Mesa and Coronado Heights.

Straightaway cross-country flight of about 90 miles, without landing, from the vicinity of Santa Ana, California, to North Island.

"We were flying Jennies—Curtiss JN-4Ds with the OX-5 engine—and a few Martin TT trainers. Of course, all the planes of the same model didn't necessarily fly the same. The ships were numbered and each of us had his favorite. Unfortunately it was generally the same Jenny we all preferred. The Martin TTs were two years older than the Jennies and were going out of service so we didn't have much flying time in them.

"Our technical training included a course in motors under George Hallett, in which we disassembled the OX-5 and reassembled it to learn something about the internal combustion engine. Did the same thing with propellers that were metal-tipped. And our principal text book was Grover Loening's 'Military Aeroplanes.'

"When we began our flight training there were only 40 acres that had been cleared on North Island. We were expected to do some of the maneuvers—like spiraling down with turns both right and left and landing with a dead stick—so as to land five out of six times within the 150-foot circle.

"On one such trial my coveralls caught in the pulley wheel of the aileron. I had to bank the ship up sharply to unroll the aileron pulley. By the time I got my coveralls free of the sprocket wheel I found myself at 400 feet directly over the spot where I was supposed to land. I knew I couldn't hit the spot from that low altitude so I just headed out into the wind and landed in the sagebrush, which was part of the hunting reserve of Adolph Spreckles, whose company owned North Island.

"In the flying class ahead of me were Joseph T. McNarney, Lieut. E. L. Hoffman (of parachute fame), Clint Howard and Lieut. Delos Emmons. I'd met Emmons six years earlier when serving with the National Guard under General Tasker Bliss on the Mexican border below San Diego.

"TECHNICAL TRAINING course in motors under George Hallett (center)."

Erickson/National Archives

43

Ryan Aeronautical Library

ARMY AVIATION area at North Island, San Diego, became Rockwell Field in 1918.

"Soon after I had soloed, those boys were all watching from on top of what we called the 'poop deck' of a little one-story building. I came in to land and skidded a little. Hoffman said I needed right rudder and Emmons said I needed left rudder. Dargue, who was the officer in charge of training, asked 'who said left rudder?' Emmons said, 'I did.' Dargue felt that Emmons was wrong and ordered, 'Come down here and get in the airplane with Fleet.' So we took off and flew around because Dargue must have thought Emmons would benefit from seeing my landing. Anyway, he couldn't tell me then that I was wrong. I didn't need any telling anyway; I caught onto it myself. Emmons became pretty much stuck on my method of flying and after that we often flew together.

"One day when flying with Emmons our motor quit right after we passed over a Navy cruiser in the harbor. Nothing to do but put the Jenny down in the water. The Navy fished both of us out."

Erickson/National Archives

"HANGAR FLYING" on the flight line at North Island as Army officers await their turns to fly.

North Island's status as a military base had been in limbo for years but a month after America's entry into the war, a joint Army/Navy Board recommended its purchase for $7 million and Congress passed the enabling legislation which President Woodrow Wilson signed. An agreement for joint tenancy of the island by Army and Navy training schools became effective August 16, 1917. In November, Lieut. Earl W. Spencer established and became the first commanding officer of the Naval Air Station. By a quirk of fate his wife, Wallis Warfield Spencer, achieved international notoriety as the Duchess of Windsor, for whom Edward VIII, the former Prince of Wales, abdicated the British throne in 1936 to marry 'the woman I love.'

"When the war broke out," Reuben resumed, "Col. Alexander L. Dade, Cavalry, who had succeeded Col. Glassford as Commanding Officer, SCAS, immediately began to clear North Island. During a smallpox scare the Army quarantined all of us on the island.

"I was officer-of-the-day on one occasion and suggested to the medicos that I be permitted to take the five hundred men down the island for a walk. We armed every man with two barrel staves, and organized a long straight line with each man stretching out his two staves to touch those of the man next to him. I gave the order to 'charge' as we started the drive to rid the island of rabbits, and headed south on the island to its narrowest point. We chased the rabbits—and innocent quail—down to the far end of the island through the brush. The barrel staves not only found good targets but a number of cadets and enlisted men got socked too, with a number of them ending up in the hospital. Every man had a couple of rabbits. It was a very successful maneuver because we had plenty of fresh meat for a couple of days."

Life at North Island had its social protocol—and its light moments. "Army regulations," Reuben related, "required all officers to call on their commanding officers within 48 hours of their arrival on base.

"Lieut. G. C. Furlow, a National Guard officer from the mountains of Tennessee, came around to my tent one day and said that he'd gotten a note from Colonel Dade wanting to know why he hadn't complied with Army regulation so and so. We looked it up and it was the one requiring the proper social call.

"Furlow said, 'What will I do? I don't understand what it means to call on him.'

"I said, 'It's getting about time for us to call on the Dades again, so this afternoon slip your white collar inside your OD [olive drab] blouse and you can go with Mrs. Fleet and me.'

"'Well, what do I do?'

"'You don't do a thing. You just stand around and talk to anybody.' So we went.

"When we arrived Mrs. Dade said, 'Lieut. Furlow, do you like San Diego?'

"'Yes, sir,' was his embarrassed reply as his collar wilted right down with perspiration. She asked him another question and again it was 'Yes, sir,' as Mrs. Fleet and I tried to rescue him from his discomfort.

"Mrs. Dade sized Furlow up properly as coming from the back country. Actually he had been a tight wire walker in a circus in the South. He was probably the best of all us fliers at that stage of the game. He went into an unintentional spin and managed to come out of it okay!"

Obviously relishing the recollection which it brought, Reuben continued: "One day Colonel Dade asked if I thought I could land on the Army's Camp Kearny drill field near what was later the Miramar Naval Air Station. I told him, yes sir, I could be there in half an hour if he'd be sure there were no soldiers drilling on the parade ground.

"There were five Curtiss Jennies in our group and we landed without incident. As soon as I left my plane I was hailed by an artillery captain. It was Peter B. Kyne, the famed author, who had lived at Hoquiam, about 14 miles from my home in Montesano.

"I took Kyne for his first airplane ride and at the same time he became the first passenger to take off and land at Kearny Mesa. Later that day I made a number of artillery spotting flights."

Major H. H. (Hap) Arnold's name, of course, has long been associated with the Army's Rockwell Field at North Island where he was twice commanding officer; 1919 and 1922-24. But even in 1917 he was able to wield considerable influence, as Fleet related. "One day Clint Howard, later Arnold's brother-in-law, came in to mess and said, 'I just got a telegram from Hap offering me any post I want when I graduate. How would you like that?' I said, 'I'd like that fine!'"

On August 8th five Jennies of the Sixth 1917 cadet class left North Island five minutes apart for the 114-mile cross-country flight to Venice, near Los Angeles. With Lieut. Furlow as pilot and Fleet as observer they made the northbound trip in 2 hours 12 minutes. On the return, with Fleet as pilot, the time was 1 hour 58 minutes. Along the way they reported seeing a huge forest fire raging in the Capistrano Mountains.

Next day Reuben made the required 60-mile triangular flight to La Jolla, Lakeside and return to North Island via Coronado in an hour and a quarter.

"That same day," Fleet recollects, "four months after arriving for training and a week ahead of my class, I graduated as a Junior Military Aviator (JMA) with wings No. 74. I'd entered as a Captain in the Washington National Guard, then transferred to the regular Army with the same rank the day the war

SIXTH 1917 J.N.A. CLASS S.C.A.S. SAN DIEGO, CAL.

Officers, left to right: Capt. Wright (Oregon), Lieut. Furlow (Tennessee), Shields, Lt. Col. Turner (U.S.M.C.), Lieut. Smith (New Mexico), Capt. R. H. Fleet (Washington National Guard), Capt. Stroup (Kentucky), Lieut. Scheleen.

Harold A. Taylor

began. But when I qualified as a JMA and graduated from the Signal Corps Aviation School I received the rank, pay and allowances of Major—the next higher grade."

The accomplishments of a home town boy were not lost on the residents of Montesano, Washington. "Wins coveted qualification by same energy, courage and brain which marked his progress from childhood in Grays Harbor," heralded the Grays Harbor Post, adding that "The sacrifices of this patriotic young citizen, in what he believes is his duty to his country, is one of the marked examples of patriotic devotion shown by men from the Grays Harbor country."

In a somewhat subdued, rather rare display of humility, Reuben wrote his parents: "You must not feel elated over my success; since taking up [Christian] Science I have come to realize that everyone has the power to do what is required of them if they have the proper understanding. Therefore, one should not be praised for making good, and in fact I think we should all be mighty careful always not to appear bragging; we are entitled to no credit for doing our duty."

A variety of assignments came to Fleet because of his natural leadership and his sound business experience. "It is giving me," he wrote, "a mighty valuable education along all lines, administrative and otherwise, in connection with aviation, but I am literally swamped with work."

Records of the post exchange at Rockwell Field were in bad condition because of the frequent turnover in officers delegated that responsibility. Fleet conducted a thorough audit and established new record-keeping systems. Three enlisted men were charged, two with stealing, the other with issuing a bum check. Reuben was pressed into service as their defense attorney before a court-martial.

MONKEY WRENCHES at the ready, Portuguese fliers pose with instructor George E. A. Hallett, second from left.

Erickson/National Archives

JUNIOR MILITARY AVIATOR No. 74 and his seven year old son, David Girton Fleet. San Diego, 1917.

David G. Fleet

46

AERO-REPAIR DEPARTMENT, North Island. "It is great to see what they can do with metal and machinery."

"As soon as I had my wings," Fleet continued, "I was assigned to the 18th Aero Squadron, Training, acting as commanding officer of the 260-man unit in place of Major Henry J. Damm who, along with Oscar Brindley, has been ordered East to test the new Liberty engine at McCook Field. I've been made officer in charge of the machine shops and am catching on as rapidly as I can. It is great to see what they can do with metal and machinery.

"In this department they can make almost anything on earth that is made out of metal. I'm supposed to put in two hours of manual labor daily myself in the experimental and repair departments. The result is I've just turned out some very fine fittings. I've about half completed a strut which I intend to send to Ned [Bishop] as a sample of what they use in the Curtiss machine.

"It takes all afternoon to tune up and repair the aeroplanes used every morning. If the number of planes and the number of men were doubled we could fly in the afternoons, too, although the air is always rough then. The rougher it is, the harder it is to fly and the more on the alert one has to be to keep the plane on an even keel."

Although most training was in Jennies, Reuben had occasion to fly other aircraft based at North Island. He was not exactly enthusiastic about the Standard biplane.

"This is a ship," he wrote, "that nobody likes particularly as it weighs nearly a ton and a half and has only a 125 h.p. motor, which roars like a boiler factory in the air. It handles just like a 250-pound woman would if you tried to dance with her.

"The name is deceiving for the Curtiss JN-4 A and B models are 'standard' as far as training ships are concerned. Flying a ship like this on a rough day makes one more tired in 15 minutes than an hour of flying in a training ship.

"The other Squadron, the 14th, is commanded by Major Thurman H. Bane. I also assist Bane as instructor in aeronautics, about which I know nothing except for what I had learned from studying Grover Loening's book.

"I found myself instructing because I had solved a problem in a different way than had the rest of those in Major Bane's class. I stayed afterward and convinced Bane that my answer was correct and that his, which all the rest of the class had solved in the same way, was wrong. Next day he announced that my solution was correct and he explained it on the blackboard to the class.

"Aviation is pretty new and all of us are interested in aerodynamics and mechanical design problems. The word from overseas that machine guns had been synchronized with the engine to fire through the propeller arc during aerial dog fights was particularly intriguing. We couldn't figure how a gear arrangement could interrupt the fire long enough to allow the propeller blade to pass by the bullet trajectory. We thought the propeller would surely be shot off. It was a lively discussion, in which Clint Howard took a leading part because of what he considered to be his superior collegiate education."

47

WITH THE START OF THE YEAR 1918, Major Fleet, along with Lieut. Col. Bane, was ordered to new duty at Signal Corps aviation headquarters in Washington, D.C.

That left an important logistics problem—Mrs. Bane's Persian cat. Since Bane was Fleet's senior officer, Reuben drew the assignment of transporting the cat by airplane to their next station. Reuben recalls that for those days it was a long, long transcontinental journey from San Diego for the Jenny, for the Persian cat and for him.

At Washington, Fleet and Bane were to serve under Colonel Hap Arnold who had just been selected as Executive Officer of the newly named Air Division. In the same headquarters group were Major Delos Emmons and Lieut. Col. Byron Q. Jones.

Fleet was assigned as assistant executive officer to Jones, the chief of training. Jones' executive officer, Lieut. Col. John C. P. Bartholf, who was a class or two ahead of Fleet, was on sick leave in the hospital so Fleet actually served as executive officer for flying training. In February, Bertholf was reassigned to San Diego to head up pilot training at Rockwell Field.

"It was an assignment I was happy to have because I had developed a keen interest in pilot training," Fleet recalls. "Up to that time the Aviation Service had a spotty record and perhaps something could be done to improve it. Approximately two-thirds of the 73 Army aviators who preceded me had been killed in early Signal Corps aviation training, which suffered several times the casualties of any other branch of the Army. Motors were unreliable, airplanes frail and quick to spin, trainees often being unable to right their craft. Parachutes, of course, were not available."

Some of the major improvements in the very early days of training at North Island had come about through the work of B. Q. Jones and Oscar Brindley, a civilian instructor. In fact, flying was then so hazardous that only unmarried lieutenants under 30 years of age were eligible for training. Colonel Reber had persuaded Orville Wright to lend Brindley to the Signal Corps. The latter had been the Wright company's test pilot and instructor and so altered the training program at North Island that the record of fatal accidents, though still bad, was vastly improved.

The early Curtiss JN-2 was the standard plane not only for training but for general operational use. Pilots considered the planes so unsafe they recommended they should no longer be flown, especially with a passenger. Capt. V. E. Clark, in charge of engineering and inspection at North Island grounded all of them. They were replaced for training by Martin TTs and they, in turn, by the JN-4 Jennies in late 1916.

Based on an April 1917 visit to Europe by a commission headed by Lieut. Col. Raynal C. Bolling, the decision was made to concentrate American war production on two basic types—trainers, principally the JN-4D with the bulk of production by Curtiss, already building for the British; and the British-designed DeHavilland DH-4 observation planes and reconnaissance bombers, the largest quantity of which were constructed by Dayton-Wright.

Aircraft engine production was concentrated on the 400 h.p. Liberty which powered the DH-4, the only U. S. aircraft to see service overseas with the American Expeditionary Force. Pursuit and bomber aircraft for American fliers would be produced by the French and British.

During the eight years preceding the war, less than $1 million had been voted by Congress for military aviation. Three appropriations in 1917—$10.8 million in May, $43.5 million in June and a whopping $640 million in July—finally got the American military aircraft production program into high gear.

FLEET ARRIVED in Washington at a time of rapid expansion of training facilities. In the year between July 1917 and June 1918, more than 38,000 young men volunteered for flying training in the Army. "Jones and I," he recalls, "built 34 primary training schools and two advanced training schools for bombers, two for pursuit pilots plus two for aerial observers and for the Army pilots who were to carry the observers. Combat training of American flying personnel was carried out in France, England and Italy.

"Cadets in primary training received six to eight weeks instruction totaling 40 to 45 hours of flying time, usually in Curtiss Jennies. After receiving their commissions and Reserve Military Aviator (RMA) ratings, the pilots received a 25% monthly flying pay bonus. Later, at advanced schools, they were trained as pursuit, bomber or observation pilots.

"A total of 14,835 cadets were assigned to primary schools of which 8,688 received RMA ratings. During training there had been 278 fatal accidents.

"Many of the training schools are famous to this day—Kelly and Brooks Field at San Antonio and Ellington at Houston also in Texas; Mather at Sacramento, and March Field at Riverside, both in California; Langley Field, Virginia; and, of course, Wilbur Wright Field, Dayton, Ohio.

"Early during my assignment I flew up to New York to visit the officer-in-charge of flying at our school at Mineola, Long Island—Thomas Hitchcock Sr., prominent New Yorker and father of the famous polo player of that name. Hitchcock flew me all over Manhattan, the first time I had seen the metropolis from the air.

"Through Hitchcock I was to meet banker and transportation tycoon August Belmont who took a fancy to me too, and became a very firm friend. Belmont, like the Vanderbilts, Whitneys and Astors, was an early aviation enthusiast. He had helped finance the Wright Company and it was on his Belmont Park property that the important 1910 Air Meet had been held.

"My immediate superior, B. Q. Jones, was sent overseas in April to inspect aircraft the British and French were using. There he selected planes which were shipped back to the United States to be considered for reproduction for use by our pilots. When he returned he was placed in charge of testing and proving Air Service equipment. Later that year he became commanding officer of Wilbur Wright Test Field in Ohio."

The Deperdussin (Dep) aircraft control system then in vogue in Europe—which was similar to the Curtiss system—had been adopted for training aircraft and most other planes. It consisted of a wheel on a pillar which could be rotated for lateral control and moved back and forth for climb or descent. A rudder bar served to coordinate directional turns.

"Jones," Fleet explained, "had earlier arranged for the first stick control and the first Hispano-Suiza (Spanish-Swiss) water-cooled aircraft engine to be sent to the United States from overseas.

"On a Sunday in January 1918, Jones and I went down to the polo grounds in Potomac Park in Washington to fly the stick-control in a Jenny. He had given the Curtiss Company orders to install the stick instead of the 'Dep' wheel control but Curtiss had put it only in the front cockpit. Jones said, 'I know you can fly it, Fleet.'

"'I can do anything under orders,' I told him. 'Give me orders and I'll fly it.'

"'Alright, go fly it!'

"When I was warming up the engine, he hollered at me, 'Don't you take off if you don't think you can make it.'

"'I can make it,' I replied.

"We had learned always to fly with the left hand on the 'Dep' control. Now I had the throttle on the left, so that when I opened it I had to handle the stick with my right hand—just opposite of what we were used to. So, as soon as I had opened the throttle, I grabbed the stick with both hands for the takeoff and as I got into the air I tried the new control system and liked it pretty well. I flew for maybe half an hour and found myself feeling so comfortable and confident that when I landed I reported my favorable response to Jones and we decided to adopt it for all American ships. Both the Curtiss and Standard companies adopted stick control and others soon followed.

"A week later, on January 26, I tested the first Hispano-Suiza engine, also in a Jenny. I took the plane to 3,000 feet, cut the engine and did five spirals to the right just as we had done in training. Then the engine froze on me and I was up there with a dead stick over this little spot of only about 40 acres where I had to land. I had to be extremely careful because the landing area at Potomac Park was inside the quarter-mile track and there was a tree in the center and a band stand on the other end inside the track. It sort of spoiled it for landing. But I managed to get it down, although some darn fool ran out and the wing knocked him down as I landed, but he was unhurt."

QUALIFYING FOR MILITARY ratings usually took some study, time-consuming preparation and training, but Reuben Fleet, one fine spring Sunday morning in 1918, found himself a fully qualified Balloon Pilot by nightfall—all by accident. As he tells it:

"I came down to Potomac Park to take a free balloon flight with an instructor who also had five other officers whom he was instructing or giving a ride.

"We took off and soon found ourselves floating south over Virginia. All during the flight the instructor was showing me how the balloon operated; how we could get various air currents at different altitudes and control our direction by that means.

"Perhaps 50 miles down into Virginia we saw a large estate and our instructor suggested it would be a good place to land for lunch as traditional Southern hospitality might be extended visitors from the sky. Our unexpecting hosts invited us in and provided a wonderful dinner.

"We had tied the balloon to a tree and asked a group of colored 'boys' to get in so as to hold the basket down. After a wonderful chicken dinner, two of the officers and I went outside and started to get into the balloon. The colored boys, who were packed in like sardines, assumed it was time for them to depart. As the human ballast jumped out the balloon gave a lurch, broke loose and we three were airborne. As the temperature had heated up during the long noon hour, the gas in the balloon had swelled up and given it greater buoyancy.

"As the balloon rose rapidly I asked, 'Which one of you is a balloon pilot?' It was a real shock when they replied, 'This is our first ride! We thought you were the pilot because the instructor was giving you all kinds of information all the way down here.'

"'Well,' I said, 'I guess I had better take charge. The trick of it is, we will see if we can get back to Washington, or near there by sundown.'

"We maneuvered the balloon to where we caught a current of air more or less going toward Washington. Hours later we finally crossed the Potomac River and as we did so the cold air from the river caused the balloon to deflate considerably and it looked like we

San Diego Aero-Space Museum

*"A HURRIED and wholly unexpected departure left
the others with no means of transportation."*

were going to go down in the water.

"Under my orders, the two lieutenants grabbed the sand bags and threw them overboard. It was too late to dribble it out gradually as through a flour sifter. We made it across the Potomac and came to a small clearing of perhaps five acres. I pulled the rip cord and down we went. We hit but bounced up into the air again as the balloon had not yet lost all its buoyancy. Again I pulled the cord hard and fast. The bag ripped open and we settled down for good this time.

"Of course our hurried and wholly unexpected departure from the Virginia plantation left the others with no visible means of transportation. I can imagine what must have been said as they came outside after dinner to find that we had 'stolen' their balloon.

"Now, the requirements to become a balloon pilot were he had to make a free flight of eight hours or more without assistance from any balloonist. I qualified because we had flown about nine hours coming back to Washington, and had landed within seven miles of our take-off point that day. So I was rated a Balloonist and immediately the Chief of the Lighter-than-Air Section asked for my transfer to his command; and it looked like I was going to get it whether I wanted it or not.

"I went down to see the Chief and told him that I certainly didn't want it; that I didn't have to serve because I had two little children, and that if he put me in Lighter-than-Air I would resign from the Army. Colonel Chalmers G. Hall, who was in charge, didn't want to see me leave the service on that account, nor did others in Army Headquarters, so I got the balloonist rating but didn't have to take the transfer.

"The real payoff, however, was the transportation allowance I was able to collect from the government. They owed me mileage from our landing site back to our takeoff point. Seven miles at 7 cents a mile. I collected 49 cents for the day's outing."

ONE DAY WHILE FLEET'S unit was getting the pilot training schools started, there was a call to his office by a Congressman from Colorado who wanted him to establish a primary school in that state.

"I asked him where he wanted it in Colorado," Fleet recalls, "and he said 'anywhere' but preferably in his own congressional district. Then I inquired what was the lowest elevation in Colorado, and he said 4,500 feet.

"'Well,' I said, 'we are using OX-5 engines in training and they take ten minutes to get up to 3,000 feet. Now, if we had to start out at 4,500 feet we would possibly be able to make only one flight an hour with that kind of horsepower. Therefore, Mr. Congressman, it's impractical.'

"'You either put a flying field in Colorado,' he replied, 'or I'll get your ass kicked out of here.'

"Jones was in the next office and heard the Congressman explode all over me. Ink-well in hand, Jones burst in and barked out, 'That officer (Fleet) knows his business and he told you the truth.' At that point the ink-well sailed across the room and splattered on the wallboard behind my desk as Jones railed at the Congressman, 'Get the hell out of here!'

"Later the Congressman had a picture taken of the ink-spattered wall, preferred charges against Jones and as a result Jones was reduced in rank from Lieut. Colonel to Major for six months."

MAJOR FLEET KNEW PLENTY about pilot training, but when Colonel Arnold added the training of aerial observers to the assignment, Reub was perplexed.

"Hap, I never saw an air observer in my life and therefore I don't think I should have to take responsibility for their training."

"Well," replied Arnold, "none of us have either. You have got the job and I want you to take it."

So, in addition to his other work, Fleet took on a new job. But some days later Reub was greatly agitated by a memo from Arnold which he found on his desk.

"Major (Clint) Howard will be your commanding officer for the training of air observers. When you get ready for him, send for him."

As Reuben later recalled, "That made me mad and I took the memo around to Arnold.

"'I just got this note from you this morning. If you are going to charge me with successful operation of these schools, you had better at least give me a voice in the selection of the commanding officer. Captain Deverre, detailed by the French to help indoctrinate us in air observer training, says that Howard has got the 'hookworm' and never gets on the job until 10:30 in the morning!'

"But Arnold was not to be budged. 'Major Howard,' he said, 'is going to be the commanding officer. Do you understand that?'

"'Yes sir.' So out I went, and as I did Delos Emmons said, 'You damn fool. Didn't you know Howard is Hap's brother-in-law?'

"I sent Howard a wire giving him orders to come in for a conference. Next morning Hap and I were in the elevator going up to our office.

" 'Hap, I guess I owe you an apology. Yesterday I didn't know Howard was your brother-in-law.'

" 'You don't owe me an apology at all, Fleet. I decided to give that kid a chance to make good. If he doesn't, all you've got to do is say so and out he goes.'

" 'Or, out I go. And I don't care which.'

" 'No, Reub, out he goes!'

"Howard came on in for the conference and stayed with his brother-in-law that night. Next morning when he came in Clint says to me, 'Fleet, I know that you didn't pick me for this job.'

" 'No, I didn't.'

" 'Well, are you going to give me a square deal on this job?'

" 'Certainly.'

" 'Are you going to give me the things I ask for on this job?'

" 'Yes, within the bounds of reason. You know, Clint, you rank me but I've got this assignment and therefore I've got to run it. And I'm going to run it to the best of my ability.'

" 'Well, then, when do you want me to start in?'

" 'Today. Take the boat down to Langley Field and start in tomorrow morning at 5:30.'

" 'But, Mrs. Howard isn't here yet.'

" 'Clint, we've got a war on. Give me the dope about her and I'll have an officer meet her and get her down there. But we can't hold back a war, you know, just because Mrs. Howard isn't here.'

"Several days later Howard called up and told me he wanted Henry Miller for officer-in-charge of flying.

" 'My goodness, Clint, you don't want that. He's got the 'hookworm' worse than you have and he's a playboy.'

" 'Well, that's all right. If you don't give me the man I ask for you can't hold me responsible.'

" 'Let me tell you something. I'll hold this line open for three minutes and at the end of that time I'll ask you if you still want Henry Miller. If you say you do, knowing how I cautioned you about him, why I'll send him to you.' Then, after a pause—

" 'So, what's your decision?'

" 'I'll take Henry Miller.'

"So I sent Miller down there and will say for both of them they certainly did a wonderful job. They were cautioned, but did the job so well that Miller got a chance to go overseas."

Blank-Stoller

MAJOR R. H. FLEET, Executive Officer for Flying Training, Signal Corps Aviation Section.

BY THE TIME AMERICA'S pilot training program was organized and growing, the report that the British had a more successful program was gaining considerable coinage. More startling was the initiative of the British aviation mission in the United States, as described by Major Fleet:

"The British came to see me at my office in Washington and said they were doing a better job in training than we were, so I said, 'Colonel, how would you suggest that we prove that statement of yours?'

" 'Well, you give me ten students and I'll train them our way against ten students you train, and we'll see which is the better method.'

"So I got in touch with August Belmont and he agreed to let us use his nursery farm at the Belmont Race Track out on Long Island. We had our Captain Frank Coffman draw out ten names and give them to the British; then we took ten names for the American training group. Three of our best instructors were selected; the British picked Colonel Robert Smith-Barry, a Major Scott and First Lieutenant Sully.

"Our system involved designating the best 5 percent of our fliers to train the others. The rest we sent overseas to combat. Many of the youngsters were virtually uncontrollable; they flew under bridges, looped over them and didn't obey orders. They were young and active and full of vinegar; war gave them a chance to work it out of their system.

"The special group of students was sent up to New York in April and the next day all started training at the improvised flying field at the Belmont nursery. Frank Coffman logged the time the British spent, and we spent, on each student. Among them the British happened to draw a man 34 years old, four years older than the normal age limit, and he was the slowest learner they had.

"In a few weeks the British sent down word that they had all their men trained, so I flew up to Long Island. I had to make a couple of turns around the field before I could land because the landing strip was so small.

"I flew with each of the men the British had trained, including the 34-year-old student; and we still hadn't finished up the American-trained group of pilots. So we had a conference.

" 'To what do you attribute your success, Colonel Smith-Barry?' I asked.

" 'To the line of patter we use with our speaking tube and to the Avro machine,' he replied.

"Well, we discounted what he said about the Avro airplane, figuring it was just Smith-Barry's desire to boost a British product. We chalked that down as not having any bearing. But they had taught the men to forward-slip and side-slip into that little field, which was a maneuver we didn't use.

"The British proved that their trainer and their system of instruction was indeed superior, and I was anxious to go abroad and visit Smith-Barry's School of Special Flying at Gosport, England, to learn for myself more about their methods. Before the year was out I was to have that opportunity."

11*R.A.F. Central Flying School Museum*

"AVRO MACHINE," said Smith-Barry, "was key to British pilot training success."

THE AMERICAN-PRODUCED British DeHavilland DH-4 bomber was to be powered by a new American aircraft engine. Engineers from the automotive industry, headed by Jesse G. Vincent of Packard Motor Car Co. and E. J. Hall of Hall-Scott Motor Car Co., joined with Army engineers in the design of the new Liberty engine. The original 8-cylinder 300 h.p. design was tested but did not prove powerful enough. When redesigned as a 12-cylinder engine it produced the required 400 h.p. By late spring 1918 it was ready for testing. Lieut. Col. Bane picks up the story as described in his diary:

"On May 2, 1918, Lieut. Col. Henry J. Damm and Major Oscar A. Brindley were killed testing the first Liberty engine in a DH airplane at South Field in Dayton, Ohio. Lieut. Col. Thurman H. Bane, Majors Reuben H. Fleet and Albert D. Smith met there, inspected the wreck, and determined the cause of the accident to have been a removed spark plug dropped on the lower wing which [lodged between] the wing trailing edge and the aileron, preventing banking of the airplane when the motor missed and caused pilot Brindley to turn back to the field from which they had taken off. Col. Damm's diary showed, 'South Field is too small for this test-flying.'

"Major Smith was on crutches with a broken ankle caused by his crash of a French Nieuport airplane, and so I designated Fleet to complete the test of the second Liberty engine in another DH, inasmuch as every delay counted, and the President had announced, 'America will win the war with aviation,' and that 'this is a war to end all wars and make the world safe for democracy.'

"Fleet insisted that the DH airplanes be trucked to Wilbur Wright Field to afford more runway and airfield. There he took off, flew the ship beyond the field's length, took it to 6,000 feet, banked it with gentle and then steeper banks, looped it four successive loops with power on, then stalled it deliberately and kicked it into a spin which he came out of 800 feet from the ground. Upon landing we gave him hell for spinning down so low, until he peeled off his shirt and wrung out the perspiration, remarking that he'd pass up lunch."

"I DESIGNATED FLEET to complete tests of the Liberty engine in the DeHavilland DH-4."

1*Ryan Aeronautical Library*

UNBEKNOWNST TO MAJOR Fleet, who at the time was traveling between Washington and Dayton to investigate the Liberty-powered DH crash, the War Department on May 3, 1918, issued an order to the Air Service to inaugurate the first U. S. Air Mail Service—with only twelve days notice.

Reuben played an important role in that historic but ill-prepared event as he related with almost total recall to Air Mail Pioneers on their golden anniversary fifty years later:

"Aerial Mail Service between Washington and New York each way [was to be flown] every day except Sunday, to depart both terminals at 11:00 a.m. beginning Wednesday, 15 May 1918. Intermediate landing and mail service to be provided at Philadelphia by both north and south bound airplanes. Airline distance between north and south terminals—218 miles.

"The order was issued by Newton D. Baker, Secretary of War, at the request of the Post Office Department, under direction of President Woodrow Wilson. A. S. Burleson was the Postmaster General; Otto Praeger, Second Assistant Postmaster General was in charge of transportation of all mail.

"Never before had mail been carried anywhere in the world by air at an announced time to and from designated places on a schedule operation irrespective of weather.

"The order came as a complete surprise, although I learned from President Wilson on inauguration day of the mail that the Cabinet had been discussing establishment of an Aerial Mail Service for several months. Bids had been called for but none were received; and, upon recommendation of Colonel E. A. Deeds, Air Service Production, that the training would be valuable to Army pilots, had decided to order the Army to fly it.

"Agreement to operate the Aerial Mail Service jointly by the War and the Post Office Departments was dated 1 March 1918, and Congress had appropriated $100,000 but we in the Air Service knew nothing of this until the order of 3 May.

"Upon recommendation of Colonel H. H. Arnold, I was appointed Officer-in-Charge of the Aerial Mail Service, in addition to my duties as Executive Officer for Flying Training.

"Colonel Arnold was entirely too busy in his new job as Assistant Director of Military Aeronautics, to bother with either the aerial mail or with the training of aviators. One of his great virtues was that he selected assistants carefully and required them to run their 'shows' without questions or assistance. Our country was at war and since Major General William L. Kenly, the newly appointed Director of Military Aeronautics, was not a flier, there was lots of work for Colonel Arnold to do with constant cablegrams from European fronts and airfields overseas.

"On 6 May, Secretary Baker phoned me to come to his office for a conference. I reported the Air Service had no airplanes capable of flying non-stop from Washington to Philadelphia or from Philadelphia to New York, and requested postponement to gain more time than eight days to obtain Curtiss JN-6H airplanes modified for mail service.

"Secretary Baker invited Postmaster General Burleson to his office; Burleson went into a rage over the suggestion for deferment, stating he had already announced to the press that an Army Aerial Mail Service would get started on 15 May, and that it had to start then, even if war work suffered.

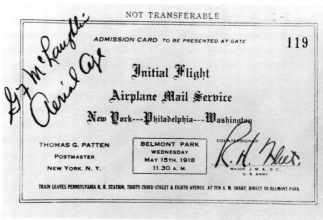

General Dynamics/Convair

THE PRESS had already been invited.

"Secretary Baker was sympathetic with my recommendation but the fact that the press had been advised was governing, and the War Department had to do it even if its aviators had to land in meadows enroute and retank with gasoline, oil and maybe water.

"It was agreed that I would run the job until I had the service inaugurated and in such shape that it operated without failure for ten days; then I could reassume my other work.

"Without leaving Secretary Baker's office, I telephoned Colonel Deeds, and requested him to order six JN-6Hs from Curtiss Aeroplane and Motor Corporation on Long Island, leaving out the front seat and the front control, and substituting in the front cockpit a hopper to carry mail; also installing in each airplane, double capacity for gasoline and oil, the six airplanes to be delivered to us at Mineola Air Field in eight days.

"Curtiss accepted the telephonic order and agreed to have the six airplanes ready at the sacrifice of suspending delivery of trainers during this period.

They proposed to use two regular 19 gallon gasoline tanks and two regular 2½ gallon oil tanks, hooking together each pair of tanks to double their capacity. The normal range of a Curtiss JN-6H airplane trainer with a gasoline tank carrying 19 gallons was 88 miles in one hour and twenty minutes at cruising speed of 66 miles an hour, reduced by head-winds and accelerated by tail winds.

"I then telephoned my friend Major August Belmont, owner of Belmont Park Race Track on Long Island, and requested permission to use his Park for the aerial mail serving New York City, as the Army did not want to interrupt training of aviators at Hazelhurst Field in Mineola where Major Thomas Hitchcock was Officer-in-Charge of Flying.

"On 13 May I went with five other aerial mail pilots (leaving Lieut. George Boyle in Washington) to the Curtiss factory at Garden City, where the mail planes were reportedly ready. Mechanics, engineers, and we pilots worked night and day, and yet on the afternoon of 14 May only two airplanes were flyable.

"I had personally selected and detailed for the Aerial Mail Service, Lieutenants Howard Paul Culver, Torrey H. Webb, Walter Miller, and Stephen Bonsal and the Post Office Department had requested that Lieutenants James C. Edgerton and George L. Boyle be detailed by us for the Mail Service.

"Edgerton's father was purchasing agent for the Post Office Department; Lieutenant Edgerton had just graduated from primary instruction as an aviator at Ellington Field. Lieutenant Boyle's father-in-law-to-be was Judge Charles C. McChord, Interstate Commerce Commissioner who had 'saved the parcel post for the Post Office Department' against private express companies bidding and fighting in court for the business. The Post Office Department requested that Lieutenant Boyle fly the first aerial mail from Washington, and Lieutenant Edgerton fly the first into Washington.

"I left Lieutenant Webb in charge at Belmont Park and the Curtiss plant, with Lieutenants Miller and Bonsal helping and in reserve. Webb was instructed to get the other four aerial mail airplanes ready, and to fly one from Belmont Park with the aerial mail at eleven the next morning south to Bustleton Field, which the Philadelphia postmaster had selected for Philadelphia. Edgerton at Bustleton Field would relieve Lieutenant Webb there and fly on to Washington, while Lieutenant Culver would relay the northbound aerial mail from Philadelphia to Belmont Park in New York.

"Edgerton, Culver and I left Belmont Race Track for Philadelphia on the afternoon of the 14th. I assigned Culver and Edgerton each an aerial mail plane and I flew an ordinary Jenny trainer without extra fuel tanks because only two aerial mail airplanes were ready by afternoon of 14 May.

"The weather was frightful; it was so foggy we pilots could not see each other after take-off; the masts of boats in New York Harbor were in fog. I climbed through the fog and came out at 11,000 feet, almost the ceiling of the airplane. I flew by magnetic compass and the sun until I ran out of gasoline and the propeller stopped.

"I glided in the direction of Philadelphia, and came out of the clouds with 3,000 feet to spare. I selected a farm and landed, buying a five gallon milk can of ordinary gasoline from a farmer. We had lots of trouble pouring it in the gasoline tank without a funnel and without a chamois skin to strain it. Perhaps three

"I LANDED at Potomac Park - the mail was due to start twenty-five minutes later."

gallons got in the airplane and darkness was coming. I inquired where Bustleton was, took off, flew toward it, ran out of gasoline again, and landed in a meadow two miles from Bustleton Field. As no telephone was available, I commandeered a farmer to drive me to Bustleton Field, and sent Culver with aviation gasoline to get the airplane and fly it in.

"There were so many things wrong with the airplanes and their motors that we worked all night to get them in better commission; for example, one gas tank had a hole the size of a lead pencil and we had to cork it up with an ordinary bottle cork, as there was no time or facility to repair it. By 8:40 the next morning, one mail machine was flyable and I took off for Washington, where I landed at 10:35 AM at the Polo Field in Potomac Park—the mail was due to start twenty-five minutes later.

"I had delegated Capt. B. B. Lipsner, who was not an aviator, and had been detailed by Air Service Production at his request to the Aerial Mail Service, to have aviation gasoline at the Polo Field in Washington. He failed in his mission and didn't have a drop of gasoline there. We drained gasoline from a British airplane and two other American airplanes that were on the field, and filled the aerial mail airplane.

"President Wilson was there with his wife; also Mr. Burleson, Otto Praeger and the Japanese Postmaster General. President Wilson said, 'Tomorrow I want to extend this service to Boston.' I replied, 'Mr. President, please do not order this until we can get the equipment and personnel.' He said, 'I want you to come to the White House right after the aerial mail airplane takes off and bring Secretary Baker with you.'

"As there was no aviation field in Washington, we had to use the Polo Field in Potomac Park for take-off and landing. It was surrounded by a race track outside of which was a row of beautiful trees about 30 feet high.

"Four days before the aerial mail was due to start, I requested permission from the Park Commission to cut down a lone, non-symmetrical, ugly and hazardous tree that was out in the field. They asked when we needed the tree removed and I said, 'Three days.' They said it would take them three months to act.

"I went to the field and ordered mechanics to cut down the tree six inches below the ground, fill over the stump with cinders, tamp it hard and pull the fallen tree outside the race track. Another obstacle was the bandstand at one end of the field, about which nothing could be done. The lone tree had caused Colonel Clarence C. Culver (no relative of Lieut. Culver) to crash and he had been hospitalized for weeks. Colonel Culver was in charge of our important development of radio.

General Dynamics/Convair

"Later, Secretary Baker directed me to report to his office and asked if I had had a tree cut down at the Polo Grounds at Potomac Park. When I answered, 'Yes sir,' Secretary Baker asked if I didn't know one had to have permission from the Park Commission before cutting down a tree in Washington. I told him the Park Commission had said it would take them three months to act, so I acted. I continued, 'I didn't ask for this job, Mr. Secretary. I am in charge of training of all Army aviators in the United States, with 34 fields operating and students crashing every hour of the day, so if you want me to run this aerial mail job also, leave me alone and I'll run it!' Secretary Baker said, 'You know your business, Fleet—continue to run it and I'll back you from hell to breakfast.'

U. S. Army Signal Corps

MAP BEFORE THEM, Reuben Fleet, right, gave Lieut. Boyle "the correct compass course to Philadelphia."

"At 10:45 AM, Lieut. Boyle's fiancee, Margaret McChord, was there with an armful of red roses. Even as I strapped my map on his leg and gave him the corrected compass course to Philadelphia, she kissed him goodbye and waved him off. He got lost in the air, landed in a plowed field near Waldorf, Maryland, 25 air miles from takeoff, and flipped the plane over on its back, breaking the propeller. He telephoned me at the office of the Second Assistant Postmaster General for instructions. I directed him to bring the mail back to Washington and we sent it by air the next day.

"The Post Office Department then requested that Lieut. Boyle be given a second chance. On this trip I accompanied him in another airplane 40 miles on the correct compass course, cut my throttle, asked him if he was okay and could carry on. He yelled back, 'I'm okay.' He landed, lost and out of gas, near the mouth of Chesapeake Bay, retanked with gasoline and took off for Bustleton Field. He crashed near Philadelphia Country Club without hurting himself, breaking a wing of his plane. He delivered the mail by truck to Philadelphia.

"The Post Office Department then requested that 'Lieut. Boyle be given a third chance and, if he fails, the Post Office Department will take responsibility for his failure.' Relying on Secretary Baker's statement that he'd back me from 'hell to breakfast,' I replied, 'The request is denied. Lieut. Boyle is relieved of all duty with the Aerial Mail Service and is being sent back to flying school for further training in cross-country flying. If the Post Office Department wishes to place the Aerial Mail Service in proper light before the public, it will take responsibility for Lieut. Boyle's two previous failures; the Chief of the Aerial Mail Service had no voice in Lieut. Boyle's selection.' Lieut. E. W. Kilgore was selected to replace Boyle.

"While the Post Office Department had also requested Lieut. Edgerton, he certainly 'made good.' He relayed the southbound mail from Philadelphia into Washington the first day, and it was a wonderful feeling to see him land beautifully at Potomac Park, bringing in the New York and Philadelphia mail the afternoon of inaugural day.

"The Post Office Department had asked how much postage it should charge. I inquired if the idea was to make the aerial mail self-supporting and if there was a limit. Mr. Praeger said, 'We want it to stand on its own feet; our limit is 24 cents,' which I then recommended. Such a stamp was printed and used on the first aerial mail letters.

"The first four days we were filled with mail and then patronage dropped steadily. We carried ordinary mail up to capacity and reduced postage to eight cents and had new eight cent stamps printed. We equipped the terminal post offices with rubber cancellation stamps 'Delivered by Aerial Mail,' and the press and business people began to praise us everywhere. It took four days to get all four route segments through without failure and then, after ten days with a perfect record, we persuaded Secretary Baker to relieve the Army of aerial mail duties, turning over to the Post Office Department temporarily the pilots and mechanics, the airplanes and fields, and Captain Lipsner of Air Service Production who had requested the detail.

"When the first plane had left Potomac Park for Philadelphia, I left for the White House with Secretary Baker. I asked him earnestly to oppose extension of the service to Boston next day without our having time to prepare, and explained we had had to neglect war operations to handle the existing aerial mail assignment.

"Secretary Baker supported me and no announcement of extension of the aerial mail service to and from Boston was then made to the press. However, Boston round trip service was begun on 6 June 1918.

"President Wilson presented me with a Hamilton wrist watch engraved to commemorate the occasion. The watch and six similar ones for the other pilots were donated by the Hamilton Watch Company, 'manufacturers of the watch of railroad accuracy.' My watch still runs [1968] and keeps good time.

"The airplane which Lieut. Webb flew into Bustleton field from New York and which Lieut. Edgerton relayed to Washington was No. 38278 and that which I flew into Washington from Philadelphia on the morning of the inauguration of the aerial mail service and turned over to Lieut. Boyle was No. 38262.

56

"All the aerial mail planes were doped fabric covered as to wings and fuselages; structure being wire-braced. They were open cockpit biplanes, properly called JN-6Hs, each airplane being powered by a Hispano-Suiza 150 horsepower single engine. There were no parachutes; every pilot rode his airplane down to earth on a forced landing. All pilots wore helmets, breeches and leggins, goggles, and leather jackets.

"There were no maps of much value in existence at the inauguration of the aerial mail. Major E. Lester Jones, Chief of our Geodetic Survey, made up maps for us to use. The state maps of New York, New Jersey, Pennsylvania, Delaware and Maryland were all different scales and they showed only political divisions with nothing of a physical nature except cities, towns, rivers, harbors, etc.

"We had to fold maps of the entire United States in a 'strip' to have everything on a uniform scale. Naturally, the maps contained little detail. The magnetic compass was inaccurate and was affected by metal on the airplane; there were no compass bases to use in compensating each compass. Pilots of this early day had to have a natural sense to fly between given points at a designated hour irrespective of weather. We should, therefore, not criticize Lieut. Boyle too severely for his failures. He simply lacked enough training to do the job and the Air Service could risk no more than two trials to suit the Post Office Depart-

ment before relieving him for more cross-country instructions.

"The whole Administration was interested in our experiments and there was no question but that my friend, Colonel Deeds, was right in recommending that the Aerial Mail Service would be valuable training for our young aviators. Our pilots, however, had had cross-country training and commanded everyone's respect. The Army pilots flew the aerial mail for the Post Office from 15 May 1918 to 12 August 1918 when it was taken over by the Post Office Department. I severed my command at the close of the second week, to carry on with other duties.

"Otto Praeger, Second Assistant Postmaster General in charge of transportation of all mail, should be credited with fighting hard for Air Mail in our country. He was ably assisted by Chief Clerk George L. Conner.

"What an age in which to serve!"

Lieut. Paul Culver well understood the key role Reuben Fleet had played in establishment of the air mail service. "Major Fleet," he wrote, "was in complete charge of the entire project and the other pilots were soon to know why. His dynamic personality and bustling activity were contagious. We knew immediately we were working with a man who was really going to make things happen, or blow his top in the attempt."

AFTER LIEUT. BOYLE'S shaky start, Major Fleet got the air mail on schedule and returned to his other duties.

By THE TIME FLEET had finished the air-mail assignment and some advanced flight training at Ellington and Brooks Field in Texas, and was again back in Washington, he needed a rest—or at least a change of scene.

"I was so tired out," the Major later recalled, "that I suggested a detail to the field, preferably out somewhere at one of the schools.

"Major Emmons said that we were going to put our largest training activity in Sacramento, California, and that after two months leave to rest, he was going to head it. He asked if I would open Mather Field as officer-in-charge of flying and commandant of cadets. Get it running so that it would be operating efficiently when he came to take command.

"It was June 20 when I arrived and I was there for three months. Sacramento proved to be too hot for Mrs. Fleet and the children so I procured quarters for them at Alameda on San Francisco Bay. For myself I had bachelor quarters at Mather Field but was able to visit with my family over the week-ends.

"At Mather Field we were allowed to put in our own course of instruction. We decided that we had so many primary-field pilots trained and awaiting assignment at Camp Dick in Texas, that we would train primary pilots of high quality rather than pilots in quantity. I laid out a course of 93 minimum hours of instruction which guaranteed a well-trained officer.

"Facilities were quite primitive since Mather was only a few months old and like many other airfields was hastily developed with dirt runways and crude hangars during the early days of the war. We started out with JN-4D Jennies. Four of them had been assembled for us by the local Liberty Iron Works."

Night flying was a little known art and Fleet spent considerable time at it himself while at Mather. Then he introduced night flying into the training schedule by teaching five of the regular officers himself and checking them out as instructors.

Military radio was virtually unknown in those days, one of the few installations being in Fleet's office at training headquarters in Washington. Use of carrier pigeons was still an accepted method of message transmission.

The most unusual training innovation which the Major introduced at Mather Field was the art of aerial launching of carrier pigeons. It was a deadly serious matter; deadly for the pigeons if not properly done.

"We put in a four-hour course," Fleet recalls, "to teach pilots how to release the pigeons without tearing their wings off. The technique was to release them in still air; that meant training our pilots to pull their planes up into a stall; then launch the pigeons on their flight."

Although Major Fleet had a reputation of being a hard-nosed administrator and disciplinarian he was not exactly lacking in humor—at least the dry wit variety one expects of the British.

Fleet's son David, then a lad of eight, recalls this incident:

"Because the weather was hot and the field dusty, it was the custom to use a water cart drawn by two mules to wet down the takeoff and landing area. Father always instructed cadets to 'S' their planes before takeoff—that is, taxi their planes in the form of the letter S in order to be sure the area ahead of the plane was clear of any obstruction.

"After being duly cautioned, one of the lieutenants saluted, wheeled about and went out the door of father's office. A few minutes later I heard a loud crash. When the dust settled I saw the plane partially nosed over where it hit the water cart, and one of the mules lying on the ground.

"Father, who had quite a temper in those days, jumped out of his chair and leaped to the window. The veins in his neck stood out as his face grew red as a beet. I ran out the door and across the field to where the lieutenant was just pulling himself out of the wreck. Brushing his clothes off, he started walking toward the office to report the accident.

"Deciding it would be worth the risk to find out what Dad would say to him, I ran back. My father was seated at his desk, still livid with rage. The lieutenant marched in, saluted smartly and awaited the explosion. Father got up, stared at the man for a full minute and then snapped, 'You're grounded for a month! It's just a case of one ass hitting another!' "

After his two months leave, bachelor Emmons reported to Mather Field in August and it was while there Fleet introduced him to Billie McKim. He fell in love with her and soon she became Mrs. Billie Emmons. With Emmons in charge, Fleet was able to resume his regular work.

"On my return to Washington from Mather Field," he explained, "I was reassigned on temporary duty to Dayton to take charge of testing of foreign military aircraft which B. Q. Jones had arranged to have imported from overseas for evaluation. There were 33 airplanes to test and I jumped right into the task. I shared it with Major A. D. Smith, who had been one of my instructors in San Diego; Howard M. Rinehart; Harold T. 'Slim' Lewis and Benny Whalen.

"After this assignment I was involved for several weeks with a group working on a new standard training course for pilots.

"As I was anxious to get overseas, particularly to observe and fly at Smith-Barry's special school at Gosport, England, I asked Colonel Arnold for appropriate orders.

"At that time, officers for overseas duty were requested by name and then only by General William (Billy) Mitchell and General Patrick, who were in charge of the Army Air Service overseas.

"Arnold said, 'Fleet, I want to go overseas too, so you go up and see the Chief of Staff and get orders for both of us so we can go together. Among other things, I've seen the tests of Boss Kettering's Bug—his pilotless flying bomb—and I think the information may be of interest to General Pershing. Fix it so that when we get there we can order ourselves wherever we figure we'll be most needed and effective.'

"So I went up to see Major General Peyton C. March, Acting Chief of Staff, who was a personal acquaintance. I had made quite a hit with him in the way I had handled the training of colored aerial observers at Ft. Sill, Oklahoma, one of our advanced schools.

"A Britisher I had put in command of the school at Ft. Sill sent me a 400-word telegram, the contents of which, if made public, would be very embarrassing. I phoned Major Dargue, officer-in-charge of flying, and gave him instructions which solved the problem. General Marsh was most appreciative. He signed our overseas orders.

"Before going overseas Colonel Arnold was anxious to inspect the submarine base at New London, Connecticut, so I got an open cockpit Jenny at our base on Long Island and flew 'Hap' the 110 miles up there. Just as we arrived opposite New London the Jenny developed engine trouble and I had to make a forced landing on Fisher's Island. We phoned the Navy, which sent a boat over for Arnold so he could complete his mission.

"By the time Arnold returned I had replaced the spark plugs and checked the engine out. There was a telephone pole line at the end of the area where I should have taken off into the wind, so it was necessary to make a downwind takeoff but the return trip was without incident as far as flying was concerned. However, Arnold came down with the flu immediately afterward as a result of that trip."

COL. H. H. ARNOLD was marched lockstep up the gangplank by Reuben Fleet and his aide.

N EARLY TEN THOUSAND troops were scheduled to depart from New York with us on the 'Olympic' in mid-October," Reuben continued, "but the influenza epidemic was at its height and 1500 troops with the flu had to stay behind in hospitals.

"Our problem was how to get the very ill Arnold aboard. His aide, Major John B. Reynolds, teamed up with me. I put Arnold just behind me, extending my arms backward around him."

Reuben stood up, arm thrust behind to illustrate, and continued, "Major Reynolds grasped my wrists. Thus supporting Arnold we marched lockstep up the gangplank to get him aboard. Then we put him to bed immediately in the best suite aboard because he was so ill; in fact, we were afraid he might die on the trip

across the Atlantic. I gave him rubdowns every day and did all I could to get him as well as possible by the time we arrived in Southampton.

"Colonel Arnold, as the SOPA—Senior Officer Present Afloat—was in command of all the troops. We couldn't let others know how ill he was. Second in command was Lieut. Col. Charles H. Swift, board chairman of the Swift packing company, an ordnance officer, whose civilian life habits hardly fitted him for command responsibility. Consequently I, as a Major, did all the staff work enroute in Colonel Arnold's name and performed the necessary ceremonial duties without revealing his illness. By the time we got him overseas he was on the road to recovery.

"Some days before we boarded the 'Olympic' Arnold had received a cable from General Pershing stating that of all the troops going overseas, the Air Service officers and Chaplains were the most undisciplined and poorest in appearance. Before we debarked at Southampton, Hap made it clear to me that this condition must be corrected.

"There were seven of us dining together at every meal—that is, assuming Arnold could make it to our table. The others were Majors Clifford B. Harmon and

August Belmont, and Captain Kendall, an officer unknown to us but apparently an executive of the Consolidated Coal Company. Harmon was a balloonist; he had married the daughter of Commodore Cornelius Vanderbilt.

"Major Reynolds had been recruited from industry. He had been manager of the Indianapolis Chamber of Commerce and was commissioned a Major and assistant to Colonel Arnold to handle his extensive correspondence, including that with congressmen and senators.

"Colonel Swift and I had the suite adjoining Arnold's. Swift had spent a week in New York before departure outfitting his large foot locker with needed equipment. His pajamas were so diaphanous that you could squeeze them in your hand and have no material showing between your fingers. He had never shaved himself in his life. I had to get a man up every morning to shave him. Mr. Gillette had given him a gold razor but he never used it. Swift saw me shave with my $1 Star razor and offered to trade me, but I was used to mine and wouldn't trade for his gold one.

"One night Captain Kendall said, 'Gentlemen, I will bet you the best dinner we can get in London that I will shake hands with Mr. David Lloyd George, British Prime Minister, and with His Majesty, King George VI, within an hour after we get to London.' So Major Harmon said, 'I'll take that bet.' The next night I was to learn that Capt. Kendall would lose his wager.

"We had agreed that in case of an emergency such as a German sub attack, we would meet at a designated station on the starboard side on the top deck. Of course we cruised at night without lights. The night of October 23, with no advance warning, the ship suddenly stopped dead in the water.

"I groped my way forward to our agreed meeting place. Out of the darkness came a whisper of the first word of the countersign. I answered, whispering; next came the second word, and I again responded. Then came the third word and the officer whispered, 'I have come after Colonel [Edward M.] House.' He was President Wilson's confidant and personal representative to negotiate an Armistice with the Central Powers.

"I said, 'He is not aboard.'

"Just then somebody touched me on the shoulder and said, 'Stand by. Colonel House is not on your manifest but here he is. I am the Captain of the ship. Let us by.'

"I stepped back and heard Colonel House whisper, 'Where is Mr. Lloyd George?'

"Out of the darkness came the response, 'He is waiting for you in Paris. He flew the Channel this morning.'

"So we lowered Colonel House down in the darkness as he was to be transferred to another ship. Less than a month later the Armistice was signed.

"Of course there in the dark I learned why the ship had stopped and that Mr. Lloyd George was not in London. Captain Kendall had lost his wager but did not then know it."

Soon after the 'Olympic' docked at Southampton on the 24th, Colonel Arnold was removed by ambulance in the drizzling rain and was on his way to a military hospital near Winchester. Then he heard a noise in the distance, growing louder by the minute.

"It was Major Fleet," wrote Arnold as he described the scene to his wife, "marching his Chaplains and Air Service Officers from Southampton to Winchester, at attention, in the rain, in the dark, at eleven o'clock at night.

" 'One, two, three, four! Damn you, Chaplains, keep in step. One, two, three, four! Damn you, Chaplains, keep in step.' It was about twelve miles from Southampton to Winchester, but Fleet was making soldiers of them."

"As soon as we got to London," Fleet recalled, "I went out and obtained for each of us a little ration stamp that entitled us to two meals a week with meat, or four meals if we had hare or foul like pheasant or chicken. Right off Major Harmon started to invite everyone he knew in London to join us for dinner at Capt. Kendall's expense. Included was Claude Graham-White, England's first aviator, a friend of Harmon's since they had both participated in the 1910 Belmont Park Air Meet, and Ethel Levy, wife of George M. Cohan, composer of 'Over There.'

" 'The dinner's on me,' Kendall announced. 'I did shake hands with the King but was unable to see Mr. Lloyd George because he is not in London.' Of course, I was the only one who knew he was in Paris, but said nothing about it.

"Harmon came to dinner wearing a pair of wings on his left breast twice the size of the wings any of us wore. In no uncertain terms Hap said to me, 'Tell him to take off those wings!'

" 'Well,' I said, 'you don't want me to do that at this dinner do you, Colonel? It would be very embarrassing. We could tell him afterwards.'

" 'With those thick glasses of his,' Arnold explained, 'he couldn't even see to land an airplane. He's only entitled to a balloon observer's one wing. But let it go. Of course we can't do it here.'

"Then, talking to Kendall, Arnold asked, 'How come you could see the King and expect to meet Mr. Lloyd George?'

" 'Well,' Kendall said, 'because we are fiscal agents for the British government.'

BECAUSE OF THE SUCCESS of the British pilot training program under Colonel Robert Smith-Barry during the competition some months earlier at August Belmont's nursery farm, Fleet was eager to get on with the principal purpose for being overseas.

Colonel Arnold flew across the Channel to inspect flying activity at the front; Fleet stayed in London to make arrangements to visit the School of Advanced Flying which had been established by Smith-Barry.

"I went over to the British Air Ministry," Fleet related, "and was ushered around until I got to see the man in charge. I made it clear that I didn't want just any training school; I wanted to visit and be trained at the original one at Gosport established by Smith-Barry. Assured it was the correct school, I asked an official at the British Air Ministry if they would take me on.

" 'Well, we'll write down there and find out.'

" 'Don't write because we don't have time! Just pick up the phone and call them at my expense! I grabbed the phone and handed it to him and he called up Major Sidney E. Parker, who was Acting Commandant of the School. Parker agreed to take me.

"I took the phone and said to Parker, 'Come up here and pick me up in the morning, please.' He agreed.

"Next day we met at Hendon, just outside of London and he flew me 70 miles southwest to Gosport on the English Channel near Southampton. It was a good thing we didn't waste any time because the Armistice came along very much sooner than we had figured.

"They housed me in an underground fort near the waterfront, and I got busy right away on my flight lessons."

The Royal Flying Corps' School of Special Flying at Gosport, England, was indeed something special. Certainly it reflected the character of its unique founder, Colonel Robert Raymond Smith-Barry.

On the outbreak of war, Second Lieutenant Smith-Barry was sent to France, only to suffer two broken legs in the crash of his B. E. 8 'Bloater' when its engine failed. With the German army advancing, he was told that he and others in the hospital at St. Germain could not be evacuated by the French.

Unwilling to become a captive of the Germans, Smith-Barry shouted for a cab, dragged himself downstairs and into the horse-drawn carriage. As the Germans entered town from the east, Smith-Barry departed out the west side, eventually getting back to England.

Eight months later, aided by a walking stick to ease a permanent limp, Smith-Barry took a pilot refresher course, then returned to the war front in France.

Appalled at the combat losses overseas, many of which he attributed to inadequate training, Smith-Barry began to campaign for better initial instruction to stem the flow of incompetent pilots then being sent

R.A.F. Central Flying School Museum

ROBERT SMITH-BARRY as a second lieutenant in the R.A.F. fought for better pilot training methods.

to France as 'Fokker Fodder.'

Smith-Barry had strong feelings which he did not hesitate to express: With dual controls and a planned syllabus as a guide, pupils could take charge of the aircraft gradually. New pilots should not be prevented from getting into dangerous maneuvers, but rather should be put into them, then shown how to get out of them. Aerobatics should be encouraged. Communication between instructor and pilot should be improved. Stick-wagging and hand signals were not adequate. Pilots who had learned bad flying habits in combat should be brought back for refresher courses. And he believed that the mental attitude of an instructor is reflected in all of the pilots he turned out.

After a series of studied reports and recommendations to Major General Hugh M. (Boom) Trenchard, chief of the British air staff, Smith-Barry summed up his thoughts in a postscript to his letter of November 21, 1916:

'. . . the best way to make use of the above principles would be to start a School for turning out Instructors in Flying, with the idea of all Instructors eventually going through it.'

R.A.F. Ministry of Defence

A month later he was ordered back to England and assigned the task of setting up at Gosport, on the south coast near Portsmouth, the kind of school he had proposed.

Three essential elements were the heart of Smith-Barry's program. The Avro biplane trainer; extensive dual instruction under specially trained pilots; and a means by which the instructor could talk to his student while in flight.

The Avro (A. V. Roe & Co.) biplane trainer had made its appearance in 1912 and by 1916 had evolved into the 504J model. Powered with a 110 h.p. Gnome Monosoupape rotary engine, it became the standard ab initio trainer of the R. F. C., and was followed by the 504K model. In all, some 8,000 Avro 504s were built.

The Avro was extremely serviceable and trouble free; it could perform all aerobatic maneuvers safely. Wings were staggered for better control of spins. With its narrow undercarriage incorporating wheels and forward-projecting skid, with the dihedral (upward slant) of its wings and with wing-tip skids, the Avro was ideal for teaching side-slips, cross-wind takeoffs and short field landings.

A flexible tube with earphones for the student at one end and a funnel-shaped mouthpiece for the instructor at the other provided a simple but effective one-way 'phone' through which the instructor, over the racket of the engine, could explain every control movement and response of the plane as it happened. In time the Gosport speaking tube was widely adopted.

Almost from the first a marked improvement was evident in pilot proficiency as newly enrolled students were completing the course in nine weeks instead of the usual fifteen. Even combat veterans back at Gosport for retraining were converted to Smith-Barry's methods, wondering how they had survived the bad habits they had learned at the war front.

One who learned for himself the superiority of the School of Special Flying was Reuben Fleet.

"Having spent three weeks at Gosport as a student myself," he said, "I found that properly instructing others was indeed a highly skilled and specialized profession.

"The Avro machine, to my surprise, was a very important element in the training program because it was better than any plane I had ever flown for training. You could side-slip it right in for a pinpoint landing—something you couldn't do with the Curtiss Jenny—even if you knocked the wing-tip skids off the 504.

"The 'Gosport tube' was a great help too and I soon developed the 'line of patter' with the novice pilot which the British found so useful: 'You will observe the stick control in front of you there. Take hold of the stick and follow my movements through. I have one that moves with yours. If you pull the stick back, the nose goes up. Now push it forward, but after you level off don't let the nose get above the horizon. Push the stick to the right. See how the airplane banks in that direction. Pull it back to neutral and it will keep the bank. Pull it further left past neutral. See how the plane rights itself and gets out of the bank . . .'

"From my experience at Gosport I knew a good deal more about the art of instruction and about the kind of training plane I wanted to build when I got back to the States.''

BY NINE O'CLOCK on the morning of November 11, everyone at Gosport knew the Armistice was supposed to take effect at eleven o'clock that day—the eleventh day of the eleventh month. "By nine o'clock," Reuben recalls, "all the officers on the post were drunk—except me.

"I went around to Major Sid Parker and asked him to lend me a plane to fly up to London so I could be in the world's largest city for the celebration. He agreed, providing I would fly him up as he said he was too drunk to fly himself. He ordered his own ship out to the flight line. We removed the controls from the rear cockpit.

"I took off with Parker and his adjutant both standing up in the rear cockpit with their arms around each other, their bodies exposed to the wind and elements from the waist up. We flew on up to Hendon and by the time we landed they were fairly well sobered up. No wonder!

"Taking a cab into London, I went to the Washington Inn for American officers. While I was having a hair cut, who should come in but two hometown friends from Montesano, Washington—Steve Conners, who had flown a Bristol fighter for the Royal Air Force, and Elver Rogers, also flying Bristol fighters with the Canadians.

"With these friends, and eleven others, we spent the night together at the Savoy Plaza Hotel, where I had taken a room—but in order to reach my room we had to walk carefully through the lobby to avoid stepping on the drunks there. A young officer from the Navy was one of our group, Lieut. Comdr. Ralph Barnaby, whom I was to see frequently after we were back in the States.

"The next night was the Armistice Ball held at Royal Albert Hall in London. It was a gala occasion, with an orchestra of 125 pieces. My partner was the beautiful dancer, Irene Castle, whose husband Vernon was in the Royal Flying Corps but had been killed nine months earlier while in Texas. She danced an exhibition with an Italian that evening and I danced an exhibition waltz with the wife of Colonel Carlton Allen, the British Air Attache at our London Embassy.

"A month after the Armistice, Colonel Arnold, Major Belmont and I were ready to return to the United States. We were to depart on the 'Baltic' from Liverpool.

"We'd booked passage on the four o'clock train to Liverpool but when I got down to the station with Arnold's baggage and mine I found there was a six o'clock express train which got to Liverpool ahead of the earlier departure. I changed reservations and called Arnold to let him know he had an extra two hours for business where he was.

"Out on the street I hailed a taxi driver and told him I had two hours until train time and would like to go over and see an area named for my forebears—Fleet Street, originally known as Fleet Bridge Street.

"He said, 'Is your name really Fleet?'

" 'Yes. Fleet Street and the Fleet River are named after us—my ancestors.'

" 'Well, that's my name too.'

" 'Oh, come on now. You're just a liar, my friend.'

" 'No, I beg your pardon, sir.'

"Whereupon he pulled out a long paper showing his membership, in the name of Fleet, in the Grenadier Guards which was London's oldest regiment. He had only one good arm; a hook on the other. And one leg; a peg on the other. He said he was shot down in the war and when he recovered a little they commandeered him in this service and hadn't let him out yet.

" 'Are there many Fleets here?' I asked.

" 'No, there are not many, but there's a community near London called By-Fleet and, of course there's Fleet Street, the center of newspaper publishing, but I'm not particularly up on Fleet family history.'

"My taxi driver friend told me London was founded two thousand years ago at the junction where the Fleet River becomes a tributary of the Thames. He took me over and showed me where the Fleet, now encased in concrete, was running into the Thames. We had time to go into Ye Olde Cheshire Cheese tavern where Dr. Samuel Johnson, the English writer and lexicographer, always lunched. There the porter took us down another level where he raised a manhole cover. He lit a match and dropped it a dozen feet to where we could see the Fleet River running in what appeared to be a sewer pipe.

"At Liverpool we boarded the 'Baltic' and departed

on December 11. Arnold and I had a stateroom together; he had the lower berth, I the upper. The 'Baltic' was the ninth largest ship afloat, but it was slow.

"In the morning the steward would shake the covers as we lay asleep and say, 'your bath is ready, sir.' I'd drop down from the upper berth and run down the corridor to the swimming pool for the swim I always tried to get daily no matter where I was. When I'd come back to our stateroom Arnold would usually be still asleep. He hadn't yet fully recovered from the flu.

"With time to spare and an opportunity to relax, Arnold organized a chess tournament of 64 entries. He and I played the final match, and I made the mistake of beating him. Then we organized a trap shooting match over the aft end of the ship and shot birds together. Again I had the poor taste to beat him. I shouldn't have!

"We arrived back in the United States on December 21st to see the Statue of Liberty, which looked pretty good to us. Major August Belmont had quarters separate from us but we usually dined together. He had gone abroad with the mission of obtaining supplies for the A. E. F. and keeping Spain out of the war.

"As we entered New York Harbor to the accompaniment of bands and of fireboats spraying water in salute, Major Belmont's card was at each plate inviting his dinner shipmates to the Winter Garden and afterward to the Brooke Club, which was the favorite of the '400.'

"After we landed, Belmont's chauffeurs met us and drove us to the theater. Just before the play was over his cars came again to pick us up and drove us to the Brooke Club where we had an extravagantly sumptuous supper—starting with terrapin soup at $4 a serving. The wine glasses tapered down one after the other for two feet at each place. The silverware ran out three or four feet from each place setting. It was a dinner long to be remembered.

"August Belmont invited Colonel Arnold and me to stay at the Club for several days as his guests. However, it was December 23rd so Hap and I excused ourselves to catch the Federal Express as it came through New York from Boston at 2:30 a.m. It put us into Washington bright and early in the morning of the 24th.

"I immediately applied for 30 days leave, which was the limit I could get and left to visit my wife and children at our home in Montesano, Washington.

"On Christmas Day I was westbound home on the train; not a too pleasant prospect for the train crew, however. I ordered a turkey and shared Christmas dinner in the diner with three fine guests—the engineer, pullman conductor and the train conductor."

Gittings

FOXY OPPONENT at the chessboard, and competitive in any endeavor, Reuben Fleet played a smart game in every mental and physical challenge.

MAJOR GENERAL CHARLES T. MENOHER, newly appointed to succeed Major General William L. Kenly as Chief of the Air Service, was agreeable to seeing Major Reuben H. Fleet soon after the latter had returned to Army Headquarters from leave in the State of Washington.

"You tell me, Major Fleet," the General began, "that you'd like to stay in the Air Service even though the war is over. Just what is it you'd like to do?"

"Well, General," Fleet replied, "while going through the British training school at Gosport I became so saturated from the experience that I figure I can now design an airplane especially for training that will be better than either their Avro machine or our Curtiss Jenny—the superiority of which we can conscientiously claim.

"I'll be delighted to remain in the Army provided I can be sent to the Engineering Division at McCook Field to have charge of the development of a new training plane that will be better and safer than what we now have."

"All right, Fleet," General Menoher replied. "Write your own orders just that way."

Service at McCook Field—under his friend Col. Thurman H. Bane, who had just been appointed Commanding Officer—would be interesting duty for the ambitious Major Fleet.

Again, with the change of station, there was the matter of Mrs. Bane's Persian kitty. Again Reuben was in charge, this time sharing a drawing room on the Washington-Dayton train with the cat.

Fleet was in for a shock when he arrived at McCook Field, January 25, 1919.

"When we got to Dayton," Fleet recalls, "we found everything in a terrible turmoil. Contractors were there yelling for their money, but there was no one to pay them. The dollar-a-year men from industry who were running the Engineering Division had quit or were quitting. They left everything just as it was as they beat it back to their respective businesses. The Contracting Officer, Major H. E. Blood, was gone. The Chief of the Division, Colonel Jesse G. Vincent, had returned to his post as chief engineer of Packard Motor Company. Other departing automobile executives were Howard G. Marmon and C. W. Nash.

"McCook Field was in horrible shape, as usually happens when a facility like this shifts back to a peacetime pace.

"We phoned General Menoher to tell him the situation and in a few days he came out for a personal inspection. On the recommendation of Colonel Bane I was detailed as business manager of McCook Field and Contracting Officer for the Air Service with my headquarters in Dayton at the Engineering Division because everything we contracted for was tied into engineering of some kind.

McCOOK FIELD'S Commanding Officer was Col. Thurman H. Bane with whom Fleet had served at San Diego.

"General Menoher offered me the job providing I would stay with it until I had it running to my own satisfaction and to the satisfaction of all concerned.

"I told him, 'If you give me carte blanche, I'll take it, and I'll accept the responsibility.' His reply was that 'I don't know legally whether I can or not, but as far as I can do so I'll give you carte blanche.'

"So, for the time being I had to give up the training plane project to get things at McCook on a business-like basis. It was a job on which I had five general attorneys, four patent attorneys in Dayton and three patent attorneys in Washington. Also, I was in charge of the Inventions Board which met every week to consider inventions, even those which apparently came from insane asylums."

Speaking more rapidly and fiercely as he thought about the urgency of the situation, Fleet continued. "We had about six thousand firms contracting with the Engineering Division for everything under the sun you can imagine. Many required formally negotiated contracts; others were handled in a routine manner through the purchasing group we established.

"We would get over a thousand letters a day, all of which had to be catalogued, referred to the proper section, and then answers prepared. Often that meant sending me the whole file so I could review the record before putting my name to the answer which had been prepared for my signature.

"I was greatly interested in new designs and new materials . . . new and better methods of fabrication and construction. It was to be for me a treasure store of ideas. We dealt with everything from Oriental silks for parachutes to new alloys like duralumin which would have the advantages of lightness like aluminum with the strength of steel. We were concerned with aircraft engines, control systems for planes, methods of handling bombs, machine guns, controllable pitch propellers, Army-Navy standards, fuels, bullet-proof gasoline tanks and development of the turbo-supercharger. They are a few examples of the broad range of products with which we dealt.

"My job wasn't necessarily to test these things; we had a whole force of test pilots for that. But where I had drawn the contract and was handling the business negotiations, I became the point of contact whenever we asked contractors to come into McCook Field. Then I would call in the technical man; if it was power plants, for instance, George Hallett and maybe one of his assistants would sit in. Sometimes it would be the chief engineer, H. S. Martin, and later C. W. (Clint) Howard. Or perhaps Mac Laddon if it involved large aircraft."

Isaac Macklin Laddon had joined the Engineering Division of the Air Service when it was still located in the greenhouse of the Smithsonian Institution in Washington. His immediate superior there was Donald W. Douglas. Laddon had been recommended for the job by the Chief Engineer of the Cadillac Motor Car Company for whom he had worked as an experimental engineer after graduation from McGill University in Montreal. When Colonel Deeds moved the Engineering Division to McCook Field, Laddon worked as assistant to John Roche, the chief civilian engineer. Later Laddon became the head of Design Section Two in charge of large aircraft design.

It was not long before Reub Fleet and Mac Laddon clashed.

After World War I the Army designed airplanes to its own requirements and then contracted for their manufacture by the aviation industry under competitive bidding. One such design was Laddon's GAX twin-engine ground attack triplane of 1919. Major Fleet called for competitive bids for ten GA-1 production aircraft. The contract was awarded to Boeing.

"I got married in Toronto in January 1920," Laddon remembers, "and my bride and I had planned a two weeks honeymoon. Meantime, as I found out later, Fleet was raising hell because I wasn't available. 'Where's Laddon; he's the engineer on this job,' was his complaint. When we returned, Colonel Bane took me in to meet Reuben for the first time.

" 'General Fleet,' Bane said, 'I want you to meet 'Admiral Laddon.' It was Bane's way of inviting two strong-headed characters to have at each other and settle their differences. We did."

A pilot at heart, Reuben fortunately was able—required—to continue his active flying career with at least four hours time each month at the controls. Soon after arriving at McCook, Major Fleet and Capt. Earl White piloted a DeHavilland DH-9 to Hazelhurst Field, Long Island, setting a new American long-distance and speed record of 664 miles in four hours thirty-three minutes flying time.

Fleet organized and conducted a special refresher course for pilots at McCook which he patterned after the British Gosport system. Top Air Service pilots were his students in this special course. Lieuts. John A. Macready and Oakley G. Kelly, later to make the first non-stop transcontinental flight, were among Fleet's students, as were Lieut. Leigh Wade, round-the-world flier; and Major Rudolph W. (Shorty) Schroeder, who pioneered high-altitude flight.

Although not expected to do any test flying, Reuben found it hard to resist climbing into the cockpit of test planes, especially if any equipment for which he had contracted was involved. "To be able to talk intelligently," he said, "and to thoroughly know what I was talking about, I had to get into the air as much as possible.

"Jesse Vincent, former head of the Engineering Division, who had returned to his pre-war job as chief engineer of Packard, represented that he could build an engine better than the 'Liberty.' He felt he could do so especially if he didn't have to follow the edicts of others who helped him design the 'Liberty,' as had E. J. Hall of Hall-Scott, and 'Boss' Kettering of General Motors who was domineering in a sense but a hell of a good engineer—probably the best of the three.

"One day he came running up to my office on the third floor and said, 'I left our new 1237 engine running down there with a mechanic. Come on and fly the 1237. You will be immensely pleased with it.'

"So I grabbed my helmet and goggles and went down and flew the Fokker plane, which Vincent had

GAX TRIPLANE, a Mac Laddon design, is hangared at McCook Field with other new planes being tested.

Air Force Museum

66

OFFICER CORPS at McCook Field, 1922, had many aviation 'greats' including names like Fairchild (1), Fleet (2), Wade (3), Howard (4), Kelly (5), Martin (6), Dichman (7), Lackland (8), Tyndall (9), Macready (10), Hallett (11), Bane (12), Hegenberger (13), Aldrin (14), Nelson (15), Harris (16), Sutton (17) and Kenney (18).

brought down from Detroit, with the new Packard engine in it. While I was flying, I saw Lieut. Col. Muir Fairchild preparing to take off in another Fokker like it. This one was powered with a German BMW engine. I landed right alongside of him.

" 'Muir,' I said, 'what are you going to do with that airplane?'

" 'Take it up and test it for the flight line. See if it's okay before I release it to other pilots.'

" 'Well, let me take it up.'

" 'Reub, you know the regulations are that it has to be released by one of us test pilots.'

" 'Well, to hell with the regulations. I have just finished that Fokker with the 1237 Packard engine and the two airplanes are the same type.'

" 'Okay, Reub, take it!'

"So I got in and taxied out for takeoff. I opened the throttle wide and took off. Right over the bridge across the Miami River the engine quit. Only then did I become fully aware of the fact that everything on the instrument panel was in German.

"I ruddered down to the right to keep from going into a spin and leveled off, turning into the wind. It looked for sure like I was going to hit the dike that kept McCook Field protected from the river. I goosed the throttle and the engine caught briefly; that took me over the dike and the trees on top of it, right on down into the airport. When I taxied back to the flight line, Muir rushed up saying, 'I should have told you! Never open the throttle during takeoff beyond that line there—until the engine is going good and strong. But you certainly handled that ship like a million dollars when you got in trouble.'

" 'John Macready joined in with, 'You sure did. We were all praying for you.'

"You see, this was just an example of how impossible it was for the staff officers like me to keep posted on all the wrinkles of all the airplanes we had. You know, more than 170 planes of over 70 different types were being tested or in service at McCook in mid-1921."

One of the new aircraft brought to McCook was the Loening PW-2A pursuit, a new monoplane developed from the M-8 of 1918 and designed to climb 10,000 feet in just nine minutes.

"It was," recalls Fleet, "the first American monoplane we had. Shorty Schroeder flew it first; then I decided to try it out.

"When I got up to about 19,000 feet I turned on the oxygen for the first time and took a whiff. It was like the finest swig of liquor that I've ever had. Tasted like a million dollars. It really revivified me wonderfully. Then the oxygen tube blew off and I couldn't fasten it back because of my parachute harness and belt.

"I had already spent about 40 minutes to get that high so I thought, well, I've gone this far—I'll just keep on going, as I wanted to find its absolute altitude. Well, minutes later I woke up spinning over Dayton; my ears were simply bursting. That's what woke me up. I looked at my aneroid barometer and found I had 17,000 feet, so I grabbed the controls and pulled the PW pursuit out of the spin. Then, because my ears hurt so badly, I played around for 40 minutes in that altitude to get the pressure equalized in my ears before I brought it down gradually and landed. The recording aneroids showed I had gotten to about 24,-000 feet before I passed out."

There was a twinkle in Reuben's eyes as one recollection after another seemed to come to mind. He hurried on.

"FIRST FLIGHT, de Bothezat helicopter, December 18, 1922. It remained *in the air 1 min. and 42 seconds." - Col. Bane*

"Among strictly research aircraft types we had at McCook was the Army's first helicopter. Its potential had been brought to our attention by its designer, Russian-born Professor George de Bothezat. It was the first helicopter I had heard anything about. He was so secretive that he wouldn't let anyone but the chief of the division in on what he was doing.

"De Bothezat wanted me to pay him $5000 for a look at it and then when I saw it, if it looked good, I could pay him the rest of the money. I told him I couldn't pay out Uncle Sam's money that way. I had to know what I was doing.

"Colonel Bane, to whom de Bothezat had sold himself, told him that as the Contracting Officer I was responsible to the government for the money; that I couldn't pay anything out for something I hadn't seen or studied, and that he would have to let me in on the deal.

"Of course he did, including all kinds of technical data and drawings that were way over my head, but which Bane understood. Finally we let a contract to de Bothezat to instruct us on how to build a helicopter. We built it. I was down there when it was flown. Bane himself flew it and raised it about five feet from the ground. Then I took a shot at it and could get no higher. That was about all it could go.

"We contracted with companies all over the country for new designs they brought to us which they thought would meet the needs of our Air Service commands. Generally we contracted for three airplanes, the first one for static tests to be sure it was strong enough and safe enough to fly. In any case I was more concerned with negotiating and administering the contracts than with the design of the airplanes.

"McCook Field was going through an exploratory period and in my opinion we placed too much emphasis on the design of the planes rather than on the requirements of the Air Service customer. When I got into industry I proposed that we change that by having the user tell us what he required, then we would have the engineers design the airplane but allow the customer to dictate changes that might be necessary. The engineering had to be subordinated to the customers' requirements and I think that was the proper way."

PROF. GEORGE DE BOTHEZAT (left) *with Col. Thurman Bane;* (right) *Majors George E. A. Hallett and Reuben H. Fleet.*

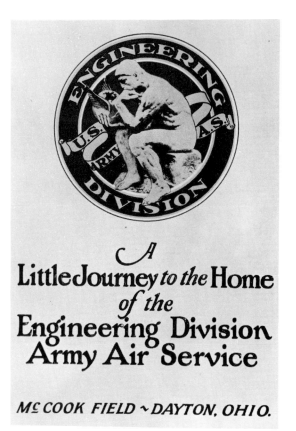

A Little Journey to the Home of the Engineering Division Army Air Service

MC COOK FIELD ~ DAYTON, OHIO.

THE NEED FOR AN ADEQUATE AIRCRAFT engineering organization, which became apparent soon after U.S. entry into the war, led to the establishment of the Engineering Division at Dayton. South Field was then being used by the Dayton-Wright Airplane Company, whose executives Charles F. Kettering and H. E. Talbot, Sr., objected to sharing it with the Army.

As a consequence North Field was selected instead and construction there got under way on October 10, 1917. Nineteen days later, Lieut. Col. Virginius E. Clark, pioneer aeronautical engineer and father of the famed Clark 'Y' airfoil, reported for duty. McCook Field opened officially on December 4 of that year and many employees of the Airplane Engineering Department were able to vacate their temporary quarters in downtown Dayton.

The Engineering Division had the difficult task of keeping post-war aviation progress alive on budgets which were a starvation diet compared with the flood of funds which had been made available for war production. Annual appropriations for the Army and Navy combined dropped precipitously from the war-time level of over a half billion dollars, as orders for over 60,000 planes were cancelled, to only $50 million in 1920 and 1921; then in 1922 declined to only $33 million.

Most of the wartime aircraft industry was dismantled by 1920. For years the Air Service would be using equipment left over from the war. Surplus planes and engines were in such abundance that most of the civilian demand for years would be met from war surplus stocks.

In such an austere atmosphere it was difficult to maintain momentum in new aircraft design and developments. Yet the work of original design, prototype construction and rigorous testing continued at McCook Field.

Design section heads included I. M. Laddon, who had gone to McCook in 1917, and Alfred V. Verville, a pioneer designer for the Curtiss and Thomas airplane companies.

Grover Loening, whose brother Albert had been Fleet's commissioned assistant at the training command in Washington, and Igor Sikorsky were representative of engineers from industry whose ideas had a major influence on aircraft design in the early twenties.

Sikorsky, the great Russian designer of multi-engine warplanes, came to the United States at almost the exact time Reuben Fleet took over as Contracting Officer at McCook Field. Sikorsky arrived bearing an introduction from General Patrick of the A.E.F. to General Billy Mitchell and his deputy, Colonel E. A. Deeds of the Engineering Division. The Russian designer hoped to interest the American government in his aircraft designs.

A letter of introduction from Lieut. Col. B. Q. Jones to Colonel Bane of the Engineering Division made Sikorsky's purpose clear: "Inasmuch as the Air Service is at present particularly interested in the design of a super-bomber, there is no doubt that the arrival of the most experienced designer of super machines in the world will be of very great interest to the Engineering Division."

Soon after his arrival in Dayton, Sikorsky signed a contract, with Reuben Fleet acting for the U.S. Government, to furnish "preliminary study and general views of two types of multi-seater airplanes for three 700 h.p. engines." It was Sikorsky's first job in the United States and netted him the sum of $1500 for his six weeks at McCook Field.

In retrospect, Fleet remembers that "Sikorsky, the White Russian who had come to the United States, was the politest, nicest gentleman you ever saw. In this respect he always reminded me, in later years, of Bob Gross of Lockheed. He was so polite."

A major factor of great long-range influence in military aviation was the fight for recognition of air

BARELY CLEARING Miami River dike, Fleet managed to get his Fokker back onto McCook Field.

power waged by the impetuous General Billy Mitchell. When Mitchell's bombers from Langley Field, Virginia, sank three German vessels, including the powerful battleship 'Ostfriesland,' off Chesapeake Bay in July 1921, the future of military aviation was assured.

Between 1919 and 1922, McCook Field engineers designed and built 27 airplanes of various types. In addition the embryo aircraft industry contributed many new designs. Among aircraft developed during the period were the Thomas-Morse MB-3 pursuit biplane and the Loening PW-2A strut-braced pursuit monoplane. Gallaudet contributed the PW-4 all-metal biplane and the DB-1 day bomber, an internally-braced monoplane, the largest all-metal plane which the Air Service had attempted to develop; and Dayton-Wright developed the TA-3 side-by-side trainer.

A McCook Field in-house design by Mac Laddon was the CO-1 corps observation monoplane, a full-cantilever high-wing design which was the first all-metal military plane, featuring principally duralumin construction with steel for the more important structural members. Two were built by the Engineering Division; another had been contracted to Gallaudet.

Another advanced design was the Dayton-Wright PS-1 'Alert' airplane, a monoplane with retractable landing gear, which was based on the earlier Dayton-Wright 'R. B. Racer.' It was designed for maximum climb in minimum time for the purpose of defending service airdomes from hostile air attack.

Yet another development of Dayton-Wright, which had employed Colonel V. E. Clark as chief engineer when he left the Engineering Division, was a Clark-designed shipboard amphibian which won first prize in a U. S. Navy competition in 1922.

Always Fleet managed to remain in the vortex of activity, negotiating contracts with manufacturers, purchasing materials from suppliers, rubbing elbows with engineers, lawyers and pilots.

But, in the stiff bidding competition which has always been typical of the aircraft industry, the developer of a new design did not necessarily get the production contract.

In 1921, Boeing Airplane Company of Seattle was low bidder among six manufacturers competing for an Army contract for 200 of the Thomas-Morse designed MB-3 biplane pursuits. It was the first sizeable production order for new aircraft since the Armistice. Proximity to prime sources of aircraft spruce lumber was an important factor in Boeing submitting the low bid. As Contracting Officer, Major Fleet signed the order which gave a needed shot in the arm to the struggling Boeing company in his home state of Washington.

AIRCRAFT PISTON ENGINES, like human beings, find at high altitude (as Reuben Fleet had done) that they are starved for enough oxygen to perform as effectively as at sea level. One of McCook Field's tasks was to tackle that problem and Reuben was soon involved.

A pioneer in the field was Dr. Sanford A. Moss of General Electric. The engine's exhaust gases, he knew, could be used to drive a compressor which would pump air under pressure to the engine induction system. Thus the plane's engine could maintain its sea level power output even at high altitude.

The theory was sound, but the technology, particularly in the field of metallurgy, would take years of work to be successful. At McCook, Dr. Moss found staunch allies in Major George E. A. Hallett, chief of the power plant section, and in Major Fleet.

"I began the negotiations with General Electric," Fleet explained, "and let all the contracts. Dr. Moss, a brilliant, bearded engineer with a squeaky little voice, came down to Dayton and the only people he dealt with—always in my office—were George Hallett and me."

Of Fleet, Hallett says, "I don't know what we could have done without him. It was he who found ways to place experimental contracts sometimes in spite of the prescribed red tape. And I remember how hard he had to press General Electric to make improvements in turbo-supercharger design and production.

"Our test pilots were very important, too, as the designers had to rely heavily on their ability to report how the engine operated because the planes we used were equipped with very few instruments."

Major 'Shorty' Schroeder, chief of flight test at McCook, set a world altitude record of 33,113 feet in a test of a supercharged LePere biplane in February

1920. Tragedy was barely averted when oxygen failure at maximum altitude caused Schroeder to spin uncontrolled for 30,000 feet. Almost blind from the effects of sudden change in pressure and the freezing cold, Schroeder finally regained control and landed safely. In September the following year further improvements in superchargers made it possible for Lieut. John A. Macready to break Schroeder's record with an ascent to 37,670 feet.

It was said that General Billy Mitchell was always lukewarm on the subject of superchargers until a visit to McCook Field. There he was given an Orenco fighter without a supercharger, while one of the pursuit pilots flew a supercharged version. They had intended to 'dog fight' from 10,000 feet up to 20,000 feet, but the General found he was no match for his adversary above 12,000 feet. After landing they switched planes, and Billy Mitchell easily had the upper hand. From then on, he was an all-out advocate of superchargers.

For his part, Reuben Fleet not only administered the contracts and prodded the contractor; he also did some of the test flying himself.

"The GE turbo-supercharger," Fleet recalls, "had been heating up to white heat and it was warping all out of shape. I decided to do my test flying after dark to take advantage of the cool night air in keeping temperatures down. When I landed after the first night flight I was able to make out my report from the light of the glow of the overheated turbo-supercharger. When it cooled it warped all over like mischief.

"Later on General Electric succeeded in making a supercharger out of stainless steel which didn't warp. When Dr. Moss and GE's government contracts man, Pat Spain, died, General Electric lost the art of making stainless steel superchargers. They had an awful time regaining the art. They had to go through the process all over again with new men to try and find how Dr. Moss had made it out of stainless steel so that it wouldn't warp."

Years later in Major Fleet's office in San Diego, he and George Hallett were recalling the early days of superchargers with General Electric president Charles E. Wilson. "We all owe a great deal to you, Reuben," said Wilson. "We just got an order for $125 million worth of superchargers! You are the man who kept us in the turbo-supercharger game and I am deeply grateful." For years General Electric had the field to itself and maintained that leadership until the gas turbine (jet) engine made the gas turbo-supercharger obsolete.

With testing of new Army aircraft centered at McCook Field, many significant records were established there. In one of the early endurance flights, Lieutenants Macready and Kelly remained aloft over

David G. Fleet

GEN. BILLY MITCHELL became a convert to advantages of turbo-supercharger after 'dog fight.'

Dayton in 1922 for more than 36 hours, as recorded by Orville Wright.

An historic date in parachute development at McCook was October 20, 1922 when Lieut. Harold R. Harris became the first Army pilot to be saved by a chute when he bailed out after his PW-2A monoplane went out of control.

Engineering Division planning also helped initiate the round-the-world flight of 1924 by four Air Service World Cruiser planes especially designed by Douglas Aircraft Company to Engineering Division specifications.

FIRST TURBO-SUPERCHARGER was tested in LePere biplane. From left, pilot John Macready, Dr. Sanford Moss, Major George E. A. Hallett and technician Adolph Berger.

U. S. Air Force

EARLY PARACHUTE *tests* over McCook Field
brought new safety for pilots.

After Major Fleet had formed Consolidated Aircraft, General Patrick gave him an opportunity to recommend pilots for the flight. His choices were Lieutenants Leigh Wade, Erik Nelson and Jack Harding—all from McCook Field. Later Wade and Nelson were to work for Consolidated. Among those chosen by General Patrick were Lieut. Lowell Smith and Major Fred L. Martin, flight commander. The others were Lieut. Leslie Arnold, alternate pilot, and two technical sergeants.

Two of the four planes completed the 26,000 mile round-the-world journey.

Fleet had experienced a demanding four years in his job at McCook Field, and he had learned a lot. "I felt," he said, "that by then I was as well qualified technically as any engineer we had in the Air Service, even though most had gone to college, as had Clint Howard, who had an additional two years at M.I.T. after graduating from West Point."

Mac Laddon, recalling their days together at McCook, says that "Reuben's drive and business ability were widely recognized, but I wouldn't say that a lot of people loved him. They respected him but he was a pretty abrasive guy. He had one characteristic which certainly didn't endear him to me.

"He had an old Franklin automobile—with an air-cooled engine—in which we often rode together. His mind was always on so many things he was in the habit of turning around and talking to people in the back seat while driving. He gave us all the willies!"

As A LEGISLATOR in Washington State, Reuben took an early interest in politics. Though shunning it as a career he was always on the political perimeter.

Senator Wesley Jones of the State of Washington was calling from the 1920 Republican National Convention in Cleveland. Would Reuben Fleet go to Idaho Senator William Edgar Borah's home in Washington, D.C. and feel him out about accepting the nomination for Vice President?

Borah, though honored, was perplexed by Fleet's report that his friends from the Pacific Northwest could get him the nomination. Pacing the floor, the Senator observed that "the vice presidency would deprive me of the greatest forum in the world—the United States Senate—where my vote wouldn't even be counted except to break a tie."

Senator Borah agreed to think it over; he'd have an answer for Fleet in the morning.

Next morning when Fleet came for breakfast at Mrs. Borah's invitation, she reported that the Senator had "not slept a wink;' that he still had not reached a decision. The Senator protested again that to accept would be to "take away my forum." The Major had no alternative but to tell Senator Jones that Borah would not accept the nomination.

So, it was Gov. Calvin Coolidge of Massachusetts instead of Senator Borah who became Warren G. Harding's running mate and succeeded to the presidency in 1923 on the latter's death.

ALTHOUGH DEEPLY ENGROSSED in his work at McCook Field, the Major never failed to maintain close ties with his parents, to whom he was deeply devoted. There was always the prospect that he might return to Montesano and resume his business career in real estate and timber.

On a trip to Portland, Oregon in January 1920 he disposed of some property holdings in that area, then wrote his parents suggesting that when his father was ready to take life a bit easier he would like to buy the controlling interest in his father's Grays Harbor Abstract and Title Insurance Co.

"Relative to Mother," he wrote, "she loves me so devotedly that she grieves continually when I'm not around. Instead she should be the personification of joy itself. I can't be with you all always, but I'm making good and getting ahead all the time.

"Never have I had such pep, such energy, such health; been so alive and keen. You folks take it easier, avoid rushing and enjoy yourselves continuously in the thought of how happy, how fortunate and how prosperous we all are.

"Above all, I enjoy everyone's respect and friendship and I'll try some day to make a fit successor to the best man I ever knew, for you're my ideal of a man, Dad."

WHAT WAS IT LIKE TO WORK with and for Reuben Fleet? Helen K. Schunck, who was in the Contracting Office at McCook Field and had been secretary to Anthony H. G. Fokker, the famed Dutch designer, wrote about her former boss in 1930:

"Major Fleet's [assignment] was a man sized job! Its duties consisted of purchasing all the airplanes, engines, and aviation accessories used by the entire Air Service.

"The man in charge had, first of all to be absolutely aboveboard, one whose integrity could not be questioned, for certainly if there was a chance for graft anywhere in the Service it was here. Next, he had to be a good horse-trader; he had to make every dollar go as far as possible, for the Air Service at that time was only the stepchild of the General Staff and of Congress. There were no five year programs then!

"Suffice it to say that the men in the industry still tell what a hard-boiled customer Fleet was! And they also say, with a laugh, that he is just as hard-boiled now when he is selling his own product! — Which only goes to prove that one's attitude depends upon the side of the fence one is on.

"He gave himself as unstintedly to the Service as he gives himself to his own business now. We, who worked closely with him, knew that when the day was too short to accomplish all our work, we worked into the night. The last few days of our fiscal year, he and all of us worked all night long!

"I remember one occasion when the office force left the Field at 5:30 A.M. And all of this activity was for the purpose of spending money! You see, every cent of the appropriations that remained unspent on July 1, reverted to the Treasury of the United States; and it wasn't wise to allocate all of the money early in the year, for aviation design in those years (1919-1922) was really less stable than it is today.

"Possibly the mention of one appropriation only will explain just a little of the situation we were in. The Engineering Division was allotted the sum of $10.00 per quarter of a year for telegrams! How did we get around that? By a gentleman's agreement with the contractors that all telegrams from us would be sent them collect, and, of course, their answers would be prepaid; and that they would be charged to us on a purchase order under some such term as 'bolts and nuts,' or anything else applicable to their particular job.

"Now you can understand why we needed a man of Fleet's type as Contracting Officer.

"He drove his associates by the force of his own zeal. There were no loafers on his force; but, in turn, he was much more interested in the contents of their pay envelopes than the average Army Officer whose own pay is regulated by statute—regardless of his worth to the Service.

"McCook Field always sent Major Fleet to Washington when promotions were in order. The Air Service was known for its stringent methods, and the story goes that Fleet's success in bringing back an approved list was due to his getting the man with the deciding voice, blocking his way by sitting directly in front of him, and then talking him into submission.

"All was not pleasant working with him. Being of a nervous, flamboyant temperament, it was inevitable that there would be occasions when he would go on a rampage when things went wrong. I remember one occasion particularly when he threw everything off his desk—ink and all—because his secretary refused to work overtime. Whenever he had occasion to refer to any of the papers which had been among those on his desk that day which, of course, were sadly marred from their nose-dive with the ink, he smiled and remarked — 'This went through the war!'

"He wasn't ashamed of his outbursts; he rather gloried in being able to get away with them. But he was absolutely fair; if one were shouted at one day, and Fleet found he was wrong about it, he never forgot to apologize. It takes a big man to apologize to a subordinate.

"He is tender hearted. One Christmas when various groups at McCook Field decided to play Santa Claus to the poor of Dayton, Fleet not only contributed money generously, but he made a personal investigation of the families assigned to us to see what was most sorely needed, and on Christmas morning he personally delivered our gifts! I've seen him approached by hungry men on the street; he doesn't give them money, but he does take them to dinner. He is basically a real philanthropist.

"He is an individualist,—an egoist, too; what successful man is not? He loves to do the conspicuous thing; keep people waiting for him for hours; secure a table in a restaurant where reservations have long been exhausted; obtain admission to a big football game without tickets; convince the Police Department the traffic cop was wrong in moving his car, and insist and have it driven to the spot from which it was moved.

"He is a delightful companion,—amusing, interested in people and in things; at home anywhere; enjoying everything except inactivity. He likes campfire suppers, and will even wash the dishes after one—and do a thoroughly good job of it.

"As for hobbies, unless one could call his business that, I don't believe he has any.

"The cares of his large business are showing on him a bit; he has learned that gates were designed to be walked through, instead of jumped over. He has been tremendously successful, and has not yet nearly reached his zenith.."

WHAT WAS IT LIKE to be married to Reuben Fleet?

It would not be unkind nor inaccurate to say that the Major was married more to his work than to his wife. Suave, amusing and charming with women, Reuben was nonetheless completely engrossed in business. He did not intend to slight nor ignore Elizabeth Girton, the home-town girl from nearby Aberdeen, Washington whom he married in 1908. Always Reuben provided bountifully for his wife and family.

But the very nature of the hard-driving executive—Reuben Fleet or anyone else—often alienates him from family and makes him a stranger at his own hearthside. Hours are long; pressures are great, and out-of-town business trips an absolute necessity. For business success, the leader must lead, often at the peril of his personal life.

A devout Christian Scientist of high ideals, Mrs. Fleet was disinclined to overlook the human frailties of a dynamic military officer and executive whose devotion to business and long working hours left too little time for wife and children. It was, perhaps, a classic example of opposites who, early in life, had been attracted to each other. The young, naive wife could hardly keep pace with the driving ambition of her husband.

The Major's desire for female companionship was satisfied in part, almost unconsciously, by secretaries and clerical help at McCook Field. Reuben and his staff worked late and because public transportation was poor he frequently drove his secretaries into town, but his fellow officers never gave that courtesy much significance.

When first assigned there, Major Fleet and two other officers lived with Col. and Mrs. Bane—and her Persian kitty—in their large quarters until their wives could relocate in Dayton. Later when Elizabeth Fleet joined her husband their social life seldom included officers and engineers from Reuben's Air Service circle. As a friend observed, "Reuben was married, but he wasn't working at it."

In any case, Fleet had been quoted as saying, not irreverently, that "Only Jesus Christ was perfect enough" to meet his wife's high expectations of what a husband should be.

Daughter Phyllis had been born in 1909; son David arrived on the scene a year and six days later.

"My family had joined me in San Diego," Reuben reminisced, "soon after I came to North Island to learn to fly in 1917. We rented a house across the bay near Balboa Park. We started flying soon after daylight when the winds were light so I had to leave home very early while it was still dark, walking to the street car line which would take me downtown for transfer down Broadway to the waterfront to catch a

REUBEN and Elizabeth Fleet with son David and daughter Phyllis. "I was too engrossed in business."

small motorboat for North Island. Then, during the smallpox epidemic, we were all quarantined on the base for quite a period.

"When I reported to the Chief of Training in Washington, D.C. in January 1918, the Quartermaster packed our household goods and Mrs. Fleet and the children joined me; then in September when my next duty assignment was at Mather Field in Sacramento the family had to move again. It was too hot there for Mrs. Fleet so she and the children—Phyllis was nine; David, eight—went down to Alameda on San Francisco Bay where I rented a house for them. Since it was only 65 miles away I was able to spend week-ends with them.

"She went back to Montesano, Washington, our birthplace, with the two children while I went overseas with Hap Arnold. Fortunately we had retained our home there and I was able to join my family on thirty days leave when I returned from Europe after the Armistice.

"As soon as I got established in Dayton I rented a house and Mrs. Fleet and the children moved there. She didn't like it particularly and after two years she decided she wanted to go to California to live. Together we went over a map of California and selected Redondo Beach as the place for her to go with the children. When she got there, though, she found Hermosa Beach nearby was better for her and she rented a house and stayed there with the children. Later she filed for a divorce.

"By the time I resigned from the Air Service and launched my own business in Rhode Island our son David, then twelve, had joined me. I wanted him to learn something about what his father was doing. We lived at an old maid's place—Miss Arnold, I believe—and boarded at Mrs. Allgren's. David spent a great deal of time with George Newman's sons, George Junior and Denny, during his first year in high school. They had a great time together. When we moved the business to Buffalo, I put David in Culver Military Academy where I had gone as a youth.

"Constantly moving around made it difficult for both parties to the marriage. Our piano crossed the continent so many times that it, too, was hardly worth saving.

"I seemingly was too engrossed in business to be a success as a husband and father. I think that is about correct; but looking back at it I don't think it was any good. I have always been intensely interested in the business affairs I was conducting, and so far I guess I have never made any serious business error.

"But in order to make a go of business I had to neglect my family terribly and that was probably the reason we got a divorce. It was an interlocutory decree and I told Mrs. Fleet that it could only be made permanent by her application. However, if she chose to make it permanent I made it clear that I would never marry her again.

"I agreed to pay her $250 a month until the youngest of our two children, David, was one year past the legal age of 21. But I doubled the alimony payment to $500 a month and instructed my bank in Montesano to charge my account $500 a month and credit her account until I countermanded that order, if ever. That arrangement has never been changed and I always keep a balance sufficient to meet that obligation. I agreed when I married her to take care of her as long as I live and she lives, and that's what I do to this day."

THE CONSTRAINTS OF A MILITARY CAREER and the endless red tape of governmental bureaucracy did not sit well with Reuben Fleet. The Army was not the place for a self-centered, highly-energized, often ruthless maverick. And, in any case, the Major's pet project, developing a superior training plane, was still to be accomplished.

Then, too, the military establishment was being squeezed down in scope. Major Fleet was reduced in rank to Captain. He was prepared to give up his promising career as a military officer. Probably it was Colonel Bane who had recommended at this juncture that Fleet be awarded the Distinguished Service Medal for his dedicated service at McCook Field.

An endorsement of approval from Major General Patrick, Chief of Air Service, went forward to the War Department. It read, "I concur heartily in all that is said of Captain Fleet. This officer has been under my personal observation for more than a year. He is one of the most able, conscientious, and loyal officers I have ever had under my command. I regard it as unfortunate that he feels it necessary to apply for his discharge. I shall regret his separation from the Service."

Things came to a head on Thanksgiving Day, November 30, 1922, as related by Reub:

"The Air Service was being reduced drastically. Commissioned officers were losing one rank. I didn't care to remain in the Army as a Captain and besides I had my job done to the satisfaction of myself and all others concerned.

"General John J. Pershing had written and expressed the hope that I would remain in the Army. The Assistant Secretary of War, Jonathan M. Wainwright, offered to restore me to a Major in the permanent establishment if I would remain in the service. He explained that if he was unable to do that by his own order he would seek legislation from Congress to do so.

"But I concluded that my job had been completed and I wanted to leave the service and carry on with the design of the training plane as I had originally intended when I went to the Engineering Division nearly four years earlier but had been unable to carry out due to the internal conditions in the Air Service.

"Thus it was that Col. Bane, chief of the division, Major Hallett, chief of the power plant section, and I met in my office on Thanksgiving morning and announced to the press that we were all resigning. Col. Bane took retirement and retirement pay. George Hallett and I, like other officers who left the service, were granted a year's pay but without flight allowance. We both resumed our careers.

"When the news dispatches got around, I was offered three jobs in industry. I took the one with Gallaudet largely because of the contacts it offered, which I felt would be of value down through the years."

What was it about Reuben Fleet that drove him endlessly to achieve his self-set goals in life? Much as he was a self-starter, he had also acquired a sense of obligation to meet the expectations of his distinguished pioneer colonial family.

BOOK III

"ABSOLUTE CONFIDENCE IN MYSELF"

1887-1917

LIKE THIS WOODSMAN in the forests of Grays Harbor, Reuben was "one of the very few men who could size up and cruise timber to accurately estimate its possible lumber yield."

"ABSOLUTE CONFIDENCE IN MYSELF"

THAT REUBEN HOLLIS FLEET WAS PROUD of his English heritage there was little doubt. It crept into our conversation frequently as he reminisced not only about his aviation career but more particularly when he recalled some incident from his younger days.

One spring day in 1974, when the Major came into the sunny living room of his Point Loma home after his usual morning swim, our conversation turned to his Southern Colonial background and distinguished English forebears.

"My ancestors," he began, "came to Virginia in 1607 and settled in Jamestown, the first permanent English settlement in the United States. Captain Henry Fleet, of the British Navy, brought John Smith and the first colonists across the Atlantic to this crown colony.

"Captain Fleet remained in this country and explored the five tidewater rivers of Virginia; the James, the Muttaponi, the Rappahannock, the Pamunkey and the Potomac. He went ashore at the falls of the Potomac, where Washington, D.C. is now, and was captured by the Indians and remained their captive for about five years. He learned their language and became interpreter for the Colony of Virginia. The family settled in King and Queen County, Virginia, and called their home 'Greenmount.'

"Father, David Wacker Fleet, was born there February 10, 1851; too young for the Civil War. His eldest brother, Fred, was a Confederate Colonel and signed the parole of the Confederate soldiers who surrendered under General Robert E. Lee at Appomattox in April 1865.

"Father graduated from Aberdeen Academy at West Point, Virginia, and then from Virginia Military Institute, class of 1874, in civil and mining engineering. He taught math and Latin in a public school at Lexington, Kentucky, and then at his eldest brother's military academy at Mexico, Missouri. This burned down and the Culvers of St. Louis asked Colonel Fleet to take his cadets to Culver, Indiana He took 72. The Culvers then built Culver Military Academy.

"Father was employed by the Government as a civil engineer and left Independence, Missouri, for the West, where he helped sectionize the Territory of Wyoming. He was then employed by James J. Hill, who was building the Great Northern railroad into the Northwest. A Congressional Act had been passed under which transcontinental railroads were granted every other section of land for twenty miles on each side of their track, excepting sections 18 and 36 of each township, which the Act reserved for school purposes. The Northern Pacific eventually built to Pacific Ocean tidewater on Grays Harbor, Washington Territory, and founded the City of Ocosta on Grays Harbor Bay.

"Father had resigned the railroad to enter private engineering practice. He surveyed and founded the City of Aberdeen, Washington, in 1884, naming it after his preparatory school in Virginia.

"Mother, Lillian Florence Adella Waite, was born near St. Charles, Illinois, in 1859. Her father, mother, 4-year elder sister and she started West in an overland wagon in March 1861. They reached Virginia City, Nevada, and stayed there to rest the frail mother, 32. The two little girls washed clothes and handkerchiefs in the creek at Virginia City for the miners who happily gave them gold nuggets and Indian arrowheads.

"After four years they again started West in the overland wagon, reaching tidewater at Napa, California, where the mother passed on and was the first person buried in Napa Cemetery. The others carried on to San Francisco; Mother, then only 5, being raised by a family named Hollis. Mother's father, Nelson Waite, accumulated sailing ships and general merchandise, and sailed North to Astoria at the mouth of the Columbia River and to Willapa Harbor and Grays Harbor, in Washington Territory, where he established stores.

"In Montesano, ten miles east of Aberdeen, Father met Mother, who had come from San Francisco to audit her father's books in Montesano, Washington Territory. They were married in 1884, and I was born in Montesano, March 6, 1887."

CONCLUDING THAT THERE WAS a more interesting story to be unearthed about Reuben's parents and his own boyhood in the rough logging country of Grays Harbor in the late 1800s, we went there to reconstruct as best we could those pioneering days.

Reuben's father, David W. Fleet, ten years old when the Civil War broke out, recalled having heard the guns of that war at the family home in Virginia. David's brother, Colonel Alexander Frederick Fleet, was on the staff of Gen. Henry S. Wise, Commander of the 26th Virginians. At one time, 15,000 of General Sheridan's Union troops were encamped at 'Greenmont,' the Fleet plantation. Despite the fact that the family had joined with the Confederacy, the Fleets were shocked by the assassination of Abraham Lincoln.

The same urge that brought David Fleet's ancestors to America lured him west to new lands. After military schooling and work as a government and railroad surveyor, Fleet found himself in the Pacific Northwest.

While visiting the Territorial Legislature at Olympia in 1883, Fleet, then 32, first learned of the harbor discovered in 1792 by Captain Robert Gray where "timbered hills rose from the shore, one behind the other into the blue distance." Knowing that any heavily forested area with a good harbor and access to the sea would have a fine future, Fleet hired a buckboard and left in late September for Montesano, located on the Chehalis River at the head of tidewater in Grays Harbor. (George Vancouver, the English explorer, had left off the apostrophe in Gray's when making his charts.)

Three days after arriving in Montesano, then the largest community in the region, Fleet laid out the new Dabney-Byles addition to the little town of 300 population. Although the railroad was yet to push its way into the area, Montesano was then an active center, for timber claims were being taken up and the tremendous logging and lumber industry was just beginning. So, too, was the area's first newspaper, the Vidette, which welcomed the addition to Montesano of Fleet's "valuable experience as a practical and highly educated civil engineer, for whose services there must be an increasing demand."

The newly arrived civil engineer promptly became a property owner and built his own office building. With a new-found friend he prospected timber in the woods of Township 18, then borrowed an Indian canoe which he paddled down the Wishkah River to its confluence with the Chehalis where both flow into Grays Harbor. Here, beginning in December 1883, he platted townsites for men holding government grants on either side of the Wishkah River. The plat for the 700-acre wilderness west of the river was filed February 16, 1884. The site became the present city of Aberdeen.

Aided by copious rainfall, the seemingly endless timber stands attracted settlers by the hundreds who came to log the great reserves of cedar, spruce, fir and hemlock. The abundance of salmon and shellfish brought scores of other settlers. Soon dozens of sawmills and canneries were added to the bustle on the waterfront. Ships were arriving daily from San Francisco, Astoria and Puget Sound bringing in supplies and returning with all kinds of wood products as well as fish and hides.

An early arrival in Washington Territory was Nelson Waite, a San Francisco merchant who had settled in Montesano and opened a hardware store in 1878. He also bought and sold lumber, shipping to San Francisco. Having met Nelson Waite, David Fleet soon made the acquaintance of his daughter, Mrs. Lillian Waite Favor, who had lost her first husband in San Francisco. In September, after just a year in Montesano, David Fleet and Lillian Waite were married.

Fleet was soon named City Engineer; then County Auditor, for Montesano was the seat of Chehalis County. In 1886 he was reelected Auditor in the Democratic

BIRD'S-EYE VIEW OF GRAYS HARBOR, WASHINGTON.

victory of that year. He later served as Montesano City Clerk.

David and Lillian Fleet's son was born March 6, 1887 and named Reuben Hollis Fleet. "I'm not sure that I was their first child," Reuben told us. "I think I was the second; the first one dying at birth, but I'm not sure of that. A year and a half later, there was a daughter, my sister Lillian, born September 21, 1888. We were both born in Washington Territory."

As the Grays Harbor area grew, the senior Fleet used his engineering skill to survey timber lands and was soon buying and selling property on his own account. Combining his knowledge of lands and titles, through two terms of service as County Auditor, with his civil engineering experience, Fleet formed The Grays Harbor Abstract Co. in 1889, maintaining the most accurate set of title records in the county.

Being at the head of navigable waters on the Chehalis River, Montesano was regularly served by the steamer service which touched all major points in Grays Harbor. It was two and a half hours by steamer to Aberdeen but only a rough road provided an 11-hour trip in a "good spring wagon in quick time" between Montesano and Olympia. Then, in late 1889, the Tacoma, Olympia and Grays Harbor railway, which was tied in with the Northern Pacific, built west to Montesano. With the railroad came a minor real estate boom.

The first train pulled into the station at Montesano

on November 11, 1889, the same day that President Benjamin Harrison signed the proclamation making Washington the forty-second state. Two years later rail lines were extended to the new city of Ocosta on the southern shore of Grays Harbor which the Northern Pacific had picked as its western terminus.

Aberdeen, with its plank-and-sawdust streets and population now grown to 1500—and its sister city Hoquiam, two miles west on the north shore—were bypassed by the railroad, but public spirited citizens banded together and in 1894 built the three-mile link to join up with the main rail lines.

BY 1893 DAVID FLEET was a very prosperous, heavily invested property owner. Like others he was engulfed by the financial Panic of 1893. Six hundred banks and 15,000 businesses throughout the country failed. One-third of all U.S. railroads went bankrupt.

President Grover Cleveland called a special session of Congress. The Aberdeen Herald wrote of the excesses of "over-production, inflation and extravagance." Stores in Aberdeen offered everything at 20 percent discount and free roundtrip railroad or steamship fare anywhere in the county for all who did ten dollars worth of shopping. Things were tough all over.

Reuben was six; sister Lillian just four, when the roof fell in on their father. Mrs. Fleet and the two

81

ON PLANK-AND-SAWDUST *streets* of Aberdeen the local livery stable lines
up its horses, drivers and 'rolling stock.'

William D. Jones Collection

LUMBER COMPANIES operated *their own railroads to bring logs from forest*
(above). *CIRCUS PARADE* (below) *brings out Montesano residents to see the*
fun.

Arthur M. Furnia, Jr.

children left for ' Greenmount,' the family plantation in Virginia, where they remained for five months. To make ends meet, David Fleet resumed his work as a civil and mining engineer, as told by his son:

"Dad went broke despite financial statements I saw in which he considered himself worth more than a million dollars. He lost all of his property in the State of Washington for a $4500 mortgage and promissory note which he had given on a piece of land. In those days the mortgagor could obtain a deficiency judgment against all your property. When the holder of the note foreclosed he got all of Dad's property—bare land, timber and farm lands, and town property.

"You could hardly give away property during the Panic; the best lot in town wouldn't bring even $100. It made times very tough for all of us. From a prosperous family we changed to a poor one, having to live on what little Dad didn't have tied up in business. From six until I was thirteen I didn't have a decent pair of shoes.

"Dad went to Alaska where mining and civil engineers were badly needed. It took him months to get far up the Yukon River to the site of the gold strikes. At that time Alaska wasn't even sectionized so it was very difficult to precisely describe and get title to a claim you had staked out, once you located gold. You had a big job to describe it correctly and be sure that you had it. As a civil engineer Dad had plenty of work from the gold seekers during the year he was in Alaska.

"Dad had managed to save a timber claim in Lane County, Oregon, near Eugene and when he returned from Alaska managed to buy the adjacent claim so that he had 320 acres of timberland there. He made a substantial come-back, resumed his abstract business and was pretty well fixed in his later years."

At the turn of the century, Grays Harbor was a rough and tumble, roaring lumber community; the center of timbering in the Pacific Northwest. Just entering his teens, Reuben was already showing the independence and self-reliance which characterized his whole life.

Reuben always managed to keep occupied at something that paid off financially. At ten he made his business debut in the poultry industry, which was just getting started then in that area. For years he had kept a vegetable garden and raised chickens— brahmas, leghorns, barred Plymouth Rocks; now he was ready to step out. Sending to Illinois for a setting of Peacomb Plymouth Rocks, he hatched three roosters and one hen out of that, and with that one hen's eggs established the breed and made a big hit with them in Chehalis County. "Even in my adult years I've never heard of a better chicken than the Peacomb," Reuben recalls with pride.

YOUNG REUBEN FLEET in dress and fancy button shoes would be deprived of such luxuries in Panic of 1893.

"I was always able to find summer jobs. When I was 13, I started work in a shingle mill, twelve hours a day, from six to six, and had to walk a mile and a half each way to the sawmill on the Chehalis River. I got six bits—75 cents—a day the first summer I worked. Next summer I got to be a packer of shingles at 7½ cents a thousand. The best day I ever had I packed 42,000 shingles—168 packs at four packs per thousand shingles. That came to $3.15 for the day's work."

Life was not all work and school for Reuben. At seven he was sneaking away to the nearby Wynooche River where, in quiet eddy water, he virtually taught himself to swim, a sport he enjoys to this day. Then, too, his father was one of the great marksmen of the Northwest and taught his young son his favorite sport of trapshooting.

When Reuben, his sister and their Mother went to Virginia to spend the summer of 1893, the World's Columbian Exposition was just opening in Chicago. The big hit with Reuben was the giant Ferris Wheel. His mother had recently trusted him with a new knife but he could not resist the temptation to carve his initials into the seat of the car in which he and Lillian rode. (Half a century later on a trip to Vienna, Austria, Fleet saw a Ferris Wheel which reminded him of the one he rode in Chicago. Out of curiosity he examined car after car and, not necessarily to his surprise, found the initials he had carved before the turn of the century.)

William D. Jones

CHILD LABOR in shingle mills was common at turn of the century in Grays Harbor County. Note two boys at left.

Reuben and his sister attended public schools in Montesano. When it came time for graduation from the eighth grade he took the State examination and scored the second highest in the county. First place went to a brilliant girl from Aberdeen, Elizabeth Girton, daughter of the publisher of the Aberdeen Herald. Seven years later they would marry.

BIRDSEYE VIEW of Montesano, Washington where Reuben "walked a mile and a half each way to the sawmill on the Chehalis River."

William D. Jones

COL. ALEXANDER FREDERICK FLEET (center) and his Culver Military Academy staff seem to have stepped out of the Civil War three decades earlier. Fleet was Culver superintendent from 1896 to 1910.

AFTER THE CIVIL WAR, Colonel A. F. Fleet of the Confederate Army headed west in pursuit of an academic career which would take advantage of his training at the University of Virginia as a classical scholar with outstanding qualifications in foreign language.

For twenty years as professor and administrator at colleges and universities in Missouri, Colonel Fleet built a solid reputation as an educator including service as the acting president of the University of Missouri.

In the fall of 1890, when he was 47 years of age, Colonel Fleet founded the Missouri Military Academy at Mexico, Missouri. It was during this same period that Henry H. Culver, a St. Louis industrialist, established Culver Military Academy, but development of a sufficiently large enrollment at the Culver campus on Lake Maxinkuckee in northern Indiana was difficult.

After five successful years, in which it became the leading secondary school in the state, Colonel Fleet's Missouri Military Academy was destroyed by fire in September 1896. That brought a prompt, useful suggestion from H. H. Culver whose school had had a similar fire the year before: "You have the boys and I have the buildings. Let's get together." Ten days later, Colonel Fleet, a staff of five, and 72 cadets arrived in Indiana to augment Culver's meager enrollment of 29 cadets. Colonel Fleet was immediately named superintendent of the combined schools.

WHEN REUBEN, NOW 15, finished his summer job in the shingle mill, his father decided it was time to send him away to military school—Virginia Military

Institute where both the senior Fleet and his older brother, Fred, had been schooled.

"I was on the train going into Chicago," Reuben recalls, "to make connection east when I got a wire from my father telling me to visit his brother at Culver Military Academy where he was in his sixth year as superintendent. There Uncle Fred arranged for me to attend Culver instead of V.M.I. Apparently my uncle provided the education, which amounted to a great deal, as I don't think my father paid my tuition fees.

"I was sort of a roughneck from the west while Uncle Fred was a scholarly southern officer and gentleman. Soon after I arrived he gave me an ancestral chart, tracing the Fleets to the founding of London. He impressed me with the high quality of those who made up the distinguished Fleet family. Having done so, I know he hoped I'd carry on in the same tradition. He went over the family tree with me. It didn't make any particular impression on me at the time; I was probably pretty much self-centered."

As is typical at four-year military academies, Reuben Fleet stuck pretty much to his books and military drill the first two years as a Private in Company "C" but in his last two years he was everywhere and in everything. Always looming in the background was Uncle Fred Fleet, the Culver superintendent, ever aware of charges of nepotism should his nephew shine too brightly.

A classic scholar himself, Colonel Fleet gave great emphasis to Latin and the Romance languages. Other cadets may have taken the business or scientific course as a major branch of study, but Reub was enrolled for the Latin course.

"Language," Reub explained, "is our method of expressing our thoughts and receiving the thoughts of

85

TREMENDOUS SUCCESS *in life was predicted for Cadet Reuben H. Fleet by the Commandant of Cadets at Culver Military Academy.*

Culver Military Academy

others. I felt I should know as much as possible about communicating ideas with others and since Latin was the basis of so much language that I should concentrate on its study."

In his final year at Culver, young Fleet's literary interests came to the fore as Editor-in-Chief of the cadet newspaper, C.M.A. Vedette. Also, he served as associate editor of the Cadet Annual, and before that he had been the Vedette's athletic editor.

As editor-in-chief of the Vedette, Fleet was also its business manager. Never timid, he decided to solicit advertising support of national firms. Because Armour and Company, meatpacker, sold regularly to Culver, Reub sent a letter right to the top. Back came a reply from J. Ogden Armour enclosing a check for $100 but asking that the advertisement not appear lest other less enterprising advertising managers use the precedent to solicit similar support for their schools.

"So," says Fleet, "I showed I could put the school paper on a paying basis. I asked the quartermaster at Culver to let me keep the advertising rake-off and that in turn I would pay the cost of printing the school paper. He told me, 'No, we can't do that, but you have demonstrated to us how to do it.' So, you see, he wouldn't let me keep any of the money."

Forensically, Reuben was never at a loss for words, serving as captain of the debate team. At commencement exercises in 1906 he was one of the principal speakers, giving a glowing presentation on "The New West." Perhaps, he was projecting his own image in paying high tribute to the 'westerner' as the 'unconventional, aggressive type that is making the New West loom large in the world's horizon.'

Reuben also early developed a keen interest in poetry, "especially if it has rhythm." Favorites—perhaps because of his father's year in Alaska--were the works of Robert W. Service, poet of the Yukon gold rush. Occasionally, young Fleet tried his own hand at writing poetry but the results were not spectacular. Even so, in later years he could not resist the temptation to take pen in hand as in the case of "The Persian Kitty" [belonging to Col. Bane's wife] and her Tom Cat friend, who speaks—

"You need to escape from your backyard fence.
My dear, all you need is experience."

New joys of living he then unfurled
As he told her tales of the outside world
Suggesting at last with a luring laugh
A trip or two down the Primrose Path.

The morning after the night before
The cats got back at the hour of four
The look in the innocent eye had went
But the look on her face, was that of content.

The niceties of common courtesy and proper use of the language dictated that Reuben Hollis Fleet should be called "Reuben," but it was inevitable that fellow cadets at Culver would shorten it to "Reub" which they wrote and pronounced as "Rube."

Throughout his life it was clear that Reuben was never exactly pleased with his given name. His parents, happy to have a healthy boy child after apparently losing their firstborn, chose—as an appropriate Biblical name—Reuben (Gen. 29:32), based on the Hebrew "Behold a son!."

"Only an ignoramous," Fleet always insisted, "or someone who wanted to give the impression that he was well-acquainted with me, would call me 'Reub.' I was never called anything but Reuben when I was living in Montesano. I just don't like the name 'Reub.'" Nonetheless, to most people—usually out of his earshot—he was always "Rube" Fleet, though by no stretch of the imagination could that nickname even remotely imply that he had any attributes of an awkward, unsophisticated country bumpkin.

The discipline of military drill and the privileges which went with rank appealed to young Fleet's authoritarian nature. After two years as a private, Reub became first sergeant of Company D and in his final year was selected as Captain of Company B and the Corps of Engineers.

The Culver cadet on guard duty early one morning at the main gate was faced with a problem. It was 4:30 a.m. and the visitor wanted "to present my compliments to your Colonel. My name is William Jennings Bryan."

Just why the perennial presidential nominee, a notorious early riser, presented himself at that hour remains a puzzle, but the cadet on duty was alert enough to refer the matter to Cadet Captain Reuben Fleet who hurried to the main gate.

"I cannot disturb the Colonel at this hour," Fleet explained, "but if the matter can wait until 5:30 a.m. when the first gun salute goes off, I'd like you to join me in the Library until then." After an hour's visit with the young cadet, Bryan paid his courtesy call on the Colonel, was invited to stay for breakfast and in turn suggested that Captain Fleet join them. Bryan agreed to address the cadets at chapel that morning and, as Fleet recalls, "His was the most melodious voice I had ever heard; it rang undistorted through the chapel, for in those days there were no electronic gadgets to enhance the volume of that famous voice. There was no noise of any kind as the cadets sat enthralled as 'The Commoner' spoke."

Perhaps Bryan merely wanted to get an impression of Culver. Several months later his son was enrolled as a cadet.

A solidly-built six-footer, Reub was a natural athlete. He was fullback on the football team as well

'ROUGH RIDER' hats and uniforms worn by Culver cadets of Company 'B' led by Capt. Fleet, center, were a carry-over from the Spanish American War.

Culver Military Academy

as center on the basketball team and participant in six events on the track team.

Social activities as at any all-male academy were naturally restricted. "There were no girls there," Reuben recalls, "so we imported them for the commencement ball and perhaps the Christmas ball or something like that. The girls were mostly friends of the various cadets but since I came from Washington State clear across the country I couldn't have any girls from my home town as it took nearly a week to get there." Even so, he was assistant manager of the Hop Club.

At the time, Culver was considered one of the six most distinguished private military academies in the country. Some of its cadets had already been graduated from such outstanding universities as Stanford. One example involved Dan and Emilio Madero, sons of Francisco I. Madero, Mexican revolutionary idealist. He wanted his sons to have solid military training as well as their academic work at Stanford.

Because Madero was advocating insurrection against Porfirio Diaz, Mexico's recurrent president, the United States government would not enroll his sons at West Point or Annapolis. "So," Reub says, "here I was on the football team with the two Madero boys who were graduates of Stanford.

"It was a peculiar thing that the varsity football team averaged 23½ years old, with the oldest player a family man 26 years of age. The reason was the Spanish-American War, followed by the Philippine Insurrection. This kept a lot of young men away from schooling so that when they returned to civilian life they entered Culver as much as four years later than their classmates."

The final two years of academic training at Culver were equivalent to the first two years of college. So high was its standing that entrance to nearly all universities at the Junior level was automatic. Reuben's plans were to attend Stanford.

Culver was a stimulating four year experience for the rough westerner from Washington State. "I gained absolute confidence in myself at Culver because I graduated second officer in the Battalion. If it hadn't been that my name was Fleet—with Colonel Fleet, my uncle, the superintendent—I'd have been head of the cadet organization. But I graduated next to the head of it and when I graduated, the commandant of cadets, in shaking hands with me, said that I could have embarrassed him a number of times, but never did." With a self-conscious chuckle, Reub added, "He predicted I'd make a tremendous success in life."

REUBEN HAD A GOOD CHRISTIAN background during his early years in Montesano. "Father was a Baptist," he explained, "and Mother was a Congregationalist, but neither denomination had a church in Montesano. So our parents attended the Presbyterian Church, and my sister Lillian and I attended the Sunday School.

"To a certain extent Mother's religion was expressed in a little couplet she taught us: 'For we must share, if we would have blessings from above. Ceasing to share, we cease to have. Such is the law of love.' "

Colonel Fred Fleet, also a Baptist, was of a strongly religious nature. This was reflected in Culver's daily chapel services in which an impressive element was the Colonel's beautifully conceived and spoken prayers. Frequently he quoted from the Psalms, a large number of which he had committed to memory.

Despite his family background, Reuben was a skeptic, influenced no doubt by a group of his disbelieving classmates who considered themselves intellectual leaders among the cadets because they questioned Christianity. Naturally the agnostics banded together. Yet Reuben's personal views changed drastically as a result of two experiences.

"One day during our senior year at the parade formation preceding dinner I was in command of the battalion when one of our non-religious associates, First Lieutenant Norman B. Comfort, a classmate from St. Louis, had obtained permission to miss dinner formation to go on the lake in a canoe.

"When the Star-Spangled Banner was being played he sat upright at attention in the canoe and doffed his cap on his left shoulder. A sudden gust of wind upset the canoe and he spilled into the freezing water.

"I instantly quit the formation and ran as hard as I could down to the pier where I kicked a rowboat loose from the ice that was holding it to the pier, rowed out as fast as I could and grabbed my friend by the hair. I could not pull him aboard, but another boat quickly came alongside. We pulled him out of the lake and rushed him to his room where we piled him under blankets to try to warm him. As soon as he could talk I asked him whether he had uttered a prayer to God to save him when he was in the water and he said he had."

The impression on Reuben was profound. Somehow the drowning man—any man in deadly peril—instinctively calls out to God for help. There must, after all, Reuben thought, be something to religion. But young Fleet was influenced even more by a Christian conference he attended at Lake Geneva.

"Culver had employed a YMCA Director especially to coach the many unbelievers. He was Wylie Miller, graduate of De Pauw University and an excellent athlete. He wrote my father a letter telling him I was quite influential among the cadets and was doing a great deal to nullify his work in the Corps of Cadets. He recommended that my dad instruct me to go to an early June conference of delegates from the principal colleges of the Middle West at Lake Geneva, Wisconsin. Dad sent me $150 and wrote that much as he loved me he would rather bury me than have me a disbeliever in God. He requested that I attend the conference, which I did.

"At Lake Geneva the best speakers in the country addressed the aggregation and one of them asked all who did not believe in the divinity of Jesus Christ to stand. I stood and six others joined me. We seven would meet after the lectures near midnight and as a demonstration of our I-don't-care attitude would dive off a 40-ft. platform into the lake. In the meantime, we seven were singled out by the various leaders and speakers for personal audiences.

"I am happy to say that during the entire conclave I never heard an oath. In the toilets, where dirty verses generally appear on the wall, there were Bible and religious verses. I remember one, 'If Jesus Christ was only a man, and only a man I say, of all mankind I would cling to him and cling to him alway.'

"Suffice it to say, the conference was a success so far as I was concerned and I ceased my disbelief and am proud now to say that I was wrong.

"Even the little couplet my mother had taught us went pretty much over my head when I first arrived at Culver as a cadet but after the conference I so completely changed that mother's couplet then meant a great deal to me.

"When I returned to Montesano I joined the Methodist Church during a revival meeting there. It was the first opportunity I had to join a church but before long I didn't find that church satisfactory. In later years I attended the Presbyterian Church and Mrs. Fleet and I now [1974] belong to the Palm Springs Community Church which formerly had a Presbyterian affiliation."

Perhaps, for a long period, Reuben's interest in religion was intellectual and emotional rather than spiritual, and certainly in the course of a lifetime some of the ten commandments were shaken up more than a little. Despite Reuben's frequent Bible quoting, we were told by someone close to the family that "only in recent years has he made a real effort to live a Christlike life."

EACH SUMMER REUBEN had come home to Montesano to work. On his return after graduation from Culver in 1906 he decided against going to Stanford immediately as he had planned. "I felt," he recalls, "that I ought to be older when I went to college in order to appreciate it better; also, as an

TEACHER FLEET, right, poses with his Brady School pupils which included three boys whom he "gave a good thrashing."

athlete, I'd be much stronger in another year or two.

"So, I took a brush-up course which my old high school teacher in Montesano was giving. After a week of this schooling I took the State Teachers Examination and won it with the highest grades in Chehalis County. I was offered my choice of any rural school in the county—rural because one had to teach one year 'rural' before he could teach in any other school.

"I selected the school six miles away at Brady. I had pupils in every grade from first to eighth. I taught two little children how to read and write and found it very fascinating.

"Three boys, about 16, thought they were big enough to quit school. I gave them a good thrashing and told them I hadn't come up there just to waste my time, and that they'd have to stay in school. One girl, quite developed, continued to whisper in school and I sent her home after telling her I couldn't put up with that kind of pupil.

"I got $60 a month for teaching and $10 for doing the janitor work; then at night I trotted the six miles home and kept my father's abstract books after dinner, for which he paid me $20 a month. So I was making a total of $90 a month."

After some months, Father Fleet sat down with his son for a serious talk about the future.

"Reuben, there is nothing for you in school teaching, so if you won't go to college now, you had better quit teaching and learn my business."

"Well, Dad, I can't afford to quit unless you pay me. How much would it be?"

"Fifty dollars a month."

"Oh, I'd be foolish to give up $90 for $50, and anyway I believe the school board is going to give me a

$10 raise at Christmas—that'd be $100 a month total."

"Now, my boy, I figure you owe me some consideration."

"Well, if you put it that way, I'll work for you for nothing."

"No, I'll pay you every cent you're worth—$50 a month."

So, at his father's request, Reuben was permitted to resign his teaching position after he helped train a replacement man teacher for the Brady school.

Some months later, March 6, 1907, Reuben celebrated his twentieth birthday. It was time, he thought, to strike out on his own. So he went to his father with a proposition.

"Do you have any objection, Dad, if I sell real estate on the side?"

"No, Son, that's alright, just so you don't neglect my business."

"So," Reuben recalls, "I took a quarter-page ad in the Vidette to announce myself in the real estate business. The headline I wrote for the ad attracted a lot of attention. It read, 'Over 20 Years in Chehalis County—Consequently Familiar with Values and Property.' Of course I hadn't been in the real estate business 20 years, but it was no exaggeration that I'd been in the county that long and did know values because of my association with my father."

The brash, self-confident young realtor continued to write controversial copy for his ads in the Montesano newspaper. One which leaned pretty heavily on Reuben's interest in religion twisted the parable of the talents to his own use. It was the precursor of the hard sell he used all his business life. Under the headline "Improve Your Talents!" his parody concluded:

"And it came to pass that the youth went into the market place and with a few shekels did proceed to buy up the earth.

"Railroads and rumors or railroads heareth he, and lo, it came to pass that great masses of people flocked into the country round about him and dwelt there.

"And albeit, many were they who wouldst buy of this lad, for his talent had multiplied many times, and dollars would not now court what common cents wouldst then win."

The ad's tag line was

"The Best Security on Earth

is the Earth Itself"

It was signed R. H. Fleet, for at this juncture in his career, Reuben for reasons of his own preferred the initials to his given name.

To some extent young Fleet, of course, was benefitting from affiliation with his father's Grays Harbor Abstract Co., for he continued to emphasize his access to "the oldest set of abstract books in the county."

Reuben's father did not agree that "the best security . . . is the earth itself."

"I don't believe that statement, my boy," he told his son. "United States Government Bonds are the safest investment; they pay 4%. If you salt down $100,000 worth of them they will keep you as long as you live. Salt down $300,000 worth and they will take care of you and any family you could possibly have."

Business in Montesano was doing well—stimulated in part by the increased demand and price for lumber as San Francisco started to rebuild from the 1906 earthquake—and Reuben's own business was beginning to prosper too.

ALONG WITH HIS REAL ESTATE business, Reub had developed another interest—the Washington National Guard, which had its nearest armory in Aberdeen. It provided an opportunity to continue the military career he had enjoyed as a cadet at Culver.

"I would catch the train once a week and go to Aberdeen where we met and drilled. After drill I was able to stay all night at Elizabeth Girton's widowed mother's place; then would catch the early morning train back to Montesano. It wasn't very long before I could drill down anybody in the Company."

Nor was it very long before the romance with Elizabeth became more serious. "Elizabeth was a very charming girl," Reuben told us, "and the day I was twenty-one I asked her to marry me. She agreed, and we announced our engagement." Six weeks later, April 29, 1908, they were married at the home of her parents, Mr. and Mrs. John J. Carney in Aberdeen. (Elizabeth's father, James F. Girton, was publisher of the Aberdeen Herald. Some years after he died his widow married his partner, J. J. Carney.) The newlyweds honeymooned on Puget Sound, then returned to Montesano to reside with his parents until their new bungalow could be built.

Fleet had gone to see A. D. Devonshire, president of the Montesano State Bank, and asked if he could borrow $1500.

"Well, Fleet, you already have money on deposit with us, don't you? How much?"

"Eighteen hundred dollars."

"Well, you don't need more. That's enough to build a house. Mary and I lived in a two-room house for the first ten years of our married life."

"Mr. Devonshire, I don't want to have to build a house every ten years. I want to build this house to last me indefinitely, so I want to do it right. I propose to spend the $1800 I've got here and $1500 more that I'd like to borrow from you."

"Alright. I'll let you have it."

Work got under way on the honeymoon bungalow. Reuben paid his construction bills as they came due until the $1800 was gone; then he went round to Mr. Devonshire for the additional $1500.

"I'll get you the check, Reuben, and you give me a mortgage on the house. How would you like to pay it back?"

"On or before three years."

"Young man, you ought to pay something every month."

"Well, I'm in business for myself and I can't necessarily afford to make a payment every month."

"How much would you have to pay if you were renting the house you're building?"

"I suppose it would be at least $25 a month."

"Then why don't you agree to pay me $25 or any multiple of $25 every month. When the three years are up you'll be practically out of debt and we can renew the note for what you still owe."

"I guess I can do that, Mr. Devonshire."

"You draw up the papers and bring them over here."

"What about the rate of interest?"

"Well, what is your idea on that, Reuben?"

"When I've borrowed from the bank before I've always paid 10%, but since I'm giving you a mortgage on my home for security, I think 8% is enough."

The deal made, Reuben got up to leave for his office to draw up the papers. Mr. Devonshire called after him.

"Come back here, Reuben. Now if you want to borrow that money at 6% you can do so."

"I don't want to borrow it at that rate, Mr. Devonshire. At 8% I am paying every cent it's worth, but if I took it at 6% I would feel I owed you something more."

"Alright, have it your way!"

Before long the new bungalow was nearly completed so that Reub and Elizabeth would be able to move into their own home.

Meanwhile, the shrewd young realtor, then 21, was putting together a business deal.

"I got an option for $1600 on a piece of land that Mr. Devonshire owned. I knew that when he found out what I was going to do with it he would want to get his option back and raise the price. He called me over to the bank.

"These people, Reuben, can afford to pay $10,000 for that piece of ground. I'd like to get my option back."

"No, Mr. Devonshire, I won't give it back."

"But, Reuben, am I not accommodating you?"

"If by 'accommodating' me you mean the money you're lending at 8%, you're getting what it's worth. If you want your money, all I have to do is go across the street, borrow it there and pay you back. I'll do that if you want me to."

"You mean you won't give the option back?"

"No, sir."

"Well, I feel pretty badly about that."

"You see, Mr. Devonshire, that's why I wouldn't accept your offer of 6% interest. I didn't want to be under obligation to you because of some special consideration you'd given me."

Before the house was finished, Fleet needed $400 more to complete the project. He borrowed from his father and soon paid him back. Meantime, he got completely out of debt by capitalizing on the option he wouldn't turn back to the banker.

Six days before Reuben and Elizabeth's first wedding anniversary their daughter Phyllis was born. A year and six days later son David Girton Fleet put in an appearance. With a growing family to support Reub began to concentrate even harder on business success.

As they discussed one of his real estate deals, Elizabeth told her husband, "It's your business to make money and my business to take care of the children. If you think you have confidence in a deal, I wouldn't care what anyone else said; I'd go ahead and do it. I'm willing to sign anything you say."

HONEYMOON BUNGALOW still stands neat and pleasant 67 years after Reuben built it for his bride.
William Wagner

To Elizabeth, taking care of the children included their religious upbringing. Herself a Christian Scientist, she and the children regularly attended meetings of the Christian Science Society in Montesano as they grew up. With the influence of his own parents still strong, Reuben at this stage was more inclined to look at religion philosophically than to follow its spiritual precepts and strictures. Anyway, business success was the name of the game.

REUBEN FLEET HAD A KNACK for putting together real estate deals, each one unique in some respect, but all adding to his reputation as an astute negotiator—and to his growing net worth. Whether timberland, city property, tidelands, farm property, oyster beds, tax delinquent or school property, Reuben seemed always to come out on top.

The Flora Metcalf home and ranch on nearly 200 acres adjoining the city was for sale. Reuben took an option on it for $27,400. Mrs. Metcalf would take back a mortgage for $15,000 but Reuben would have to borrow the balance of $12,400. Again he went to see Mr. Devonshire.

"What does your Dad think about this? If he endorses the paper I'll let you have the $12,400."

"No, I won't let Dad do that."

"Well, Reuben, the ranch isn't worth any such money as you're apparently willing to pay."

Questioning his judgment raised Reuben's dander.

"I didn't come over here to find out what the ranch is worth. I came here to find out whether you'd lend me $12,400. That's the point!"

"Tell you what I'll do. Talk it over with your Dad, and with your wife. Come back tomorrow and if you still want the money—and you think it's okey—I'll let you have it."

Elizabeth Fleet's consent was readily forthcoming. Reuben explained to his father the details of the loan and of his plans to market the property.

"Well, son, you are past 21. I'll not advise you. If I advised you not to buy it and afterwards concluded you might have made a chunk of money, you'd blame me. If I advised buying it, and you went broke on it, you'd also blame me. The only advice I'll give you is this—if you do buy it, don't let any grass grow under your feet in getting out of debt."

"Dad, that's pretty good advice."

Reuben bought the Metcalf Ranch. Right off he sold 104 acres of bottom land for $150 an acre—$15,600. The option provided that as he made partial payments to Mrs. Metcalf on the mortgage she would release additional acreage. Promptly the upland was surveyed and cut up into 2½ acre parcels. The only automobile in town was pressed into service as salesman Fleet went to work.

"I got seven prominent men in Montesano to go out by automobile with me and look at the property. Each 2½ acre tract had 100-foot frontage on the main road and was on the crest of a hill. I suggested they place their houses so as to have only a half acre front yard as a garden which they'd have to mow and trim; the two acres in the back would take care of their cows, vegetable garden and things of that kind.

"The Judge of the Superior Court was one of my guests. "Reuben,' he said, "if you'll take my paper for it, I'll take this tract nearest to the city.' I told him, of course I'd take his paper. Each of the other men bought a tract then and there.

"Shortly after that I sold the 50-year-old house and five acres for $5000. That brought me completely out of debt with all bills paid, $650 in the bank and 52½ acres left.

"I subsequently sold the 52½ for $200 an acre. So I made $11,650 in 26 days on that deal."

Not bad for a 23-year-old real estate operator in a small western town.

"That deal," Reuben recalls, "gave me such a wonderful reputation that I began to get business to beat the band from all kinds of other people."

Fleet was soon specializing in timber, and that ran into big money. "Having been born and raised in the tall-timbered country," Reub related, "I was one of the very few men who could size up and cruise timber to accurately estimate its possible lumber yield.

"I did all my work on foot, hiking into the forest and sleeping and eating with nearby settlers or out in the woods alone. When you got into the forest—especially 15 or 20 miles from any habitation—the trees were often so thick you couldn't see the sun.

"At times I've spent up to four days looking for a section corner to be sure I was on the right land. The corner might be, say, 'a cedar tree from which a spruce bears South 15° 30' East at a distance of 20 feet; from which a fir bears North 18° 30' at a distance of 35 feet.'

"You see, those were the Government field notes which were available to everyone; those original field notes located everybody's property in the tall timber. If you were well acquainted with a particular section of the county, as I was, I was able to start from section corners of a good many pieces of property I already knew. That made the work easier and brought me more and more business.

"It was great outdoors work, but I had to do the written work at home at night."

One of the logging companies came to Fleet with a problem. They wanted a 20-foot right-of-way for their railroad over the narrow part of the 20-acre Farre property which was an odd shape, being half a mile long, but only a sixteenth of a mile wide facing the road. They were willing to pay $1000 for access across

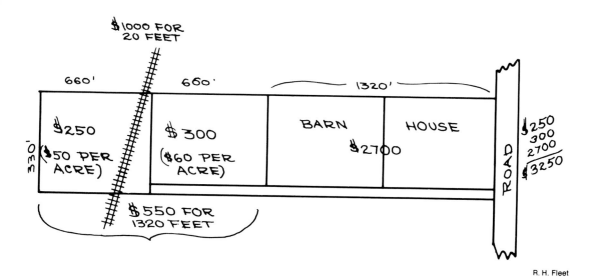

$1000 FOR 20 FEET

660' 660' 1320'

$250 ($50 PER ACRE) $300 ($60 PER ACRE) BARN $2700 HOUSE ROAD

330'

$550 FOR 1320 FEET

$250
300
2700
$3250

R. H. Fleet

the 330-foot width at the back of the land. But Farmer Farre didn't want the noise of the logging trains and insisted the company buy the entire 20-acre property for $3000. Things were at a standstill until Reuben got into the deal.

Advertising the property for $3000, he began to get calls but only for five or ten acre parcels. That's what he expected. Reuben talked Ferre into dividing the property into four 5-acre parcels. The house lay on the property closest to the main road. The barn was on the next five acres. An easement one-rod wide gave access to the two back five acre parcels.

"I'd drawn up new options," Reuben related, "to replace the original one of $3000 for the entire 20 acres. We priced the rear five acres to sell at $250 and the next five acres at $300. The logging company bought both parcels. The option for the ten acres where house and barn were located was for $2700, and I soon sold it. Farre got a total of $3,250 for his property instead of the $3000 he asked.

"The logging company's ten acres, a quarter of a mile long by 330 feet wide, cost them only $550—and they could put the roadbed anywhere they wanted—although they had been willing to pay $1000 for just a 20-foot right-of-way.

"That deal made me such a good reputation that I began to get other business from people who were prominent in the timber game. There was real money to be made, for our county—a cruise showed 22 billion feet of standing timber—was the heaviest timbered in the state."

As THE TIMBER INDUSTRY GREW, so did the lumber mills on the Grays Harbor waterfront, and with that growth came labor trouble. However, should any violence break out, there was always the National

Guard in Aberdeen on which to fall back in a real emergency.

"When I got out of Culver," Reub recalls, "I joined the Second Washington Infantry of the National Guard. Those who graduated at the top of their classes from the six most distinguished private military academies were entitled to commissions as second lieutenants in the regular Army when they reached 21.

"By then I was making money so fast that I decided not to go into the regular Army but to do my military service in the National Guard. So, I entered the competitions and was selected Second Lieutenant of Company G. In a year or two I worked up to First Lieutenant; then to Captain of the Company.

"Father was a fine marksman; probably the best trap shooter in the county, and at Culver I had been able to improve my own skill with the rifle. As Captain in the National Guard I took a very active interest in shooting, was a member of the rifle team and coached my men in shooting. All but two men in Company G qualified as expert riflemen—the best rating you can earn. The other two were from military families and it would have been a shame to deprive them of their right to belong to the National Guard, so I retained them in the Company and kept on training them but I never could get them beyond the sharpshooter grade."

The I. W. W.—Industrial Workers of the World—was a militant labor organization, headed by William D. (Big Bill) Haywood. It had sprung up among miners in the Northwest; then broadened its base as 'one big union' advocating violence against capitalists.

Fleet recalls that "The I. W. W. became well organized in the county. They were very active and very dangerous, threatening to burn down the enterprises on the waterfront at Aberdeen, Hoquiam and throughout Grays Harbor. They were discontented with wages, powers-of-labor, overtime and everything

93

TROUBLE on the waterfront at Aberdeen came to a head when I.W.W. threatened the peace of Grays Harbor.

William D. Jones

else. There had been some incidents of arson.

"The situation became so bad that Sheriff Ed Payette appealed to the Governor to call out the Washington National Guard, as he felt his department was unable to handle the situation."

At noon on March 10, 1911, Capt. R. H. Fleet received orders from the Adjutant General at Seattle to hold Company G in immediate readiness for mobilization on short notice. The Company was to be brought to full fighting strength to be ready for service at any minute. As a precaution drills were to be scheduled three times a week. Captain Fleet, however, believing that the National Guard should not handle the assignment, got hold of the Governor, then called on his neighbor Sheriff Payette.

"Ed, the Governor tells me you have reported your inability to handle the I. W. W. situation, so I've got to handle it as Captain of the National Guard in Aberdeen. I suggested to him that I could do this better as a civilian than as a military officer.

"I told the Governor that all in our Company are citizens of the county, intensely interested in tranquility, and suggested that he permit me to discuss with you my suggestion that you deputize me as a sheriff with the right to deputize my company members, also as your deputies. We'd serve without salary and for the emergency only. As civilians we could settle the trouble without bloodshed which I feared if handled by uniformed National Guardsmen. The Governor acquiesced, telling me to use my own best judgment in handling the trouble."

As Reuben talked, the Sheriff bristled. "I don't need your help, Captain Fleet."

"Well, you're going to get it anyway, Ed, because you've requested aid from the State. So why not deputize me and my men and we'll run the I. W. W.s

out of the county without bloodshed?"

Reluctantly, the Sheriff agreed. Fleet picks up the story;

"We got a list of the I. W. W. membership and their addresses. I divided Company G into squads of three deputies each and sent my men to each labor agitator's place of residence to seize him and bring him to the Armory.

"Next day when we had them all assembled—there must have been about 50—we made a speech to them, telling them to get the hell out of the county and never come back; that if they did they'd likely be killed when they returned. We made it clear that we refused to accept the kind of danger they represented in our midst.

"They had to leave Aberdeen on the elevated roadway paralleling the railroad. We armed each of the Guardsmen deputies with a barrel stave instead of a rifle and made the I. W. W. members run a gauntlet as they were hurried out of town to the accompaniment of a beating which really scared the living daylights out of them."

As they scurried out of Grays Harbor—leaving personal belongings, girl friends, and wives, if any, behind—the I. W. W. group reportedly headed south for Mexico, where the Federal government would have to cope with them. But Captain Fleet had not yet seen the last of the problem.

April first the Adjutant General ordered Captain Fleet, together with an officer from Spokane and two from Seattle, to report to San Diego to join in "maneuvers" on the Mexican border as members of a brigade under famed General Tasker H. Bliss. Captain Fleet was named regimental adjutant. Four officers were also detailed from the State of Oregon. (The Montesano Vidette noted that "Captain Fleet will

CHEHALIS RIVER Bridge at Aberdeen over which labor agitators beat a hasty retreat from Captain Fleet's National Guardsmen.

receive the pay of a captain in the Regular Army, which is $6.66 per day.")

The National Guard teams from Washington and Oregon would be able to keep track of the labor agitators who were reportedly in Tijuana, 16 miles south of San Diego, preventing their return if necessary. In addition the Guardsmen would serve with Army troops on the border protecting U. S. interests during the revolution being lead by liberal Gen. Francisco Madero against the entrenched dictatorship.

Captain Fleet and his brigade lived in tents on the American side near Tijuana, making occasional patrols along the border. One three-day march took them to Alpine Heights. Here Reub found the location—between San Diego on the ocean, and mountains inland from there—just about right to provide a near uniform temperature. He camped with a man who owned 30 acres of olive trees. "He told me," Fleet recalls, "that he'd been sent there as a sick man with tuberculosis, and given six months to live. That had been 29 years earlier, and it convinced me the San Diego area was certainly a healthy place to live.

"I became enamored with the area and its climate and said to myself that if I could so arrange my business life as to spend it in San Diego, I'd certainly

TENTS, WAGONS and automobiles of American troops stationed at the border opposite Tijuana, Mexico, May 9, 1911.

GLENN H. CURTISS'S seaplane is pulled into water of San Diego Bay for first hydro-aeroplane flight in history, January 26, 1911.

do so. I did arrange it, but not until 24 years later."

At the time, Reuben was not aware of it, but aviation was making some of its first, very tentative advancements on North Island and in San Diego Bay. Glenn H. Curtiss made the first seaplane flight there on January 26, 1911 and had established a flying school. The foundation was being laid for a future aircraft industry in San Diego.

Eight years earlier, December 17, 1903, the Wright Brothers of Dayton, Ohio had made the first powered flight, but neither Cadet Fleet nor anyone else at Culver Military Academy in the neighboring state seems to have noted the event.

Reuben's tour of duty in San Diego with the Army was relatively brief. The Mexican insurrection forces under command of the father of the Madero brothers, Reuben's classmates at Culver, were victorious on May 25, 1911 when President Porfirio Diaz retired into exile after 34 years of dictatorial control.

Captain Fleet returned to Montesano to his wife and growing children and to his prosperous real estate and timber business.

BASED ON THEIR EXPERIENCE with Fleet on the Ferre property for railroad rights, the logging company approached him on another important transaction. They had their eyes on an adjacent property and asked Reuben to see if he could buy it for them for $100,000. The instructions were verbal.

Reub went to the owner and obtained an option to purchase the timber land for $100,000. Meanwhile the logging company had second thoughts about their offer and decided that perhaps it could be obtained for less. Fleet knew the owner well and was sure he would not take less than $100,000; in fact that he might well sell it to someone else for even more.

"Gentlemen," Fleet told them, "you can't back out of the deal even though I don't have your offer in writing. I have already made the offer to purchase the property for the figure you quoted."

"Alright, Reuben, we'll go across the street to attorney Ove Nelson and have him handle the deal; maybe he can buy it cheaper." The logging company officials thus found themselves in an embarrassing position, and decided against having Nelson represent them. Fleet made the deal as originally discussed; but it continued to disturb him. He went to see his father.

"Reuben," he said, "you had given your word on it. You can't afford to break your promise under any circumstances. Always remember that. I'm proud, my boy, that you insisted on not going back on your word. Never do."

Not long after, the Weyerhaeuser lumber interests, through George S. Long, their manager, offered Fleet the job of buying their timber in Chehalis County. They had already paid Reuben $5400 that year in commissions, but wanted him to work for them at a $10,000 yearly salary.

"Mr. Long," Fleet replied, "I don't want to work exclusively for Weyerhaeuser. I would rather run my own business; then where I get timber in your neck of the woods, and am not otherwise obligated, will submit it to you. I'll do so for my regular 5% commission unless I have already gotten it from the seller; in that case you won't owe me anything."

In one three-day period over Christmas, Fleet earned a tidy $6750 commission on a timber transaction by playing a hunch that a Hoquiam banker would not keep a confidence. It was a crafty ploy by Reuben in which he neatly baited a trap.

Fleet had bought a half section of heavy timber property in township 16-6; and also wanted to acquire the adjacent half section which was owned by the bank's vice president.

"I purposely took the deeds to the half section," Fleet recalls, "to the home of the president of the Hoquiam First National Bank.

" 'Before I give you these deeds,' I told him, 'which I'm hoping to place in escrow with your bank, I want you to swear to me that you will not tell a single soul anywhere that you are acting as an escrow agent for me.' He agreed to that.

"I particularly didn't want the vice president of the bank to know I was buying the other half section. That's why I made the president give me his word that he would tell no one. However, that's exactly what he did, telling his vice president that I no doubt would soon be wanting to buy his half section, too.

"The day after Christmas I went straight to the banker. 'Do you have those deeds for me?' I asked him. He told me he did. 'Did you tell anyone?'

" 'Well, I told Mr. Kellogg here.'

" 'He owns the adjacent half section, doesn't he?'

"Kellogg interrupted long enough to admit his ownership.

" 'But, Mr. Adams, you pledged your word you wouldn't disclose the fact that I had the property in escrow. You've broken a confidence.'

" 'Now I don't give a damn how the two of you arrange it, but I'll give Mr. Kellogg $150,000 for his half section and that's all. You and Kellogg get me the

deed or I'll advertise what kind of an escrow dealer you are.' "

Relating the transaction, Fleet admits that "I set the trap for them because I knew I was going to have trouble buying that half section. They walked right into it."

When Hoquiam High School needed some additional ground adjacent to their buildings, one of Fleet's timber clients told the School Board that Reuben was the best man in the county to tackle the job for them.

"A representative of the school," Fleet related, "came up to Montesano and employed me for the job. I immediately got an option from Harry Hermans, the original platter of that part of Hoquiam, for any vacant lots I needed at $500 each. There were all kinds of houses situate on other property the school wanted.

"I then went to one of the owners with a proposition. I told him I'd move his home into the fourth block from the school, giving him a new foundation and new plumbing connection. I'd pay all the expenses and he'd have a much better home. It would also be an advantage to him for his own school district to enlarge its quarters.

"The owner was agreeable. The City Council gave us moving permits and we put his house on rollers and moved it to the new location. We did the same thing with others in the neighborhood and in three or four months we had the whole task accomplished."

It was another example of Fleet's ability to come up with an ingenious solution to almost any problem put before him.

REUBEN AND ELIZABETH FLEET had been married five years and were raising two children, but his sister Lillian at 24 seemed headed for spinsterhood. Not that there weren't beaux.

"One day," Reuben recalls, "she told me of the various proposals of marriage she had received, and we discussed the qualifications of her various suitors. I asked her if love didn't enter into her consideration of these men.

" 'Of course, love enters into it, Reuben, but I think I can learn to love any of those we are talking about.'

"I told her I thought Ned—Edward K.—Bishop was my preference. He was about 15 years older but a well-educated, well thought of lumber man. His grandfather had built the Chicago and Alton Railroad from Chicago down to Alton, Illinois.

"Of course, she had some wonderful suitors; one was the founder of the Metropolitan Building Company in downtown Seattle. But she ended up marrying Ned Bishop March 25, 1913. He owned the E. K. Bishop Lumber Co. of Aberdeen and was a specialist in spruce."

When the war came along in 1917, there was a de-

C. H. Clemons 1904   Wm. Maloney   Geo. Arland   Joe Bernard   E. K. Bishop   Dan McCloskey (Maloneys bro-law)   Ben Kesterson   Geo. Ninemire

William D. Jones

*PROMINENT TIMBER MEN of Grays Harbor area stop for a sandwich lunch.
Reuben's sister married E. K. 'Ned' Bishop.*

mand for tremendous quantities—ten million feet a month—of clear, straight-grained airplane spruce in wing beam lengths. To get the needed supplies the government set up the "Spruce Production Division." New companies were formed to bring the spruce out from virgin timber tracts and those who knew the choice locations from personal contacts covering many years experience made huge fortunes. The Bishops were among them, for he was the largest supplier.

"Ned," Fleet recalls, "sawed nothing but spruce. He would pick the spruce logs out of any raft, pick them up and take them to his mill in Aberdeen. He paid a premium for the spruce he selected for in those days spruce was essential for airplane ribs and spars. Because it was light, strong and resilient, spruce was considered the very foundation of the airplane. It was essential, for which no suitable substitute was then known. Among others Ned supplied Boeing in Seattle, Vought on Long Island and later on my own company—Consolidated in Buffalo."

Frank H. Lamb of Hoquiam, owner of the Lamb Timber Company and later president of the successor Wynooche Timber Company, describes in his memoirs some of the problems in obtaining rights of way for logging railroads:

"In these long drawn out negotiations with the Wynooche Valley farmers I secured the assistance of Reuben Fleet and shared with him many amusing experiences.

"One rancher, by the name of White, was a tough nut to crack. He did not want a logging railroad through the middle of his little farm and I did not blame him much, but I could not afford to route the tracks around his property.

"It was a cold winter day with the snow a foot deep when we found Whitey out in the barn early one morning. Fleet and I argued with him out in the cold past lunch time and to late in the afternoon before he finally deigned to invite us into the house. It was dark and the oil lamps had been lighted before we finally secured his signature and that of his wife to an option for the rights that we sought.

"Before starting out to buy any rights of way, I had listed them all in a notebook with the maximum price I intended to pay for each. I had a miserly widower by the name of Burgess down for $700. Always on a first visit with him several hours would be spent in general talk. Then he'd bring out some wretched hard cider after which he always asked you to come back a week later. You just couldn't do anything with him on a first call.

"After Fleet and I went through lengthy arguments with him on our second visit, Burgess agreed on a price of $450. True to form, Burgess then said, 'Now boys, if you had been good traders, I would have sold for $350.' I was tired of his ribbing so replied, 'Yes, and if you had been a good trader you could have had $700, for that is what I had you down for.'

98

"I showed Burgess my notebook and a more crest-fallen rancher you never saw. I think the experience shortened his life some years. Fleet said I was foolish for he would stick us the next time. I hoped there would not be a next time, but on a later occasion my partners could not put up with Burgess' brusque methods. They turned the negotiations over to me, and I think I paid for my former satisfaction.

"In the spring of 1916 we began construction of the Wynooche Timber Company's railroad and the logging camps. The demand for spruce for airplane construction became very insistent for much of the material was going to the Allied nations in Europe. We had about 50 million feet of the finest spruce that ever grew. We were just in time to take advantage of the huge war demand and good prices."

ONE OF THE PACIFIC NORTHWEST'S pioneer fliers was Terah T. Maroney of Great Falls, Montana, who had built his first plane in 1911. Planning to become an exhibition pilot, he enrolled in the first class of the Curtiss Flying School in 1912 at San Diego and bought a factory-built Curtiss plane.

By 1914 he was flying out of Lake Washington, Seattle. An early passenger was a former Grays Harbor lumberman, William E. Boeing, whom Reuben Fleet had known casually during his summers home from Culver Military Academy.

Not until after Reuben graduated from Culver in 1906 had he learned of the Wright Brothers' flight three years earlier; nor had he known of Glenn H. Curtiss during his short stay in San Diego in 1911.

Like most youngsters, however, Reub was handy with kites and savvy enough to "make them out of cedar and fly them with No. 8 thread, because a thousand feet of string would be too heavy.

"I was fascinated with kites, probably more than any other boyhood activity, especially having the wind blow my paper messages up to the kite.

"Of course I also tried the usual stunt of making a bedsheet do for a wing in jumping from the second story of the barn into the hay. Another favorite pastime was lying on my back watching the seagulls effortlessly soaring in an offshore breeze."

Little wonder, then, that an article about Terah Maroney's flights on Lake Washington brought a quick reaction from the 27-year-old Fleet who made a hurried trip to Seattle to get his first personal taste of aviation.

Reuben doesn't remember paying for that first flight in the 100 h.p. flying boat, recalling that "I must have bummed a ride from Maroney. In any case I was greatly impressed and became an aviation convert immediately."

After that, Reuben flew every chance he got. Such an opportunity came when Bill Boeing arranged for him to fly with Eddie Hubbard, an early Boeing test and mail pilot, who had been taught by Maroney.

Tacoma was nearer home and Reuben was delighted when he learned that G. W. (Al) Stromer had built a seaplane and was flying there. "I flew with him whenever I could and arranged for one of the first practical demonstrations.

"I got Stromer to fly from Tacoma with the payroll of our National Guard unit to where we were encamped at American Lake, 15 miles away.

"Stromer landed on the lake, then taxied in to shore where he and I took the seven cash sacks containing the payroll and tied them to my tent cot. I put a guard on duty there all night and as acting paymaster paid off the whole encampment the next day.

"I was convinced it was really the best way to get the payroll out there although I was unable to make the flight myself because the airplane just couldn't carry me in addition to those heavy cash bags.

"Later on I took flights with Stromer when he and I had the chance and could spare the time."

Frank Wiley

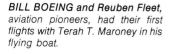
BILL BOEING and Reuben Fleet, *aviation pioneers, had their first flights with Terah T. Maroney in his flying boat.*

FLEET'S TALENTS as an aggressive young businessman did not go unnoticed among the good citizens of progressive Montesano. In 1909, at the age of 22, Reuben became city clerk.

Montesano had much of which to be proud. It was the county seat and in 1910 built a stately new Courthouse. Reuben continued to grow in stature in his home town, which he was soon vigorously promoting as president of the Chamber of Commerce.

County seat though it was, Montesano lacked an adequate City Hall. Reuben rallied his fellow citizens, leading a campaign to raise funds to build a handsome Spanish-style city hall and fire station. Friends like attorney Ove Nelson and Gaston Moch, both of whom had served as city officials with Reuben, joined in the campaign going house to house soliciting financial support. In June 1914 the new $16,000 City Hall was ready for occupancy.

When we visited Montesano in September 1974 we looked up Ove Nelson, then a vigorous 94, to learn what he could tell us about his friend's early career.

"Well, for one thing," he told us, "when Reuben was City Clerk and I was City Attorney, each of us got $12 per month as salary, but of course we had our own businesses, too.

"Reuben was pretty shrewd and very ambitious. He had good contacts and the drive needed to get around on real estate and timber deals. He was as aggressive a pusher as I ever met, and would concentrate on any goal until he achieved it no matter what. Reuben was real good for Montesano—even had the City Hall built up here in 1914. He was a manipulator of that, too."

Politics was clearly just around the corner for young Fleet.

"When I was about 20," Fleet told us, "I became a Republican instead of following blindly in the footsteps of my father who was a lifelong Democrat. I felt I had to make decisions for myself.

"I saw firsthand how cheap foreign labor was affecting Grays Harbor business; I believed in a tariff to protect goods from such competition.

"In Canada there were four mills—sawmills and shingle mills—which employed only Hindus working at just $1 a day for 12 hours work. Even the Canadians didn't like the cheap Hindu labor because they didn't earn enough to spend anything with local merchants except for food.

"When the British ship 'Annie Larson' came into Victoria Harbor with a thousand Hindu laborers aboard, the Canadians trained a cannon on her and told them not to land; that if they tried they would blow the ship to bits. They claimed they were Britishers, that they came from the British Dominion of India and as such were entitled to go from one British country to another.

MONTESANO FIR
17 JUN

ABOVE:
IVAN CALDWELL, BERT SCHOFIELD, TOM BROWN, PERRY McGEE, CHARLES WILDER, RAY DOUGLAS, 2 UNIDENTIFIED

STANDING:
CLARK CALDER, COBE WARTMAN, OSCAR MOAK, GEORGE SELLS, DR. MOAK, BILL CALDWELL, JOE CHENE ERNIE PARSONS, HARRY LATIMER, FRED PICKERING, ALBERT SCHAFER, REUBEN FLEET, Chm., CLAUI ELVIS EATON, VERNON WHITE, BILL BUSH, HARRY PICKERING, HERK SHOREY, GEORGE GAUNTLETT FRANK BYLES, LLOYD PICKERING, BERT RESLER. Building Committee Underlined.

William D. J

MONTESANO FIRE DEPARTMENT gathers to honor Reuben Fleet (X) and others who sparked construction of new City Hall, still in use 60 years later (below).

William Wa

STILL IN HIS TWENTIES, Reuben was a civic leader in his native Montesano elected to the State Legislature to try and retain the county seat for his home town. He's shown here with the committee he headed which raised funds for Montesano's new City Hall. Top row, Dr. S. L. Moak, Claude Pickering, Gaston Moch, Albert Schafer, Lloyd F. Pickering. Below, R. H. Fleet and George W. Gauntlett.

"Victoria remained steadfast. So they went over to Vancouver and there, too, cannons were trained on the 'Annie Larson' and again the ship was not permitted to dock.

"The cheap Canadian lumber and shingles simply flooded the midwest states out of Chicago. In Grays Harbor we paid two or three times what the Hindus got and we had a terrible time competing with the Canadian product. It was tough going for us all the time. I felt we needed a protective tariff, and that's what made me a Republican."

Chehalis County had its own internal dissension. Aberdeen had become the metropolis of the County, but the seat of county government remained in Montesano. It turned into a bitter fight which would probably be settled by the State Legislature in its 1915 session.

A lot of proposals were offered; trial balloons were floated by the various proponents. "They proposed," Fleet recalls, "to move the county seat to Aberdeen, so we got Hoquiam, their neighbor four miles west, to side with us from the east end of the county to nullify that effort.

"Next it was proposed to make Hoquiam the county seat and we got enough Aberdeenites to join with us to stop that. Then they suggested it be located between Aberdeen and Hoquiam, but we convinced people it was no good putting the courthouse in a swamp between the two cities.

"Thus it was that friends asked me to run for the State Legislature in November 1914 to represent Montesano in the county seat matter and try and establish harmony in the county."

On other matters due to come before the Legislature, R. H. Fleet (he was still not using his given name) was equally outspoken. The Grays Harbor Post, which was supporting Fleet, published his platform in its October 31 news section:

"I believe we have far too many laws, and would favor repealing many rather than making more. I also believe that it is time we sent men to the legislature who pledge themselves to strict economy in state appropriations. Any measure that carries with it an appropriation must be desirable way beyond the extent of the taxes it causes to get my vote."

In the election three days later, Reuben won election as a State Representative from the 29th District by a big plurality, leading the entire field. The ever-confident Fleet thanked the voters through the columns of the Post advising them that "I have the nerve, the energy, and the ability to make good." No one ever doubted that Reuben had the nerve.

Aberdeen did not quickly forgive the county seat issue. Reuben was a member of the Elks Club there and was invited to leave the lodge because he had fought them so hard. He did what he could to appease them but would not resign. Fifty years later he was still a member.

When the matter finally got before the legislature, meeting in Olympia early in 1915, the bill introduced by other members of the Chehalis County delegation had a new twist.

"They proposed putting the court on wheels," Reuben recalls, "and holding sessions at places other than the county seat. I managed to hold it from being voted on until the next to last day of the 60-day session. That day it passed over my protest.

"Governor Ernest Lister called me in and told me confidentially he was opposed to the bill. He thought it was wrong to hold court anywhere in the state other than the established seat of justice in every county. He assured me he would veto the bill."

One positive action did come out of the session. On March 15, 1915 the name Chehalis County was changed by the legislature to Grays Harbor County. The matter was settled.

"The whole experience had been so distasteful," Reuben said, "that I lost any desire to ever again run for public office. I determined in my own mind that I was an autocrat and had to have things run my way. If I couldn't, I didn't want anything to do with them."

Political quibbling was not Reuben Fleet's forte in the Legislature. Aviation was. Here is his account of what were, for him, exciting days:

When I got to the legislature, that gave me sort of an official opportunity to exploit aviation.

Since I was a Captain on the active list of the National Guard I was made Chairman of the Military Affairs Committee of the House. Some of my colleagues on the seven-member committee said that if I would fly around the Capitol building for half an hour, they would support any bill that I would bring in to help aviation.

The first Sunday I was in Olympia I got Al Stromer to fly down from Tacoma, land in the water near the Capitol, taxi up to the shore to refuel and take me on as a passenger. For 35 minutes we flew around the Capitol, naturally getting a great deal of attention. The Daily Olympian reported we had 'taken a spin in the hydro-aeroplane around the flagpole of the capitol and some of Olympia's other skyscrapers.'

With the encouragement of other committee members I introduced a bill to appropriate $250,000 for aviation in the Washington State National Guard. I selected that figure so as to be greater than that of the Federal government. The bill was referred to our committee and unanimously recommended for passage; then the Speaker of the House sent it to the 23-member Appropriations Committee of which I was also a member. They, too, passed it unanimously and sent it to the Rules Committee which put it on the calendar for action. The final vote in the House was unanimous approval.

"I have the nerve, the energy, and the ability to make good."

News wire dispatches went all over the country announcing that Washington State was to have aviation in its National Guard. That attracted a lot of attention in Washington, particularly with the Aviation Section of the Signal Corps of the U. S. Army, which had been created only seven months earlier. By mid-1914 the United States had lost leadership in military aviation having only about two dozen serviceable aircraft compared with 100 in the British Royal Flying Corps and still larger numbers in the French and German armies.

Head of the Signal Corps Aviation Section was Lt. Col. Samuel Reber. He came hot-footing it out to Seattle. Finding that the State Capitol was in Olympia and the legislature still in session he came to see Governor Lister. The Governor sent for me. I asked Colonel Reber if he would like to meet with and address the legislature as a whole. He said he would and agreed to submit himself to interrogation.

We agreed to have him address the legislature next night with the Governor and his staff present, and with me presiding at the joint meeting with the Senate in the House chambers.

In his speech the Colonel said it was the height of folly for one State to consider adopting aviation when the Federal government had seen fit to spend only $225,000 on aviation for the biennium. I then began the questioning, which went like this—

"Colonel, are you really the head of the Aviation Section of the Army Signal Corps?"
"I am."
"Are you, yourself, a flier?"
"No, I am not."
"Have you ever been up in the air?"
"Yes, twice."

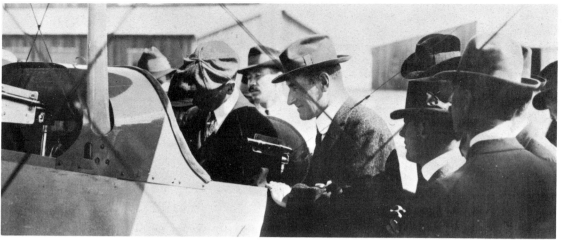

COLONEL REBER, peering into cockpit, learns some mysteries of aviation from Glenn H. Curtiss (wearing cap) at North Island. Fleet found Reber was less than enthusiastic about flying.

"Couldn't you see, when you were up in the air, where the 'enemy' was; how wonderful aviation is as a new source of information which is helpful to those below who are supposed to engage the enemy?"

"No, I couldn't see a thing."

"Why couldn't you see anything?"

"Because my eyes were closed."

"Why were they closed?"

"Because of the wind. I was terrified."

"What were you doing?"

"I was holding on to two braces and praying to God to get me down."

"Did you ever make any other flights?"

"Yes, I made one other flight."

"What did you do then?"

"I did the same thing. My eyes were closed and I didn't see anything. I just wanted to get down alive. If the Lord had intended mankind to fly, he would have given him wings. There isn't one man in a million who could ever learn to fly."

"Colonel, I don't want to be disrespectful particularly, but I want to remind you that where there is no vision the people perish; that's what the Good Book says. (Proverbs 29:18) I consider you haven't had any vision at all. Aviation was invented in the United States and Europe is using it good and strong and we have been very dilatory in using it.

"Now, if you would get together with our Military Affairs Committee and let us open your eyes to what we think is the proper attitude for our U. S. Government to take, we will drop our bill.

"We think you have been absolutely derelict in your duty; that you haven't had the vision to go ahead at all. You haven't got the confidence you should have in your own subject; in your own activity."

Our committee helped write the bill which proposed that the Federal Government appropriate $13 million for aviation instead of $225,000 and offered to train one representative of the National Guard of every state how to fly.

We really pepped Colonel Reber up because he perhaps realized in his own mind that he had been derelict in his duty. He ended up being sold. The Army finally got the bill for $13,281.666 through Congress in August 1916.

AT THE END OF THE 14TH legislative session of the relatively new State of Washington, R. H. Fleet returned from Olympia to his prosperous real estate and timber business in Montesano.

Reuben's adventures in raising oysters is a good illustration of how a casual transaction can lead along an intricate path to a completely unrelated business. Here he tells what happened—

"As I walked in the front door of the Court House in Montesano, the County Treasurer was selling tax delinquent property. 'Ninety-six lots in all,' he called out. ' What am I offered?'

" 'Ninety-six dollars,' I said, as I continued on up the marble steps. At the landing I stopped and called back, 'What was that I bought?'

" 'Ninety-six lots in the Townsite of Bay City.' It was on the south shore of Grays Harbor next to Ocosta.

"Just then, out from the courtroom, came Frank Morgan, a lawyer from Hoquiam. He asked, 'What was that you just bought, Reuben?' I told him.

" 'What will you take for a half interest?'

"Jokingly, I replied, 'Ninety-six dollars.'

" 'I'll take it,' he said.

" 'Don't be a goose, Frank, you don't even know where the property is.'

" 'Don't worry, Reuben. I'll take it on general principle. I'll pay you the total consideration for a half interest because you are lucky and well-informed on real estate. Take the title in your name and send me a quitclaim deed to an undivided half interest, which I won't record.'

"Two years later a stranger walked into my office and asked if I was R. H. Fleet. Assured that I was, he asked what I would take for Block One of Bay City Townsite. I asked him what he wanted it for and he said that was his business.

" 'How many lots are there in Block One?' I asked.

" 'Twelve.'

"From his answer I surmised he had looked the property over carefully, so I said, 'How does $100 a lot strike you?'

" 'I'll take it,' he replied.

"So, I said, 'Look after my front office, please, while I make out the deed and run up to the house to have my wife sign and acknowledge it. Whom should I put in as grantee?'

" 'A. M. Hall; of Olympia.'

"We went over to the Montesano State Bank and had the $1200 purchase price transferred into my account. The transaction completed I asked, 'What are you going to do with the property, Mr. Hall, now that you have it?'

"His reply was a brusque, 'Wait and see.'

"I called up Frank Morgan in Hoquiam. 'Remember that property we bought in Bay City for $96? Well, I'm sending you a check for $600 for your half of Block One.' I explained who had purchased the property and he told me to send back the deed and that he'd send a new one omitting Block One.

William D. Jones

"Well, Mr. Hall established on Block One the only whaling station on the west coast. He had a local shipyard build four whaling vessels at $50,000 each. He would steam out of Grays Harbor, shoot several whales, and blow them up with compressed air, putting on each one the flag of his vessel. When he had four or five he would tow them into the whaling station and boil the oil out of them, letting the scum float in the salt water off the whaling station.

"The State of Washington had recently surveyed the tidelands, giving the up-land property owner priority to purchase the tideland at the cost of the survey. The State also classified the tidelands as to use and designated those in front of the whaling station as oyster lands.

"As Mr. Hall had passed up his right to purchase his frontage tideland, I organized the Grays Harbor Oyster Company. Six of us put up $2500 each, bid in the tideland and had a carload of oysters shipped in from Baltimore. We dumped them overboard on the oyster tideland.

"We continued this for several years but could not get the oysters to propogate, probably because the water was too cold. So we had to replant each year.

"I suggested to Mr. Hall that he buy us out for the $15,000 we had invested because the scum from the whaling station made the oysters very difficult to sell even though they became full-grown each season. But he claimed the whale scum was great food for the oysters. So we sued him for $15,000, plus costs.

"We took the jury down to see the oyster beds. Dynamite Jim, the oyster bed keeper, rowed the jury out to the beds, washed the scum off some oysters and opened them for each juror to eat. About half the jurors tasted the oysters; the other half turned away in disgust. We got a judgment for the $15,000, and we still owned the oyster beds.

"Later that year I took a guest down to shoot ducks in Mallard Slough, two miles south of the whaling station. He was Congressman Joseph W. Fordney, one of my best timber customers from the east and Chairman of the House Ways and Means Committee.

"The north wind blew the scum and odor down toward Mallard Slough. The ducks were so greased with the scum they could not fly. We might as well have been shooting at mud hens. Congressman Fordney got so sick from the offensive odor that we had to give up the shoot. When we got back to the upper harbor I called Mr. Hall. He said, 'For goodness sake, don't sue me. I'll look into it.' "

WHALING STATION at Grays Harbor provided food for oysters but led to lawsuit. For Fleet the incident was just another facet of his real estate business.

The Grays Harbor Commercial Company at Cosmopolis was using city lots in the 160-acre Riverside addition on which they piled lumber to air-dry it. The taxes were entirely out of proportion to the land use. If they could obtain the only three lots to which they didn't have title—they were owned by Gustavus P. Wagner—they could petition the County Board of Commissioners to vacate the whole addition and assess the property as four 40-acre tracts.

The job of buying the three lots was turned over to R. H. Fleet. Reuben's letters to Wagner, who lived in isolated mountain country in Oregon went unanswered. It would require Fleet's personal charm and ingenuity to solve this one.

Arriving in Medford, Oregon, Reuben paid a visit to the postmaster who was able to identify Wagner as a gold miner living some eighty miles north in the mountains, but who seldom came out. Fleet inquired where he might employ a notary public who could drive him out to Wagner's mining operation.

Jack Smith, an Oregon notary, had a team of horses and a surrey for just such trips and was hired. Before leaving, Reub went to the local banker to cash a $300 check and obtained 15 gold coins of $20 each.

"The first day," Fleet recalls, "we drove about 60 miles before dark, and resumed the drive next morning. Around noon we came to the miner's home and found it to be a one-room cabin made of split cedar slabs, hand planed with a smooth draw-knife. Though it had but two windows and a door, the cabin was immaculate.

"We looked around for the owner and finally found him working with a shovel and pick in his diggings down the mountain. We watched him for perhaps ten minutes, then 'hallooed' to him. He quit work and came up the mountain to meet us.

"I told Wagner my reason for being there was that he hadn't answered my letters. Again I explained that though the land was really worth nothing except for air-drying timber, because at high tide and with freshets it overflowed, we wanted to buy his three lots.

"He told me I was right about the land alright because he had been employed there when the manager of the sawmill fired him. It was because of the manager, he said, that he was now out alone in this lonely country and wouldn't do anything to help him.

"I explained that the manager was only an employee of the company, just as I was, and he had been, and that he would not be helping the manager, but instead would be helping the company with its tax problem. It would also save a lot of unnecessary work by county employees.

"While we sat around the table talking I took out five of the $20 gold coins and played with them. That caught his attention, and he asked if he could see one. I passed all five over to him.

" 'I am a gold miner,' he said, 'and can take out at least $20 in gold quartz any day that I want to work. But, somehow, I find the $20 coins more fascinating.' I knew then I had a deal in the making."

It was at his winter home in Palm Springs in March 1974 that Reuben told me the story of the Oregon gold miner. "You know, William, you asked me one time about my interest in poetry. Well, here was an occasion, where it came to practical use.

"If I had not known Robert W. Service's poem, 'The Spell of the Yukon' by heart I would never have been able to make this deal. I recited it to the miner from memory since I had read it a few times on one of my early trips to Alaska and appreciated its beauty as one of the literary gems of that great country."

As he told the story, Reuben leaned back in his comfortable arm chair, hands clasped behind his head and began:

William Wagner

I wanted the gold, and I sought it;
  I scrabbled and mucked like a slave.
Was it famine or scurvy—I fought it;
  I hurled my youth into a grave.
I wanted the gold, and I got it—
  Came out with a fortune last fall,—
Yet somehow life's not what I thought it,
  And somehow the gold isn't all.

When Reuben had finished all nine stanzas—gesturing as he spoke in a strong, resonant voice—we asked him to tell us how his meeting with the miner ended.

"Well, my miner friend was attentive as could be. He asked where in the world had I gotten that poem.

" 'I'll tell you what, Mr. Wagner. I'll send a copy of Service's poems about the gold rush to you—and give you those five $20 coins—if you'll give me a deed to your property. My driver, Jack Smith here, is a notary public and can take your acknowledgment.'

" 'Yes, but if I do that I would no longer be a freeholder and I believe every man should be a freeholder.'

" 'I understand, though I never before knew a person refuse to sell because he would no longer be a freeholder. But when I get home to Montesano I'll send you a quit-claim deed to three lots in Westport that I bought for taxes some time ago. Westport has some future to it, whereas your three lots in the Riverside addition in Cosmopolis are virtually worthless—and you can still keep those five $20 gold coins.' "

Reuben got the deed. It was recorded January 4, 1916.

THE $13 MILLION APPROPRIATION for the Army Signal Corps' Aviation Section had been passed by Congress in August 1916. When it came time early in 1917 to implement the provision for training aviators from the various state National Guard units, Reuben promptly applied—as did 83 other Guardsmen from the State of Washington, for the examination was given wide publicity.

After a three-day mental and physical examination by a board of Regular Army officers, four men—Reuben included—were passed, all commissioned officers of the Guard.

Captain Fleet suggested to the State Adjutant General that he confer with the War Department and get it to agree to have the four officers go before yet another Army board two weeks later at a different post to select the State's single representative.

"One man," Fleet recalls, "apparently lost his nerve when getting that close to the appointment and didn't appear. Another was found to have a sinus condition and was eliminated. That narrowed it down to me and to Captain Alexander, 26, captain of the Company at the University of Washington where he was a student."

Captain Fleet was called in to see the Adjutant General.

"Captain," he said, "I'm going to give this appointment to Alexander."

"General, I'm disappointed to hear this. I don't want to beat Alexander out because he's an awfully good man, but why are you going to appoint him? I was Chairman of the Military Affairs Committee which initiated this idea; I was a member of the Appropriations Committee which got this program funded. I have done more for the National Guard of Washington than anyone I know of the last year or two. Why turn me down?"

"Because, Captain Fleet, Alexander is a bachelor and you're married and the father of two children. I understand the War Department will not permit married men to learn to fly in the Aviation Section of the Signal Corps. It's too dangerous."

"But, General, when an officer trained as an aviator gets his pilot rating he is then free to marry and to have children; and besides, my children are well provided for. Why don't we tell the War Department that we've got two officers, both Captains, and well qualified; and ask that if any state doesn't avail itself of the opportunity, that we be given two appointments."

That seemed agreeable to the General.

"Let me write the telegram for you," Captain Fleet offered as he slipped into his superior's chair. As Reuben wrote, the General looked over his shoulder. "Reads okay, Fleet. Send it off."

Only 11 National Guardsmen throughout the country were selected. The State of Washington got two. Captain Fleet and Captain Alexander.

By late Spring 1917, Reuben was certain the United States would soon be in the war in Europe. He closed the business he had run for ten years in Montesano and left for the Army's pilot training school at San Diego and a lifetime career in aviation. In 1922, after five and a half years as a military officer, Fleet returned to civilian life but continued in aviation as an aircraft manufacturer. Then, in 1929, with six successful years as head of his own company—and the leading builder of military training planes—Reuben was ready to take the next giant step in his career.

BOOK IV

"A STRONG BELIEVER IN COMPETITION"

1928-1935

"A STRONG BELIEVER IN COMPETITION"

BY 1927 REUBEN FLEET HAD ACCOMPLISHED what he had set out to do—design and build the world's best and safest primary training plane. Satisfying as that was, the Major sought new goals to conquer.

The market was developing for large multi-engine military aircraft and when the Army announced a competition for a twin-engine heavy night bomber, Fleet aimed to get his share. His first move was a most strategic one. He opened an office at Dayton and in March hired as manager I. M. (Mac) Laddon, who had been in charge of Design Branch 2 (heavy aircraft) at McCook Field. Laddon; Roy Miller, in charge of structures; and Bernie Sheahan headed the small group of Consolidated engineers in offices near Wright Field. Earlier Fleet had optioned land opposite the Army's new Wright Field facility for a Consolidated design and research center but surrendered with great reluctance to Air Corps objections that a location so close to its own engineering center would give him an unfair advantage.

Laddon recalls the controversy: "Reuben and Brig. Gen. William E. Gillmore, in charge of Wright Field, really went at it. Gillmore thought we didn't belong there adjacent to Wright Field as Consolidated would be getting all our competitors' secrets. Fleet literally wept—he was so upset about having to move. I said, 'What the hell are you crying about? You really don't have to be here. Let's move downtown.'

" 'Well,' Reuben replied, 'it never hurts any to turn on a little emotion now and then.' "

In this instance it may have been emoting rather than emotion on Fleet's part but on other occasions the tears were genuine with no question of the real depth of the Major's feeling.

Laddon's Consolidated team immediately went to work on the design of Model 11 for the night bomber competition. Four other companies were also after the business.

In April Fleet decided to team up with another company—Sikorsky Manufacturing Company of Long Island, New York, whose founder, Igor Sikorsky, already had a great deal of experience in designing large aircraft.

In 1926 Capt. Rene Fonck, famous French ace, had come to the United States looking for a plane capable of flying from New York to Paris nonstop. He hoped to win the $25,000 prize posted by Raymond Orteig for the first such flight.

Fonck selected an advanced version of a plane Sikorsky already had in the works. The new ship would be an all-metal tri-motored sesquiplane, the S-35. The top wing would have a

COMMODORE FLYING BOAT 'Cuba' used by NYRBA (New York, Rio and Buenos Aires Line) on its pioneering routes down the east coast of South America.

span of just over 100 feet.

The small underfinanced Sikorsky company was beset with pressures which were not at all compatible with the personality of the usually thorough Russian designer. The flight's backers were so anxious to beat the pending winter weather over the Atlantic that they urged Sikorsky to eliminate many essential tests. Pressure on Sikorsky also came in the form of advertising tie-ins which would provide badly needed financing.

With an improvement in weather over the ocean, Capt. Fonck decided on a dawn takeoff September 20, 1926. Between rows of spectators the heavily-laden plane roared down the runway. The slight tailwind blowing at dawn would lengthen the already long takeoff run.

One untested feature of the huge S-35 was an auxiliary landing gear to be dropped after the plane was airborne. Halfway down the runway one of the auxiliary landing gears broke, dragging behind so that the plane could neither take-off nor stop in time to avoid a crash. The S-35 plunged down a steep slope. The crack-up was followed by a ball of fire. Fonck and his American co-pilot, Lieut. Lawrence Curtin, fought their way clear. Two crewmen in the aft fuselage died. Everyone agreed when Sikorsky said, ''We needed more time to prepare for the flight.''

With new financial backing Fonck returned to the United States and again chose a Sikorsky plane for his projected flight. His new craft was the S-37, similar to the S-35 but this time with two instead of three engines. And this time a proper test program would be conducted. However, the reason for the flight evaporated in thin air when Charles A. Lindbergh flew the Atlantic solo May 20-21, 1927 in the single-engine Ryan 'Spirit of St. Louis' monoplane. Fonck's S-37 'Ville de Paris' later became the 'Southern Star' and flew in South America for American International Airways of Argentina.

It was the S-37 design which became the basis of the joint Consolidated-Sikorsky effort to win the Army heavy bomber competition. Reuben Fleet was in-

CONSOLIDATED and Sikorsky joined in building the 'Guardian' twin-engine bomber developed from an earlier Sikorsky design for French ace, Capt. Rene Fonck.

terested in Sikorsky's design because the earlier S-35 model had been demonstrated to the government at Bolling Field, Washington, just prior to Rene Fonck's ill-fated transatlantic attempt. The big trimotored biplane's performance on two engines had then attracted favorable attention.

"In April 1927," Laddon recalls, "Fleet received word from Igor Sikorsky that he didn't have the facilities for construction of anything more than a prototype. Therefore, if Fleet would go in with him, Consolidated could get all the production if the team won the competition.

"I said to Reuben, 'Before you draw up the contract be damn sure that while we'll offer Sikorsky all the design assistance we can, the final design responsibility will have to be his.' While Sikorsky was a great inventor he was really not a good engineer."

Fleet then entered into a contract with Sikorsky to buy one twin-engine bombardment biplane based on the S-37 design. Included in the $50,000 purchase price was a license to build additional aircraft on a royalty basis provided a government production contract was received. Consolidated would furnish engines and instruments. As Sikorsky had very minimum facilities, Consolidated would be the prime contractor but agreed to subcontract back to Sikorsky 30 percent of the airframe work.

"For the Army competition," Fleet recalls, "we had Sikorsky build a prototype. Consolidated, under Mac Laddon's direction, would be responsible for the armament installations and the structural stress analysis. These were fields in which Laddon and Roy Miller were recognized experts.

"We called the plane the Consolidated-Sikorsky Guardian. Financial interests, headed by Frederick B. Rentschler, later chief executive of United Aircraft, were investors in Sikorsky but because the company was doing poorly they would not permit Sikorsky and Michael Gluhareff, his chief engineer, to refine the design."

Fleet hired Lieut. Leigh Wade—an old friend from McCook Field days—as the company's test pilot, and when the plane had been completed at Roosevelt Field, Long Island, Wade and Laddon went there for the first flight.

"After we'd climbed into the cockpit and started to taxi out," Laddon remembers, "I suggested to Leigh we check the controls: 'Let's have right aileron.' The proper aileron responded. 'Now left aileron.' Again the controls responded properly. 'Right rudder.' Instead we got left rudder.

"The Sikorsky mechanics had hooked the rudder up wrong. The control cables were reversed—that's the way they did it in Russia—so that it was like on a sled, when you wanted to go left you pushed the right part of the rudder. We had to stop and change the cables

over. Igor climbed aboard with five or six of his people and Leigh took off with me in the right seat. Everything was okey in flight except it didn't have any performance. It was slower than billy-be-damned."

Later Leigh Wade and Fleet went down to Long Island intending to fly the 'Guardian' to Washington, D. C. to show it there before taking it out to Dayton. The plane was powered by two Pratt and Whitney 525 h.p. Hornet engines, with fuel tanks in the nacelle behind each engine.

"As we approached Washington," recalls Fleet "a cam ring on the engine on my side broke while we were over the Aberdeen Proving Grounds. We brought the plane's speed back almost to a stall. I shut off all ignition on my side and waited a few minutes until I felt confident there was nothing that would cause a spark. Then I pulled the emergency ripcord which jettisoned the fuel so that we would be lighter in landing at Aberdeen. The Lord must have been holding us by the hand. The gasoline poured out behind the engine but we didn't catch fire.

"We got a Pratt and Whitney mechanic down to fix the engine and later flew on down to Washington. We

"THE GASOLINE POURED OUT behind the engine but we didn't catch fire." The Lord, Fleet said, was holding him and Leigh Wade by the hand.

sucked hind teat in the competition because our own stress analysis picked the design to pieces. It was the first time anyone had used enormous duralumin tubes for structural members. Miller found that some members were twice as strong as they need be; others were only 50% as strong as they should be to meet Army requirements.

"Fred Rentschler hadn't let Sikorsky spend the money necessary to correct the deficiencies in the original S-37 design and made us take the same structure as in the Fonck plane.

"We could not successfully sell the airplane as we did not have full confidence in it. We came out third place in the competition, which was won by Curtiss with its B-2 Condor bomber.

"The 'Guardian' was for us a failure but it taught me some of the frailties about going into airplanes that had wing spans of one hundred feet or more. After that I moved Laddon, Miller and our group of Dayton engineers to our headquarters at Buffalo and started them on a new project.

"Meanwhile Sikorsky had attracted attention with its S-34 and S-36 amphibians and plans for flying boats. Rentschler wanted to sell me the Sikorsky corporation because it was a loser to them and because it was in the big boat business in which we were also taking an interest."

Although Fleet had previously tangled with General Gillmore, Chief of the Air Corps Material Division, they remained good friends. After visiting the Buffalo factory, the General wrote Reuben that "I am very strong in my feelings that your organization is fast becoming one of the real assets to the Army Air Corps, and I know that in time of emergency you will be a tower of strength to us."

The age-old military-industry problem of what courtesies constitute improper influence was as much on people's minds in 1928 and it has been ever since. General Gillmore wrote that "The hotel in Buffalo would not listen to my paying for the room. I appreciate the courtesy but apparently the clerk thought it should be charged to you since you had reserved the room. Please let me know how much I owe you."

In reply Reuben explained that "My daughter is living with me and my apartment is not large enough to entertain guests, so I must use the hotel or Athletic Club."

AFTER THE ABORTED Consolidated-Sikorsky 'Guardian' venture, Fleet and Laddon got started on a new tangent, the design and production of flying boats, a field in which Consolidated was to become the international leader for more than a decade and the major World War II supplier.

CAPT. HOLDEN C. RICHARDSON,
Naval expert on flying boat hull design.

While the Army was conducting its twin-engine bomber competition the Navy began preliminary design specifications and layouts for a new long range patrol bomber. Departing from the tradition of biplane patrol craft, the new plane would be a huge monoplane with perhaps 100-foot wing span. The engines would be the latest air-cooled radials; construction would be all-metal except for fabric covered wings, and an operational range of 2000 miles and cruising speed of 110 miles an hour would be sought.

The hull lines would be provided by Captain Holden C. Richardson of the Bureau of Aeronautics, one of the world's leading authorities on flying boat hulls. In 1919 he had supervised design and construction of the NC transatlantic flying boats at the Curtiss Buffalo plant and had accompanied Comdr. John H. Towers on the flight of the NC-3 the following spring.

NC FLYING BOAT of 1919 which participated in first trans-Atlantic flights was forerunner of later designs.   Warren D. §

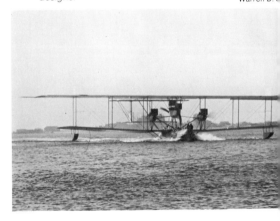

But this Navy competition was to be different. For the first time the design of a patrol plane was not to be wholly controlled by the Navy's aircraft design teams or the Naval Aircraft Factory. And, for comparative purposes, the Navy's Philadelphia factory would build a PN flying boat of its own.

Mac Laddon had some valuable flying boat design experience to contribute. While at McCook, the Engineering Division's own designs for large aircraft began to taper off and Mac then had time for some independent work. Colonel Bane had no objection to Laddon moonlighting for aircraft companies on his own time and getting paid by them for his work.

In the cellar of his home Laddon had outfitted a small engineering office where he and Bernard Sheahan, from Design Branch No. 3, used to work together. With Louis Marsh, a visiting engineer from Boeing who was familiar with hull requirements, Laddon designed the Boeing PB-1 biplane flying boat whose tandem Packard engines turned both tractor and pusher propellers.

The new Consolidated engineering team went to work, designing around the Navy's general specifications and hull lines. Laddon and Roy Miller moved from Dayton to the Buffalo plant and soon had 30 engineers and draftsmen on the job.

"When we closed the Dayton office," Reub told us, "the Army, in the person of Clint Howard, butted in and wanted us to make Mac Laddon our chief engineer. Well, we also had Joe Gwinn. Actually the Army had very little work for us except for trainers, and Gwinn, who was a very novel engineer, was in charge of engineering on them.

"When Howard asked me who was going to be chief engineer I told him, 'I'm going to take that responsibility. I'm not going to make Laddon chief engineer. We've got Gwinn and Laddon and we're going to play one against the other to see who earns the chief engineer's job. In the meantime we've got both of them to advise me.' "

On February 28, 1928, Consolidated won the Navy sponsored design contract and order for a prototype aircraft. It was designated the XPY-1—first experimental patrol plane by Consolidated. (Y was the letter symbol for Consolidated, Curtiss already having the C designator.)

The new plane, Fleet decided, would be called the 'Admiral' "after Admiral Moffett, because it represents the culmination of aircraft engineering by the Naval Aircraft Factory and by industry."

Assisting Admiral Moffett in working out contract details with Major Fleet were Adm. Emory S. Land, Capt. Marc Mitscher and Capt. S. M. Kraus.

In announcing the $150,000 contract award, Edward P. Warner, Assistant Secretary of the Navy for Air, expressed the hope that development of the new long-range patrol boat would help stimulate the development of commercial airline routes.

XPY-1 'ADMIRAL' prototype is moved from hangar into Anacostia River at Washington, D.C., for first trial flights.

San Diego Aero-Space Museum

HUGE for its day, the XPY-1 had a wing-span of 100 feet, carried crew of five, was powered by two 425 h.p. Wasp engines.

The XPY-1 was, in fact, designed to be convertible to carry 32 passengers in a 60-foot cabin. But, as a reconnaissance patrol plane, it would carry a crew of five. Pilot and co-pilot would be in the open bow cockpit, and the navigator-bomber in another open cockpit further forward, with a radio operator and mechanic gunner astern.

The two 425 hp Wasp engines were mounted on struts between the high wing and the hull. Atop the wing center section the Laddon-patented design had provision for an emplacement for a third engine, if necessary. Fourteen feet outboard of the hull were two Richardson-type pontoons for stability on the water. They were supported by struts to the wing and hull.

Construction of the XPY-1 got under way at Consolidated's Buffalo plant in March. No one there had ever worked with such a huge craft before.

"Sixty percent of the plant engineering area," Laddon recalls, "became a loft for laying out full size on the floor, the lines of the hull and wing. We had no end of trouble with fabrication of the aluminum alloy flying boat. This type of construction was completely new to the workers and the problems encountered and solved were legion—difficulties with forming the metal sheet stock, with heat treatment, with rivets and so on.

" 'Captain Dick' Richardson wanted to make certain major changes in our design. I told him that in my opinion they would not contribute to the performance of the boat and wind tunnel tests confirmed my opinion. After that we were permitted to go ahead with our own version.

"Later, Secretary Warner was adamant in stating that in no event would the Navy accept the flying boat unless it was faster than the twin-engine one we proposed. He wanted one with a top speed of at least 135 miles an hour, and that was the reason for the emplacement for the third engine atop the wing."

In November, with assembly of the newly named 'Admiral' flying boat progressing rapidly, Secretary Warner came to Buffalo for a personal inspection. After checking out progress with Reuben Fleet and Lieut. Leigh Wade, Consolidated's recently hired chief pilot, Warner said, "We expect great things of the new boat and it is much needed. Its development is epochal and may lead to many things in aviation." Then he announced that "if flight tests are successful the Navy will buy 32 next year," and said that the planes would be ordered to the Hawaiian Islands.

In late December the XPY-1 'Admiral' prototype was ready for its first test flight, but Reub Fleet was less than pleased about his Buffalo location. Ice in the Niagara River and on Lake Erie made flying impossible, a mid-winter condition which was to haunt Fleet and the Buffalo business community for the next six years.

"When we built what was the country's biggest plane up to that time," complained the Major, "we couldn't put it in the water. There was no place in Buffalo to do so.

"And, we couldn't find a box car big enough to take some of the disassembled sections, so we loaded the parts on three flat cars. The last piece of deck plating was riveted to the hull after the plane was loaded. Then we had to route the flat cars all around the country in order to avoid bridges and tunnels because the parts were so large.

"We also had to send fourteen men along to reassemble the ship before the Navy test flights at Washington. It cost probably $10,000 to ship the plane out of Buffalo and turn it over to the Navy. Of course we couldn't continue to make them in Buffalo if we had to do that with every one."

Mac Laddon went down to Washington over Christmas to take charge. When the rail flat cars arrived December 26, the major assemblies were swung onto barges in the Anacostia River by a huge locomotive crane and towed across to the Naval Air Station where the XPY-1 was assembled.

On the morning of January 10, 1929, the 'Admiral' was ready for its first test flight. Few commercial pilots with experience on flying boats were to be found so the Navy made Lieut. A. W. Gorton available. Mac Laddon, as he always did on the first flight of every airplane he designed, accompanied the test pilot as observer. Next day another series of Consolidated test flights were run. Surprisingly, the huge wing enabled the XPY-1 to land 5 m.p.h. slower than comparable Navy biplane boats. The plane was declared ready for its first official demonstration for the Navy Test Board.

On January 22, in scattered snow flurries, the XPY-1 took off from the Anacostia River with Lieut. W. G. Tomlinson as pilot, Captain Holden Richardson as navigator and with Secretary Warner as a passenger.

"The big plane," reported the New York Times, "roared down the river on a 10-mile wind . . . lifted easily after a 650-foot run and climbed quickly. Two Navy Corsairs, one with photographers, swooped after it in formation." The flight went well. Afterward Richardson told a reporter, "The boat is very stable. It felt good to have something solid under foot." Secretary Warner spoke of "a long step forward" for the XPY-1, with improved performance, marked the end of the biplane era in large Navy aircraft.

FIRST DEMONSTRATION flight of XPY-1 'Admiral,' was made January 22, 1929 with Assistant Secretary of Navy aboard as passenger. Note open cockpits in bow.   Warren D. Shipp

But Warner still insisted on a top speed of 135 miles an hour. The third Wasp engine was installed atop the wing to increase the 'Admiral's' performance and a flight test program conducted in August but Laddon was the first to admit that "it was, in many respects, a real monstrosity." The third engine made it nearly impossible to hangar the plane with its increased height, and servicing at sea by tender was treacherous.

TRI-MOTOR VERSION of XPY-1 *"was, in many respects,"* said Mac Laddon, its designer, *"a real monstrosity."*

U. S. Navy/National Archives

WHEN FORMING CONSOLIDATED AIRCRAFT Corporation in 1923, Reuben Fleet had written that the company "does not bid against others to manufacture their designs."

"When you ask a foster parent," he reasoned, "to mother and father a child when the natural parents are living and watching, no good will come of such an arrangement." The Major's viewpoint was not arbitrary; he had negotiated many such arrangements while Contracting Officer at McCook Field and knew from experience the often unsatisfactory results.

Thus it was that Fleet had some misgivings when the Navy in June 1929 announced it would accept bids from qualified companies to produce nine 'Admiral' flying boats to Consolidated's Laddon-Fleet design. By that time Consolidated had invested half a million dollars in engineering costs in excess of its original $150,000 development contract for the XPY-1 prototype.

Recalling his quandry, Reub said that "we had to bid so as to recoup our investment in development of the first ship. Glenn L. Martin had bid against us and the Navy had to give him the contract because with no engineering cost he was able to bid a half million dollars under Consolidated. We of course objected to Martin's copy of our data. The Navy didn't give them our drawings so with only the benefit of external details they worked up their own engineering drawings.

"But in the end, Martin lost his reputation because he was 28 months in building the nine planes and the Navy learned then the fallacy of taking bids from other than the originator of the design."

The Martin contract called for a developmental prototype (XP2M-1) and nine production planes similar to the Consolidated 'Admiral.' Three were given the designations P3M-1 and six were model P3M-2.

During the two years Martin was producing to the Consolidated flying boat design, Laddon and his engineers were studying modifications for a follow up design for Navy patrol boats and were more than a little disturbed to see some of the same proposed improvements showing up on the Martin flying boats. But on May 26, 1931, Fleet and Laddon received the go-ahead on the prototype of an advanced model, the XP2Y-1. After that they were never again, as Fleet said, "sucking hind teat" on flying boat business.

EVEN BEFORE MARTIN WON the Navy flying boat production order, Major Fleet faced a real dilemma. Not only had he run up a half million dollar engineering expense on which he could not yet collect; he had purchased raw material in anticipation of the order and the tight production schedule Secretary

Warner had mentioned when visiting Buffalo. If he didn't get the Navy order he would be in deep trouble.

There was, however, one ray of hope. Part of the original concept for the flying boat was its convertibility to commercial passenger flights. In fact it had been reported that the Detroit and Cleveland Navigation Co. might inaugurate flying boat service by the Spring of 1929 on Lake Erie between Detroit, Cleveland and Buffalo.

Never one to let the grass grow under his feet, Reuben was covering his flying boat bet in every way possible.

Late in 1927 Fleet had had a talk with Capt. Ralph O'Neill, a World War I ace, who wanted to represent Consolidated in South America. One of O'Neill's dreams was to establish an airline between North and South America and he hoped to do some work on this idea while selling Consolidated trainers. Instead O'Neill made a similar deal to represent Boeing just as Lieut. Wade was later to represent Fleet's interest.

To help sell the flying boat concept for long-distance mail and passenger service, Consolidated printed a sales brochure describing the potential of the 'Commodore,' a commercial version of the Navy's 'Admiral' patrol plane. A prime prospect for 'Com-

A LEVIATHAN of the AIR

CONSOLIDATED · AIRCRAFT · CORPORATION · BUFFALO · N · Y ·

The COMMODORE

modores' was the then-expanding Pan American Airways and through his old friend Col. Thurman H. Bane, then living in New York City, Reuben tried to set up a meeting with Juan Trippe, the dynamic head of the airline. "We feel sure," Fleet wrote Bane, "this is the job for Pan American and will appreciate your making an appointment for us with Mr. Trippe whenever he returns from Europe."

Then, long before Martin won the production contract, Fleet placed two other bets on commercial airline operation as the impetus of Lindbergh's transatlantic flight opened up a whole new world of commercial aviation possibilities.

Under Postmaster General Harry S. New, international airmail contracts were being expanded. In February 1929, flying a Sikorsky S-38 amphibian for Pan American Airways, Charles A. Lindbergh opened up Foreign Air Mail Route No. 5 from Miami to Cristobal in the Canal Zone.

Bids had also been advertised by the Post Office Department for an extension of airmail service from Cristobal to Santiago, Chile.

On the last day of February, Consolidated submitted a bid to carry the airmail on the new route extension.

Also bidding on the route was Tri-Motor Safety Airways, Inc.

As a further hedge, Reuben Fleet three days later signed a contract with Tri-Motor Airways for a million dollars to build six 'Commodore' Flying Boats for use on South American airmail routes.

How Fleet succeeded in the airline business is a story in itself.

The year 1929, in fact, was one of great activity—and of personal tragedy. Another pioneer aircraft company was absorbed by Consolidated; two new aircraft designs were introduced; and shares in Consolidated became available to the public for the first time as the stock was listed for trading on the New York Curb Exchange.

Reuben Fleet, who could handle any situation, discovered that he too was fallible and not immune to personal trauma. Piloting a new 'Fleet' commercial biplane trainer, he experienced an engine failure and subsequent crash in which his passenger was killed. And in October came the stock market Crash of 1929, heralding the Depression of the early thirties.

Each episode became an important chapter in the Fleet saga.

BY THE END OF 1928, after 5½ years in business, Reuben Fleet had converted Consolidated Aircraft's initial $25,000 investment and first year profit of $202 into a viable, money-making corporation. It had done over $6 million in business, 96% of which was with the Army and Navy. Earnings had totaled $2,118,552, representing a respectable 33.4% profit on sales, despite having to furnish the Army 50 trainers for $1 each by way of refund on claimed excess profits. All of the earnings had been plowed back into the business, then still owned almost entirely by Fleet and his sister, Mrs. Lillian Fleet Bishop, with a small percentage held by other directors.

A summary of Consolidated's business through 1928 looked like this:

	Army	Navy	Other	Total	Net Profit	Profit As % of Sales
13 Mos. Ended June 30, 1924	$ 210,975			$ 210,975	$ 202	00.1%
15 Mos. Ended Sept. 30, 1925	593,695			593,695	156,421	26.3%
15 Mos. Ended Dec. 31, 1926	949,626	$ 168,409		1,118,035	276,947	24.7%
Calendar Year 1927	717,752	564,504	$ 2,214	1,284,470	591,459	46.0%
Calendar Year 1928	1,617,584	1,295,722	225,284	3,138,590	1,093,523	34.8%
	$4,089,632	$2,028,635	$227,498	$6,345,765	$2,118,552	33.4%

As the aircraft and airline industry began enjoying the expansion which followed Lindbergh's flight, and as the stock market continued to boom, Major Fleet sensed that it was time to take the public in as partners in Consolidated Aircraft. The ability of Fleet's enterprise to earn a handsome profit was beyond question, a matter of great importance to Wall Street.

Knowing of stock exchange requirements that a certain minimum number of shares had to be listed and available for trading by the public, directors changed Consolidated's capitalization from 600 authorized shares of $100 par value to 750,000 shares of no par value. To get enough shares to list, the company multiplied the original 250 shares held by Fleet and his sister by 2200, giving the company a capitalization of 550,000 shares outstanding.

Arrangements were made with Pynchon & Co., New York investment bankers who had been involved in the Gallaudet Aircraft financing, to handle the first public offering of Consolidated shares. From Major Fleet's own holdings, 82,175 shares were purchased by Pynchon & Co. and offered to the public at $25 per share. The offering was oversubscribed six-fold and Consolidated stock was admitted to trading on the New York Curb Exchange on February 21, 1929. Initial trading was at 33½ per share.

"The present owners," the Pynchon announcement said, "are convinced that all aviation companies must depend upon public support for their proper growth and development and that public participation in ownership is the best method of guaranteeing support of an industry growing so rapidly. Purpose of this sale is to establish a market for the stock."

Since it was Reuben Fleet personally who was selling the 82,175 shares, the transaction did not provide any new financial capital for the company, but it did net the Major close to $2 million.

George M. Pynchon, Jr. and Preston Lockwood of New York, and Francis Dean Schnacke of Dayton, went on the Consolidated board of directors, where they joined Fleet and three other company officers, Whitman, Newman and recently-hired Lawrence D. Bell.

"In those days," says Reuben, "it was the custom of some companies to put a man well-known in aviation on their board. For instance, Irving Air Chute Co. put me on as a director, along with General Patrick, without my knowledge or consent and they gave me an option on 1000 shares of stock at the market price. I resigned their Board, sold the stock and made perhaps eleven or twelve thousand dollars gross on the deal. I just didn't care to identify with any company in aviation other than our own."

In reinvesting all of the profits of Fleet's enterprise to provide Consolidated with adequate working capital and facilities, Reuben and the other original investors had not received any cash dividends on their initial investment. There are, however, more ways than one to skin a cat.

"WE HADN'T BEEN IN BUSINESS in Buffalo very long," Reuben told us, "before we realized we were spending hundreds of thousands of dollars annually with suppliers in the Niagara frontier area. Often their prices were high, delivery was late and quality was poor. Sometimes they spoiled the material we furnished or maybe they misinterpreted our drawings. We decided to overcome that handicap and eliminate the middle man.

"We had been purchasing items like turnbuckles, bolts, nuts, various machined parts and things of that nature from perhaps 200 suppliers around Buffalo. They charged us 100% of their labor estimate, 100% thereon for overhead and 20% of both items for profit, making the cost to us about 240% of the labor estimate.

"In October 1927 I organized Tonawanda Products Corporation, of which 80% was owned by Consolidated Aircraft and 20% allocated to employees of Tonawanda. We formed Tonawanda to be a major parts supplier to Consolidated, which not only did the engineering but also the inspection. Where a supplier was late with our requirements, it might upset our own production schedule. But with our own subsidiary we could direct it to give preference to our work and thus not upset our delivery schedules.

"Tonawanda was directed to operate at the cost of labor, plus 60% for overhead and 10% of both for profit. This meant 176% of labor cost for the finished product against 240% for outside suppliers.

"We invested $25,000 in machinery and rented quarters for Tonawanda Products right near our own Buffalo plant, which also greatly reduced our transportation problems."

To head Tonawanda as president and treasurer, Fleet chose Charles T. Leigh, assistant to Consolidated's factory manager. Chuck Leigh had recently come from a position as superintendent of Grays Harbor Construction Co., Washington, the area where Fleet had grown up, to oversee construction of a new building.

Consolidated's machine shop foreman, Henry R. Golem, who was born in North Tonawanda and had worked for the Curtiss plant in Buffalo, was named vice president. Secretary of the new corporation was Fleet's secretary, Lauretta Lederer Golem, Henry's wife. Henry's young nephew, Howard, was also employed by Tonawanda Products.

"When we did want to buy from outside suppliers," Fleet recalls, "we found we could get rock-bottom prices because they knew we could do the work ourselves at Tonawanda. Often we were able to buy from these outside sources at prices far lower than they gave our competitors.

"On one occasion when we were ready to place parts orders for several hundred airplanes I sat down with George I. Stitch the head of one of the big aero supply manufacturing companies from Long Island who had come over to see us.

" 'George,' I said, 'I figure there is 10% profit in this $5000 order for your company. Now I know that's contrary to your prices to other customers. For instance, on this bolt which is a perfect fit in the wing spar, you put a few scratches on it so the Air Force will think you had to turn it out of bar stock. Then you plate it and sell it to them for $1.40, whereas it cost you, say, 3 cents. Now I know that because I've been down to your factory and seen all the ways you do it. You know it, and I know it.

" 'Since we now have our own parts factory I want you to take this order down to the hotel and figure if you can accept it for $5000 flat for the whole works. We won't price the individual items—you just do that in your own way. We'll pay you $5000 for the works, but we want the goods delivered the same as if we were paying for $1.40 unit price.'

"George says, 'You've got me there Reuben. We'll be happy to do it; and keep your mouth shut about how we manufacture our stuff.'

"I said, 'I've never told anybody.'

"You can see how successful we were in operating competitively through our ownership of Tonawanda. We earned $225,299 the first year and Tonawanda paid twenty dividends of $25,000 each during its first five years."

At the time Major Fleet was arranging for the first public offering of Consolidated shares to the public, he also formed Frontier Enterprises, Inc. as a holding company for various Consolidated Aircraft subsidiaries. Frontier held 225 of Tonawanda's 250 outstanding shares. Frontier also operated the company airport at Tonawanda and owned the Niagara-from-the-Air sightseeing business.

Then, to promote pilot training and the sale of planes to the public, Fleet organized National Flying Schools, Inc., with Leigh Wade, Consolidated's sales manager, as its operating head.

The great Falls of the Niagara River had long been a prime attraction for tourists, but from the air got scant endorsement from David W. Fleet. On a flight with his father as passenger, Reuben banked the plane steeply to give the senior Fleet a better view, "Straighten it out, son! I'll look at the Falls when we get down."

WHEN REUBEN FLEET and James H. Rand, Jr. agreed in January 1929 to underwrite two-thirds of the expenses Capt. Ralph A. O'Neill incurred in promoting an airline in South America, the die was cast for the creation of the New York, Rio & Buenos Aires Line, Inc. Its 7000 route miles would make it the world's longest commercial airline and the first to make extensive use of flying boats—the Consolidated 'Commodores.'

And that first step would get Major Fleet off the hook, permitting Consolidated to recover its engineering costs on the XPY-1 flying boat and use up the stock of materials it had bought in anticipation of a production order from the Navy.

> " . . . the logical answer is big flying boats: almost every large city has a good harbor . . . "

The backgrounds of the three men—Fleet, Rand and O'Neill—were quite different but they did have a mutuality of interest which culminated in the foundation of NYRBA (the airline's acronym).

Jim Rand, a fellow Buffalo business man was head of the Remington Rand Corporation, makers of typewriters and other business machines. On a visit to Ford Motor Company, one of his company's major customers, Rand had been invited by Henry Ford to inspect Ford's new aircraft manufacturing division and fly in its new plane. Rand was so pleased by his flight in the Ford trimotor transport that he ordered one on the spot.

Not long afterward, Rand formed a new company, hopefully to operate an air transport service, possible between New York and Washington. As a compliment to his new Ford plane, Rand called the firm Tri-Motor Safety Airways, Inc.

After his return from flying with the U.S. Air Service in France, Capt. Ralph O'Neill, a pre-war mining engineer, was invited by President Adolfo de la Huerta to organize the Mexican air force and serve as technical consultant on aviation to the government.

O'Neill's five year stay in Mexico stimulated his interest in the future of aviation in Latin America and the possibilities of air transportation throughout the Western Hemisphere. He believed the real potential lay on the east coast of South America where nearly all the commerce and population was concentrated. There, the French Aeropostale and German Condor airlines were already operating on a limited basis, as was SCADTA, a Columbian airline operated by German settlers.

Obtaining a contract from Boeing to demonstrate their airplanes in South America afforded O'Neill the opportunity to also promote his ideas of an airline linking South and North America.

Unlike Pan American Airways, which saw the west coast of South America as the logical and shortest route, O'Neill confined his studies to the east coast, which offered far greater traffic and the advantage of many harbors, river deltas and bays, making possible operating the route with flying boats.

Because of his wartime service, O'Neill was well known in Army and Navy circles in Washington. Before leaving in March 1928 on his sales trip to South America for Boeing, O'Neill stopped to see Admiral Moffett and discuss his ideas for the airline.

"What flying equipment do you have in mind for use in commercial operation?" asked the Admiral.

"Sir," O'Neill replied, "the logical answer is big flying boats; almost every large city in the Caribbean and on the east coast has a good harbor and on an average they are about three hundred miles apart."

"Well, Captain O'Neill, I think we may be coming up with something to fit the bill. Reuben Fleet's Consolidated Aircraft recently won a design competition for a new flying boat and we'll be testing it at Anacostia within nine months. It's a big boat. One-hundred-foot wingspread with bracing to outrigger pontoons and a hull sixty-two feet long. Of course we haven't flown it yet, but you ought to keep it in mind."

Conferences with Post Office officials, especially W. Irving Glover, Assistant Postmaster General, were less promising. Glover made it clear that the government would favor a one-company monopoly in Latin America if necessary to meet the competition of airlines sponsored by foreign governments. That probably meant that Pan American Airways, then operating landplanes between Key West and Havana, had the inside track as it was flying this country's only foreign route.

The name Pan American had originated with John K. Montgomery and Richard B. Bevier, two wartime pilots who incorporated under that name to seek an airmail contract for their landplane operation between Key West and Havana—the same route over which Aeromarine Airways had previously operated a passenger service with flying boats.

During the same period the first contracts for domestic airmail service were being awarded by the Post Office Department. The 192-mile New York-Boston service—Contract Air Mail Route No. 1—went to Colonial Air Transport, whose principal mover was Juan Terry Trippe. A former Navy pilot and founder of the Yale Flying Club, Trippe was associated with influential Wall Street interests.

Outmaneuvered, and convinced by Trippe that the government and financial contacts of newly formed Aviation Corporation of the Americas, of which he was a key executive, assured their winning the important Key West-Havana contract as an opening wedge to

JUAN TERRY TRIPPE
"the leading figure in U.S. foreign airline operation."

Latin America, Montgomery and Bevier merged their Pan American Airways into AVCO. In March 1927, PAA became AVCO's airline operating subsidiary; later with massive support from Washington and as this country's chosen instrument in airline matters in Latin America it virtually dictated airline matters in Latin America for many years.

Such were the obstacles which O'Neill was to face, though it was difficult at the time to fully evaluate them.

On March 8, 1928 President Calvin Coolidge signed the Foreign Air Mail Act. And in March, Ralph O'Neill sailed aboard a Munson liner for South America to demonstrate Boeing planes and to explore the potential for his proposed airline.

On a cross-country flight in a Boeing fighter, O'Neill had a near-fatal crash north of Montevideo, Uruguay which ended with Boeing cancelling his contract. But his proposals to government officials in Brazil, Uruguay and Argentina for air mail service were well received. If Argentina, in particular, would grant a contract, O'Neill felt the others would follow. Buoyed by the prospect, he booked passage on the next steamer and returned to New York.

His lawyers in Buenos Aires were soon pressing O'Neill to obtain the strong financial backing the Argentine government insisted upon before a contract would be awarded. With Wall Street pouring money into post-Lindbergh aviation projects, financing for the proposed airline should have been no great problem. But O'Neill hadn't taken into account Pan American's strong influence.

When financing did appear to be available, the prospective investor often sought the advice of Richard F. Hoyt of the Wall Street firm of Hayden Stone & Company. Unfortunately Dick Hoyt and his friend Cornelius Vanderbilt (Sonny) Whitney were Juan Trippe's closest associates in Pan American Airways and always succeeded in squelching O'Neill's deal.

Since Reuben Fleet's Consolidated Aircraft would no doubt be supplying the flying boats for the proposed airline, O'Neill put in a call to Buffalo. Yes, Fleet would meet him in New York City on his next trip. Seeing an opportunity to sell some 'Commodores,' Fleet agreed to match the first half-million dollars of capital that O'Neill got firmly committed.

Another six months passed. Meantime Fleet tried to get to Juan Trippe, since he felt Pan American was an equally good prospect for 'Commodores.' Colonel Thurman Bane, his contact in New York, had written:

"My dear Fleet:

"I'm from Missouri, as usual, and should like to know its [Commodore's] weight and predicted performance. As you probably know, your high powered salesmanship alone will not sell it. The present is not the opportune time to discuss flying boats with Juan Trippe."

However, when Bane visited the Buffalo plant in November he was convinced of the merits of the Consolidated design.

Finally, in January 1929, word came from Buenos Aires that President Hipolito Irigoyen would undoubtedly sign the contract to fly mail from Argentina to New York. And Uruguay was expected to grant a similar contract almost immediately.

Meantime, O'Neill had been in touch with Jim Rand, an aviation enthusiast whose company had a natural interest because of its many sales offices in South America.

Things came to a head in Buffalo when Fleet and Rand met. The Navy's first 'Admiral' flying boat had just recently taken to the air and the contract to carry mail for the Argentine government to New York was clearly available if a new company could be formed and financed.

"Rand was a good friend who was enthusiastic about flying and would often come around and ask my advice on aviation matters. He and I agreed to help form the new company and to personally pay two-thirds of O'Neill's expenses, including a survey flight down the 'mutton leg' east coast of South America. That would make it a three-way partnership.

"Jim suggested that he raise the money. 'That's my specialty,' he said, 'Fleet, you design and furnish the flying boats, and let Ralph manage the operation,' Each of us had his forte. We felt it was a combination you couldn't beat.

"We would issue 50,000 shares of bonus stock between the three of us for promoting the company, for our knowledge of aviation, for the airmail franchise and for everything of that character. We split the stock three ways: 16,667 shares were mine; same amount to Rand and 16,666—one share less—to Ralph.

CONSOLIDATED AIRCRAFT CORPORATIO

Safety—Durabil. Reliability

2050 ELMWOOD AVE
BUFFALO, NEW Y

WITH SIGNING of contract for transport flying boats, 'Commodore' began to appear on Consolidated letterheads.

"Tri-Motor Safety Airways was selected as the company through which we would initially work. Because 'safety' had a negative connotation and since the 'Commodores' were twin-engined, not tri-motor planes, we decided on a new operating name—New York, Rio and Buenos Aires Line, Inc.

"Assured of sound financing, the formal airmail contract with Argentina was obtained March 1. The next day Consolidated Aircraft signed a contract with Tri-Motor for six 'Commodore' boats for $150,000 each. With spare parts, the contract came to an even one million dollars. Then, just before President Herbert Hoover took office, Postmaster General Harry S. New awarded the Canal Zone-Santiago, Chile airmail contract to Pan American Grace Airways. Obviously, NYRBA was going to have to hustle against such competition.

"O'Neill had gotten to Buenos Aires ahead of Pan American and sewed up the Argentine government which agreed to pay us $10 a pound for airmail destined for North America, the contract to be good until 25% of all their northbound mail was carried by air, by us. To assume that such a high percentage of mail would ever go by air made us feel we had almost a perpetual contract. Later O'Neill sewed up Uruguay and Brazil in the same way.

"Dick Hoyt offered us—Rand, O'Neill and myself—a quarter of a million dollars each for our interest in those contracts. They wanted us to take it and for Jim and me to join the Pan American board, but they didn't want Ralph because he had fought them so hard. Rand thought the mail contracts with the South American countries were worth $50 million.

"I wanted to accept Hoyt's offer, but Rand and O'Neill voted against me. I figured a quarter of a million in hand was better than several million in the bush, but Ralph said, 'I have always been a soldier of fortune. A quarter of a million is nothing to me compared with the possibility of making several million, so I vote with you, Jim, that NYRBA go ahead as planned, on its own.'

"At that time costs for O'Neill's survey trip were $14,430, so Rand and I had each made an investment of $7,215, with Ralph nothing.

"Among those from whom Rand eventually raised some $6 million was Lewis E. Pierson, chairman of the Irving Trust Company He and other investors were aware that we held 50,000 shares of bonus stock. Pierson's son-in-law was Dick Bevier.

"After Bevier and Montgomery had sold out to Trippe, who became president of Pan American Airways, they decided to again compete with him and formed American International Airways. That new firm bought a twin-engine Sikorsky land plane similar to the Fonck biplane built for the transatlantic flight, and bid on the Canal Zone—Santiago mail contract. American International also bought a million dollar interest in NYRBA and had representation on its board of directors."

At Rand's urging William B. Mayo of Ford Motor Company was added to the NYRBA Board and six trimotor Ford landplanes were ordered for the Santiago-Buenos Aires run over the Andes.

At Buffalo, work on the 'Commodores' moved briskly along. O'Neill frequently visited the plant to become familiar with the huge new flying boats. Designed to carry up to 32 passengers, the final arrangement provided for 22 passengers in two 8-passenger com-

partments and two drawing rooms each seating three. The crew would consist of pilot, copilot and a combination radio operator/steward. Ample space was also available for mail, express, radio gear and lavatory.

Fleet contracted for the services of Frederick J. Pike, interior decorator, who set a new standard in beauty and comfort in the plane's luxurious appointments. Each compartment had large picture windows and was paneled in a different pastel color of waterproof fabric. The usual imitation leather seats were replaced by fabric upholstery. In every way the 'Commodores' were the finest, largest transport planes available, and years ahead of their time.

To complete arrangements for landing facilities and service, passenger handling and for traffic offices and representation, O'Neill left in mid-June in NYRBA's S-38 Sikorsky amphibian on a final survey flight to South America. Six additional 'Commodores' were then ordered by NYRBA for the same unit price as for the original six.

HULLS of first two 'Commodores' and wing center section of one of the passenger transports make their appearance on Consolidated's first production line for multi-engine aircraft.

General Dynamics/Convair

By September O'Neill had returned and the first of the 'Commodores'—the 'Buenos Aires'—was ready to try her wings. The color scheme was spectacular. Wings of bright coral, hull a rich cream to the water line and black below. A gigantic caterpillar crane mounted on a power barge carefully lifted the 'Commodore' over the sea wall where it had been assembled and into the Niagara River-Lake Erie harbor on September 28 for her first flight with Consolidated's Leigh Wade and Lieut. William S. Grooch, former Navy pilot now working for NYRBA, at the controls.

Two days later, Grooch and Wade, with the latter in charge until the 'Buenos Aires' was officially delivered and accepted, flew at low altitude over Manhattan through a rain storm. In that weather Grooch wanted to bring the flying boat down at Port Washington on Long Island, but Wade had been instructed to land off Miller Field, an Army airport on Staten Island, and did so, but the heavy sea and cross swells pounded the boat against the too-narrow ramp as it taxied in, opening several seams in the hull.

By noon October third the hull had been patched and Grooch and Wade were in the air for Washington.

Landing off the Anacostia Air Station, a Navy crew hauled the plane out of the water, washed it down and moved it into place alongside a bunting-wrapped stand where Mrs. Herbert Hoover was to christen the first inter-American transport plane in the presence of diplomats from 21 Latin American republics.

But Reuben Fleet, who played such a key role with his plane and his financial backing of NYRBA, was not on hand for the ceremonies. His first serious accident as a pilot had him confined to a hospital in London, Ontario. In his place, Mac Laddon and Larry Bell represented Consolidated.

When Mrs. Hoover arrived for the christening of the 'Buenos Aires' O'Neill was in for a rude shock. Secret service men shouldered him aside as Mrs. Hoover, accompanied by Juan Trippe, walked to the platform. There Pan American's Trippe stole NYRBA's show as described by O'Neill:

"He stood in front of our airplane rattling on to the effect that Pan American Airways would establish an eight-hour passenger and mail service to Buenos Aires. 'If Trippe has the Post Office Department in his pocket,' asked Grooch, 'what chance do we stand to

FIRST COMMODORE, 'Buenos Aires,' is lowered by barge crane into Niagara River-Lake Erie harbor for initial flight September 28, 1928.

CONSOLIDATED AND NYRBA officials at roll-out of first 'Commodore' flying boat. Left to right, Consolidated's George Newman, Mac Laddon and Leigh Wade; Col. Ralph O'Neill, president of NYRBA; Larry Bell, recently named general manager of Consolidated, and William Grooch, NYRBA chief pilot. (Reuben Fleet was in hospital in Canada after near-fatal crash in new trainer.)

get a U.S. Air Mail contract?' "

Early the next morning a working party arrived from the Buffalo factory to repair the 'Commodore's' hull. Several days later Grooch and O'Neill taxied out from a cove of the Anacostia River and took off for Miami with stops scheduled enroute at Hampton Roads and Charleston. By noon the next day they were in Havana where a sightseeing pleasure flight had been planned for the family of President Gerardo Machado. It ended in near disaster.

With O'Neill ashore on business and Lewis Pierson's son in the copilot seat, Grooch taxied out with Mrs. Machado, her family and friends, mostly ladies, aboard.

In the hot, dead air of the harbor, and with 30 passengers aboard, Grooch could not get the plane off the smooth water, so he taxied out to sea and bounced the beautiful new 'Commodore' off the waves and into the air. Again, in landing, Grooch set the 'Buenos Aires' down just outside the harbor in the swells that were booming against Morro Castle. The pounding was too much for the plane's hull. Hysteria broke out when water started gushing into the cabin just after the plane landed. Grooch taxied into the harbor and beached the plane.

MRS. HERBERT HOOVER christens 'Buenos Aires' at Washington, D.C. Note open cockpit in bow for pilot and co-pilot.

That accident required major repairs to the 'Buenos Aires' and meant that additional strength had to be built into the hull of all 'Commodores.' Admiral Moffett agreed to let Consolidated and NYRBA use Navy facilities to make the modifications. Grooch flew the crippled plane back to the Pensacola, Florida, Naval air base. It was ten days before the 'Buenos Aires' was again in the air to pick up its passengers at Havana and continue south through the West Indies.

Meantime, the second flying boat, 'Rio de Janiero,' was flown to Port Washington, New York by Wade, dismantled and put on display November 10 in Madison Square Garden, where it attracted great attention. Like other 'Commodores' to follow, the 'Rio' had an enclosed cockpit, as the tropical sun and rain made the original open cockpit arrangement impractical.

To try and offset some of Juan Trippe's influence with the Post Office Department, NYRBA offered the position of chairman of its board to William P. MacCracken, Jr., then Hoover's assistant secretary of commerce for aeronautics. On December 4 he assumed his post as chief executive of NYRBA. That day the third plane, 'Havana,' after repairs to its ice-damaged hull, was flown from Buffalo to Long Island.

William B. Wheatley, former airline pilot, was at the controls as the new Consolidated test pilot, succeeding Leigh Wade who had left on a training plane sales trip to South America. "The temperature at Buffalo," Wheatley explained, "was below freezing and I remember that the spray, incident to the takeoff, froze on the windshield. I considered using the hand fire ex-

tinguisher to break the glass in order to see out. However, I was able to see through a small corner of the glass, and finally melted the ice off part of the windshield immediately ahead of me by holding by bare hand against the inside of the glass."

In October, two more 'Commodores' had been ordered, bringing the total to 14, plus six single-engine Consolidated 'Fleetsters,' some of the latter to be equipped with pontoons.

After the successful display of the NYRBA flying boat in Manhattan, it was reassembled at Port Washington and on November 23 the 'Rio de Janiero' with O'Neill aboard left for Buenos Aires. All went well until Fortaleza on Brazil's north coast. To give NYRBA crews experience in flying the 'Commodore,' O'Neill rode as a passenger. Again, in a rough water takeoff, the hull took a severe beating but it was a motor mount this time which failed when a wave hit the propeller causing the engine to shake loose and the propeller to cut into the cabin. The 'Rio' would be grounded for a month.

As Consolidated and Navy pilots were learning, handling a large flying boat on the water was more of a problem than piloting it in the air from point to point.

On its inaugural southbound flight, with NYRBA company personnel aboard, the 'Havana' also ran into trouble. Coming in to land at Paramaribo, Dutch Guiana a fuel line on the port side burst and caught fire, Capt. Robin McGlohn beached the plane on the muddy banks of the river and extinguished the flames. NYRBA's New York office phoned Reuben Fleet at home that night and two days later a new left wing was

SECOND COMMODORE, 'Rio de Janeiro,' prepares for first flight *November 6, 1929. Note new enclosed cockpit to protect pilots from the elements.*

General Dynamics/Convair

on a southbound steamer. Before the plane went back in service the name on the hull was changed to the Spanish 'Habana' to soothe local feelings.

Such were the initial growing pains and bugs. Then the situation brightened.

Northbound airmail service out of Buenos Aires was inaugurated just two weeks before the March 1, 1930 deadline stipulated in NYRBA's contract signed a year earlier with the Argentine government. Operations soon settled down to regularly maintained schedules after the 'Cuba,' which brought the first mail into Miami February 26, joined the first three 'Commodores.' Travel time had been cut from 20 days to seven days.

In May, the speedy Consolidated 'Fleetster' was put on the northbound mail run. A day after the weekly 'Commodore' left Buenos Aires, the 'Fleetster,' carrying the mail, would fly north at night to overtake it at Florianopolis, half way to Rio, thereby cutting a whole day from the mail schedule to Miami.

"There were few hotels down around the 'mutton leg' of South America," Fleet explained, "until you get to Rio, so the people who went on those early flights often slept aboard. The Coca-Cola executives were among our first customers and they were very loud in their praise of the line. Even when they reached Rio and then to Sao Paulo and Montevideo they preferred to sleep on the boat rather then ashore."

To expedite delivery of the 'Commodores' Consolidated gave up on Buffalo with its inclement weather and shipped assemblies for nine of the huge flying boats to Langley Field, Virginia. The company leased space from the Navy in its seaplane hangar and sent 18 employees to handle assembly of the 'Commodores.' Here they could be flown and tested by Bill Wheatley during the winter months in the open water of Chesapeake Bay. Delivery flights out of Buffalo

General Dynamics/Convair

THIRD COMMODORE, 'Havana,' flies over Statue of Liberty in New York Harbor before delivery to NYRBA for airline service to South America.

127

'ARGENTINA,' used by National Geographic Society on expedition
to South America, joins a sister 'Commodore' in harbor at Rio de
Janeiro, Brazil.

resumed in June with testing of the 'Miami' by Wheatley.

One more operational incident with the 'Commodore' did attract unusual attention. On a scheduled overland run from Cienfuegos, Cuba to Havana in the 'Porto Rico,' with 18 passengers and mail aboard, Capt. Herman E. Sewell had both engines quit. That meant a crash landing of the huge flying boat on land. Landing on the sugar cane parallel to the furrows, Sewell skidded the plane's hull to a safe stop with no injury to passengers and relatively minor damage to the boat, except to the right wing.

Although flying schedules were being maintained at a reliable routine, there was much pulling and tugging going on within the NYRBA organization and between NYRBA and Pan American. As always, the PAA triumvirate of Trippe, Hoyt and Whitney was aiding and pushing the 'chosen instrument' policy of President Hoover's new Postmaster General, Walter F. Brown—there would be a single U.S. flag airline overseas.

Montgomery and Bevier, with $1 million invested and with MacCracken's tacit approval, were trying to wrest operational control of NYRBA from O'Neill, the rugged individualist whose sole investment was his dream and his untiring work. Jim Rand sat somewhat on the sidelines watching his own financial empire shrink in the disasterous stock market slump.

Although concerned primarily with the sale of the 14 'Commodores' and a goodly number of Consolidated 'Fleetster' single-engine transports, Reuben Fleet was aware of the forces at work in NYRBA behind the scenes.

"Pan American eventually got a route into Buenos Aires, and Argentina, anxious to get another line in there, split their business between NYRBA and PAA. We found that instead of the North Americans exploiting the South Americans, they were exploiting us. They could play one against the other.

"We decided that consolidation of our two companies would be in the national interest, and the Post Office Department had made their position clear that there should be just one U.S. operated airmail line. Then, too, the Depression had hit all of us badly and Rand was unable to raise any more money.

"We hired lawyers to write us briefs on a consolidation with Pan American. We paid Elihu Root's firm $35,000 for its written opinion; another $25,000 to the firm with which Dean Acheson was associated; and Bill MacCracken, our attorney, received $35,000 for his brief on the matter. The briefs were given to Hoover's Attorney General, William D. Mitchell, who drafted his own brief for the President, who then authorized the consolidation.

"Juan Trippe was the dominant factor and we backed him good and strong. He was a charming, wonderful man and the leading figure in U.S. foreign airline operation for decades.

"Pan American was kept as the operating company. All the investors turned their stock in for Pan American shares in a $4 million stock transfer. It was a paper transaction as they put up no cash, merely exchanging their shares for NYRBA shares. My 16,667 shares of NYRBA had cost me only $7,215, but in the Depression PAA stock had slumped badly. It wasn't worth anything like the quarter of a million dollars each we had earlier been offered, because all stocks were terribly depressed and the country was so panicky over them that it was doubtful how much they were worth. But, whatever PAA stock was worth, it was clear profit, so I decided to use it as gifts to charitable organizations and for years and years I was giving PAA shares away until all were gone.

"For Consolidated, the NYRBA project paid off handsomely. We sold 14 'Commodores,' 10 'Fleetsters,' and 10 'Fleet' trainers and made a profit of $208,000 for our company on the deal. And, of course, we got back all our development cost on the original XPY-1 'Admiral' flying boat.

"Above all else we established that in 15 months we could produce 14 flying boats modified for commercial service. Martin took 27 months to produce their nine copies of the 'Admiral' for the Navy. That taught the Navy a good lesson which they never, never forgot—don't alienate the original designer from his design by giving it to someone else. Always thereafter, they patronized Consolidated on flying boats no matter what happened."

In mid-August 1930 agreement had been reached to merge NYRBA into Pan American, which then took over the contracts from NYRBA and Tri-Motor Safety Airways for the remainder of the 'Commodores' to be delivered. For years thereafter the Consolidated flying boats rendered excellent service on PAA's Caribbean and South American runs.

In his 1934 Annual Report to Stockholders, Fleet was able to write, "Consolidated 'Commodores' have flown more than five million miles of scheduled passenger and mail flying in the service of Pan American Airways; to our knowledge no passenger or person has ever been hurt in a 'Commodore' in the five years they have been the backbone of that great American company's service from Miami to Buenos Aires."

Ryan Aeronautical Library

'COMMODORE' was featured by Pan American on special envelopes designed to promote use of air mail.

Nine years after the 'Commodores' were built, 13 of the 14 planes were still in service with Pan American, one having burned in a hangar fire. Average flying time exceeded nine thousand hours each. Appropriately, one of the five 'Commodores' operated by Panair do Brazil held the international license PP-PAA.

In 1945 Pan American sold the tenth 'Commodore' built to Bahama Airways, Ltd. Twenty years after it first flew it was still carrying passengers on a scheduled airline route between the Outer Islands and Bahama.

PAA PUBLICITY photo of early thirties has Caribbean vacationers using Commodore as a swimming float.

Warren D. Shipp

AN INTERESTING POSTSCRIPT to Postmaster General Brown's autocratic handling of airmail contracts, domestic as well as foreign, also involved Reuben Fleet. When Franklin D. Roosevelt assumed the presidency, a congressional investigation under Senator Hugo L. Black of Alabama was looking into the awarding of domestic mail contracts. As a result, President Roosevelt, on February 9, 1934, cancelled all domestic contracts and directed the Army Air Corps to fly the mail effective February 19.

The result was disasterous. Trained for combat flying, not daily scheduled transport operation, Army pilots one after another crashed and were killed in the inclement weather and unfamiliar operational conditions. Even before the Army started its service on February 19, three pilots were killed in one night while en route to taking over their assignments. A fourth crashed but escaped death.

In the first week, five pilots were killed and six more critically injured. Accidents continued throughout the next weeks. When Lieut. Fred I. Patrick gave his life, Reuben Fleet could no longer contain his outrage, brought on by the death of his flying colleague from Brooks Field days and by the inappropriateness of trying to have the Army assume a role for which it was not properly equipped.

In a sulphurous wire to his friend President Roosevelt, Reuben gave full vent to his spleen. Asked much later to provide a copy of that wire, Fleet begged off on the explanation that he would never reveal that such a brutal communication had been received by the President. But on another occasion he had been willing to talk about it briefly.

"Lieut. Patrick was one of my bosom friends. I sent Roosevelt a telegram, the likes of which he never got before in his life. I wasn't in the Army, and by God, it just burned me up. I told him he was a murderer and

Lieut. Fred I. Patrick

he better quit it.

"He called me on the phone long distance.

" 'Of all the telegrams I have ever received in my life, Reuben Fleet, that is the worst.'

" 'Well,' I said, 'Mr. President, I meant every word of it. And you'd better quit that. The Army is not equipped to do that job.' "

" 'All right,' he says, 'I'm going to take your advice. And I'll tell you something else. Never again am I going to move on aviation matters without consulting you first.' "

Many similar protests were received by the White House and within weeks steps were taken to restore the service to private contract operation. Then Roosevelt got in touch with Fleet and asked that he serve as an advisor on airmail matters to the new Postmaster General, James A. Farley.

Much of the blame for the Army airmail fiasco fell on Major General Benjamin D. Foulois, chief of the Air Corps, who many believed accepted the ill-advised assignment in part because it might focus attention on the Air Corps' needs to keep pace with commercial aviation advancements.

For Major Fleet there was a macabre sense of justice to the tragedy. Only a few months earlier he had spent a Saturday afternoon in conference with Secretary of War George H. Dern extolling the leadership qualities of his friend Lieut. Col. Henry H. Arnold and recommending in most urgent terms his selection as chief of the Air Corps to replace Foulois.

While the Major would never later fully discuss his advocacy of Arnold for the top Air Corps post there is no doubt that his many and frequent discussions with President Roosevelt played a key part in the latter's selection of Arnold four years later on the eve of World War II.

THOMAS-MORSE O-19 observation plane carries the mail over hazardous Rockies as Army understandably bungles effort at scheduled airline operation.

U. S. Air Force

THE MARKET FOR PRIVATE AIRPLANES virtually exploded after Lindbergh's inspiring New York to Paris flight in May 1927. Consolidated Aircraft, however, offered only a line of military training planes. And it was an accepted fact in aeronautical circles that planes designed and manufactured to government specifications were too big and expensive for sale to private owners.

Reuben Fleet was not about to let opportunity pass him by.

His scorecard on training plane orders was a good one and by mid-1929 deliveries of completed aircraft, including those exported, looked like this:

Model	Total
#TW-3	20
#PT-1	224
NY-1	127
0-17	32
PT-3	264*
NY-2	179
Total	864

With water cooled engines
* Includes 50 at $1 each for U.S. Army

Now Fleet would try and come up with a plan to tap the opportunities in the private aircraft field equally as well.

Joe Gwinn, who had come to Consolidated from the original Gallaudet company, had been placed in charge of training plane engineering after Ginny Clark had departed in mid-1927. Gwinn saw the potential in commercial planes and got a go-ahead from the Major to build a prototype of a new cabin plane around a design he and Fleet favored.

The Model 10 was a strut-braced high-wing monoplane powered with a 225 h.p. Wright Whirlwind engine. The five-place plane had two distinctive features, a triangular shaped fuselage and an overhead control stick. The first flight was made August 10, 1928.

Instead of the conventional oval or rectangular fuselage, Gwinn had designed a triangular shape with the peak of the triangle at the top. It was felt it would give improved visibility from the cabin and would be cheaper to build.

The simplified control system eliminated cables and pulleys. Ailerons and elevator were operated by means of single push-pull tubes with an overhead control stick. The design of the system materially decreased cost, but none of the pilots liked it even though a stirrup grip was put in in an effort to conventionalize the overhead stick control. It was just too dangerous for pilots to master.

Factory manager George Newman said that, "I remember the overhead stick and after many attempts, and a few close calls, it was changed to a conventional stick operating from the cabin floor. We just were not able to cope with the unfamiliar motion of the overhead arrangement."

"I was forced to admire Gwinn's ingenuity," Fleet recalls, "but I finally decided to abandon the airplane, lest we have an accident with it. Even the triangular

General Dynamics/Convair

TRIANGULAR FUSELAGE of Model 10 business plane of 1928 proved too radical for post-Lindbergh private aircraft market. Fleet felt the 'time was not right for its innovative features.'

fuselage was so unconventional that it did not attract buyers who considered it 'ugly' and possibly not rigid enough to carry the tail surfaces. It was best to put Model 10 to sleep as the time was not right for its innovative features.

"Joe Gwinn was possibly the most original engineer in the aircraft business. The only trouble with Joe was he had a screw loose in his makeup. He would always overlook something that would trip us up unless I held him by the hand; then I could detect the oversight and call it to his attention so it could be fixed.

"When the business got so exhausting that I simply could not hold his hand anymore we just kept him on the payroll to do nothing but study. It was cheaper to pay his salary than give him a group of workers with nobody to check his probable deficiencies.

"After we had him on the payroll for about three years without any work, I called him in one day. 'Joe, what have you created; what have you got now?'

"He showed me a design similar to what later became the Gwinn Aircar, but said, 'I want a 51% interest in it.'

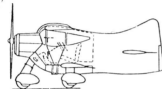

" 'Well, Joe,' I said, 'I never heard of such a thing. You designed this plane all on our time, and during that period you never had a reduction in salary. You've had our equipment and facilities and have observed everything we are doing just the same as if you were on a regular production job for us, rather than just study work. Regardless of the 51% interest you think you should have we would never produce that airplane. It would never sell.'

" 'Why?'

" 'Just its looks, if nothing else. It hasn't got that attractive an appearance. You can't sell a thing that looks crazy.'

"I paid Joe $105,000 for his 1% stock interest in Consolidated Aircraft that he had bought from me years before for about $600. Later he built the Gwinn Aircar in Buffalo with his own money and employed Frank Hawks to test it. In a demonstration flight at East Aurora, New York, Hawks and a passenger were killed in August 1938. That stopped the whole project."

Only the one Model 10 Consolidated triangular-fuselaged cabin monoplane was built. No application for an Approved Type Certificate was processed, but the plane was operated briefly on sightseeing flights by Niagara-From-The-Air. Finally the airplane was dismantled and stored in the attic of the hangar on Military Road, which Bill Wheatley and George Newman jokingly referred to as 'Joe Gwinn's Museum.'

HEDGING HIS BETS as usual, Reub Fleet had not neglected the possibility of adapting his experience with military trainers to private and commercial flying.

"We had worked hard to reduce the cost of our military trainer," he related, "so that we could sell it commercially as a product built to Army-Navy standards, but I despaired of ever getting it down below $6000 to where we could sell it as a commercial product.

"One weekend early in 1928 I called in four of our key people and asked them to meet me Monday with their suitcases packed for a week away from the office. 'Tell your wives,' I said, 'that you are going on a special mission with me.'

"On Monday, George Newman, factory manager; Leigh Wade, test pilot; Joe Gwinn, acting chief engineer; Ralph Oversmith, material supervisor, and I got into my car. The five of us drove down to the Buffalo Athletic Club. I said, 'Boys, we are going in here for breakfast.'

"While we were eating, I had the bellboys take our luggage upstairs to the suites we had engaged for the men. I explained to them that we had come there for the purpose of designing a training plane that we would sell commercially to private owners and operators of civilian flying schools.

"We wanted a junior version of our PT-3 'Husky' military trainer which was a big airplane with a span of 36½ feet, empty weight of 1750 pounds and was powered by a 225 h.p. Wright Whirlwind engine.

"The specifications we were shooting for in the new commercial open cockpit biplane trainer were that it weigh not over 1000 pounds and be powered by the Warner 'Scarab' 110 h.p. radial engine. Efficient simplicity and rugged construction was the goal.

"We laid out the fuselage and 28-foot-span staggered wing with chalk on the carpet of the sitting room in my suite. If we got a line we didn't like, we'd rub it out with a bath towel and replace it with a better shape. It was folklore in our business that new airplanes were first sketched on the back of an old envelope. Ours was probably the first sketched full-size on a carpet.

"The four men I'd selected were all intensely interested in the new project. Newman looked at everything from the factory standpoint. Joe Gwinn looked at it from a structural and engineering angle. Leigh Wade and I were both fliers and saw it from the pilot's viewpoint. Ralph Oversmith recorded all of our decisions. Each evening Lauretta Lederer, my secretary, would bring us pertinent information we needed from the factory. When we finished two and a half days later we had the most complete directive have ever seen for a new airplane.

"We felt the 'Husky Junior' would soon be ready to take off as a new product line."

'HUSKY JUNIOR' *scaled down version* of popular PT-3/NY-2 'Husky' military trainer won a lasting place under 'Fleet' name as popular trainer/sports plane.

General Dynamics/Convair

To run static tests on the 'Husky Junior', Consolidated attempted to hire the temporary services of a specialist employed by the Army at Wright Field but ran afoul of the strong objections of General Gillmore who wrote that "a man cannot work for the government and also work for contractors who are dealing with the government." Of course, in this instance, the 'Husky Junior' was a commercial project, not a government contract.

"When we got back to our normal work schedule," the Major explained, "I placed an order for 100 Warner engines. I told the Warner engine people I expected them to sell me stock at market price in their company in proportion to the value of the engine orders we contemplated giving them. If Warner was going to make a profit on our business I wanted to be a stockholder in their company and get some of our money back that way. They thought they had us by the tail and wouldn't do it.

"W. B. (Bert) Kinner of Kinner Motors out on the West Coast heard about our new plane and went after our engine business. He offered to sell us both engines and whatever stock we wanted. I bought 1000 engines from them, and at the same time purchased 240,000 shares of Kinner stock."

Perhaps because he had a hand in its design and development, Leigh Wade was particularly enthusiastic about the new plane's flying characteristics. "Up to then," he said, "all trainers had too much inherent stability built in, so that the student was not really getting the feel of the airplane.

"I insisted that the 'Husky Junior' have neutral stability; and we got it. Others thought we couldn't get such a design past the Department of Commerce inspectors of the Aeronautical Branch unless the plane had 'hands off' stability. I knew it would hold its position in smooth air once we had it flying straight and level.

"In the first day of acceptance tests the air was bumpy and the inspector was not satisfied with the plane's stability. I told him if he would fly early the next morning in calm air he'd find that it met the criteria. He did; and I won my point.

"To me it was the finest training airplane that's ever been built."

General Dynamics/Convair

STATIC TEST of 'Husky Junior' *brought out top company officials. Fleet and Laddon, third and fourth from right, and Joe Gwinn, far right.*

133

"FINEST TRAINING AIRPLANE ever built," was Leigh Wade's evaluation of 'Fleet' biplane, shown here in seaplane version.

Consolidated management soon found, as have all companies, that developing new planes does not come cheaply. Fleet recalls that "By the time we rolled the first Model 14 'Husky Junior' out of the factory and obtained its Approved Type Certificate in November 1928 we had $173,000 tied up in development costs.

"We flew the first three planes over to Chicago where they were having an important show of new aircraft models. Leigh Wade and I were flying together, but he'd dozed off and was sound asleep in the front cockpit. I checked my map and found we were just passing over Cassopolis, Michigan. I knew it was Leigh's home town. I banked the plane and started to spiral down. Throttling the engine back, I hollered, 'Cassopolis.' As Leigh woke up he was startled to see his home town staring him right in the face. He almost broke up laughing.

"As we were flying back from Chicago the adjustable setting for the horizontal stabilizer on my ship came loose and it flopped back and forth all the way to Buffalo. It was a terrible feeling. You see, Gwinn didn't have a positive lock on the stabilizer adjustment. He always and forever overlooked something that would trip us up unless I could catch him. Of course that was the first thing we fixed on all the planes when we got back to the factory.

"Leigh Wade and I shared test flying the 'Husky Junior.' Flying was my business and I always managed to keep my hand in even though some people thought that as the 41-year-old chief executive I should give it up. But how else could I evaluate our new designs?

"We had sold the three planes at the Chicago Air Show and booked orders for a whole lot more for future delivery. The new project was off to a good start but the other directors, especially Newman, were less enthusiastic because they doubted whether a factory that was accustomed to building for the government could ever produce a commercial airplane which could be sold profitably.

"At this time our investment bankers were getting ready to offer Consolidated stock to the public and list our shares on the New York Curb Exchange. They didn't want to include what they considered to be a 'loser' in our product line. So I said, "All right, I'll take the 'Husky Junior' out, buy it for myself and pick up the $173,000 tab. Which I did.

"The military knew the name 'Husky,' which is what we called the Army PT-3 and Navy NY-2 trainers, but 'Husky Junior' didn't mean anything to the public. I'd bought the commercial trainer business for myself and as I was fairly well known— and because the dictionary word 'fleet' was appropriate—I changed the plane's name to 'Fleet.' In February I organized Fleet Aircraft, Inc. which purchased the design and manufacturing rights to the 'Husky Junior.'

"Temporarily the new plane was to be manufactured for me by Consolidated. Fleet Aircraft gave them a cost-plus contract to build 110 planes.

"For sales manager we had Lawrence D. Bell whom I'd selected because of his experience. He'd been general manager for Glenn L. Martin, first in Los Angeles and later in Cleveland, but when I hired him in July 1928 Larry was back on the West Coast selling second hand goods in a store in Los Angeles.

"Although planned for the commercial market, the 'Fleet' had been built to government standards. Soon the Army took a shine to it. They became very interested and insisted on my selling it to them. I told them, 'I haven't got all the bugs out of it yet and, therefore, I don't like to sell it to you. I doubt that it will ever make a hit with you fellows. It's only a hundred horsepower and you are accustomed to twice that horsepower.'

"Clint Howard, then chief engineer for the Air Corps, said they would never buy another ship from us unless I sold it to them. That didn't leave us much choice but I still hesitated because I knew they would condemn the 'Fleet' if we hadn't eradicated all the bugs that always appear to be part of the aeronautical engineering profession. They bought 16 'Fleets' a bit later on and called them PT-6s. Equipped with a

MILITARY VERSION of popular 'Fleet' biplane was the U. S. Army Air Corps' PT-6, though quantity purchased was small.

U. S. Air Force

135

NAVY N2Y-1 was equipped with 'skyhook' to catch trapeze for mid-air retrieval by dirigible 'Akron' in these 1931 tests.

skyhook arrangement, the 'Fleet' N2Y-1 was also purchased by the Navy and operated from aircraft carriers in mid-air trapeze retrieval and launch trials by the dirigibles 'Akron' and 'Los Angeles.'

"Fleet Aircraft and Consolidated did business under the same factory roof in Buffalo. Because I owned 100% of Fleet and a lesser percentage of Consolidated, I had to lean over backwards favoring Consolidated on everything. I found that having two companies under one roof with different ownership was no good. When the 'Fleet' Model 14 bid fair to take away the training business of Consolidated Aircraft and replace the $6000 military model with the less expensive 'Fleet,' I

had to correct that.

"The other directors of the company also saw that the 'Fleet' was likely to be adopted by the Army, and perhaps by the Navy, and they naturally wanted to get it back. I said, 'All right, boys, we'll hold a directors meeting and you can have it back for whatever the books show I've got in the 'Fleet.' I don't want to make any profit out of it.'

"So, just six months after I personally took the new plane over, the company issued me 19,000 shares of Consolidated stock to purchase all my shares in Fleet Aircraft, Inc., as well as 5000 shares of Kinner Airplane and Motor Co., plus my stock in National Flying Schools, which I had organized to promote pilot training and 'Fleet' trainer plane sales, and 100 acres of land in Canada I had purchased.

"With our large purchase of Kinner engines, their shares went up and up on the stock market. I began to sell, not all in one gob but let it out gradually so it didn't depress the stock. When we'd sold all the Kinner stock we had a handsome profit. It was enough to pay for the engines. In effect we got them for free! Of course we'd taken a risk in placing that 1000 engine order, but we had confidence in our product and history proved it was a smart business move.

"The 'Fleet' was a go from the start. Its rugged construction, sturdy wings and good flying characteristics attracted an enthusiastic following, especially among flying school operators. In aerobatic maneuvers it was unsurpassed. We sold it for $4985.00, including engines and propeller. We paid 25% commission to our dealer/distributor organization so we got $3738.75 net for it—and made money. With the coming of the Depression, business slacked off and we reduced the price a thousand dollars. We had engines coming out of our ears. But no problem. We'd made enough money on Kinner stock to pay for the Kinner engines."

Air shows at the expanding number of new airports around the country became a great spectator sport in the early thirties. The nimble 'Fleet' biplanes could always be counted on to put in an appearance and make a great showing.

Performing outside loops was a particularly demanding maneuver for both airplanes and pilot, and demonstration of this capability was often used to prove the excellent design and rugged construction of new planes. The writer's first exposure to the 'Fleet' was in 1930 when handling publicity for the opening of the new Curtiss-Wright airport at San Mateo on the San Francisco Peninsula. As a sure-fire attraction we had hired Paul Mantz, famed movie stunt pilot. Flying his Kinner-powered 'Fleet' Model 14-2, Paul established a new world record of 46 consecutive outside loops. It was typical of the demonstrations of precision aerobatics which helped make the 'Fleet' so popular with pilots of that era.

REUBEN FLEET'S ENTHUSIASM was always infectious and especially susceptible to his dynamic vision was his capable and devoted secretary who had worked for him since his first days in Buffalo. The invitation to accompany the dashing Major Fleet on a 15,000 mile, month-long sales trip in the sporty new 'Fleet' trainer could not easily be turned aside.

There also must have been some raised eyebrows when the Major first let it be known that his secretary was going to accompany him on the long, cross-country trip to visit aircraft dealers and manufacturing plants. One associate, unnamed, understood that Reuben, a grass widower, was taking Lauretta along to meet his parents in Montesano, Washington. But strong-minded Reuben Fleet neither sought the approval of others in this or other matters, nor was he swayed by their disapproval—if indeed there was—once he had made up his mind.

In preparation for the trip, planned for August, Lauretta Lederer Golem began taking flying lessons at the company's airport at Tonawanda. While the flight training was going on, the Golems had a guest arrive at their North Tonawanda home. Dorothy Mitchell had come up from Yonkers, New York, for an early summer visit with her mother's brother, Henry, and his wife, Lauretta.

Dorothy had met Reuben Fleet by chance some months before in Manhattan when Lauretta, his secretary, had accompanied him on a business trip. Dorothy and a date were dancing to Fred Waring's music at the Pennsylvania Hotel when they literally bumped into the Major and his secretary. Now, as a courtesy to their out-of-town guest, the Major hosted the Golems and their niece Dorothy Mitchell at the Buffalo Trap and Field Club.

"During the evening," Dorothy recalls, "the conversation often turned to the cross-country trip Reuben and Aunt Lauretta were planning. They were understandably excited. Perhaps my uncle was apprehensive, and so far as I was concerned I couldn't help but feel a touch of envy for Lauretta, but the two of us were only spectators. Reuben and Lauretta were the stars of the show.

"I think there was some general understanding among Reuben Fleet's associates that he expected to marry Lauretta—that the relationship was a personal as well as business one. You see, Uncle Henry was a sportsman, perhaps more interested in trap shooting, hunting and fishing than in his marriage. So Lauretta decided to take a job as a secretary. He was aware of the feeling between his wife and Reuben. He understood it and there was no great conflict. He was willing to give her up.

"Reuben always laid the cards out on the table. When he asked Lauretta if she would marry him, he told Henry, 'I intend to marry your wife, so you had better be good to her or I'll take her away from you.' He told him right out. It worked out with no problems. Of course, while Reuben was going with Lauretta, Henry was going with Lorraine, whom he later married."

All went well on the westbound trip. Everywhere the new 'Fleet' was received with real enthusiasm, especially after knowledgable pilots had an opportunity to fly the new sport trainer themselves.

There was an occasional jarring experience such as at Kansas City. "We had flown into Fairfax Airport," Reuben told us, "and took a taxi to the American Eagle aircraft factory. There we discovered Victor Roos, one of their engineers, working with a complete set of engineering blueprints for the 'Fleet' trainer.

"I asked him where he got them; he said he wouldn't tell me. 'What do you think,' I inquired somewhat heatedly, 'of copying another company's design?'

" 'Well,' he replied, 'if you are going to copy, you might as well copy the best.'

"I said, 'Let's see how you are doing with your airplane. Is that it?'

" 'Yes.'

"So I looked it over quite carefully. Driving back to the airport I said to my secretary, 'He has made a mistake in that design. It will probably trip him up.'

"We were all preparing for the St. Louis Aircraft Show some months later. I couldn't find Victor there, but I danced with his wife and asked her where he was.

" 'Victor and I weren't able to make this show,' she said. 'My husband felt pretty bad when you found him copying your design. The taxi cab driver came back and told him he had overheard you tell your secretary that he'd made a design mistake which would trip him up. And it surely did.'

"What was the matter?" I asked.

" 'Well, he didn't like to copy your aileron design so he deviated from it and made his own. That's the reason we couldn't make this show.'

"Actually that was not the mistake which I had spotted, but of course I said nothing to Mrs. Roos.

"Later came the Chicago Show and Victor Roos did

not appear at it either. I know that the American Eagle was a fair commercial airplane, although in my opinion, not in a class with the 'Fleet.' "

Flying into San Diego from Phoenix, Major Fleet could not but reflect on his days as a student aviator at North Island twelve years earlier. Nor, in a prophetic way, was he unaware that San Diego's year-round good climate was in bold contrast to the severe winters which hampered flying boat operation at Buffalo.

After Lindbergh's transatlantic flight, the City of San Diego passed a $650,000 bond in November 1927 to develop a new land and sea airport on tidelands near the heart of the city. In August 1928 Lindbergh Field was dedicated.

The next month found Major Fleet in Los Angeles attending the National Air Races. A fellow Washingtonian, Edgar N. Gott, president of Keystone Aircraft Corp., and before that with Boeing and Fokker, took Reuben around to the San Diego booth and introduced him to Thomas F. Bomar, head of that city's Chamber of Commerce aviation department. Fleet somewhat abruptly reminded Bomar that he didn't need any sales pitch on San Diego—he was already familiar with the city and its advantages as a possible factory site—but agreed he would talk the idea up with his directors.

It was the first contact by San Diego civic leaders in their years long effort to get Consolidated to move from Buffalo to their more equable climate.

Now, a year later, Major Fleet had flown into town on his nation-wide tour in the new 'Fleet' trainer. "If the municipality will sell Lindbergh Field," he told a Chamber of Commerce meeting, "I'll purchase it at any time for $1,000,000 cash." Six years later he would be relocating Consolidated Aircraft cross-country to that same airport.

LINDBERGH FIELD, San Diego, looked like this in 1929 when Reuben Fleet offered a million dollars. In foreground, buildings where 'Spirit of St. Louis' was built.

Moving on to another field of interest, Fleet told his San Diego audience about his thoughts on transoceanic air travel.

"There is no profit in carrying gas," he said in reference to the success of recent refueling flights, "and I believe that in the very near future floating airports will be established in both the Atlantic and Pacific oceans where aircraft winging their way to Europe and Asia will refuel from floating bases."

Making demonstration flights and lining up dealers along the way, the 'Fleet' sales tour flew into Portland, Oregon. There Reuben met and made arrangements with a pilot flying from Vancouver Airport, across the Columbia River from Portland, to become a demonstration pilot and Pacific Coast representative for 'Fleet' sales. He was Gordon E. Mounce, an Air Corps pilot and flying service operator, who later became Consolidated's European representative.

THE LAST LEG of the long but successful sales trip was to be from Detroit to Buffalo. Just after lunch the sturdy Whirlwind-powered 'Fleet' took off for home. To avoid the longer flight around the southern shore of Lake Erie or the more hazardous overwater trip across the Lake, Reuben and his secretary headed east on a land route over Ontario, Canada.

Keeping the shoreline in sight five miles off the right wingtip, Lauretta Lederer was at the controls in the rear cockpit. Reuben always chose the front cockpit, considered more dangerous in case of a bad forced landing as the engine might be pushed back into the forward cockpit. With 80 miles already clocked, the 'Fleet' was flying over West Lorne when the engine sputtered. One cylinder had failed. Reuben immediately took over the controls. To this day, 45 years later, the Major is reluctant to discuss what happened next beyond, "I was over trees and hobbled over an opening, then banked up to slip the plane in for a landing. If I had twenty feet more, I would have had the ship out." Instead the plane crashed.

It was the Major's first serious accident in 13 years of flying. The date was September 13, a Friday.

The accident occurred on the farm of Russell Reid who saw the 'Fleet' plunge to the ground.

"We were both conscious," Reuben recalls, "after we cracked up and were lying on the ground. I asked Lauretta how she was and she said, 'I'm okey.' I told her there would be someone through there pretty soon to pick us up and that she should go in the ambulance and I would follow in a truck if they had one. Two doctors had been called to the scene and they sent her in the ambulance. I followed by truck, but the jolting

caused me to pass out and I was unconscious for days."

Both Major Fleet and his secretary were taken to Victoria Hospital in London. David Fleet, then 19 and just out of Culver Military Academy, rushed to his father's bedside in London. "Dad looked like a rotten banana," Dave said, "he was so bruised and broken. Over and over he kept asking for Lauretta."

Next day Mrs. Lauretta Lederer Golem, 31, died of a broken neck and injury to her spinal cord. It was Tuesday before Reuben was informed of his secretary's death.

Lauretta's valise in the baggage compartment had been thrown forward in the crash. It slammed into her head, breaking her neck. Fortunately, Reuben was less critically injured. Obviously moved by the recollection, Reuben continued, "When I recovered consciousness the doctors said there wasn't a bone in my body in the right place. I asked for a telephone and phoned the osteopath I had in Dayton when I was an Air Service Officer and asked him to come up to London. I figured because he had given me many treatments in the past he would be able to adjust my bones correctly so they would heal, but the hospital wouldn't let him touch me. All we could do was visit together."

Two weeks after the accident a coroner's inquest was convened. The principal witness was Major Fleet. His leg in a cast, he was on crutches and had to be assisted into the witness box by William B. Wheatley, Consolidated test pilot.

The distraught Major explained that when the engine began to miss at 750 feet altitude he had taken the controls.

"I first flew straight ahead, edged to the south in order to find a suitable landing place. As the motor continued to miss I lost altitude and at a height of 475 feet I ascertained for sure that a forced landing must be made. I realized I must do one of two things. I could either fly straight ahead and land with the wind, or turn and land into the wind. At this time I had sufficient power to inveigle me into making the turn. I banked around on a turn of about 180 degrees, so that I was flying due west. There were two trees directly in the path of my flight.

"I tried to get the motor to carry me over the top of these, but in so doing lost flying speed, so that there was nothing to keep the plane in the air, and veering to the left, it dived almost straight downwards."

The motor had stalled after making the turn, said the witness.

Major Fleet, according to newspaper accounts, burst into tears when asked if he remembered seeing Mrs. Golem immediately after the accident.

"When I regained consciousness I asked where she was. They told me she was beside me. I tried to crawl over to where she was lying. I . . .''

At this juncture, the news report continued, the witness was unable to suppress his emotions, and tears streamed down his cheeks. It was several minutes before he was able to reply by stating it was the next day before he knew that his secretary had been seriously injured.

At the inquest Wheatley testified that he had personally tested the plane before Reuben and Lauretta had left on the sales demonstration trip. An examination of the engine after the accident, he reported, showed that a rocker valve had failed in one of the cylinders.

REUBEN FLEET'S ACCIDENT and seven weeks hospitalization in London could hardly have happened at a more critical time. Before he and Lauretta left Buffalo a series of complex corporate moves had been set in motion. The company's stock was now being publicly traded, creating new considerations in relations with the investment community.

A commercial version of the Navy flying boat, the 'Commodore' was being manufactured for an airline to South America in which Fleet had a financial interest. Work was well along on the swift new 'Fleetster' passenger/mail plane. Negotiations had almost been concluded to acquire the ailing Thomas-Morse Company.

Consolidated executives flew back and forth between Buffalo and Victoria Hospital in London for key conferences with their stricken leader whose emotional strain was at least as difficult to cope with as were his physical injuries.

Larry Bell, the experienced Glenn L. Martin aircraft manufacturing executive, though with Consolidated for only a little over a year, was placed in overall charge as General Manager of the whole company. Ray Whitman was named Assistant General Manager.

"Larry took over," the Major said, "and was running the factory while I was gone. Normally I put Newman in charge when I was away but he always came up with a thousand different questions at the last minute and could never decide anything. Like a cow's tail, you know, which switched all over.

"Newman never could get going. You see he needed someone to direct him all the time. He couldn't make that final decision himself because he always had so many unresolved questions to consider."

Soon after the accident the company announced that "Fleet and Newman are retiring to policy and planning posts. They will retain their titles but will not participate actively in management of the company."

Understandably, the Major tended to downgrade the whole incident and in business letters said he had just gotten out of the hospital as the result of a minor airplane accident. However, once on the road to recovery, Fleet decided to take his parents on an extended cruise aboard a Panama-Pacific liner from New York through the Panama Canal.

"The death of Lauretta," Dorothy Mitchell wrote of her aunt, "haunted him with a sense of guilt and bereavement for many years to come. When he reached New York with his parents he telephoned me. He was on crutches, still desolate. He wanted to talk about Lauretta, and because I had loved her dearly, Reuben obtained some measure of comfort by sharing his grief with me.

"Then, before their departure, I was introduced to Mr. and Mrs. David W. Fleet, Reuben's father and mother, for the first time. I found them completely charming."

The long ocean cruise with his parents through the Caribbean and up the west coast of Central America and Mexico helped Reuben regain some semblance of direction in his life.

Before continuing the cruise north to the familiar Seattle area, the Panama Pacific liner 'Virginia' was scheduled to put into San Diego. Reuben got off a wire to Tom Bomar of the Chamber of Commerce. Would he meet the ship and have a seven-passenger car and driver available for a day's sightseeing?

"Our party," Bomar reminisced, "included Reuben, his parents and a young Army officer and his bride whom the Fleets had met on the cruise ship. We decided to go across the border to Agua Caliente for lunch in Mexico. It was mid-December and I purposely drove them along Harbor Drive where the Major could see men in shirtsleeves working in the shipbuilding yards. He had just come from the snows of New York and I impressed on him that you didn't need a building out here; he could assemble his airplanes out in the open.

"Reuben and his parents enjoyed the brief San Diego visit and I know we had him seriously thinking about the desirability of moving the company out of Buffalo."

Distraught after the tragic loss of Lauretta, his devoted secretary; divorced from his wife and 'married' only to his business these many years, Reuben Fleet found himself a lonely man in his few contemplative moments. The void had to be filled.

BACK IN BUFFALO, Reuben Fleet began to pick up the remnants of his business career and, to the limited extent he had a personal life, what remained of that.

So the children might be near their father and have some meaningful relationship with him, Mrs. Fleet, though divorced from Reuben, had moved to Buffalo in 1926 with Phyllis and David. However, she and Reuben did not see each other; in fact Elizabeth Fleet made it a point to absent herself from any affair he might attend.

After two years of high school in Redondo Beach, David was ready for Culver Military Academy and that was an added reason for leaving California. Summers Dave worked at the Consolidated plant. Then, because his father wanted a graduate engineer in the family, Dave enrolled at Cornell University at Ithaca, New York after graduating from Culver in 1929, but soon proved that engineering was not really his field. His sister Phyllis (somewhat against her own wishes) was also studying engineering at Cornell—the only woman in her class.

Dorothy Mitchell continued her recollection that it was "in December Reuben called me from Buffalo to invite me to a New Year's Eve party, because, as he put it, 'You might like to spend the holiday season with your Uncle Henry.' Henry still grieved over Lauretta, and I felt that perhaps Reuben's suggestion was a good one. I accepted the invitation, recalling how we had taken a fancy to each other in our meeting a year earlier and again the past summer.

"It was during the holidays that he persuaded me to move to Buffalo and take over Lauretta's job as his secretary. 'You have no idea how many things I have to do,' he told me. 'Now that Lauretta is gone I don't know how I'm going to manage.'

"At first I was appalled at the thought of working for him. I didn't know anything about the business, to begin with, and to make matters worse I had no love for secretarial work. There was one argument which I was sure was unassailable— I didn't know shorthand. I felt that a secretary who couldn't make 'pot hooks' surely wouldn't be of much use to the head of Consolidated Aircraft; but Reuben was unconcerned.

" 'Who cares? Shorthand or no shorthand, you can help me. Anyway, I need you more as a social secretary.'

"My job teaching a dancing class at the Women's Institute in Yonkers, a sort of day school for the children of working mothers, had seemed like an ideal arrangement. Nothing, or no one less than Reuben Fleet, could have made me change my mind. I hadn't realized yet how persuasive Reuben could be, but before he had finished talking I found myself on his side. To work as his secretary suddenly seemed both logical and desirable. Who wanted to teach a bunch of little kids how to dance? Not I.

"I turned in my resignation to the Women's Institute and was soon on my way to Buffalo, a desk at Consolidated Aircraft . . . and Reuben Fleet.

"I had expected a great deal of dull paper work in connection with my new job, but I was to discover that monotony was never a part of the routine. My first assignment as Reuben's secretary was to brave a blinding snowstorm, fight my way down to the train station and leave for Ithaca, New York, where Reuben had left his new Stutz Benz stranded.

"His daughter Phyllis, a student at Cornell University, had just had an emergency appendectomy. He drove to the University; but after assuring himself that Phyllis was in no danger, he had taken a plane back to Buffalo. Now it was up to me, and my six-months-old driver's license, to get the Stutz Benz safely back to Reuben's garage.

"When he mentioned it to me I assured him that I couldn't do it. 'It's not possible,' I explained. 'You must make some other arrangement.'

" 'You'll get along fine,' he told me. 'Your train leaves in an hour.'

"The drive back from Ithaca was a horror. The Stutz Benz and I, disliking each other, crept through a blinding snowstorm that never subsided by a single flake until I reached Buffalo.

" 'I knew you could do it all the time.' Reuben told me the next day.

"I was beginning to learn for myself what my Aunt Lauretta had told me about the Major: to him all things were possible because he doubted nothing. The most beautiful part about his philosophy was that it worked!

"The next assignment Reuben had for me, and I was beginning to feel as if he were manufacturing jobs to keep me busy, was compiling a list of names for Christmas cards. He wanted to know what cards he had sent and what he had received. It seemed like a strange employment, and before I was finished my woman's intuition told me that Reuben didn't really want a secretary—he wanted company. My intuition was right.

"When summer came, we were engaged to be married. By then I was learning that anything connected with Consolidated came first with Reuben. Although his courtship was ardent as demonstrated by a steady stream of flowers and candy, he was unpredictable as to the priorities on his time and I spent many a solitary evening glaring at the clock.

"But Reuben was completely honest and forthright. Before we were married he told me that his business came first in his life.

"Later I was to learn that unless a wife was deeply involved in Reuben's business affairs there was a tendency for her eventually to get pushed into the background."

Reuben had an affinity for secretaries as we shall see. First there was Lauretta; then her niece Dorothy. Finally there was Eva, his wife now for some 28 years.

THOMAS-MORSE AIRCRAFT CORPORATION

CABLE ADDRESS
"TOMASAERO"

Thomas

MANUFACTURERS OF
AIRPLANES AND ENGINES

ITHACA, N.Y.

General Dynamics/Convair

F. TRUBEE DAVISON, the Assistant Secretary of War for Air, was troubled. The Thomas-Morse Aircraft Company of Ithaca, New York, had done a good job in building six metal versions of the Douglas O-2 observation biplane under contract to the Army. Now the Army was ready to place an order for a production quantity.

What troubled Secretary Davison was that Thomas-Morse had been relatively inactive for several years except for experimental designs of metal aircraft. Their production capability had been highly questionable since their wartime success with the 'Tommy' Scout and the immediate post-war MB-3 pursuit.

Trubee Davison thought he might have a solution for his problem.

"They called me down to Washington," Reuben Fleet began after a brief chuckle, "because they didn't have any confidence in Thomas-Morse. The War Department didn't think they were equipped to produce this aircraft in quantity and in that respect they were correct, of course. Would we see if we could buy Thomas-Morse out? If we could, there was a 70-plane order awaiting Consolidated.

"So I went up to Ithaca to see Frank L. Morse of the Morse Chain Company which owned Thomas-Morse. He had just sold the parent company to Borg-Warner for about $18 million. He had several small activities operating under the same roof as the chain company, including the Barr Morris Typewriter Company and other firms of various nature, including the aircraft company. Obviously he had to make some kind of disposition of these odd companies and that's what bothered the War Department.

"To get away from others, Morse and I drove up to an overlook point above the football field at Cornell University. While we were talking another car drove up next to us and a fine looking woman stepped out to walk her two beautiful dogs. It was the famous dancer, Irene Castle, whom I hadn't seen since we danced together at the Armistice Ball at Royal Albert Hall in London eleven years earlier. I don't remember why she happened to be there at Cornell.

"After a brief visit with Irene and her third husband, Morse and I got back to business. Yes, he would sell the company. We wanted only its designs, not its physical plant. So we made the deal and it was closed in August 1929.

"We paid 6000 shares of Consolidated stock for their designs and another 4000 shares to B. Douglas Thomas, their fine design engineer, who would not otherwise have joined Consolidated. We made him

B. DOUGLAS THOMAS, brilliant chief engineer of Thomas-Morse, in front of famed S-4 'Tommy Scout.'

General Dynamics/Convair

president of our Thomas-Morse subsidiary after we moved their work to Buffalo from Ithaca since they had neither adequate facilities or a suitable airport there.

"When B. Douglas Thomas joined Consolidated it served to highlight a basic philosophy of mine about organization. You'll recall that Ginny Clark left the company in 1927 and that Major Leslie MacDill of the Engineering Division at Dayton was after me to appoint a new chief engineer.

"Well, I am a strong believer in competition, not only between companies but also within my own organization. I appointed Thomas the project engineer of Unit No. 4, the Thomas-Morse group. Unit No. 2, multi-engine heavy aircraft, was headed by Mac Laddon. Joe Gwinn was in charge of Unit No. 1, trainers; also Unit No. 3, the development of aircraft for the private owner market. All reported directly to me.

"Our military customers were critical but I had proven that my system induces each project engineer to make his best showing for the boss, not for just another engineer. I told Wright Field, 'If you've got any complaints, come to me.'

"It was the mid-thirties before we appointed a chief engineer."

THE NAME THOMAS-MORSE conjures up so much nostalgia with old-time pilots that some review of its contributions to aviation is justified in a definitive history of Consolidated Aircraft. Unlike Reuben Fleet's early dealings with the ailing Gallaudet and Dayton-Wright companies which involved only the use of facilities or design rights, Thomas-Morse was acquired as a subsidiary and its name perpetuated for several years.

The company had its origin with two English

H. M. Benner

CURTISS 'AMERICA' flying boat, large for its day - 1914 - had 67-foot span and two 100 h.p. engines.

brothers, William T. and Oliver W. Thomas. W. T. Thomas had come from London in 1909 to work for Glenn H. Curtiss at Hammondsport, New York. Three years later he and his brother Oliver formed the Thomas Brothers Aeroplane Co. at Bath, New York.

By coincidence a third Thomas from England, no relation to the brothers, joined the company in 1914 as chief engineer. It became virtually a British invasion of the then struggling American aircraft industry. B. Douglas Thomas had worked in England with Vickers and Sopwith. He had met Glenn Curtiss in London and Paris and accepted his invitation while still in England to work with Curtiss in designing the Model J training plane and later in the United States on the 'America' flying boat. The latter, financed by Rodman Wanamaker, would be seeking the prize money offered by the London Daily Mail for a transatlantic crossing. Curtiss was also developing the N biplane and Thomas helped marry the J and N designs into the JN—the famed Jenny of World War I.

MODEL J training plane which, blended with Model N, became Curtiss JN 'Jenny' of World War I.

General Dynamics/Convair

AMERICAN-BUILT T-2 tractor biplane, 24 of which were sold by Thomas Brothers to British Admiralty.

After B. D. Thomas joined Thomas Brothers he designed the T-2 tractor biplane which was so successful the British Admiralty ordered 24 of the American-built planes. In 1914 the company moved to Ithaca, New York, on the shores of Lake Cayuga. New designs were developed, including the SH-4 hydroplane for the U.S. Navy, but production seldom followed design and by 1916 the underfinanced company was in trouble. Local business interests, headed by Frank L. Morse of the Morse Chain Company and

Herman H. Westinghouse of the airbrake company, came to the rescue.

The Thomas-Morse Aircraft Company was formed in January 1917, with Morse as president, W. T. Thomas as vice president and the talented designer, B. D. Thomas, as chief engineer. At the time. B. D. Thomas was already at work on the S-4, the original Tommy Scout biplane, an advanced trainer designed to prepare American pilots for combat abroad. It won immediate Army approval.

LIKE OTHER MANUFACTURERS of that period, Thomas Brothers operated their own training school with planes such as their D-5, shown here, two of which were purchased by the Army Signal Corps in 1917 as 'corps observation' planes.

Air Force Museum

Despite the gyroscopic effect of its French rotary engine, which made looping and left turns difficult, the Scout was well suited for acrobatic training. A total of 100 S-4Bs and 497 of the highly regarded S-4C pursuit trainers were delivered by Thomas-Morse, making it the fourth largest wartime producer of aircraft. At war's end orders for 533 more Tommy Scouts were cancelled.

FOURTH LARGEST wartime producer of military aircraft was Thomas-Morse whose specialty was S-4 'Scout.'

'TOMMY' SCOUT pursuit trainer widely used to prepare American pilots for combat flying with A.E.F. in Europe.

General Dynamics/Convair

MB-1 (above); MB-2 (below)

MB-7 monoplane

MB-3 prototype (below)

MB-9, with corrugated fuselage

MB-6 clipped-wing racer (below)

MB-10 (above); TM-22 (below)

A.S.68537

TM-23 (above); TM-24 (below)

THOMAS-MORSE MB-3 biplane pursuit carries the single star of air power advocate General Billy Mitchell, in cockpit.

The Thomas-Morse MB-1 was an experimental strut-braced pursuit monoplane; the MB-2 an experimental pursuit biplane. Then came the MB-3 biplane, first flown in February 1919. It was to be the first post-war fighter ordered in quantity by the Army and the nation's standard pursuit during the twenties. The four experimental MB-3s so outclassed their competitors that when the Air Service ordered 50 planes in 1919 they did so with assurance to Thomas-Morse that an order for 200 more would probably follow. The company's response was to make a major expenditure for jigs, dies and other production equipment.

Unfortunately for Thomas-Morse the purchasing policy at McCook Field was to encourage open bidding on contracts for quantity production of existing designs. When contract award time came, Major Fleet, as Contracting Officer for the Engineering Division, placed the production order for 200 of the MB-3A version with Boeing Airplane Company, the low bidder. It gave the Seattle company a shot in the arm and the Ithaca company a jolt in the pocketbook.

Work continued on a series of advanced designs including the MB-6 biplane, a clipped wing racer modification of the MB-3 pursuit, and the MB-7 high-wing monoplane. Both were designed to participate in the 1921 and 1922 air races. These were followed by the all-metal MB-9 and MB-10 gull-wing monoplanes which gave the company invaluable experience in metal construction.

Another parasol monoplane design was the TM-22 which, like the MB-10, had a fuselage of corrugated dural. It was followed by the TM-23 and -24 biplanes. Both were small, all-metal planes with unusually large engines for their size and were planned to fill the need for military alert pursuit or observation planes. None went into production.

General Dynamics/Convair

General Dynamics/Convair

*LIBERTY-POWERED X0-6 was Thomas-Morse
metal version of Douglas 0-2 corps observation
plane.*

Finally the sought-for opportunity in metal aircraft came in the XO-6, a 1926 adaptation of the Douglas O-2 observation plane. In addition to the corrugated dural fuselage, one of the 'X' planes had wings of metal structure covered with duralumin on top and fabric on the bottom. The new observation type was the first Thomas-Morse plane to be received with real enthusiasm by the military since the MB-3. Two of the XO-6 and four of the O-6 Liberty-powered type were bought by the Army for evaluation; then the prospect of a production contract brought Major Fleet and Consolidated into the picture. But, in the process, Thomas-Morse had lost $60,000 just on the two experimental planes.

Under Consolidated ownership, but still carrying the Thomas-Morse name, three production contracts were obtained; the first being for 70 of the O-19B model powered with the 450 h.p. Pratt and Whitney Wasp radial engine. The next production order was for 71 aircraft of the O-19C type with minor modifications and a Townend anti-drag ring around the Wasp engine.

The final order for 30 of the O-19E version with the more powerful 575 h.p. Wasp engine was delivered in 1932. All models featured the same wrap-around corrugated sheet metal fuselage construction that was a Thomas-Morse hallmark. The moveable control surfaces were also of corrugated aluminum sheet.

Air Force Museum

*CONSOLIDATED 0-19 featured corrugated metal
fuselage. Prototype model below. Model above had
Townend anti-drag engine cowling.*

Thomas-Morse Aircraft Corp.

A FREQUENT VISITOR to Major Fleet's hospital room while he was recovering in London, Ontario, from his air crash was W. J. (Jack) Sanderson, formerly a Captain in the Royal Canadian Air Force, well known throughout the Dominion as an outstanding pilot. He was so warm and thoughtful in his consideration for the American pilot, who had suffered personal tragedy as well as physical pain, that Reuben decided in December 1929 to build a factory on the Canadian property he had purchased in Fort Erie, across the Niagara River from Buffalo. There Consolidated would build the 'Fleet' trainer.

There was a great deal of logic and business advantage in such an arrangement, as Reuben explained:

"When we began to get orders from foreign countries we ran into a real problem with our State Department. The government wouldn't give us a permit for longer than three months to build any plane—even the simple 'Fleet' commercial trainer—for export to any foreign government.

"You can see what a fierce enemy of mankind the 'Fleet' trainer was. It might possibly be used in the air! Our State Department was so narrow-minded that it didn't give a damn if they drove business out of the United States.

"They would give us a permit good for only ninety days. If at the end of that time conditions in the world were still stable, we'd get a new permit, then another permit good for three months, and another, and so on. But there was never any certainty in that. It took us 18 months from purchase of alloy steel and some other raw materials to delivery of the finished plane. 'Well,' I said, 'we can't do business this way. I can't afford to take that chance. I'll go across the river and put a factory there in Ontario under Canadian laws.' The U. S. government said, 'Go ahead.'

"So I went over to Fort Erie and early in 1930 built an airport and a factory. We had 400 men coming over the Peace Bridge from Canada every day anyway. Now many of them could work for Fleet Aircraft of Canada, Ltd., which we organized as a Canadian corporation in March 1930 to be operated as a wholly-

General Dynamics/Convair

FLEET AIRCRAFT of Canada, Ltd. was headed by RCAF Captain Jack Sanderson, above.

owned subsidiary of Consolidated. Jack Sanderson was selected as president.

"We arranged with the Canadian government to accept the validity of our invoices. Every day we flew there from Buffalo—just three miles across the river—dozens of times delivering all kinds of material from our parent plant and bringing other material back to the United States.

"Never was the trust granted us by the Canadian and United States governments broken because it was very important to us. I wouldn't have broken it for a hundred thousand dollars. Never, for instance, would we permit anyone to bring back liquor and things like that. The trust that both governments showed us was wonderful.

"In all, we manufactured 'Fleets' for 23 different customers, including eleven foreign governments—China, Argentina, Spain, Brazil, Portugal, Turkey, Mexico, Rumania, Colombia, Yugoslavia—and, of course, Canada, whose Royal Canadian Air Force had early placed an order for 20 trainers.

FORT ERIE, CANADA Fleet plant with group of Fleet trainers purchased by Royal Canadian Air Force.

David G. Fleet

FLEET F-10G production line at Buffalo, 1934, with Gypsy Major-powered biplanes being assembled for export.

"Before we got through we had delivered planes with a great variety of power plants—Kinners, Warners, Whirlwinds, Continentals, Challengers, Gypsy Majors and Axelsons, ranging from 90 h.p. to 170 h.p.

"There were more than a dozen different versions of the basic Model 14 'Fleet.' They were available as seaplanes as well as landplanes. Two versions were offered to appeal to sportsmen pilots, one of these having provision for two passengers and pilot, rather than the usual two-place arrangement.

"Another offered a coupe-top canopy particularly desirable in northern climes during winter months. Most popular and widely sold was the Model 14-2 'Fleet.' The 125 h.p. Model 14-7 served as the basis for the military PT-6 primary trainer. Another version, Model 10-G for the Rumanian and Portuguese governments, used the English Gypsy Major in-line engine, in contrast to the usual Kinner, Warner or other American radial engines.

"Provision was made in some export models for light armament. To meet the requirement of the Mexican Air Force for a trainer which could give virtually sea level performance at the 7100-foot altitude of Mexico City, Fleet provided a plane with 32-foot wing spread instead of the standard 28-foot wing.

"Our largest export business on the 'Fleet' trainer was with China for the Nationalist Government of Chiang Kai-shek who had employed Col. John H. (Jack) Jouett as advisor to the Nanking Aviation Bureau. He, of course, was succeeded by Col. Claire L. Chennault of Flying Tiger fame after the Japanese invasion of China in 1937."

For four years, starting in 1932, there were large annual shipments to China. Consolidated's representative at Shanghai, Carl A. Nahmmacher, reported that on arrival of the shipping boxes they were transferred from ocean liners to Chinese "junks" for transportation down the Whangpoo River to the docks at Shanghai.

The first shipment of 30 'Fleets' was transported by truck some eight miles to the Hungjao Airport where they were assembled and tested under the supervision of American pilots attached to the Chinese government in the capacity of instructors.

The Shanghai area had been heavily damaged during the Sino-Japanese conflict and facilities were minimal. Once the planes had been rigged and tested they were flown to Hangchow 120 miles to the southwest of Shanghai where the Central Aviation School was under construction. There they served as both primary and basic trainers for many years.

As was his habit, Reuben Fleet kept a hand in every phase of the company's operation. Even a single airplane got his personal attention as he explained:

"A 'Fleet' had been shipped over to our agent in Tetouan, Spanish Morocco. He died and his widow wrote me saying she had this airplane and asking what should she do with it since it was still in the crate.

"I wrote back and told her to leave it right there and I'd come over and get it as her husband hadn't paid for it as yet. One of the mechanics went abroad with me, and we took an extra engine just in case.

"We got the plane out of the crates, set it up and tested everything. Then I flew it across the Straits of Gibralter to Madrid. I always seemed to be away from home during the holidays. Christmas Day found us in Toledo, Spain. In an office there we huddled around the single radiator with a visiting Englishman. They may be used to little or no heat in England; nonetheless my English friend blurted out, 'Did you ever see such a cold place in all your life?'

"We were even glad to get back to Buffalo, which isn't exactly noted for its mild winters!"

ALTHOUGH HIS ACCIDENT in the 'Fleet' trainer and Lauretta's death was a traumatic experience for Reuben he was not one to let it throw him. Five months to the day after the accident, the Major was back in the air, again at the controls of the sporty open-cockpit biplane.

It was not long before his secretary and fiancee, Dorothy Mitchell, resumed her own interest in flying. The previous year, while visiting Lauretta and her uncle, Henry Golem, she had some dual flying instruction at Tonawanda airport. Now she tackled flying with new enthusiasm and had soon qualified for her private pilot's license.

Having a shared interest in trap shooting, Reuben laid out plans for a combined business and pleasure trip in the fall with his secretary. It was, in a way, a replay of a similar ill-fated trip a year earlier with Lauretta. This time the usual open cockpit 'Fleet' biplane would be fitted with a sliding canopy which would make the plane much more comfortable on long cross-country flights.

"Our flight south," Dorothy Mitchell related, "was planned so we might visit various trapshoots along the way. After a few days at Pinehurst, North Carolina, we took off for Punta Gorda, Florida. Rather than waste time with taxicabs, Reuben decided to find a landing field closer to the trapshoot.

"As we approached I glanced out the cockpit and discovered the field he had chosen was covered with hundreds of tree stumps that hadn't been visible until then. I was scared to death, but Lauretta's untimely death never entered my head. Everything happened too quickly.

"We came to a shuddering stop with two sharp explosions as both tires blew out. Reuben's famous temper also exploded. That left me speechless.

"The accident was minor. The incident just seemed like one of Reuben's idiosyncrasies. He loved things that were different—like landing among the tree stumps.

"Next day we continued on our way to Miami, where I met Reuben's parents for a second time; then we were off to St. Petersburg. As we left there the next morning, someone handed Reuben his accumulated mail and he asked me to take the controls while he read. He'd told me to fly northwest and assured me I'd have no trouble even though I protested I was no navigator.

"Finding nothing disturbing in his mail, and showing an undue amount of confidence in my navigation,

he decided to take a nap. When he finally awoke he asked where we were. I told him, quite honestly, that I had no idea.

"Exasperated, furious and worried, Reuben scanned the ground until he spotted the parallel lines of a railroad track. He turned around and bellowed to me. 'Follow the tracks while I look at the map!'

"Soon Reuben shook the stick vigorously, put aside the map, kicked the rudder pedals and nosed the plane steeply down so he could read the name the town had painted on the railroad station roof. That hardly solved our problem as Reuben had been consulting a map of Florida and we were over Georgia! Later we landed at a race track, got our bearings and took off for Tallahassee, Florida!"

Two days later Reuben and his secretary were in Los Angeles conferring with Gordon Mounce, the company's 'Fleet' aircraft sales representative on the west coast. Mounce had a new 'Fleet' which had to be delivered to Seattle. Reuben said he'd deliver the plane himself. It was a bad, uncomfortable decision, for Reuben and Dorothy gave up the comfort of their sliding coupe canopy model for the stock model open-cockpit 'Fleet.'

"The further north we went, the colder it got," Dorothy remembers. "At Redding, in northern California, we could bear the cold no longer. At the general store the proprietor was astonished at the two halffrozen fliers who appeared to demand 'the heaviest suits of long underwear in stock.' The woolen drawers he purchased looked better to me than French lingerie.

"After we delivered the plane at Seattle, I made the acquaintance of Reuben's sister, Lillian Bishop. Reuben had also flown Lauretta there to meet his parents, but I never felt I was a substitute for her though I did fill some of his vacant hours after she was gone. A few days later we flew back to Buffalo, avoiding both the hurdles of tree stumps and the pitfalls of plunging temperatures."

It was no exaggeration to say that Major Reuben Fleet was married to his work; that work then came ahead of all else. During the early months of 1931 Reuben and Dorothy talked seriously about their future together and finally firmed up long discussed plans to be married.

The vast majority of Consolidated's business was with the government and this kept the Major in Washington, D.C. a great deal of the time; consequently the burden of marriage arrangements—announcements, decorations, reception, guests, her wedding gown—fell on Dorothy.

"Finally," recalls Dorothy, "the great day arrived. The weather, the flowers, my dress—everything was ideal. There was but one flaw in an otherwise perfect day.

"The bridegroom was missing!"

Reuben could miss his own wedding; he could not miss negotiating a contract for his company in Washington.

It was several days later, July 7th, before the wedding took place. Bill Wheatley flew Reuben and Dorothy in a 'Fleetster' to Erie, Pennsylvania. There a justice of the peace read the brief ceremony. William K. Mitchell and Augusta Golem Mitchell, Dorothy's parents, were the attendants. The only other witness was Dorothy's cousin, Carol.

Even on his wedding day Fleet's conduct was cavalier. "Before we knew it," his bride related, "we were on our way back to Buffalo. Reuben was in a hurry to keep a golf date with the boys.

"My wedding dinner was attended by a cozy threesome—my mother, my father and myself. My husband was still at the golf club where he remained until I drove out to get him.

"A new bride or no, there were weeks at a time when I scarcely saw my husband. But now and then we were able to make arrangements to be together on a flying visit to one place or another.

"When you worked for him, it was a full-time job, often into the evening. He usually took his secretary on long out-of-town business trips, and I was as engrossed in the business as he was. He had little time, really, for a personal life not connected with his work. When my role changed from secretary to wife I found myself more and more removed from him, rather than closer to him. But his new secretary was in no way a threat to me.

"He was always in a hurry, always cursing the clock that never gave him enough time to do what had to be done. It never occurred to him that his utter disregard of time might be a personal peculiarity. He thought nothing of telephoning people at ungodly hours. When the urge to call someone struck him, he called."

Reuben was ever the aristocrat. Although his military rank was that of Major he always conducted himself like a four-star general. To him, everyone was a subordinate.

Not infrequently Reuben took his fabled terrible temper at the office home with him to his family at night. When he was angry he was capable of being very angry—and demonstrative—until the temper storm was spent.

"If anything didn't strike him right," Dorothy recalls, "there were fireworks. When, on one occasion, dinner was not on time, he stormed into the kitchen and smashed all the plates. When he went 'down' at

bridge because he felt I had bid incorrectly, he held his temper until our guests had gone. Then he picked up the card table, tore the legs off one by one and hurled them across the room.

"But such flare-ups were the exception. With the passing of the years he mellowed so that the kind, thoughtful, considerate side of Reuben Fleet was seen ever more frequently by his family and business associates."

That Reuben was also a charmer no one could deny. In the habit of barreling down the road in his Stutz in complete disregard of Buffalo's speed limit, Fleet was stopped so frequently that he kept a deposit posted in court to take care of speeding tickets.

On one such occasion, according to Dorothy, he dashed to the airport to see a new plane being tested, leaving his wife behind to explain to the officer as best she could her husband's unorthodox behavior.

When he returned, the Major explained he had to exceed the speed limit to get to the test on time. There was nothing else he could do, was there? Now, how about a plane ride?

"The policeman," Dorothy said, "wasn't the first nor the last, to succumb to Reuben's charm. Before the afternoon was over the two of them were the best of friends.

One day Reuben's car accidentally struck a woman. What could have been a disaster ended up in the most amiable fashion. Reuben took her to the hospital, sent her flowers and paid her bill. They, too, ended up as friends."

Reuben Fleet was at his charming best three and a half years after he and Dorothy Mitchell had been married. The occasion was the birth of their son Preston Mitchell Fleet, on February 26, 1935.

Already the father of a grown son and daughter Reuben was "an old hand at this business," thought his young wife. "I had rather imagined he would regard the birth of his third child with equanimity. couldn't have been much further off.

"The doctors permitted Reuben to witness the actual delivery. Every day he came to the hospital to visit and in fact spent most of the first day with me.

"He wrote his parents a long, detailed and very warm letter in which he said, 'Dorothy is simply beautiful and gorgeous. She is happier than a clam—but no happier than I. She is just a wonderful brick about everything and never complained and is such a darling companion to me . . . My hopes and plans will be that we may have another Fleet to carry on the name as well as our Dad has done . . .'"

There were unfortunate medical complications but Preston, later nicknamed "Sandy," came through alright.

"After his third day," his mother recalls, "he began to have convulsions for no reason that we could un derstand. They decided to give him a blood transfusion. The baby's father was away so the donor was Reuben's 24-year-old son, David, the baby's half brother. We pulled him through that and then we found it was the RH blood factor which was the problem. I had lost two babies before Preston so I was afraid that this was my last try. We were very grateful

that he pulled through.

"Never had Reuben been more solicitous, more considerate, more affectionate.

"Time was when I had considered that to dance, to design, to write, would provide me with the ultimate in spiritual and artistic satisfaction, but it took only the birth of Preston to teach me otherwise."

FRONT VIEW of 'Fleetster' high-wing full-cantilever monoplane emphasizes its sleek lines.

IF IMITATION IS INDEED the sincerest form of flattery, the cigar-shaped Lockheed 'Vega' monoplane with its circular plywood fuselage and wooden wings certainly influenced aircraft design after its introduction in 1927.

Consolidated, however, with its greater experience in metal aircraft construction was successful at one-upmanship. For if Lockheed could produce a monocoque wood fuselage, Consolidated would build its new high performance single-engine transport with a metal monocoque fuselage in which the outer metal skin carried most of the stress.

To meet the need for speedy mail and passenger transports for the expanding airline network, Major Fleet announced plans for the 7-9 place 'Fleetster' in March 1929 at the time he was helping organize the New York, Rio and Buenos Aires (NYRBA) Line to operate in South America.

The new 'Fleetster' Model 17 was a high-wing full cantilever monoplane capable of carrying six passengers, seated on two divans facing each other or six seats facing forward. The pilot's cockpit had provision for a second pilot or for an additional passenger.

For its day, performance was outstanding, the 'Fleetster' cruising comfortably at 150 m.p.h., with a top speed of 180 m.p.h. The 575 h.p. Hornet engine was enclosed in the recently-developed NACA cowling which provided a better airflow and increase in cruising speed by as much as 15 m.p.h. The 'Fleetster' was

one of the first planes to use this type cowling to reduce the drag and turbulence created by the exposed cylinders of radial air-cooled engines.

The patents for the plane's unique metal construction were held in the name of Larry Bell, Consolidated's general manager. Thus the 'Fleetster' became the first American production plane to have an all-metal monocoque fuselage. Like the rival 'Vega,' the 'Fleetster's' wings were of wooden construction, plywood covered.

By October work had been completed on the prototype 'Fleetster' and initial test flights were begun with Leigh Wade at the controls. After being flown as a landplane, twin floats replaced the landing gear and the plane was taken to Miami during the winter for trials as a seaplane for NYRBA.

The Model 17 had its cantilever wing directly on top of the fuselage, with the enclosed cockpit streamlined into the wing leading edge forward of the passenger cabin.

A later 'Fleetster' version was the Model 20 for airmail use with a parasol wing located a foot above the fuselage and the pilot in an open cockpit (later enclosed) aft of the passenger cabin area. Both models were available either as a landplane or as a twin-float seaplane.

Some two dozen 'Fleetsters' were built, the first significant customer being the NYRBA Line, later merged into Pan American Airways, which used them, starting in mid-1930, on airmail runs out of Buenos Aires.

The 'Fleetsters' were more effectively used by NYRBA than the two Lockheed 'Vegas' they had acquired earlier in their operations. "For some stupid reason," reports Ralph O'Neill, "after the 'Vegas' were shipped to Rio they were left outdoors in tropical heat and humidity that caused the plywood wings to corrugate."

Pacific International Airways of Alaska, Western Canada Airways and several private owners, including Col. Robert McCormick of the Chicago Tribune, were also 'Fleetster' purchasers. Later the Ludington Line operated three-passenger versions between New York and Washington supplementing its every-hour-on-the-hour service with slower Stinson trimotors.

Needing a suitable small transport to operate over short routes feeding into its main transcontinental system, TWA also decided to look into the 'Fleetster.'

John Collings, TWA's chief pilot, accompanied by Larry Fritz, another of the airline's pilots, flew in to Buffalo to try out the first Model 20 'Fleetster.' "Our pilots," Fritz reported, "were quite leery of the structural integrity of the parasol wing, so during our visit I asked Major Fleet if I might give it a test ride. The okay was given for just the normal maneuvers, but once airborne I did a series of rolls and loops that I understand had both Fleet and Collings in a fret. After I landed, Fleet gave me hell, but with a big smile since it was obvious Collings was pleased with the plane's performance."

LUDINGTON AIRLINES, operating New York-Washington service was among transport companies flying 'Fleetsters.'

General Dynamics/Convair

As a result, TWA leased seven Model 20 combination mail-passenger versions in 1932. Later all were purchased by the airline and used for several years. Three were sold in 1937 to an exporter and reportedly were used in Spain during its Civil War.

Two of the original NYRBA/PAA Model 17 'Fleetsters' were sold to Amtorg, the Russian trading company, in 1934. They were delivered to Soviet pilots Mark Slepnev and Sigismund Levanevsky at Anchorage, Alaska, and were used in searching for the crew of the Russian icebreaker 'Chelyuskin' which had

SEAPLANE VERSION of 'Fleetster,' test flown at Miami, later flew South American routes of NYRBA.

General Dynamics/Convair

TWA PILOT Larry Fritz flew Model 20 'Fleetster' in tests before airline put these new transports in service.

MILITARY TRANSPORT version of 'Fleetster' was used by Army's F. Trubee Davison, left. Pilot was Major Ira C. Eaker.

been crushed in Arctic ice. The crew was safely rescued and the Russian government issued a 15-kopek airmail stamp in 1935 that pictured a 'Fleetster' transport, commemorating the event. The planes bore Russian registrations USSR-MS and USSR-SL (initials of the pilots).

The Army Air Corps accepted one demonstration 'Fleetster' which it designated a Y1C-11A cargo transport but which was tested as a fast command transport. Major General James E. Fechet, Air Corps Chief of Staff, used it to attend Army maneuvers in California in 1930 and Assistant Army Secretary F. Trubee Davison used it for inspection trips. The pilot assigned to the Y1C-11A was Major Ira C. Eaker. Within a year the Air Corps purchased three Y1C-22 'Fleetsters.'

Another military application of the 'Fleetster' was with the Navy, which was to test it as a carrier-based bomber under the designation XBY-1.

Although the design and construction principles first tried out in the 'Fleetster' proved to be of greater advantage later on to Consolidated, Reuben Fleet himself did not have too high a regard for the 'Fleetster,' but he did use one frequently when it was

155

assigned as a company executive airplane.

"The 'Fleetster,'" he explained, "was our attempt to make a single-engine transport airplane out of metal. However, it had wooden wings and I never considered it too much of a success. Lockheed had a very clever method of molding their plywood fuselage, using an air bag to force the moist veneer against a concrete mold. When the fuselage dried it was really an egg shell without any skeleton. We found to our chagrin we couldn't do the same thing with metal that they were doing with wood; we had to have some minimum skeleton on which to rivet the exterior metal skin but there was no cross-bracing. This, of course, was before the day of large hydropresses.

"I used to fly the company's own executive 'Fleetster' several times a year down to Florida. A frequent guest was my good friend Congressman John J. McSwain, Democrat of South Carolina, chairman of the House military affairs committee and militant advocate of strong air defenses. I would pick him up at Greenville and then fly down to Sanibel Island off Fort Myers, Florida, in the Gulf of Mexico, where Thomas A. Edison lived. We'd land on the beach, taxi up high enough so the water never got to the 'Fleetster' and stay there several days to fish and rest."

Edison shared February 11 with Reuben's father as their common birth date, although the great inventor was four years older than David W. Fleet. To celebrate Edison's 80th birthday in 1927, Reuben flew his 76-year-old father to Florida for a reunion with his old friend.

Reuben recalls the difficulty of communicating with the stone deaf inventive genius. "Daddy" Fleet would write out his message and Edison would respond in the distorted monotone typical of those unable to hear the sound of their own voices.

TWO BASIC VERSIONS of 'Fleetster' are Model 17 high-wing passenger transport, above. and Model 20 parasol wing combination passenger/mail plane, below, with pilot in rear cockpit.

General Dynamics/Convair

NIAGARA FALLS is backdrop for this unusual photo of TWA's Model 20 on flight out of nearby Buffalo, New York.

HAVING RETRIEVED THEIR FLYING boat development costs through sale of the 14 'Commodore' commercial transports, Reuben Fleet and Mac Laddon launched into studies of improvements to the Navy's 'Admiral' patrol bomber. They were not about to allow Glenn L. Martin to squeeze them out of what they saw to be their own design and market.

The refined design would have an enclosed cockpit, as in the 'Commodore,' and the larger engines to be used would take advantage of new NACA streamlined engine cowls.

The original 'Admiral' flying boat had so many bracing struts and wires that it resembled a flying birdcage. In the new plane the first of many steps would be taken to clean up the exterior structure. Continued refinement throughout the years led ultimately to the graceful PBY 'Catalina' flying boats of World War II.

"The most important aerodynamic change in the new XP2Y-1 'Ranger,' Reuben explained, "was in the horizontal structure supporting the floats on each side of the hull. We simply covered the structure extending out from the fuselage and made a shoulder-high wing out of it in order to provide additional lift. We gave it as much overhang beyond the floats as possible.

Seven weeks later when procurement funds became available in July, at the start of the government's new fiscal year, the Navy placed orders for 23 production P2Y-1 'Ranger' patrol bombers even before the prototype of the new model had flown. To complete the order Consolidated leased additional production space in the former Curtiss Buffalo plant.

The three-engined XP2Y-1 was assembled outdoors on a huge concrete apron adjoining the launching ramp of the new Buffalo Marine Airport on the Niagara River. Even in late March, after a warmer-than-usual winter, the weather was as unpredictable in 1932 as in any other year.

A takeoff in the XP2Y-1 prototype was decided upon March 26 after a favorable wind had blown drifting ice to the far side of the harbor and left what test pilot Bill Wheatley considered ample space for a takeoff free from ice. But after half an hour in the air Mac Laddon noticed that floating ice was moving back into the area and a hurried landing had to be made because the wind continued to shift. A short time later the water adjacent to the ramp was completely covered with floating ice.

Things looked more promising, though still

U. S. Navy/National Archives

"The Navy was, of course, anxious to increase the range of the ship so it could, perhaps, go from the Canal Zone to San Francisco or from San Diego to Hawaii. I had also insisted that we make some of the flying boats capable of carrying their own beaching gear to give them more versatility in off-site operations."

With the added power from two 575 h.p. 'Hornet' engines and new three-bladed controllable pitch propellers, the sesquiplane configuration did not penalize speed even though the stub wings were designed to carry 2000 lbs. of external bomb stores on undersurface racks.

But, first, the Navy had once again to try the tri-motor concept on the experimental XP2Y-1 patrol bomber which went under contract on May 26, 1931.

marginal, a fortnight later, as told by Laddon.

"It was such an expense and nuisance to take a flying boat by rail to Washington that we decided, in view of the relatively warm winter, we would take a chance on flying the XP2Y-1 there.

"The airplane had our first beaching gear. In order to install it properly it had to have neutral bouyance in the water. I achieved that by taking the air valve out and putting water in the tires. When we had the right amount of water we replaced the valve and that was that.

"Unfortunately by the time we started to go down to the river for the launching the weather had turned cold and the water had frozen in the tires. It was thump, thump, thump as the wheels rolled over each time down the ramp.

XP2Y-1 'RANGER' in tri-motor configuration was abandoned for twin-engine version. Note engine installation in photo below.

"However, with Bill Wheatley at the controls and a Navy Commander in the right seat, we took off April 14 for Washington. I sat over some of the aluminum extrusions. Right before my eyes I could see these things curl up because, instead of having pressure on them, we had suction when the hull rose in the water as the wing began to lift the plane into the air.

"After several hours flying we had crossed the mountains and were down past Williamsburg, Virginia less than an hour from Washington, but the clouds kept pushing us down. We didn't dare go above them because in those days we had no way of communicating with the ground. We had no alternative but to turn around and head back for Buffalo.

"After six and a half hours in the air we landed smoothly on the Niagara River, but the wind had changed. Instead of the water being open from there in to the ramp, it was packed with loose ice coming in from Lake Erie.

"Larry Bell got hold of the Buffalo fire department and they tried to open the way to the ramp with hoses. But nothing worked. We were already tired and getting colder and colder by the minute. Fortunately, I had a big 40 ounce bottle of Canadian whiskey. Wheatley didn't drink but the rest of us got pretty well potted while we were waiting. Finally they sent a boat out to take us off and left the flying boat out there until 10:30 p.m. when a passageway opened up."

Three days later the flight was successfully made in three hours over the mountains to Washington in perfect weather.

PRODUCTION VERSION of P2Y-1 'Ranger' had short cowl rings
around more powerful 'Hornet' engines. Note enclosed cockpit.

On another occasion the Buffalo weather proved just as unpredictable and difficult. "The climate," Reuben explained, "made it the most ungodly place you could possibly have from which to deliver flying boats. On May 3 we hit submerged ice and ripped the bottom out of the boat but succeeded in taxiing it into the ramp. We rebuilt the bottom and tested the plane again on May 15. Again we hit submerged ice and again ripped the bottom out. It was pretty well on toward summer and yet the Niagara River was plumb full of submerged ice. After that we concluded that Buffalo was no place for flying boats.

"To get our new Navy boats to the Atlantic seaboard we had, weeks in advance, to engage the six 'well' cars that existed in the whole United States. To carry unusally high loads, the 'well' cars had been cut down to clear the rails by only four inches.

"Even with these cars we couldn't route them down the Pennsylvania Railroad because the trusses of the bridges interfered. With the high, rigid tail of the flying boats, the load wouldn't clear the trusses. In addition we had to have a vacant rail car protecting the load in front and another in the rear.

"We found we had to route the flying boat through Cincinnati and down the C. & O. to Norfolk, Virginia to get it to the seaboard.

"This left us with three choices: abandon building flying boats altogether; make them smaller than the 100-foot span patrol bombers, or build them on one of the seaboards.

"Eventually we spent ten years, as we flew around the country, picking out various places to which we might like to move. We looked at Florida, from Jacksonville south to Miami. On the west coast we considered Seattle and examined the area from Los Angeles Harbor and Long Beach down to San Diego."

Warming up to the subject, Fleet went on to describe the outcome of an evening of bridge with Paul Fitzpatrick and his wife.

"Paul was the Democratic leader of Buffalo, and of Erie County—the tail which wagged the political dog in New York State politics. It was the large population center in the west end of the state and because Manhattan, the Bronx, Brooklyn, Queens and Staten Island never could agree on anything, Buffalo held the state's political power. Anyway, he told me that

Governor Franklin D. Roosevelt wouldn't let us move out of Buffalo.

" 'Paul,' I said, 'if I am not violating your confidence, I would like to go down and see the Governor and talk it over with him tomorrow.

" 'Well, I know what you're up against,' he replied, 'and I think you ought to do it Reuben.'

"So I called up Roosevelt and made a date with him for the next day. I flew down to Albany and during the course of our talk I explained to Governor Roosevelt the situation in regard to flying boats. I told him that if Consolidated and I were going to be any good to the country in time of war I should be located on one of the seaboards south of the Mason-Dixon line where we would be unhampered by snow and ice and the added cost and time of shipping unassembled planes by rail. He was very attentive.

"We talked it over for perhaps an hour and a half and he decided to withdraw his objection. I told him, 'Of course, you don't own any stock in this company, Governor, and neither do the people of New York own much of it. Therefore, you see, we have to go where it is best for the company.'

"When I left he told me that whenever we felt it was time for the company to move to go ahead. It was my first personal contact with Franklin D. Roosevelt. He was a great personality and a beautiful talker.

"Of course the bad weather didn't affect just the flying boats. When we were completing a training plane every working day we often had dozens of pilots accumulate as our guests at the Buffalo Athletic Club waiting for better weather to fly south to Brooks Field in Texas for the Army and Pensacola, Florida for the Navy.

"While we had the advantage in Buffalo of using leased factory space without a large capital outlay, the disadvantage far outweighed that consideration and in the long run we just had to get up and go elsewhere."

EXPORT P2Y-1C model of 'Ranger' is checked out at Buffalo for delivery to Colombia.

Buffalo Evening News

THE TRI-MOTORED ARRANGEMENT in the XP2Y-1 was no more successful than in the original XPY-1 three years earlier. The 23 production P2Y-1 'Ranger' flying boats would be built with only the two engines mounted just below the 100-foot-span wing. The first operational 'Ranger' was delivered to the Navy at Norfolk, Virginia, February 1, 1933. It won immediate and enthusiastic approval, particularly for its greatly increased range.

Further design refinements were suggested by Mac Laddon on the basis of updated information from NACA on additional developments in cowling for radial engines. Consolidated already had experienced good results with NACA engine cowling on its 'Fleetster' commercial transport.

The last of the P2Y-1 'Ranger' flying boats was modified on the assembly line. Its engines, improved Wright Cyclones delivering 750 h.p. each, were enclosed in long-chord NACA cowls and raised to the leading edge of the wing. Emerging as the XP2Y-2, the modified plane showed an increase in cruising speed of 10 m.p.h. in flight test at Hampton Roads, Virginia in August 1933. December 27 an order was placed for 23 of the new, longer range model, now designated P2Y-3. Already geared for quantity production, Consolidated delivered the new order in the first five months of 1935. They were to be the last of the Navy's sesquiplane, strut-braced flying boats and were, at that time, the best patrol bombers in the fleet.

The Navy liked the new design configuration so well that it was decided to similarly modify all of the original P2Y-1 'Rangers.' For this purpose Consolidated developed a modification kit so that the Navy could make the conversions in the field. The planes so modified were given the P2Y-2 designation, the same as the prototype plane on which the modification had first been made that lifted the engines and nacelles into the wing leading edge.

Foreign sales of the P2Y type boats included one each to Colombia (P2Y-1C) and Japan (P2Y-1J) and six in 1937 to Argentina (P2Y-3A).

In all, Consolidated's total production of this basic flying boat type, including the 'Commodores' for NYRBA, came to 71 planes and revenue exceeding $7 million.

EVOLUTION OF CONSOLIDATED FLYING BOAT DESIGN

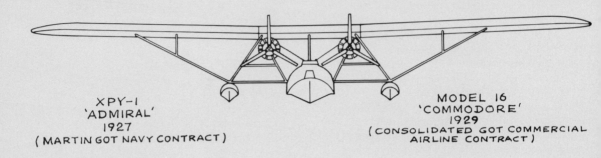

XPY-1
'ADMIRAL'
1927
(MARTIN GOT NAVY CONTRACT)

MODEL 16
'COMMODORE'
1929
(CONSOLIDATED GOT COMMERCIAL
AIRLINE CONTRACT)

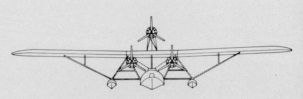

TRI-MOTOR TRIED IN
XPY-1 AND AGAIN IN XP2Y-1

P2Y-1 'RANGER' 1931

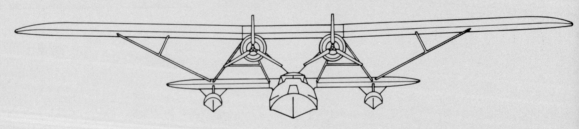

P2Y-2 AND P2Y-3
'RANGER' 1933
(NACA COWLS STREAMLINED INTO WING)

ENGINES NOW STREAMLINED into leading edge of 100-foot wing, the P2Y-2/3 versions of 'Ranger' set enviable operational record.

P2Y-3 'RANGER' cruises off-shore in Hawaiian Islands where patrol bombers were on duty.

WHEN, IN 1928, THE NAVY placed the order for the 'Admiral' patrol bomber it set in motion a new policy of developing a long-range reconnaissance capability covering the Atlantic seaboard, the Canal Zone, the West coast of the United States and from there to the Hawaiian outpost in the Pacific.

It was not until five years later that the potential of this new scouting and patrol capability was dramatically demonstrated when the P2Y 'Ranger' flying boats became operational.

A division of Navy Squadron VP-5 based at San Diego was dispatched to Norfolk, Virginia to accept six P2Y-1s to be delivered to Coco Solo in the Panama Canal Zone.

Under command of LCdr. Donald M. Carpenter the six planes left Norfolk at 5 p.m. September 7, 1933 on the long non-stop formation flight. Due to fuel line trouble one plane had to land at Miami for repairs, but resumed the flight independently an hour behind the others. All had to buck head wind and line squalls during the night.

At dusk the next day the five patrol bombers landed in the Canal Zone after flying 2059 miles in 25 hours 19 minutes. Within the hour the other P2Y-1 landed alongside the anchored patrol bombers.

The longest 'mass' flight up to that time, the planes of VP-5 had broken the record previously held by General Italo Balbo and a squadron of 12 twin-hulled Savoia-Marchetti flying boats in flying the South Atlantic from Africa to Brazil.

Meanwhile VP-10 Squadron based at Coco Solo had also been flying the new Consolidated patrol bombers which they then exchanged for a newer fleet of longer range P2Y-1s recently received by VP-5. The new planes were to be based at Pearl Harbor, Hawaii and VP-10 was to fly them there via Acapulco, San Diego and San Francisco.

The seaplane tender 'USS Wright' was dispatched to Acapulco as an intermediate service station for VP-10's planes. On October 7, the six P2Y-1s, under command of LCdr. Knefler (Soc) McGinnis, arrived at Acapulco after a 14 hour flight from Panama.

Next day there was a heavy swell in the bay but virtually no wind. After long runs, five of the heavily-laden P2Ys struggled into the air, but one plane simply could not get 'on the step.' Its propellers had been honed down for better balance and could not provide the necessary power. This P2Y had to be hoisted aboard the 'Wright' for the trip to San Diego. After a flight of 19 hours the five 'Ranger' boats landed in San Diego Harbor, where VP-10 remained for three months during which the planes were prepared for the long Hawaiian hop.

In January VP-10 flew from San Diego to San Francisco to await takeoff orders, which came on the 10th. Because the water was calm and the winds light, Navy biplane flying boats helped 'blow off' the P2Y-1s by taxiing ahead of them to break water suction and provide a 'head wind' until the Consolidated boats started to 'plane' on the water.

It was nearly two hours before the six P2Y-1 'Rangers' were in the air and had formed up into two three-plane elements led by Comdr. McGinnis and Comdr. Marc A. Mitscher, his copilot. Engine power was cut back for maximum range as cruising speed was held to just under one hundred miles an hour. Through the afternoon and night the squadron droned on, much of the time through fog; it was late morning before Diamond Head came into view. Flying time for the 2408 miles, San Francisco to Pearl Harbor, was 24 hours 35 minutes.

From Washington, President Franklin D. Roosevelt sent McGinnis congratulations for "the greatest undertaking of its kind in the history of aviation . . . a magnificent accomplishment." And in Tokyo, a Japanese Navy Office spokesman noted the increased power such aviation developments gave mankind.

General Dynamics/Convair

PATROL SQUADRON VP-10 at San Diego before group left in their six P2Y-1s for San Francisco and Hawaii.

10 JANUARY 1934, first planes of VP-10 patrol squadron take off from San Francisco.

U. S. Navy/National Archives

Rear Admiral Ernest J. King, Chief of the Bureau of Aeronautics, stressed the seaworthiness of the flying boats' ability to land and take off with heavy loads in the open sea and pointed out they could scout and patrol vast areas of the Pacific to obtain information of the 'enemy.'

A great advocate of air power who believed that airplanes should always be in a state of operational readiness, Admiral King frequently led long training flights of P2Y squadrons. The Admiral flew copilot in one of the P2Ys of VP-10 when it and other squadrons totaling 33 planes flew from Pearl Harbor to French Frigate Shoals. Later Admiral King commanded a similar patrol bomber exercise in the Caribbean.

For nearly six years, the P2Ys continued to serve the Navy as operational aircraft; finally 41 of the 46 planes (21 P2Y-2s and 20 P2Y-3s) were retired to Pensacola where they served as training aircraft for several more years.

Relatively little is known of the operation of the six P2Y-3A boats in Argentina or the P2Y-1C in Colombia.

Arrangements for purchase of the P2Y-1J for the Imperial Japanese Navy were handled by the Mitsui Trading Company and the plane was assembled in 1935 by the Kawanishi Aircraft Company of Naruo, Japan.

After test flights with Japanese crews the 'J' boat was used for design study and comparative tests against Japanese-built flying boats. It was later sold to a civil airline which operated it during World War II. One modification of the plane had been necessary. The rudder pedals needed extensions so the short-legged Japanese pilots could reach them.

U. S. Navy/National Archives

24 HOURS from San Francisco, 10-P-1 in command of LCdr. 'Soc' McGinnis arrives over Hawaii.

FORMATION OF SIX P2Y-1 'Ranger' patrol bombers make final approach to landing in Hawaii.

Fleet Air Base, Pearl Harbor

PT-11 ARMY AIR CORPS version of Consolidated's Model 21 primary/advanced trainer.

THE YEARS BETWEEN the success of the 'Husky/Fleet' series of training planes and the emergence of the great PBY patrol bombers were the Depression years for Consolidated Aircraft, as they were for the rest of the country. Not so much in terms of volume as in profitability of operations.

Airplane sales for the four years 1929-1932 totaled $10.2 million compared with $6.3 million for the company's first 5½ years in business. But while earnings during the period from the company's founding in 1923 through 1928 were $2.1 million, in the next four years the company barely broke even because of net losses in 1931 and 1932.

The year 1930 had set a new high in volume when, as Major Fleet reported, the company "produced, sold and delivered more airplanes, 309, and in total value, $4,345,171, than any other aircraft manufacturing unit in America." "Yet," he added, "the net profit was only 3% on the entire volume of business."

The impressive sales volume of 1930 was due to deliveries of 10 'Commodore' seaplanes and six 'Fleetster' landplane transports for use on South American routes; to good customer acceptance of the 'Fleet' biplanes, and to delivery of the Thomas-Morse 0-19 observation planes to the Army.

The often low profit margin on government contracts served to point up Fleet's complaint three years earlier about having had to sell 50 PT-3 planes at $1 each as retribution for the Army's claimed "$300,000 of excess profits" earned by Consolidated. In 1931 and 1932 the company had a net loss of $375,158 on sale of planes to the Army but no one in the government stepped forward to cover the company's loss.

"Our losses to the Army," Fleet wrote, "put the shoe on the other foot, and it would seem fair that it should reimburse us at least for our outlay in its behalf, even if it were to pay us nothing for two years work."

The low point for the company was 1932. Only a hundred planes were sold. Volume dropped to $1.3 million. All salaries and wages were cut 20%. Even Reuben's son David, who had been a sales pilot and service manager for "Fleet" trainers, was laid off so as not to jeopardize the job of a married employee with a family to support. Things were tough all over. Then business gradually began to pick up, though it was not until 1937 that sales volume got above the level set in 1930.

Under an Army Air Corps design competition to develop an updated biplane trainer as successor to the PT-3, Consolidated in 1931 came out with the 'convertible' Model 21 capable of handling both primary and advanced instruction. The prototype aircraft was reported to have been designed, built, static tested and ready for demonstration in only eight weeks.

Smaller than the PT-3 but larger and more powerful

DEBUT OF MODEL 21-A trainer on wintry February day, 1931. Left to right, test pilot Bill Wheatley; engineer Joe Gwinn; guest Jimmy Doolittle.

than the 'Fleet,' the '21 series' trainers had a span of 31 feet six inches, compared with 28 feet for the 'Fleet' and 34 feet six inches for the PT-3, and were available with a wide range of power plants, depending on mission. For primary training the 170 h.p. Kinner was used; for advanced work either the 300 h.p. or 400 h.p. 'Wasp Junior' was fitted. Other engines could also be used. To provide longitudinal balance involving engine change from primary to advanced configuration, the wing was moved forward to additional fittings provided.

In U.S. Army service, the Model 21 carried the PT-11 and PT-12 designations for primary training and BT-7 for basic training. Some 40 aircraft of these types were used by the Army. The Navy and Coast Guard purchased the N4Y-1 model. Later, 30 of the Model 21 trainers were sold abroad , most of them going to Colombia. The PT-11C version with 250 h.p. Wright engine and Townend cowling ring was sold to China.

Fleet Aircraft of Canada continued to supply planes for the American commercial market and to foreign military customers, but during the early thirties the volume of trainer sales was not comparable to what it had been in prior years. The Canadian-based subsidiary had a hard time making a go of it but under the leadership of its president, Jack Sanderson, the organization was held together during four very difficult years.

PROTOTYPE of BT-7 basic trainer, above. *Seaplane version for Colombia,* below, *had designation PT-11C.*

Meantime, Consolidated had moved its headquarters from Buffalo and the Canadian firm was somewhat out of the main stream of company activity. Sales had been disappointing. In nearly seven years the Canadian company delivered 112 planes and had a business volume of just under a million dollars.

With the new year, 1937, Canadian interests purchased the Fleet subsidiary and reorganized under the new name, Fleet Aircraft, Ltd. Fifty thousand shares of stock were offered to Canadian citizens but Consolidated continued to hold 35,000 of the 90,000 shares of stock in Fleet Aircraft, Ltd. Reuben Fleet and Joe Gwinn continued to serve on the board of directors.

The new company received exclusive rights to manufacture and sell 'Fleet' trainers worldwide except in the United States, China and Rumania. In addition, it acquired rights to the Model 21 line of advanced trainers, except for the U.S.

AS DID OTHER AIRCRAFT manufacturers during the Depression, Consolidated undertook a number of development projects hoping that one or more of them might lead to production orders. In this Major Fleet was as disappointed as were his contemporaries.

MODEL 18

The Model 18 XBY-1 (experimental bomber, 'Y' for Consolidated, first model) was built in 1932 as an all-metal single-engine landplane designed for use aboard aircraft carriers. It was based on the successful 'Fleetster' commercial transport design and was a unique example of a civilian aircraft in which bomb bay doors were installed in the fuselage in order to convert the plane into a military plane for bombing missions.

The XBY-1 had the 'Fleetster's' monocoque metal fuselage, the patents for which were held in the name of Larry Bell. In addition, it had a metal cantilever wing in place of the all-wood plywood-covered wing of the commercial 'Fleetster,' and was the Navy's first aircraft to employ stressed skin wing construction.

Only the one XBY-1 Navy bomber was built, but some good did come of the project. The leading edge of the metal wing contained the first integral fuel tank, a development on which Mac Laddon and Consolidated later capitalized.

T-M VIPER

Consolidated's Thomas-Morse group, under B. Douglas Thomas, came up with the 'Viper' design in response to Army interest in a biplane fighter to use the new 600 h.p. 12-cylinder twin-row Curtiss 'Chieftain' engine.

In August 1930, the Army purchased the one 'Viper' built and assigned it the XP-13 designation. Like other

U. S. Navy/National Archives

MODEL 18 (XBY-1) experimental bomber adapted from 'Fleetster' transport.

Air Force Museum

THOMAS-MORSE 'VIPER' design was reminiscent of popular WW I 'Tommy Scout.'

Thomas-Morse designs it featured a corrugated-skin metal fuselage with fabric covered wings and tail surfaces over metal structure.

The single 'Viper' was later converted to use the Pratt and Whitney 'Wasp' engine enclosed by an NACA cowling. It became the XP-13A, but neither version went into production.

MODEL 23

Another Thomas-Morse venture was the Y10-41 two-place observation type, also identified by the designation XO-932. (The 'Y1' Air Force designator indicated that a plane, though undergoing service test, was a company-financed venture involving no cost to the government.)

Essentially the plane was an O-19B powered by a Curtiss Prestone-cooled 600 h.p. 'Conqueror' in-line engine in place of the 450 h.p. radial, and converted into a sesquiplane configuration. Just the one plane for flight testing was built. Its top speed was some 50

m.p.h. more than the 140 m.p.h. of the O-19B and O-19C types. It was intended to serve the multiple role of observation, two-seat fighting or bombing missions. Typical of Thomas-Morse construction, the fuselage was covered with corrugated duralumin sheet.

MODEL 24

B. Douglas Thomas' last work at Buffalo was on the XB2Y-1, a chunky shipboard biplane dive bomber for which the Navy supplied the basic design. Performance with a 700 h.p. Pratt and Whitney engine included the ability to climb to 15,000 feet in 15 minutes, and a speed of 181 m.p.h. at 8,900 feet.

To meet the severe demands imposed on the airframe structure when pulling out of 9 g. dives at 400 m.p.h., construction had to be unusually rugged. It was on this requirement that Thomas stumbled.

"This plane," Reuben Fleet observed, "was not a success. Thomas had quite a large piece of the center structure hogged out of a block of steel. It was too ex-

MODEL 24 (XB2Y-1), chunky shipboard bomber, on which Thomas stubbed his toe.

U. S. Navy/National Archives

MODEL 23 (Y10-41) sesquiplane high-performance development of O-19 biplane series.

General Dynamics/Convair

pensive even to consider for production, and the plane just died on the vine. Soon after that Thomas resigned."

And Thomas-Morse ceased to be a separate, active unit within the Consolidated Aircraft corporate structure. To use a phrase of Reuben's, Thomas-Morse was "put to sleep" as a legal entity two years later. As with the XO-932 sesquiplane, the Thomas-Morse 'Viper,' and the XBY-1 monoplane bomber, only the one XB2Y-1 biplane dive bomber was built.

Despite lack of success on new designs, the 23 P2Y-1 'Ranger' flying boats produced for the Navy, and sales of some 130 'Fleet' and Model 21 trainers abroad, accounted for a steady but not spectacular volume of business during 1933 and 1934, permitting the company to just about 'break even' financially.

To simplify the parent company's corporate structure, all of the subsidiary companies, except Fleet Aircraft of Canada, Ltd., were liquidated, their capital accounts reduced to a nominality, and physically merged with Consolidated.

General Dynamics/Convair

Y1P-25 pursuit-attack prototype was delivered to Wright Field in December 1932. Note turbo-supercharger engine installation.

As THEY HAD in several previous cases, Major Fleet and Consolidated helped out the Air Corps by picking up the remnants of another company's poor management of a potentially good product.

The plane involved was Detroit Aircraft's XP-900, a cantilever low-wing two-place pursuit with retractable landing gear. It had the Lockheed look because, in fact, Lockheed was then a subsidiary of Detroit Aircraft Corp. The metal fuselage had been built in Detroit; the wooden wings at Lockheed's Burbank, California plant.

The Air Corps had been impressed by the performance of the Lockheed 'Altair' and had contracted for a pursuit plane based on that design. Detroit's project engineer on the XP-900 was Robert J. Woods.

Unfortunately, Detroit Aircraft in 1932 was on its last legs financially. Its only hope of survival was the XP-900; funds were available for purchase and service test of four YP-24 pursuit and four YA-9 attack planes based on the XP-900 design. Things were so austere

that Woods recalls "I rode the back seat of the XP-900 when it was delivered to Wright Field in order to save train fare. To get that far with the project, the twelve engineers on the job had put in an almost unbelievable amount of overtime for five months on half their regular pay."

Despite such heroic efforts, Detroit Aircraft folded. The Army Air Corps still liked the airplane and asked Consolidated to continue with it; this time with an all-metal version requiring complete reengineering of the wing for metal construction.

Along with the new contract, which called for one Y1P-25 pursuit and one XA-11 attack plane, Woods came to work for Consolidated.

Like its predecessor, the Y1P-25, which was delivered to Wright Field in December, was powered with a 600 h.p. turbo-supercharged Curtiss 'Conqueror' liquid cooled engine. The attack version, having a lower altitude operational requirement for its mission, was not supercharged.

DETROIT AIRCRAFT test flies its XP-900 pursuit equipped with retractable landing gear. Pilot is Vance Breese.

In an unfortunate accident in mid-January 1933, the Y1P-25 prototype was destroyed but not before the plane's excellent performance had been well demonstrated. Contracts followed for four service test P-30 supercharged pursuits and four A-11 non-supercharged attack planes.

With successful testing of these aircraft, the Air Corps ordered 50 of the 700 h.p. supercharged P-30A pursuit version for operational squadrons. This was to be the first successful application of the turbine-driven supercharger to operational military aircraft. Its supercharger increased top speed of the P-30A by over 50 m.p.h. at altitude. Reuben Fleet had played a key role in supercharger development while at McCook Field more than a decade earlier.

And, between the two World Wars, the P-30A and its successor models, were to be the only two-place monoplane pursuits to reach operational status. It was another feather in Consolidated's cap, but this time there was a catch as explained by the Major:

"Before the Army would buy Consolidated's version of the XP-900 they wanted a metal wing. Larry Bell handled the negotiations on the contract and should have told the Army we would have to charge them for the costs to develop the Y1P-25's metal wing. The word 'metal' was in the contract specifications and Larry let it get by without provision for reimbursement of the extra cost, so we didn't get paid for development of the metal wing. That oversight cost us three quarters of a million dollars!"

TO SAVE TRAIN FARE, engineer Bob Woods (in cockpit behind test pilot Vance Breese), "rode the back seat of the XP-900." On ground, Detroit Aircraft executives.

171

In its first serious labor dispute, Consolidated experienced a 57-day strike at its Buffalo plant in the spring of 1934. Pursuant to an order of the Regional Labor Board the strike was called off and settled by arbitration as had been provided under the pre-strike contract.

Soon after this, as part of President Roosevelt's New Deal, Congress passed the National Industrial Recovery Act which included creation of a National Labor Board headed by New York Senator Robert F. Wagner. Its guarantees of collective bargaining rights for employees, and government control of alleged unfair labor practices by employers, raised the Major's ire. He headed straight for Washington to give his senator a piece of his mind.

At Senator Wagner's quarters in the Senate Office Building Fleet was informed the Senator was not in or available. Reuben decided to wait, especially after a glance through a partially open door disclosed the Senator was indeed at his desk.

When Wagner left and came down the hall he was collared—literally—by the irate Major. "Now see here, Senator," he began, only to be interrupted as Wagner barked out to "get your hands off me, or I'll call the sergeant-at-arms."

"You'll do nothing of the kind! You're my senator and you damn well better listen to what I have to say."

The argument went on and on as others gathered round, but as Reuben admitted later, "It didn't do any good."

When Reuben really wanted to see someone of influence badly enough he was willing to pay for an audience—pay, that is, by making a campaign contribution.

Major Gen. Leigh Wade tells of the time Fleet asked a Senator on Capitol Hill for a five-minute interview, telling him it was worth $100 a minute to talk with him. Not surprisingly Fleet so interested the Senator that the conversation went to 12 minutes. When it was over Reuben made good on his promise with a $1200 campaign contribution for the Senator's reelection.

MAJOR FLEET CONTINUED to be a vigorous, vocal spokesman in Washington not only for Consolidated but for the entire aircraft manufacturing industry. After testimony before the Naval Affairs Sub-Committee of the House of Representatives he went on record in March 1934 in a letter to the Committee Chairman in which he expressed his strong views:

"The profit (on orders we have filled from our birth) has not been great enough to justify the risks and hazards attending the creation, detailed design, building and guaranteeing of our aircraft.

"The risk involved in attempting to estimate in advance what military aircraft will cost in its experimental stages of development, especially where it must meet constantly changing military demands, is so great that it must yield higher profits to those who are successful, than they would have right to expect from production manufacturing of staple articles, if America is to have worthwhile brains and healthy companies engaged in this line of endeavor.

"Ten and three-quarters years sees us still without a factory of our own or a wind-tunnel or an experimental laboratory, and with no dividends to our stockholders for more than five years.

"Lack of continuity of orders forces carrying costs that wipe out profits rapidly, for if we are to be a national asset we must not disband our organization between contracts. Of course profits earned on specific orders must be drawn against for losses and for payment of at least the skeleton organization of brains, trained engineers and lead men in 'lean' periods.

"If the profit on any contract is to be restricted to 10%, who will carry the overhead in lean periods when there is little or no work on hand? Such a policy would destroy the aviation industry as a business and put each company in the category of a road or building contractor—a dangerously and woefully weak prop to our country in peace times and in times of emergency.

"There is a gross misconception in the lay mind regarding negotiated aircraft contracts, namely that they are 'hand-outs' and perhaps involve collusion whereas they are awarded only after the severest competition. Government officers have then used every conceivable means of chiseling prices including threats to buy an admittedly inferior product, or to appropriate creator's design and invite formal competitive bids from other manufacturers therefor, or to have same manufactured by the Government, or to let the funds revert to the Treasury. Particularly unfair has been the government practice to try to force successful design creators to meet the prices of competitors with less satisfactory and 'cheap' aircraft.

"Your basic aircraft procurement law should be amended to recognize design rights as proprietary if you expect to encourage the creation and development of better aircraft in this country. If samples are to be taken away from their originators by low-bidding competitors who have sat on the sidelines like vultures, it is discouraging beyond words.

"You should also authorize procurement of aircraft, in cases where no one can intelligently estimate in advance their probable cost, on the basis of 'cost plus a fixed profit with a bogie saving.' Where the profit is fixed, no temptation exists to make the job run up in cost. By coupling the fixed profit with a bogie saving, the contractor gets part of all he can save as an incentive to make the cost as low as he can consistent with safe and satisfactory aircraft."

B O O K V

"NOTHING SHORT OF RIGHT IS RIGHT."

1 9 3 5 - 1 9 4 1

REUBEN H. FLEET, a man whose conviction led him "to serve God, Country, Community, fellowman, under the policy, 'Nothing Short of Right is Right.' "

"NOTHING SHORT OF RIGHT IS RIGHT."

REUBEN FLEET ALWAYS HAD a warm spot in his heart for San Diego. He had been there in 1911 on Army patrol along the Mexican border as a member of the Washington National Guard. He had returned six years later and had won his wings as an Air Service pilot at North Island.

While San Diego was a fine place to live and raise a family, its greatest attraction to Major Fleet was for business reasons. Its fine climate made possible year round flying, in sharp contrast to the rigorous winters in Buffalo which were a real detriment to Consolidated's flying boat business. Reuben knew he must move. It was only a question of when.

On his west coast sales trip in the 'Fleet' biplane in August 1929, the Major had expressed his enthusiasm for San Diego's new Lindbergh Field with an offer to buy it for a million dollars. He also was shown Mission Bay and considered the purchase of much of the adjacent land as a location for a flying school. These were all the hints Tom Bomar and city officials needed.

Before Major Fleet left San Diego, Bomar had shown him several sites and followed up by letters with detailed information on six potential locations. But Tom Bomar could not understand Fleet's apparent discourtesy in never answering his letters. What he did not know was that Reuben lay at death's door in a hospital in London, Ontario, after his accident in the 'Fleet' trainer.

Early in November Fleet had recovered sufficiently to return to his office in Buffalo. His letter to Bomar reflected the impatient Reuben Fleet his associates knew so well:

> "I have just gotten out of the hospital as the result of a minor airplane accident, and find your letter of October 25th. Thank you for the information about San Diego; you need not forward any more. I know almost as much about the town as you do, and if and when I get ready to do business with you, I know where to go—I know how to do it."

The curt letter set Bomar back on his heels. No use irritating the Major any further. Yet not too many weeks later Fleet sent a radiogram to Bomar that he and his parents would be arriving on a visiting steamer. Again Bomar saw to it that Fleet had an opportunity to visit several possible sites.

For the next two years Bomar kept up a steady barrage of San Diego material, writing the Major at least once a month and repeating over and over that he should move the Consolidated plant there. T. C. Macaulay, Chamber of Commerce manager and an instructor at North Island when Fleet was learning to fly there in 1917, kept reminding Reuben that San Diego had 14 different 'climates,' anything he could possibly want except ice, snow and strong winds.

Still his boss didn't always share Bomar's optimism. "At weekly staff meetings," Bomar recalls, "Mac's favorite joke for years was to kid me. 'Are you still working on Fleet; still thinking you're going to get him? You haven't got a chinaman's chance. Los Angeles is going to get him.' "

San Diego's northern neighbors, Los Angeles and Long Beach, indeed were not asleep at the wheel. E. P. Querl of the Los Angeles Chamber of Commerce went east to Buffalo to present his case to Fleet. In April 1933 Fleet and Larry Bell investigated plant locations in the Los Angeles Harbor-Long Beach area and were favorably disposed to enter into an agreement to move there. But first they should get in touch with San Diego.

Phoning the Chamber of Commerce, Fleet's call was taken by Major Macaulay who motioned for Bomar to get on the extension line.

"We're ready to make a deal with you," Macaulay said. "Lindbergh Field is pretty well complete and we can offer you a fine plant location and access to the new seaplane ramp."

"Well," replied Fleet, "we've been the only company of any size that doesn't own our own factory. We've leased ever since we went to Buffalo but every year have been looking for a better place—the ultimate place before we build our own factory.

"Los Angeles, you know, is after us pretty hard. That's the big—the active—area in Southern California, and we're going there. We appreciate what you fellows in San Diego have done for us but we've got an offer from the City of Long Beach that we can't turn down. They'll give us 22½ acres free of charge right at the municipal airport."

Bomar broke in angrily. "Are you drunk, Reuben?"

"Hell, no."

"Well, you're talking like a drunken man. If you'll investigate you'll find that site is under four feet of water in the winter, and your factory will be flooded. Besides, that's five miles from the water and it costs as much to haul one of your flying boats five miles as it does 500 miles. Here you're right on the water and you're not going to be flooded."

"Are you telling the truth, Tom?"

"Yes, Reuben. That site will be under four feet of water this winter."

"Okay. We'll check into it and call you back."

Right after lunch, Reuben was back on the phone to Bomar and Macaulay.

"You fellows are sure right! Larry and I will be down to San Diego in the morning to spend several days and we want to meet with your Mayor, City Manager and Harbor Commission. We'll be there to get some action."

Armed with still further material and some specific proposals, Fleet and Bell left San Diego and returned

Thomas F. Bomar

to Buffalo to present plans to their board of directors for moving the company to the west coast.

Querl of the Los Angeles Chamber got wind of what was afoot and went east to Buffalo to appear before the Consolidated board, as did a representative from Long Beach. Both had rosy offers to submit. Buffalo, too, was putting up a stiff fight to retain the factory. Seattle and Oakland had not sent agents, nor had San Diego which, however, got a lucky last minute reprieve.

It was spring vacation time and Emil Klicka, San Diego banker and chairman of the Harbor Commission, was traveling with his wife in New York State.

"I stopped in a gas station as I went through Buffalo and put in a call to Major Fleet and asked him how negotiations were progressing," Klicka said. "He told me I was about the luckiest man in the world as the directors were meeting that very day to vote on moving west."

Klicka left for the meeting posthaste. Greeted by Major Fleet, he sat down in the president's place at the directors' table and talked San Diego for one solid hour. The timing could not have been better.

At that meeting on May 29, 1933 the Consolidated board passed a resolution authorizing a conditional lease with the City of San Diego. It was just ten years since Fleet had formed the company in East Greenwich, Rhode Island.

Forwarding the notarized documents and a $1000 check two weeks later as a binder on a 50-year lease Reuben Fleet wrote that "Your Mr. Klicka appeared before our board and did his best to convince us of the merits of San Diego. Later he telephoned many times from Chicago and offered to come back to Buffalo if he could aid to hasten us to a favorable decision.

"Few cities have such business-like departments and executives as your Harbor Department and its Port Director, Joe Brennan. This increases our confidence in San Diego.

"Ordinarily it is hard for Chamber officials to win the entire confidence of those they are trying to convince but Major Macaulay and Tom Bomar have done so. These gentlemen and you are all wide awake and command our respect. It will indeed be a pleasure to join you in working for the welfare of your charming city, if we select San Diego as the most attractive of the several propositions we are considering."

The 'if' was no longer operative. The die had been cast to move to San Diego.

"Although the Depression was on," Fleet explained, "we made up our minds in 1934 just to take the bull by the horns and come. We sent Chuck Leigh, vice president, and my son David out here to build a factory."

Consolidated employed architect L. B. Norman to draw plans for a "continuous flow" assembly plant incorporating the best features Fleet had found in modern aircraft factories he had visited.

The company found itself for the first time in a position to build a plant to house the business, rather than having to try and fit the business into an existing building. The matter of plant arrangement for the new building in San Diego became the subject of careful study. So far as practical it would have all the elements of an uninterrupted production flow from raw material to final assembly.

In December 1934 directors authorized a call for construction bids and applied for a $500,000 loan from the Reconstruction Finance Corporation to help meet the huge expense and task of moving an entire plant across the country. The catch was that the limit on such loans was $100,000. Congressman George Burnham went to bat for San Diego. The increase was granted but in the end Consolidated did not find it necessary to borrow the money.

In 1935 the dream became a reality when Consolidated put $190 on the line for a $300,000 building permit for its first factory unit.

General Dynamics/Convair

'CATALINA' PROTOTYPE, the XP3Y-1, pictured in April 1935 in familiar location at Anacostia Naval Air Station, Washington, D. C., where earlier water-borne Consolidated planes were also test flown.

CONSOLIDATED REALLY HIT the jackpot with the XP3Y-1 experimental patrol plane.

As the famed 'Catalina' of World War II, the Model 28 patrol bomber, based on the XP3Y-1, was the most successful flying boat ever designed. It was the ultimate refinement of everything Reuben Fleet and Mac Laddon and the Navy had learned about long-range airboats.

"I'd taken advantage," Laddon said, "of all the mistakes I'd made on the previous ones." The broad-winged XP3Y-1 all-metal monoplane had the cleanest lines of any seaplane yet designed. Two 825 h.p. Twin Wasp engines were built into the leading edge of the wing center section which, in turn, was supported above the hull by a faired-in pedestal structure which contained the flight engineer's position. Two struts on each side connected wing and hull, but the tail assembly had no external bracing.

Laddon designed retracting floats that folded into place after takeoff and became the outer tips of the

177

wings. Lastly, the plane had integral fuel tanks, an important weight-saving innovation.

Consolidated obtained a contract October 28, 1933 for the one experimental aircraft to be entered in a Navy competition to select a new long-range patrol plane with 3000 mile range as successor to the P2Y-3 'Ranger' boats. The prototype was delivered to the Navy in the spring of 1935 just after Douglas had delivered the competitive XP3D-1.

Engines of the Douglas mid-wing flying boat were fitted on pedestals above the wing much as in the third-engine version of the earlier Consolidated XPY-1 and XP2Y-1. Later Douglas converted its entry to a high-wing design as the XP3D-2 with engine nacelles in the leading edge. Douglas got into the air first, six weeks ahead of Consolidated.

Flight tests of the Consolidated XP3Y-1 began March 21, 1935 at Norfolk, Virginia. The plane had been shipped by rail on four special freight cars from the Buffalo factory and assembled by a Consolidated crew in a Navy hangar.

Back in Buffalo, Larry Bell passed along the good word to employees:

"Just received preliminary reports of the first flight of the XP3Y-1 at Norfolk this afternoon.

"Wheatley, Laddon and crew flew the boat for an hour and report that in the preliminary tests everything functioned satisfactorily. The entire structure was without vibration and is rigid in all respects. The floats were operated in the air electrically and by hand several times with complete success. Wheatley reports ship has excellent flying characteristics.

"From these first reports the XP3Y-1 looks very good, but additional tests will be necessary to prove all features."

So successful were the tests that the Navy redesignated the aircraft mission from P (patrol) to PB (patrol bomber) classification.

Both Consolidated and Douglas planes met technical requirements but as winner of the competition with a lower price, Consolidated was awarded a 60-plane, $6 million production contract on June 29, 1935 for its redesignated PBY-1 model, the first in the series of famed PBYs. A precursor of the threat to come from Japan in the Pacific, the contract was by far the largest awarded by the U.S. government since World War I. There would be work aplenty for the new factory already under construction in San Diego.

The new flying boat design was almost too advanced for Reuben Fleet, as recounted by Mac Laddon:

"Based on our success with a fuel tank in the leading edge of the 'Fleetster,' I got the courage to build a gas-tight wing in the PBY so that the fuel cell became an integral part of the wing structure.

"Reuben heard about it when he and Gordon Mounce were in Europe demonstrating the 'Fleet' trainer. He was highly incensed and let me know it in no uncertain terms.

"Didn't I have enough brains to know about the failure of others; how when they put an outboard engine on another job it leaked like a God-damn sieve, and here I was putting a thousand gallons of gas in each wing! He went on and on and on about it to Larry

ROUGH WATER LANDING TESTS of XP3Y-1 off Norfolk, Virginia, prove new design can 'take it' in heavy seas.

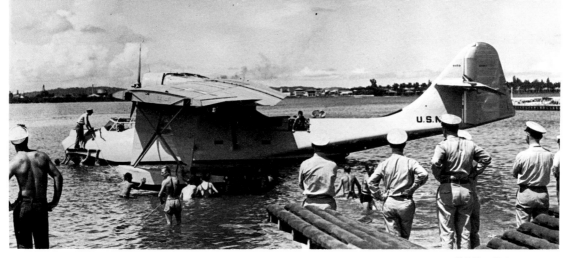

NON-STOP from Norfolk, the XP3Y-1 arrives at Coco Solo, Canal Zone, October 10, 1935.

Bell and me.

"Finally I said, 'Look, Reub, I've had enough of this; not ad infinitum but ad nauseam. Take all of the things you've said, and write 'em down on a piece of paper. Tomorrow we're gonna run up the engine on the PBY and then if it doesn't leak I want to see you eat every God-damn bit of that paper!'

"That shut him up.

"The next day we started the engines and the wing tanks didn't leak a drop. It was the first really gastight wing ever produced; it's used to this day . . . on every transport plane.

"In the 'Fleetster' we had built our tanks of aluminum alloy and mounted them in the leading edge of the wing. They were, therefore, not actually integral. We used to give them a terrific vibration test,

and they'd taken that alright. That's what gave me the courage to use the cavity in the wing of the PBY as the plane's fuel tank."

Instead of building separate fuel cells, Laddon sealed off internal sections of the wing as gasoline reservoirs. The weight saving was calculated as a half-pound per gallon of fuel capacity, adding substantially to the PBY's payload.

The first demonstration of the new airboat's greater range and carrying capacity was another long-distance flight with Lieut. Comdr. Knefler McGinnis, executive officer at Anacostia and skipper of the massed P2Y flights of 1934, again at the controls. Having flown the plane from Norfolk to Coco Solo in the Canal Zone in 17 hours and 33 minutes, McGinnis hoped to fly non-stop from there to Seattle. However, trials with max-

imum fuel load indicated the empennage dipped into the water when the pilot tried to get the plane 'on the step' for takeoff. The rudder was later redesigned and the problem eliminated.

With a slightly lighter load, McGinnis and crew took off in the XP3Y-1 prototype at 6:30 a.m. October 14 and landed 33 hours and 40 minutes later the next afternoon at San Francisco, California, having flown 3443 statute miles non-stop, establishing a new world distance record for seaplanes.

The day after arriving in San Francisco, the XP3Y-1 again took to the air, flying to San Diego to take part in the dedication ceremonies at Consolidated's new plant. The plane then went into the shop for modifications which were to be incorporated in the production PBYs. When it emerged in May 1936 as the XPBY-1, it had more powerful engines and redesigned vertical tail surfaces.

WHEN THE TIME CAME in 1935 to pack up production tooling, machinery, material, work in process and aircraft in various stages of assembly, the magnitude of the task in moving from Buffalo to the new plant in San Diego suddenly struck home.

Then, to top everything off, Consolidated had just won two of its largest contracts—in December 1934 for 50 model P-30 pursuit monoplanes for the Army, followed on June 29, 1935 by its most important order yet, 60 huge PBY flying boats for the Navy.

The moving task was of particular concern to Howard Golem, nephew of Henry Golem. As the company's traffic manager he had a budget estimate of $40,000 to which he attempted to work. One of Golem's first thoughts, when he began planning the move, was to charter an ocean-going freighter to carry everything in a single shipment via the St. Lawrence

TRAVELING TO SAN DIEGO to inspect new plant site; left to right, Gordon Mounce, C. A. Van Dusen, Reuben Fleet, David Fleet.

General Dynamics/Convair

Seaway and Panama Canal. Obviously the time loss could not be tolerated.

"These and other schemes," Golem explained, "were mainly to use as a lever on the railroads to grant us rates we could live with."

Because of his background in construction in Fleet's native Grays Harbor, Washington, the company's vice president, Chuck Leigh, was dispatched to San Diego in April 1935, along with Reuben's just-married 25-year-old son, David. Together they directed early construction of the new plant and handled unloading at the west end of the line. A thousand feet long and 275 feet wide, the new 275,000 square foot plant offered somewhat more area than the Buffalo facility at the peak of the company's use of leased space in the old Curtiss plant.

Actually the shut down of production was very brief. The Buffalo plant kept working until mid-August; the San Diego factory started some operations just a few weeks later, following Labor Day. The contents of the 157 freight cars used were made up in sequence to allow for orderly resumption of work, with the most important production machinery and parts arriving first.

The matter of housing for the three or four hundred employees and their families moving to San Diego was also a major problem. Larry Bell was trying to work out something special with Tom Bomar of the Chamber of Commerce because San Diego's 1935 Exposition, coupled with the summer tourist season, were putting a heavy drain on available rental properties.

"Several hundred families," Bell wrote, "will be driving across the country the last two weeks of August, all arriving there about the same time and without your cooperation we might run into considerable trouble when so many arrive together.

"The earning power of our employees will range from 60 cents per hour upward. The majority will doubtless require unfurnished places. I, personally, will require a three-bedroom furnished house with suitable maid's quarters. I hope to get something for $100 to $150 a month.

"We are enthusiastic about moving and are looking forward to the day we arrive."

For years Reuben Fleet had threatened to leave his leased factory in Buffalo for his own plant in a more temperate climate. Perhaps Buffalo business interests thought he was bluffing. When they found he wasn't they approached Larry Bell with a promise of financing a new company if he would remain and take over part of the plant Consolidated was renting from the American Radiator Co.

After the September 1929 crash in the 'Fleet' trainer in which Lauretta Golem had been killed, Major Fleet announced that he and George Newman were retiring to policy and planning posts and that Bell was taking over as the active operating head, assisted by Ray Whitman as assistant general manager.

Fleet had been fairly successful for nearly five years in staying reasonably clear of day-to-day management responsibility. "Larry," he said, "had been running the company since I cracked up. Even after I got back on my feet, I let him continue to run it."

In June, Larry Bell came to Reuben with a proposition: "What would you think of my resigning from Consolidated and not going with you? I'd like to stay here and capitalize on what you are forced to leave behind."

"Well, Larry," Reuben replied, "looking at it from my standpoint, it would force me back into harness. Looking at it from your standpoint, I think it is your opportunity. So, if you want to do it, it is alright with me.

"But, since this would force me to take up the management reins again, I want something distinctly understood. The organization belongs to me and not to you. I don't want you to make an offer to anybody that I want to take to San Diego."

Reflecting on his deal with Bell, Reuben recalls that "he violated it in one respect only, and that was in regard to Ray Whitman, who had long been my office assistant. Larry painted a nice picture about how Ray would be second in command and what a good opportunity that was. So Whitman stayed, but I think he later regretted it.

Lawrence D. Bell,
who stayed behind.

Textron/Bell Aerospace

"I picked 311 selected employees and brought them out to San Diego, paying their moving expenses. Another hundred, having been promised work when they got there, paid their own way. We left all the bad radicals back there in Buffalo.

VANGUARD FROM BUFFALO. Key executives after arrival in San Diego. Left to right, Ray Madison, Doc Carpenter, Mac Laddon, Roy Miller, Harry Sutton, Ralph Oversmith, Jim Kelley, George Newman, Jr., Chuck Leigh, C. A. Van Dusen, Capt. Leland Hurd, Roy Neff, Bernie Sheahan, Dave Fleet.

General Dynamics/Convair

NEW CONSOLIDATED PLANT, on San Diego's still undeveloped Lindbergh Field. Photo taken November 1935, just a month after dedication of new facility.

"There were some things we couldn't ship to San Diego; our airport at North Tonawanda, for instance. Then there was the matter of electric motors, all of which were 25-cycle. Beside Buffalo, the only other place in the world that I knew of which used 25-cycle was the Panama Canal Zone. Since it wouldn't pay to rewind these motors to 60-cycle, I told Larry I'd sell them to him for $5,000, just where they were. That would give him a plant already furnished with the electric motors that run the machinery. Then I told Bell that we'd promise him a couple of million dollars worth of sub-contract work to help him get started."

Beside Bell and Whitman, another who stayed, but who had not been with the company so long, was Robert J. Woods, designer of the P-30 pursuit plane while at Detroit Aircraft, who had joined the new Bell Aircraft Corp. as chief engineer.

The Buffalo Courier-Express, rejoicing in the announcement about Bell's new company, reported on June 30, that "it was stated unofficially that tremendous local financial backing had been swung to Mr. Bell in starting the new company, and that a large part of the local expert personnel of Consolidated, irked by the commands of Major Fleet to move to the West Coast, would remain with the new organization."

If the absence of Bell, Whitman and Woods was significant, it never became apparent as Consolidated swung into a period of greatly expanded business once it settled in San Diego.

With the move to San Diego, Fleet strengthened his corporate management by appointing three new Vice Presidents: Mac Laddon as Chief Engineer, Chuck

Leigh as Materials Supervisor and C. A. Van Duser for 20 years Glenn L. Martin's production expert, a Works Manager.

ON OCTOBER 20, 1935, San Diego ceased to b "just another Navy town" and a haven for retire folks, and took a giant step toward industrialization a Consolidated's new plant on Lindbergh Field wa dedicated.

Having just set a new world non-stop distanc record for seaplanes, the XP3Y-1 flying boat wit Lieut. Comdr. Knefler McGinnis at the controls wa flown south from San Francisco to serve as center piece for the ceremonies.

In his dedicatory address, Major Fleet pointed ou that, "Twice each year I flew around the country try ing to find a suitable location with a publicly owne waterfront on a good but not congested harbor. And i needed to be in a city large enough to furnish reasonable supply of labor and materials, and course with all-year flying weather. So today mark the culmination of a dream for a factory of our own i a city of our choice.

"Since I founded the company in 1923 we hav manufactured over $23 million of aircraft and part No holding company owns or controls us. We no have $9 million of unfilled orders which will occup the new plant at 80% capacity on a one-shift basis for year and a half. We have 874 employees now, shoul have 2000 within six months and about 3000 ne summer.

REUBEN at the microphone: "Today marks the culmination of a dream . . . "

"Our directors seriously questioned the advisability of moving here because we were in the valley of the world's worst depression. Finally we made up our minds to have faith in the future and to leave Buffalo and our friends of eleven years standing."

Then, looking to the broad future of aviation, Reuben continued, "As a force, air power does not occupy foreign soil to compel observance of edicts; it knows no boundary within its range. Just as the airplane has become man's greatest means of making neighbors of all nations, so will it surely become the instrumentality to guarantee world peace by force until the temperament of mankind changes."

AGAINST HISTORIC background of North Island and Spanish Bight where Glenn H. Curtiss flew first seaplane in 1911, the prototype 'Catalina' flies over Lindbergh Field and new Consolidated plant, lower right.

General Dynamics/Convair

CONSOLIDATED PB-2A (P-30) was first model placed into production after plant was moved to San Diego.

Air Force Museum

MANUFACTURING OPERATIONS in San Diego got under way with assembly of the first of 50 Army pursuit planes. This was the contract for the two-place supercharged pursuits expecially designed for high altitude operation. Most of the parts had been fabricated in Buffalo, greatly simplifying the task of promptly getting into production.

When the first planes left the San Diego plant they bore a new military designation—PB-2A, the PB standing for pursuit, bi-place.

The first of the PB-2As arrived at Wright Field in January 1936, with test flying continuing throughout the Spring. With the latest Prestone-cooled 'Conqueror' engine of 700 h.p. and an improved turbo-

SELFRIDGE FIELD, MICHIGAN, with 27th Pursuit Squadron's PB-2A pursuits on flight line.

Air Force Museum

supercharger, Lieut. Donald Putt reported a top speed of 275 m.p.h. at 25,000 feet and excellent controllability at all speeds. The only major criticism of the airplane was the gunner's rear cockpit position, which offered a very restricted field of fire except when the aircraft was flying straight and level.

In May 1936 the test PB-2A crashed, killing Major Hez McClellan, a close friend of Fleet's from Brooks Field days.

Since the PB-2A set some new standards of performance, it also presented some new challenges to test pilots as explained by Bill Wheatley, Consolidated's chief of flight test. "The problem was that the pilot could not accurately climb the plane at full power and constant speed, and at the same time read and write down all the instrument readings.

"If the pilot was reading instruments, the plane would either level off, or climb too steeply, and if he concentrated on his flying he missed the instrument readings. The instruments were not grouped so that they could be easily photographed, and the plane would climb so fast that if the time and airspeed were read at 6000 feet, by the time the pilot got around to reading the manifold pressure the plane would be at 8000 feet."

In their new pursuit craft, Army pilots set notable records in March 1937. Lieut. W. R. Robertson flew his PB-2A to an altitude of 39,200 over Langley Field and remained at that altitude for 20 minutes. Then his controls froze and he was compelled to throttle back so as to lose altitude and return to a warmer layer of air.

Three PB-2As led by Lieut. Col. Ralph Royce flew from San Diego to Selfridge Field, Michigan in 1 hours 10 minutes flying time, with stops enroute.

ONE OF FOUR pursuit squadrons which flew PB-2As from Langley Field, Virginia, and Selfridge Field, Michigan. Supercharged PB-2A was top performing pursuit of its era.

Four pursuit squadrons were equipped with PB-2A aircraft, the fastest planes then operated by the Air Corps. Three were located at Langley Field, Virginia, under Major General Frank M. Andrews, and one squadron at Selfridge Field, Michigan.

For the first time a turbosupercharged production aircraft had finally entered squadron service in fairly large numbers. The PB-2A's major contribution was that it paved the way for the thousands of high altitude military aircraft which were to follow.

Thus, due in no small measure to the PB-2A and to Major Fleet's determination many years earlier at McCook Field to make a success of the work pioneered by Dr. Sanford Moss, the United States entered World War II as the only power which had an operationally proven turbo-supercharger.

WHILE THE PB-2A was first to go into production in San Diego, the real challenge for Consolidated was to begin work on its largest and most important contract—the $6.5 million order for 60 twin-engine PBY-1 patrol bombers. The Navy had awarded the contract only three months before the new plant was opened.

Then, in July 1936 with completion of the order for the PB-2As, the Navy placed a second order for PBYs, this time for $4.9 million for 50 of the improved PBY-2 model. Meantime the Navy had shown interest in an even longer range flying boat, this one to have four engines. Consolidated had entered a design in the competition and in July 1936 had been declared the winner and awarded a contract for the prototype.

The pressure was on for more factory space. The experimental four-engine XPB2Y-l would have to be built in a separate building for security reasons and to avoid interference with regular manufacturing operations on the PBY twin-engine boats.

Construction of plant additions got under way promptly and by the next year Consolidated had 450,000 square feet under roof, plus 170,000 square feet of paved area which the favorable climate made adaptable to outdoor assembly.

To finance the needed plant additions, directors authorized Consolidated's issuance of 24,000 shares of convertible preferred stock in August 1936. Sale of 22,976 shares at $50 each realized $1,148,800. The remaining block of 1,024 shares was reserved for sale to selected employees.

Success followed success for Consolidated and its PBY patrol bombers. Less than four months after its order for 50 PBY-2s, the Navy awarded another $6.1 million contract, this time for 66 more planes of a still further improved model, the PBY-3 which would have 1000 h.p. Twin Wasp engines.

Two days after the latest order was received, the first San Diego-built patrol bomber, a PBY-1, was mounted on a beaching gear, towed tail-first across Lindbergh Field and launched from the bay where Glenn H. Curtiss had made the first American hydroplane flight 25 years earlier. It was October 5, 1936 when the first PBY-1 was delivered, just two weeks short of a year since dedication of the new San Diego plant.

Yet, behind the scenes there were always service problems with the customer. The earlier P2Y-3 flying boats were a cause of sufficient concern to the Navy that word had filtered up through the system to Rear Admiral Ernest J. King, Chief of the Navy Bureau of Aeronautics. That called for another of Reuben Fleet's hardsell, yet very sincere and convincing letters:

20 February 1936

My dear Admiral King: -

Our discovery from yours of 8 February that

185

you are wondering if the Navy has misplaced its confidence in relying upon us, causes us much concern.

Confidence cannot be forced—it must be earned. Our business lives on it. We would not lose it. Nothing equals a flier's confidence unless it be his distrust.

No misfortune is greater than the loss of confidence, of that moral credit which honest people give one another. We want our written and spoken word to circulate like authentic currency for we are not a hit-and-run outfit. Our aim in selling service is to win, enjoy and never lose the complete confidence of our customers.

Despite the fact that, unfortunately, we have worked eight years for nothing for the Navy and have in addition paid for this privilege, we value our Navy's complete confidence so highly that every reasonable effort on our part seems warranted to hold it. Accordingly we are forwarding our official response today through the Inspector of Naval Aircraft.

Fleet then went on to describe in detail the work Consolidated would do without charge to make requested corrections to the P2Y-1 and P2Y-3 flying boats already in service. Commenting on the task ahead on PBY-1s recently ordered, and on the losses the company had already taken on previous orders, Fleet concluded:

We are not minimizing our tremendous task in manufacturing PBY-1's, which take cognizance of all complaints and in which we are incorporating desirable changes at the cost of time and money. We are making real progress.

On the 49 flying boats we have built for the Navy our audited books show a total net loss of $89,673.93, with sufficient profit on the 16 built for others to enable us to keep going. We have hoped that we have earned a real asset in our Navy's confidence, since our boats have helped our Navy to lead the world in aviation and all are still flying with no deaths chalked against them.

Soon after that Fleet ran into Admiral King in Washington and later related how "He walked with me from the Bureau of Aeronautics clear to the front of the building with his arm around me all the while telling me that if everybody in the whole industry took one side and I took the other, he'd take my word against the bunch."

With delivery of the first PBY flying boats Consolidated began to emerge from the low sales volume,

miniscule profits and frequent net losses of the Depression years.

Through sound business practices, modest profits were reported in 1935 and 1936, the first years in San Diego. By the end of 1936, the 176 PBYs ordered by the Navy had swollen the backlog of undelivered contracts to $18 million. Employment had grown from 900 workers in 1935 to 3700 the following year.

Consolidated, for the first time, became really 'big business' in 1937 and began attracting national and international attention as a large, expanding industrial corporation.

On the New York Curb Exchange, Consolidated stock rose from a 1933 Depression low of 6 to a new high of 33-½ in March 1937. At the end of May the company's shares were listed on the 'big board,' the New York Stock Exchange. After nine years as a listed stock, Consolidated paid its first common stock cash dividend—50 cents per share—at the end of 1937.

More PBY contracts rolled in, this time for 33 of the PBY-4 type, ordered December 8, 1937, adding another $4.5 million to the backlog.

Reuben Fleet was in his glory, riding high. The only cloud on the horizon was labor trouble. Still he had suffered a severe personal blow earlier in the year.

THREE GENERATIONS of trap shooters: the ramrod-straight Fleets, 'Daddy,' son Reuben, grandson David.

David G.

His distinguished father, Aberdeen, Washington's beloved pioneer, 'Daddy' Fleet, was in declining health. Word reached Reuben while on a business trip to New York that his 86-year-old father had passed away February 23, 1937. He took the next plane for Seattle to be with his Mother and old friends at memorial services for the man his contemporaries described as "a pattern of the Southern Gentlemen' who always carried with him that distinct form of politeness which identifies them wherever they are met." (Reuben's mother died two years after 'Daddy' Fleet's passing.)

From 'Daddy' Fleet, Reuben no doubt acquired the courtly manner which so ingratiated him to the ladies but occasionally infuriated men of lesser breeding who considered such deportment pompous.

THE LONG LEGS of American survelliance and patrol capability in the Pacific began to be demonstrated dramatically—partially for the benefit of the Japanese—as mass delivery flights of Consolidated PBYs to their base stations in Hawaii, the Canal Zone and Alaska became routine.

In preparation for deployment of operational squadrons, the Navy began a training program out of the Naval Air Station, North Island, across San Diego Bay from the Consolidated factory.

The first class consisted of seven officers and 24 enlisted men under Lieut. Comdr. William M. McDade. The group, composed of experienced big boat pilots and mechanics from patrol squadron VP-6, based at Pearl Harbor, divided their time between the Consolidated plant and North Island. Soon personnel from other units of the far-ranging Navy scouting force were in the training cycle.

The first of many 'routine transfers of men and equipment' got under way January 28, 1937 when twelve new PBY-1s, with 80 officers and men, left San Diego for Pearl Harbor. Consolidated's chief pilot, Bill Wheatley, was aboard one of the patrol bombers and reported on the flight.

"There was little wind on San Diego Bay so that the several planes taking off toward the northwest did so with some difficulty because of the smooth water and heavy load. The remaining planes took off toward the southeast without trouble.

"About an hour was used in climbing to 10,000 feet and getting into formation for newsreel pictures. Finally all planes were in formation and not until then did we pass over the Coronado Strand and depart the area on our westerly course.

"For the first three or four hours we bucked a 40-knot headwind. I marvelled at the clarity and confidence Lieut. Harvey displayed in computing our position after making an observation. Neither he nor his radioman left their posts during the entire flight. One of the mechanics acted as mess boy; coffee, bacon and eggs were prepared on the electric hotplate.

"All hands were fitted out in fur boots and flying suits but we all suffered keenly from the cold. It was just above freezing most of the time, both inside and outside the plane.

"About half-way across we began to pick up a slight tail wind. During darkness it was colder and pitch black until the moon came up. It was beautiful above

GETTING INTO FORMATION off San Diego, a squadron of Consolidated PBYs head west on the long overnight flight to Hawaii.

General Dynamics/Convair

the clouds as we passed over the Navy ships spotted along our route.

"Three hundred miles from the Hawaiian Islands we flew through some clouds and rough air. About an hour before reaching Pearl Harbor we all reduced power and got into closer formation.

"Twenty-one hours and 48 minutes out of San Diego, the lead plane with a tired, bewhiskered but happy Comdr. McDade at the controls landed off the Naval Air Station. When he beached, the next plane landed, and so on until all had completed the 2553-mile mass flight.

"Navy personnel really know their business when it comes to navigation. On this flight we found that in order to be practical for long over-water flights an airplane should be at least as large as the PBY so that the pilot, navigator, radioman and flight engineer can work in comfort, and so that the relief crew can get proper rest while not on duty. As the range of our flying boats continues to be increased, comfort for off

duty personnel will be even more important.

"The automatic pilot holds the plane so much steadier than the human pilot can, that navigation is better and blind flight is safer. And lastly, even between mild San Diego and milder Pearl Harbor it is so damn cold at 10,000 feet that a heating system should be given serious and favorable consideration!"

As more PBY-1s came off the production lines Navy squadrons began to take delivery of their new aircraft and head for operational bases. Actually, the first PBYs went to VP-11, which had been formed in July 1936.

Transfer of the personnel and 12 planes of Patrol Squadron 11 to Pearl Harbor was accomplished April 12-13. In contrast to the take-off of VP-6's planes several months earlier, VP-11, commanded by Lieut. Comdr. L. A. Pope, needed only 35 minutes from the time the first plane left the ramp at North Island until all 12 PBYs had taken off from San Diego Bay and headed out to sea. After an uneventful flight, the

U. S. Navy/National Archives

NINE PBYs of Patrol Squadron 9 formed one unit of two-section 18-plane mass delivery flight to Pearl Harbor in January 1938.

planes began to land at Pearl Harbor 21 hours and 21 minutes out of San Diego, It was, the Navy said, another routine transfer of men and planes.

The 'routine' transfers did indeed become routine.

Two squadrons of 12 planes each had already flown their new patrol bombers to Pearl Harbor, Hawaii. The next two PBY delivery flights from San Diego would be to the Canal Zone.

June 21, twelve PBY-1s, under command of Lieut. Robert W. Morse, set a new record of 27 hours, 58 minutes for the longest mass formation flight, 3087 miles over Mexico and the wilds of Central America to Coco Solo. The squadron ran into thick thunderheads shortly before midnight and flew by instruments until off the east coast of Nicaragua where skies remained clear until landing at sunset at Coco Solo.

On December 8, 1937 another mass flight was made from San Diego to the Canal Zone, this time with 14 PBY-2s, under Lieut. Comdr. B. E. Grow, in the formation. Establishing a new record, the 14 ships took

off in 19 minutes. Flight time was cut to 22 hours, 20 minutes for the three thousand mile flight.

Six weeks later, January 18, 1938, a formation of 18 PBYs flew from San Diego to Pearl Harbor, Hawaii in 20 hours, 30 minutes. Lieut. Comdrs. Spencer H. Warner and W. G. Tomlinson, the latter pilot of the prototype XPY-1 'Admiral' nine years earlier, were in command of the two sections.

Fourteen flying boats were delivered to the Canal Zone September 2, 1938 and 17 to Pearl Harbor six days later. This time Patrol Squadron No. 4 under Lieut. Comdr. Aaron P. Storrs, III set a new San Diego-Honolulu record of 17 hours, 17 minutes.

Largest of the mass flights came January 10, 1939 when Patrol Wing One, comprising four squadrons—VP-7, -9, -11 and -12—and 336 men under

189

command of Capt. Marc A. Mitcher left San Diego for the Canal Zone. Twenty-five hours later, 45 planes began landing at Coco Solo, to be joined by three others which stopped enroute for refueling.

Twelve days after landing in the Canal Zone, the 48 PBYs of Patrol Wing One flew on to San Juan, Puerto Rico for fleet exercises. After completing that mission the Wing proceeded non-stop from Puerto Rico to Norfolk, Virginia to participate in a joint air exercise off the New England coast.

Two of the PBY squadrons remained on the east coast, the other two returning to San Diego via Guantanamo Bay, Cuba and the Canal Zone.

Having compiled an enviable record in fleet exercises, and with the delivery of 45 additional patrol bombers in three mass delivery flights to Hawaii, the Navy appeared well prepared for coming hostilities in the Pacific.

LANDFALL IN HAWAII greets two PBYs after 20-hour flight from west coast of United States.

BEHIND THE SAGA of the first PBY-type flying boats to be privately owned and operated lay the driving scientific interest of Dr. Richard Archbold, research associate of the American Museum of Natural History.

Scion of a Standard Oil executive, young Archbold had led an expedition to New Guinea in 1933 to observe birds, beasts and stone-age man in an environment which for thousands of years had been undisturbed by white man.

When Archbold found his studies hampered by difficulties in transporting food and supplies, "he turned to the airplane as a solution," wrote Museum Director and famed explorer Dr. Roy Chapman Andrews.

Returning to New Guinea in 1936 with a single-engine Fairchild amphibian which he had learned to fly, Archbold and his pilot, Russell R. Rogers, soon demonstrated the great advantages the airplane provided in that remote and primitive land. Unfortunately the plane 'Kono' was finally lost in a sudden 'guba' windstorm.

Determined to expand the scope of his work, Archbold was attracted by the capability of the new and by then highly publicized Navy patrol bombers to carry larger loads and increase his range of exploration. Special permission was granted by the Navy for the sale to a private individual of a PBY-1 especially equipped for all-weather flying but without armament. Consolidated accepted Archbold's order for a commercial Model 28-1 seaplane January 27, 1937. The Navy stipulated that the plane could not leave the United States until November 1, one year after the first PBY-1 had been delivered.

Christened 'Guba,' Archbold and Rogers, under Bill Wheatley's tutelage, flew their new PBY-1 to fresh water demonstration landings and takeoffs at Boulder Dam (Lake Mead) on June 18 and June 20 to Lake Tahoe, the latter being used to simulate the kind of high-altitude operations required in the interior of New Guinea.

As a further demonstration of the 'Guba's' capability, Archbold, Rogers, Wheatley and a crew of three technicians left San Diego Bay June 24, 1937 on the first coast-to-coast nonstop flight by flying boat, landing at New York 17 hours 3 minutes later. Although two professional pilots were aboard, Archbold, holder of only a private pilot's license, made the landing off North Beach Airport in Queens.

The flight had been 2700 miles, yet sufficient fuel was left aboard the world's largest privately-owned airplane to have flown on to Bermuda and back to New York.

Archbold planned to depart in November for New Guinea, but his plans were altered so the 'Guba' could be used on a mercy mission.

Sigismund Levanevsky, the Lindbergh of Russia

*PROUD MOTHERS; dis-
tinguished* sons. *Left to right:
Mrs. John F. Archbold; her
son, Dick; Major Fleet; his
mother, Mrs. David Wacker
Fleet.*

'GUBA' tries out her wings in fresh water landings and takeoffs at Lake
Mead, *above, and in first flight from San Diego Bay,* below.

and his crew of five, on a 4000-mile transpolar flight in a four-engine amphibian to Fairbanks, Alaska, had been reported missing August 13, shortly after crossing the North Pole. Major Fleet, with whom Russia had already negotiated a contract for three planes and license rights, was contacted. Would he see if Archbold would sell the 'Guba' to the Russian government? As before, the inquiry came through Amtorg, the Russian trading company in New York, and the sale was consummated with approval of the U.S. Navy.

To head the rescue operation the Russian government engaged Sir George Hubert Wilkins, Australian polar explorer and aviator. August 19, Russ Rogers accompanied the 'Guba' and veteran Canadian pilot Herbert Hollick-Kenyon, to Coppermine, base headquarters above the Arctic Circle in the Northwest Territories of Canada.

The rescue effort eventually had to be called off as the available landing areas began to be frozen over, but Sir Hubert wrote Major Fleet that in a little over a month "we covered over 19,000 miles of intensive flying . . . in this magnificent airplane . . . under the most adverse weather conditions, flying over rough and uncharted terrain and, for the most part, heavily loaded with fuel, supplies and equipment." The former 'Guba' bore the Russian designation L-2 and on the hull the initials URSS (Union Republic Socialist Soviet). When returned to New York it was disassembled and shipped by steamer to Russia.

Archbold's plans were only temporarily interrupted.

BEARDED EXPLORER Sir George Hubert Wilkins tells Reuben Fleet details of his Arctic rescue effort in former 'Guba' flying boat.

As soon as the Russians had purchased his plane, a near duplicate of the 'Guba' was ordered.

Taking delivery of his second Consolidated flying boat, a PBY-2 type designated model 28-3, Archbold, Rogers and Wheatley, on December 3, 1937, flew 'Guba II' on a non-stop shake-down flight from San Diego to Miami in 14 hours, ten minutes. In March a similar flight was made, San Diego-Miami and on to St. Thomas in the Virgin Islands. Meantime Lewis A. Yancey had signed on as expedition navigator.

By June, 1938 'Guba II' was ready to head off across the broad Pacific to New Guinea, as described by Archbold:

"When the 'Guba' lifted from the waters of San Diego Bay on June 2, we were on our way to New Guinea, over 6000 miles across the Pacific. We knew the 'Guba' would be traveling air trails never flown before. But we didn't know that before she settled down on San Diego Bay again, she would have made a complete circuit of the globe the longest way around. That flight was incidental to our third expedition to New Guinea to collect mammals, birds and plants. The 'Guba's' principal function was to transport men and supplies to the camps in the interior.

"As the success of the expedition and the lives of its members depended in many ways upon our plane, we put the 'Guba,' her equipment and ourselves through rigorous test flights. From November 22, 1937, to May 28, 1938, we made fifty-three test flights.

"The most interesting test was the one to determine how much the 'Guba' could lift on a high altitude takeoff. We had to know that because one of our main inland camps in New Guinea was to be Lake Habbema, 11,500 feet above sea level and about 200 miles from Hollandia, our coastal base.

"For that purpose we went to Lake Tahoe in California, 6000 feet high. After determining the power drawn from the engines at 12,000 feet over the lake, we made takeoffs using power not exceeding that available at the higher altitude, building up loads until the ship was barely able to rise from the water. We found she could get up with a gross weight of 23,700 pounds. When we finally took off from Lake Habbema we found we were able to carry 1800 pounds more than that.

"With our engines overhauled and new ones shipped to Hollandia, we were ready on June 2nd for the trans-Pacific flight. The flight crew included Russell Rogers, co-pilot, and Lewis Yancey, navigator.

"About 170 miles from Honolulu, we spoke for the first time with P06ZA, our own radio station in Hollandia, which reported that all was well and that the ramp for the 'Guba' would be ready on our arrival.

"We landed at Pearl Harbor an hour after daylight—18 hours and 3 minutes after leaving San Diego, which, at that time was considered something of a record.

"After an overnight stop at Wake Island, we landed at Hollandia just after sunrise of June 10. When the expedition personnel was complete we numbered nearly 200 men, including scientists, soldiers and native carriers.

"The 'Guba' enabled us to do in ten minutes work which could not have been done in two years had we used the available means of land transportation. Many of the supply flights were from Hollandia to Lake Habbema, 11,500 feet above sea level near Mt. Wilhelmina in the mountainous interior of Netherland New Guinea, 200 miles from the coast.

"We made 168 flights in and around New Guinea from June 15, 1938, to May 10, 1939, carrying 568,000 pounds of food and equipment over jungle impassable on foot. In addition to the biological specimens we brought home we had discovered a 'new' tribe of 60,000 natives in an unexplored valley of the Balim River.

"Side trips were made west to Makassar on the Island of Celebes and another south to Sydney and Melbourne, Australia. On the latter trip the governments of Australia and Great Britain asked if we would survey a new aerial route across the Indian Ocean from the west coast of Australia to Kenya, Africa, via the little-known Cosos Islands, Diego Garcia and the Seychelles.

"It would, they said, 'provide a valuable alternate route to the existing one between England and Australia by way of Singapore and Java should war break out.'"

With new engines installed, the 'Guba' left Hollandia May 12 for Sydney where final preparations were made for the return flight, with sufficient provision for stops in the Indian Ocean to make aerial and land surveys for the possible establishment of air travel bases along the route.

Capt. P. G. Taylor, an Australian colleague of Sir Charles Kingsford-Smith, joined the crew for the flight along the 'Reserve Empire Air Route' to Kenya.

Archbold resumed:

'GUBA' on 11,500-foot high Lake Habbema in interior of Dutch New Guinea. Ninety-seven expedition members including soldiers, bearers and flight crew pose atop 104-foot wing.

General Dynamics/Convair

"We left Sydney June 3rd and flew 2600 miles non-stop across Australia.

"Then six hours after leaving Port Hedland, Western Australia, on June 7 we landed at Direction Island. The longest stage of the Indian Ocean flight was between there and Diego Garcia in the Chagos Archipelago. Our arrival at Mombasa, Kenya, on June 21 created considerable interest throughout the East African territories.

"We crossed Africa to Dakar with stops at Lake Victoria, on the Congo River and at Lagos, Nigeria. We made the 3190 statute miles across the South Atlantic from Dakar to St. Thomas in the Virgin Islands in 19 hours, 33 minutes. After a stop at the World's Fair in New York, the 'Guba' again settled on San Diego Bay July 6, 1939, after 13 months of flying and having made the first round-the-world flight by a seaplane."

Among many other firsts, all incidental to the main purpose of the expedition, 'Guba' had been the first airplane to fly around the world at its greatest diameter and first to fly across the Indian Ocean from Australia to Africa.

It was a memorable record of performance by the aircraft and by Dick Archbold, Russ Rogers and their crew. Nor had 'Guba's' capability been lost on the British. World War II was brewing in Europe and the British Purchasing Commission had placed an order for a PBY so that they might run an evaluation of its capability. Rogers, Yancey and crew, home in San Diego just four days from the 'Guba's' New Guinea expedition, turned around and headed east, this time on a delivery flight of the first British PBY over the North Atlantic to England. Later the British also purchased 'Guba II,' registered it as G-AGBJ and turned it over to British Overseas Airways for three years, flying a wartime shuttle run in Africa.

'GUBA' CREW on departure from San Diego. At microphone, pilot Russ Rogers. On his right, navigator Lewis Yancey. At Rogers' left is expedition leader Dick Archbold.

THE WHITE HOUSE TELEPHONE operator was pursuing Reuben Fleet just as his plane landed in San Diego after one of his frequent trips to Washington. President Roosevelt wanted to see him immediately.

"I never even had time to shave," Fleet recalls, "before returning to Washington. The President wanted me to help the Russians establish a factory on the Black Sea to manufacture our PBYs, charging them nothing for the design rights.

"Final arrangements were made with Henry Morgenthau, Jr., Secretary of the Treasury. We were to help the Russians get started at a factory they had built at Taganrog. We gave them a license for overseas production and technical support by 18 people we sent abroad."

Obviously the Russians were impressed with what they had been able to learn about the performance of the PBY flying boats, including 'Guba I' which had been used in the vain effort to rescue the lost Polar fliers. Through Amtorg, their purchasing agency, the Russians ordered three Model 28-2 cargo-mail boats similar to the PBY-1 on February 28, 1937.

"After test flights at San Diego," Fleet explained, "the first plane was readied for shipment but, as with Dick Archbold's 'Guba,' the Russian PBY could not be delivered before November 1. The other two boats were shipped unassembled so they could be used for training in assembly operations after their delivery to Russia. Three Russian engineers spent several months with us in San Diego.

"The contract provided that the Russians would withhold $50,000 until the first Russian PBY flew to their satisfaction. Nearly two years later I was quite surprised to receive the check for $50,000 with a letter saying they had been flying to their satisfaction for some months. However, they reported the Wright Cyclone engines they were building under license over-cooled in that climate. They asked if we had any suggestions.

"We sent them drawings showing how to mount the cowls closer to the Russian-built M-62 engines so as to let in the less-cool air and hold in the heated air. That did the trick.

"The only sour note in the Russian PBY transaction had to do with two employees we sent abroad. They had solicited the job but when they got to Moscow, 600 miles short of their destination, they wired that conditions at Taganrog were impossible and asked for money to return home.

"Of course they hadn't been in Taganrog so we assured them that conditions there were satisfactory; that Garner Green, head of our Russian group, was already there with his wife and two months old baby and to proceed to their assignment.

"They came on home anyway after their one-way joy ride to Moscow, as we didn't send them the return fare. We sued for breach of contract which had provided them a 50 percent increase in salary plus expenses. One man went through bankruptcy; the other had to pay the company a $1900 judgment for travel expenses and cash advanced to him. The judge would not let him testify regarding rumored conditions about which he had learned only through hearsay."

When the Taganrog plant got into production, some 150 flying boats designated GST were built by the U.S.S.R. for Navy use before the invading German Army captured the area in 1941.

As WITH THE 'COMMODORE' flying boats of nearly a decade earlier, Reuben Fleet and his sales people began to tout the potential of PBYs in commercial airline operation.

The Navy had shown what the PBY could do on long over-water hops and Dick Archbold had made the first of five transcontinental over-land flights. Consolidated executives were quick to point out that some of the largest cities had developed on the coasts, inland lakes or adjacent to major rivers and that fine harbors were located close to city centers.

Carrying their argument further they found that it was hard to pick a route across the country which did not have as many potential 'seaports' as airports. The distance between suitable water ports was found to average somewhere between 60 and 100 miles. Too, providing beaching facilities for seaplanes on existing lakes would cost much less than to build airports for landplanes.

The real potential, however, seemed to lie in providing commercial seaplanes for transoceanic ser-

General Dynamics/Convair

RUSSIAN PBY-1 bore commercial designation Model 28-2; was test flown in San Diego before shipment overseas.

vice to Europe and to the Orient. Reuben Fleet put his people to work studying the size and configuration of future long-range seaplanes.

Not unlike the early days of the New York, Rio and Buenos Aires Line in pioneering flights to South America with Consolidated flying boats, Pan American Airways was again the major point of contention. With its 'chosen instrument' concept accepted by the government, PAA had a near monopoly on American-operated foreign airline routes.

Even now PAA was conducting Clipper survey flights for new overwater routes across both the Atlantic and Pacific. Looking beyond its Martin and Sikorsky four-engine flying boats, Pan American had ordered six giant Boeing 314 Clippers. It would be difficult to overcome their lead.

One way of possibly breaking PAA's strangle hold was to encourage a broadening of the charter of the Merchant Marine to encompass overwater air transport as well as ship service.

Mac Laddon went east to appear before the House Merchant Marine Committee in December 1937. "American Export Steamship Company," he testified, "is interested in running a transocean airline.

"In this country we need legislation to extend ship subsidies to overocean air transport. Pan American has a monopoly on transoceanic air transport and the proposals of the Post Office Department for carrying airmail over the ocean have been designed so Pan American alone can qualify."

Even as Mac Laddon was testifying in Washington, Reuben Fleet in San Diego was explaining what Consolidated envisioned for the future.

"As soon as larger engines are available we will be able to build a three-deck seaplane capable of carrying one hundred passengers and a ton of mail 190 miles an

AMERICAN EXPORT AIRLINES used Model 28-4 (PBY-4) flying boat on trans-Atlantic commercial airline route survey flights.

hour across the Atlantic. On our own initiative, and without any definite promise of business accruing as a result of experimental work, we have already invested $150,000 in the design of a new seaplane. It will weigh 50 tons, cross the Atlantic in 12 hours and be capable of carrying 50 passengers on trips up to 5000 miles.''

Whether in response to the charges by Laddon or by pure coincidence, Pan American, on December 9, really shook the aircraft industry. Invitations went out to Consolidated and seven other manufacturers to submit plans for long-range ocean service aircraft with ''stateroom accommodations for at least 100 passengers . . . capable of flying 5000 miles at cruising speeds not less than 200 miles an hour.''

American Export Lines, operators of steamship service between the east coast and ports in the Mediterranean and Black Seas, was quick to follow up on its plan to compete with Pan American. In February 1938 it organized American Export Airlines to go after the potentially lucrative transatlantic business. In September an order was placed for a Model 28-4 PBY-4 type flying boat capable of cruising 4000 miles with a crew of six and payload of 2000 pounds. It would be used to survey overseas commercial routes.

After a shakedown flight to Lake Mead on March 3, 1939 the plane was flown to Galveston, Texas and on to New York. There, on June 20, the PBY was fittingly christened 'TransAtlantic' by Mrs. Anne Towers, wife of Rear Admiral John H. Towers, Chief of the Navy Bureau of Aeronautics, who 20 years earlier had commanded the NC flying boats in the Navy's first transatlantic crossing.

During the next six weeks the American Export Airlines flying boat flew 25,000 miles in surveying air service routes between New York, the Azores, Portugal and France. In addition, the Newfoundland-Ireland-France route was flown in both directions.

No more PBYs were purchased by American Export. When the airline began regular service in 1942, four Sikorsky VS-44 four-engine seaplanes were assigned. By that time, Consolidated was completely committed to PBY and landplane bomber production for the war effort.

Consolidated used its Model 28 'dash' designation to identify these commercial sales of PBY flying boats—

28-1	1 PBY-1 type	'Guba' (eventually to Russia)
28-2	3 PBY-1 type	Russia
28-3	1 PBY-2 type	'Guba II'
28-4	1 PBY-4 type	American Export Airlines

One more commercial delivery had been made, in July 1939, this one to the British Air Ministry which had ordered one of the twin-engine patrol bombers for evaluation by the Marine Aircraft Experimental Establishment at Felixstowe (Ipswich), England.

Basically a PBY-4, it was designated Model 28-5 and carried Royal Air Force insignia and British identification NP9630. Russ Rogers, who had just returned with the second 'Guba' from Australia to San Diego via the South Atlantic, headed the crew which a few days later flew the RAF 28-5 from California via Botwood, Newfoundland to Felixstowe. It was the first North Atlantic ferry flight of an essentially military, but unarmed aircraft to Europe. P9630 was lost in wartime service 10 February 1940.

FIRST BRITISH PBY was a Model 28-5 flown by Russ Rogers in first North Atlantic ferry flight to England. P9630 was lost early in the war.

General Dynamics/Convair

FORTY-TWO PBYs had been delivered to Pearl Harbor by Spring 1938. They were to play a major role in a Pacific War Games problem—Defense of the Hawaiian Islands.

"The Navy," Major Fleet recalls, "had invited Mac Laddon and me to attend the official critique of Fleet Problem XIX and in April we went to Honolulu with our wives on the S. S. Lurline.

"On our arrival we were startled to learn that during the maneuvers ten PBYs in a squadron of 11 planes had their hulls caved in when taking off in rough seas from French Frigate Shoals, some 600 miles west of Pearl Harbor.

"After all the testing which had been done, neither Laddon or I ever dreamed that the spanking they took from the waves on take off in the open ocean would rock them back on their tails beyond the rear 'step' and bash in the aft end of the hull. But here was the evidence when they pulled into Pearl Harbor. Ten of the planes had their bottoms caved in at the aft end. Of course, the watertight compartments provided buoyancy and they landed and taxied in alright at base.

"That experience necessitated making the hulls 25 percent heavier with additional frames. We agreed to give the Navy the new parts and they agreed to install them on all the PBYs we had produced. The change was made at a cost of only 17 pounds additional weight. It was one of the most eye-opening things that ever happened to me—and one of the best because the strengthened hull was largely responsible for the fine record the PBY had during the war in landing on the open ocean to accomplish almost unbelievable rescue missions in the South Pacific."

Fleet paused for a moment, obviously gathering his thoughts before continuing on another tack.

"The Hawaiian defense force in the war games, the Blue Force, was commanded by Lieut. Gen. Hugh A. Drum of the Army to whom Admiral Ernest J. King was assigned. Drum told King that he wanted the Hawaiian Islands patrolled continuously day and night by the 'eyes of the fleet' at a radius five hundred miles from Pearl Harbor.

"Admiral King suggested that a 360 degree patrol was unnecessary as he knew from which 90 degree sector the Red Forces would attack.

" 'You might know that Admiral' Drum replied, 'but I don't, and I'm responsible for the Blue Force. I don't want to be caught napping. Don't ever count on what the enemy will do. Can't you patrol the full 360 degrees around these Islands all during the maneuvers?'

" 'Yes, we can do that with our fleet of 42 PBYs.'

" 'Well, that's what I want you to do.'

" 'You know, of course, the airplanes will not be in sight of each other if we patrol that far out!'

" 'Don't they carry radio—and radar!'

" 'Yes.'

" 'Well, is it necessary for them to be in sight of each other!'

" 'No. Not really.'

" 'Then here's what I want you to do. Take a radius of 500 miles from Honolulu and have a constant patrol around the Islands, 360 degrees.'

"The War Games were conducted accordingly. The enemy Red Force was detected and the simulated attack was made without severe 'damage' to Pearl Harbor and the Blue Force."

With the purchase of PBYs to scout and patrol the Hawaiian Islands area and the realistic Pacific War Games in mid-1938 simulating an enemy threat, the Army and Navy appear to have anticipated, and been prepared for, by 3½ years, the attack on Pearl Harbor.

ENTERING THE RANKS of large industrial corporations in 1937, Consolidated Aircraft had sales of $12 million that year and a similar volume in 1938. Then, in 1939, volume dropped to only $3.6 million. Two hundred PBYs had been delivered but no new orders for the famed twin-engine patrol bombers were then on the horizon. Employment dropped from 3700 to 1200 workers in late 1938. Was the company in financial trouble?

Not at all, explained Major Fleet in his Annual Report to Stockholders. "Deliveries were relatively low because of the large amount of new aircraft design and development, together with the start of production work on airplanes for delivery during 1940 and 1941." Fleet was able to write with unusual conviction because he had three new type aircraft under development and had just signed a $20 million Navy contract, believed to be the largest yet awarded.

"Ten of the planes had their bottoms caved in . . . "

While attention seemed to center on production of flying boats, it was the concentrated engineering activity which was to pay off for Consolidated and for the government when the world went to war in 1939.

Just as a great deal of significant activity had been packed into the year 1929, so too, a decade later, Reuben Fleet found his company involved in a variety of key projects—a four-engine patrol bomber, a radical wing design proved out on a new company-developed twin-engine flying boat, and the design of the B-24 Liberator bomber, destined to become a dominant factor in the air war. All were going on at the same time like a three-ring circus.

In these developments, Reuben Fleet invariably had a personal, often decisive role.

SINGLE-TAIL XPB2Y-1 is readied for first flight as onlookers marvel at size of huge four-engine flying boat.

William Wagner

JUST AS THE NAVY had been able to extend the operating range of its scouting and patrol capability when shifting from the Consolidated P2Y-3 'Ranger' type flying boats to the more advanced PBY 'Catalina' series, it saw a similar potential in an even larger, four-engine aircraft.

Planning was far enough along in 1936 for the Bureau of Aeronautics to award a contract on May 27 to Consolidated as winner of the design competition. The Model 29, identified by the Navy as XPB2Y-1, would be a far larger, more refined patrol bomber capable of carrying twice the load of the PBY. For production orders it would compete with a similar plane designed by Sikorsky.

Of all-metal construction, it featured a deep hull and retractable wing tip floats as in the PBY. A six-ton bomb load could be carried internally in the 115-foot wing. Power would be supplied by four 1050 h.p. 'Twin Wasp' engines streamlined into the wing leading edge.

Separated in the factory from PBY production line work, the four-engine boat was being assembled even as Consolidated and Navy engineers worked together in an effort to reconcile differences in design philosophy and detail. Navy funding for the prototype came to $600,000. Consolidated put up $400,000 of company funds.

Exactly 34 years to the day after the Wright Brothers made man's first flight, Bill Wheatley and George Newman, Jr. took the four-engine patrol plane aloft from San Diego Bay December 17, 1937 on its initial trials. Later that day the 100th PBY was delivered to the Navy. As the huge boat left the water, a factory whistle was blown and 3000 workmen poured out of the plant building to see their new plane in flight. An hour and 20 minutes later Wheatley landed but was by no means satisfied with the plane's flight characteristics. The flight test report listed 'directional peculiarities.'

It was a month before the prototype was again in the air. This time Mac Laddon accompanied Wheatley and Newman on another flight of an hour and 20 minutes.

The report this time listed 'directional peculiarities more prominent.'

Next day, January 18, 1938, Harry Sutton, assistant chief engineer, took Mac Laddon's place. The purpose of the hour and a half flight was to decide what should be done about 'directional instability.' With its single vertical fin and rudder, the plane was sadly lacking in lateral stability.

Wheatley's apprehension continued to grow.

The engineers came up with a 'fix.' Fifty square feet of vertical fin area was added by installing two elliptical fins on the horizontal stabilizer about halfway to the tips.

For forty days the XPB2Y-1 was beached to install the tail modification. That helped the directional stability problem some, but not enough. Flight testing continued but Bill Wheatley was at wit's end—and frightened. His last test flight had been really hairy. He wanted to see Reuben Fleet—and right now!

"Wheatley came into the office," Reuben recalls, "and was trembling all over. He virtually collapsed in front of my desk. He said that if he hadn't been able to get power on when he did he would have had to bail out of the new ship because of a spin it had gotten into.

"I jumped up and ran around to his side of the desk and sat him down in a chair. Then we talked it over quietly together. 'Bill,' I said, 'we've got to go up together and figure this thing out. When we get squared away at altitude I'll do the flying. Then you put it into attitudes where the tail surface can't control it with power off. If I get in trouble, you take the ship out if I can't.'

"So Bill and I got into the cockpit of the new flying boat, buckled on our parachutes and off we went.

"I flew the XPB2Y-1 for four hours and six minutes that day. It just didn't have the proper tail surfaces to handle lateral stability under reduced power. On several occasions I would have had to bail out if we hadn't been able to get power when we needed it. I simply couldn't pull the ship out of a spin without power. I came down knowing full well that if you didn't put power on you didn't have control. You'd spin in. Now that's a fatal error. No company can affort to have a thing like that because a ship must be controllable at all times with or without power."

As Fleet talked it was clear that his own piloting experience pointed the way to a clear management decision.

"I got hold of Mac Laddon who was in Washington at the time," Reuben continued, "and asked him what he had in mind; what his next move was to solve the problem. I reminded him we had a whole factory of people waiting for direction. We couldn't have that.

"Mac said he too was at his wit's end for what to do. 'If you don't have a solution for this, Mac, you'd better stay there,' I told him. 'You're on an important assign-nent and need to finish it. I'll take charge of this.'

" 'Do you think you can fix it,' he asked.

" 'Well, we've got to fix it. Of course I think I can!'

" 'More power to you.' "

"I sketched out a 'raised tail with dual fins and rudders to get the vertical surfaces in better air directly back of the inboard engines and put 7½ degrees dihedral into the horizontal stabilizer. Also I put two-thirds of the rudder on top of the stabilizer. And, by putting in the dihedral, the lower part of the rudders would never get down into the water if the plane rocked far back on the hull during takeoff.

"In Laddon's absence I called in Harry Sutton, assistant chief engineer; Bernie Sheahan, chief draftsman; Pete Larson, the project engineer and Roy Miller, chief of structures. They had instructions on what to do, including using Friese balances which avoided overhang that would induce torsion if one edge of the control surfaces stuck out.

" 'Go to work right now and design it,' I told them. 'When you get it designed and drawn up call me tonight, even if it's past midnight.'

"They called me about 11:30 p.m. I went down and looked it over carefully.

" 'Harry,' I said, 'I thought I told you I didn't want any eccentricities. Here's one right here. How about that? Turn that hinge over and you avoid the eccentricity.'

" 'My gosh,' Sutton replied, 'I just overlooked it.'

" 'That's the trouble. You're a damn good flier yourself, Harry, and ought to know better than that!'

"Sutton apologized; the draftsmen swung the hinge around the opposite direction and that avoided the eccentricity.

"The shop started on the changes in the tail next day. They made it up, put it on the XPB2Y-1, and it worked like a million dollars. It controlled the ship, and everything was all right.' "

IN TEST PILOT ROLE, Reuben Fleet helped solve XPB2Y-1 stability problems. Above, *engineers tried elliptical fins on horizontal stabilizer. Below, Fleet's solution: dual fins and rudder configuration.*

There's little doubt but what Reuben's fix of the XPB2Y-1 control problem was one of the most satisfying experiences in his aviation career.

[Perhaps embarrassed by the fact that the 'boss' had to fly the airplane himself to solve the engineering problem, the test reports of Flights No. 43 and No. 44, the latter the July 1938 first flight with the dual tail configuration, were missing from Consolidated's official files of engineering test reports on the XPB2Y-1 prototype when we checked them in 1974.—Ed.]

Reuben had kept his hand in at flying over the years. It was a definite plus for Consolidated. He felt it was more important to the company's reputation than to his own that the firm be headed by an executive capable of understanding aerodynamics from the pilot's point of view.

Some changes to the hull were also necessary so that it was not until August 24, 1938 that the big ship was turned over to the Navy for further testing and proving trials. Then it went back to Consolidated for minor modifications.

With war clouds darkening Europe and the Far East, President Roosevelt had become increasingly concerned about America's military might. Would the Army and Navy show him the state of development of new aircraft?

October 25 the word went out to the Aircraft Scouting Force from Rear Admiral Arthur B. Cook, Chief of the Bureau of Aeronautics. "We must have the XPB2Y-1 here at Anacostia by Friday—October 28." President Roosevelt would be inspecting the latest aircraft at the Army's Bolling Field and Anacostia Naval Air Station on Saturday.

Consolidated officials were notified. Consolidated mechanics worked all night Tuesday reinstalling equipment to have the plane ready Wednesday morning. But new engines had just been installed and had no in-flight check time whatever. Lieut. Comdr. Andrew Crinkley and his Navy flight crew took the big airboat up and got in five hours flight time breaking in the new engines and checking equipment. It was the longest time the experimental patrol bomber had been aloft.

By Wednesday night everything was stowed aboard—including furlined clothing and the plane's own beaching gear. The boat was ready for takeoff next morning, although the crew still did not know the plane's destination.

"The best wind," Comdr. Crinkley reported, "could be had by going north rather than the more logical flying boat route over the Gulf of Mexico, Pensacola, Florida and up the east coast.

"Permitted to pick our own course we flew northeast over Lake Mead, Salt Lake City and Omaha, where darkness set in, then on to Chicago. It was extremely cold. Even with furlined flying suits the pilots

Consolidator

PRESIDENTIAL PARTY looks over XPB2Y-1. From left, LCdr. Crinkley, President Roosevelt, Asst. Navy Secy. Charles Edison, Asst. War Secy. Louis Johnson.

huddled in blankets like Indians. From south of Cleveland, we passed over Pittsburgh, then approached Washington just ahead of a ground fog, landing in the Potomac River at one o'clock in the morning in an elapsed time of just 13 hours from San Diego.

"The President concluded his military plane review on Saturday at Anacostia with inspection of the giant Consolidated flying boat."

After several days of demonstration flights at Anacostia for pilots who had also flown the competitive Sikorsky four-engine boat, the XPB2Y-1 departed Washington on November 8th for the return over-land non-stop flight to San Diego via Nashville, Oklahoma City and Albuquerque. Flying against headwinds, the return flight took 15 hours.

Bill Wheatley, who accompanied the first mass PBY flight to Hawaii and the first flight of a seaplane, the 'Guba', non-stop across the country, also was aboard the first four-engine flying boat to cross the United States.

FIRST NAVAL FLAGPLANE was XPB2Y-1 used by Commander Aircraft Scouting Force during Alaskan survey flight.

Consolidator

The first production order for the four-engine Consolidated flying boat came on March 31, 1939 when the Navy contracted for six model PB2Y-2 deep hulled patrol bombers with engines uprated to 1200 h.p. The first of the new 'Coronado' boats was delivered December 31, 1940.

Meantime, on August 20, 1939, Commander Crinkley flew the prototype XPB2Y-1 to the Sand Point Naval Air Station, Seattle. There, four days later, the flying boat became the first Naval Flagplane when Admiral A. B. Cook, then commanding the Aircraft Scouting Force, hoisted his flag (from the U.S.S. Memphis flagship) aboard the patrol bomber.

August 26 the plane, with Admiral Cook and Nevada Congressmen James G. Scrugham, former military officer and naval consultant, aboard, left on an extended inspection of air bases and operational PBY squadrons in Alaska as far west as Kodiak and Dutch Harbor.

Pending delivery of the first PB2Y-2s, the prototype four-engine boat continued to be used for VIP transport by Admiral Cook. It was flown from San Francisco to Hawaii, where it departed on September 16, 1940 carrying newspaper publisher Colonel Frank Knox, newly appointed by President Roosevelt to be Secretary of the Navy, on an overnight flight back to San Diego.

One of the six -2 'Coronado' boats—used most for test purposes—was reconfigured to XPB2Y-3 specification as contracts for this updated -3 production model had been placed on November 19, 1940.

PB2Y-2 'CORONADO' version shows further revision of dual-tail configuration to more elliptical shape. General Dynamics/Convair

THOUGH NEITHER SCIENTIST nor inventor, Reuben Fleet was a creative thinker who could apply visionary ideas to technical problems and make his concepts work. He would provide the idea; others could work out the details.

He knew that a plane's wing is capable of supporting in flight virtually twice the weight with which it can take off. The Major felt there were two possible solutions to achieving greater take off performance. One was to take off with a full cargo load and minimum fuel; then add fuel in flight to extend the range. The other was to somehow hurl the plane forward with additional takeoff thrust to quickly achieve the flying speed at which the wing could support a heavier load.

Fleet decided to check his ideas with one of the best scientific brains in America—Dr. Robert A. Millikan, head of the California Institute of Technology, an old friend from Army Signal Corps days when the noted physicist was chief of its science and research division.

"Dr. Millikan," Fleet related, "was a fine, well-balanced gentleman who had gained world-wide recognition in 1923 when he won the Nobel Prize for Physics. I asked him to come down from Pasadena as my guest for two or three days so I could sit at his feet and talk with him."

One night before the fireplace, nursing a friendly drink together, the Major got down to what was on his mind.

"Doctor, I find that I can fly with twice the load I can take off with. Now, refueling in the air right after taking off is not yet fully developed, but I am working on that.

"Sir Alan Cobham has been studying the problem but has had to stop his experiments with a probe-and-drogue system. However, Sir Alan gave Jimmy Doolittle a report on what he had accomplished and asked Jimmy to take it to me with a request that I carry on.

"The danger in mid-air refueling is from fire. We proved that it takes three things to cause a fire: air, gas and an electric potential sufficient to set the mixture off. We began by trying to shut off the air, were successful in doing it, and have turned the information over to the government."

Dismissing air refueling for the moment, the Major sipped at his drink, absorbed some of the warmth from the fire and took off on another tangent.

"But I have another idea—that if I can use rockets and drop them the second after I get off, they will do the trick. We especially need this boost for our flying boats. Now we have to run the engines at full power for 70 or 80 seconds just to break the suction between the hull and the water. I need a man—the best man I can get—to investigate this rocket idea of mine."

The suggestion caught Dr. Millikan by surprise.

"Why, Major," his guest responded, "you have some wonderful engineers, some of the best in the world right here."

"Yes, I know I have. But I don't want to put this up to them. They would be thinking about nothing else for the next six months—until we got it worked out. We have so damn much work to do I have to keep their noses down to the grindstone and I want an outsider to do this."

"Well, Major, I think you have something very logical in your idea; but have you consulted any of your engineers?"

"Not a one. I don't want even one to even think of it, you see."

"I'll tell you what I'll do, then. I'll send Dr. Theodore von Karman down."

In a couple of weeks the noted Hungarian physicist and director of Caltech's Guggenheim Aeronautical Laboratory paid a visit to Major Fleet at his Spanish villa in San Diego.

After some preliminary discussion, the Major asked von Karman what he thought of the concept. "You've got the germ of a fine idea there. I'm just as sure of that as I am that you're sitting there."

"Well, Doctor, will you go over to Roswell, New Mexico at my expense and see what you make of the work of Dr. Robert H. Goddard? As you know, his work on rockets has been underwritten by Harry Guggenheim as the result of a proposal made by Charles Lindbergh."

"No, Major, I'm too old to go over there in that desert country, but we've got three young men working with us now on rocket studies. I'll send you Frank Malina and have him do the study you requested."

The results of the study, which cost Fleet $1000, were far-reaching, for Malina came back convinced that they had found an answer. Caltech became the first American university to treat rockets seriously. "My good friend Fleet," von Karman said, "was the first to call my attention to rockets and their possibilities. Until then neither industry nor government had shown the slightest interest in the practical side of rockets. But he saw a potential new application—assisting the takeoff of heavily-loaded planes."

Within a year of Fleet's initial interest came the government's first recognition of rockets. After a surprise visit to Caltech in May 1938, General Hap Arnold invited Dr. von Karman and Frank Malina to come to Washington to meet with the National Academy of Sciences on the use of rockets for jet assisted takeoff (JATO).

The first JATO takeoff was accomplished August 12, 1941, when Lieut. Homer Boushey of the Air Corps flew an especially equipped single-engine Ercoupe from March Air Force Base. "The plane," wrote von Karman, "shot off the ground as if released from a slingshot. None of us had ever seen a plane climb at such a steep angle."

The potential of both solid and liquid rockets for commercial and military applications was at last becoming apparent. Caltech set up the Jet Propulsion Laboratory. Von Karman, Malina and four associates put up $200 each and formed Aerojet Engineering Corporation in March 1942. Six months later, bringing Reuben Fleet's concept to actuality, a Consolidated PBY, with Comdr. C. F. Fischer at the controls, for the first time took off with the aid of JATO.

"Fleet was the first to call my attention to rockets and their possibilities" — von Karman

---

Somewhat ruefully, Fleet noted that although he had provided the initial impetus he had not been asked to participate in the formation of Aerojet. "I didn't have a nickel in it," he said. "After the war Dan Kimball, who had been president of Aerojet-General before being appointed Secretary of the Navy, told me that their JATO business one year exceeded $700 million!"

Years later, Caltech's president, Dr. Harold Brown, asked Fleet why his financial support of the Institute had been minimal.

"Well, Dr. Brown," replied the Major, "what's your thought on the matter?"

"I wonder, Major, if it could be that we organized Aerojet up here and left you out of it?"

"Maybe that very fact was one reason. But there were others. Remember that we owned a one-third interest in the Caltech wind tunnel. Well, I had to jump Dr. Clark Millikan about the fact that the Los Angeles companies always got the information first; Consolidated in San Diego didn't get it until it was common knowledge. He contended it doesn't happen, and I told him, 'Well, my boy, it certainly does.'

"So Millikan asked me if I accused him of responsibility for it and I told him that I certainly did. You see, Dr. Brown, that's a pretty good reason, isn't it, why I have never given you any donation? I preferred to give it to my home town; just as you gave data to the Los Angeles companies before you gave it to us. We owned a third of the tunnel. Why did you ignore us?"

In addition to Jet Assisted Take Off for flying boats and mid-air refueling, Reuben had another idea for long-range flight which he felt worth pursuing.

"I had an idea for a very stable mid-ocean airdrome," Fleet recalls. "It was a project of C. A. Van Dusen's and mine together. We didn't spend much money on it—just drawings and a small working model with which we proved it was virtually un-affected by wave action.

"In the days when planes couldn't carry enough fuel to make Europe non-stop, such an airdrome could be a half-way landing and refueling station. But, as the flying range of aircraft increased we abandoned it as a mid-ocean project.

"After we'd been out here in California and saw all of the complaints of people surrounding any land airport, as in Los Angeles, Van and I revived the idea. We proposed it for areas like Santa Monica Bay and Coronado Roads off San Diego where such floating platform could be located so the approach of transport planes would not be over residential areas and complaining citizens. Such a concept may yet have its day."

Ryan Aeronautical Library

JET ASSISTED TAKEOFF (JATO) was first demonstrated on private aircraft like this Navion business plane.

McDonnell Douglas

PRINCIPALS in Davis-Douglas Aircraft Co. were David R. Davis, left, and Donald W. Douglas, right, here posed on stub wing of 1920 Douglas 'Cloudster.'

THE IDEA SOUNDED SCREWY to Reuben Fleet when Walter Brookins called him, but what was there to lose in talking to an engineer with radical ideas for a new method of designing a wing airfoil? Fleet knew only too well that the quest for better aircraft performance depended on even small improvements in airfoil efficiency.

This man just might have something. At least he'd give him a polite but brief hearing. Brookins was, after all, a pioneer airman—the first civilian to be taught to fly by the Wright brothers—and had asked Reuben to see David R. Davis. That name was vaguely familiar. Wasn't it Davis who had been Donald Douglas' first partner in the Davis-Douglas Aircraft Co.? Yes, Brookins had assured him, it was the same Davis.

The slight, bespectacled Davis stepped into Fleet's office. "Mr. Davis," Reuben began, "why did you bring your new wing down to me? Why didn't you take it to Don Douglas? I thought you were associated in business with him."

"Well," Davis said, "it used to be the Davis-Douglas company. But it's now Douglas; not Davis-Douglas. That's why I didn't take it to Douglas."

"But who told you to see us?"

"Walter Brookins, my partner, told me that you could be trusted. You know, his wife was Marie Lemke who had been Colonel Bane's secretary when you were together at McCook Field. She told me we could count on you. That's why I'm here."

Davis proceeded to outline his ideas and the work he had done to prove his theories. Though not a graduate engineer, he felt there must be some mathematically perfect airfoil section.

Most airfoils had been developed by trying different sections in a wind-tunnel, then calculating which were the most efficient. That was doing things backward, Davis thought.

Instead of testing an infinite number of sections why not start with a perfect sphere and the teardrop shape formed from it as by a falling drop of water? Perhaps 'drag' could be virtually eliminated.

For years after applying for a patent, Davis continued to perfect his formula, then applied it to wing sections installed on an automobile and tested at high speed. The results were spectacularly encouraging. Now—in late 1937—he was in the office of the president of Consolidated Aircraft presenting his ideas and asking that they be tried in a full-scale airplane.

"Have you got your new method of wing design patented?" Fleet asked.

"No, but the patent's been applied for."

"Alright, then, I'll look at it."

"So," Fleet recalls, "I studied his material for quite a time while Davis sat there waiting.

'Frankly, Davis, I would never dare use your 'Fluid Foil' wing unless I had it checked by the very best technical men I've got.'

" 'Well, Major Fleet, I'm sorry, but I won't show it to anyone but you.'

" 'That does no good, Davis. I'm a practical engineer but not an aerodynamicist. I'm not sufficiently versed technically to decide whether or not we can use your wing. Of course, if it's as good as you claim we'd be interested. But it has to be studied by the best engineering brains we have. They're honest people and won't reveal your secret to others.

" 'Tell you what you do. You go down to your hotel and think about it overnight. Come back tomorrow and if you've made up your mind to submit it to my people for study, then I'll talk turkey with you. Otherwise I won't.'

"Davis concluded he had no alternative and came back the next day.

" 'There are two men, Davis, I want to have consult with you. One is Mac Laddon, our chief engineer; the other is George Schairer, one of our best aerodynamicists.' "

No chief engineer is particularly pleased when the boss asks him to analyze the ideas of some crack-pot inventor, especially one who doesn't even have an engineering degree. Mac Laddon was no exception, but he did give Davis a further hearing. Gradually the idea crept into Laddon's thinking that perhaps it was worth a try; there is always that outside chance.

The matter came to a head when Laddon called in his secretary and drafted the outline of an agreement between Consolidated and the Davis-Brookins Aircraft Corporation.

With signing of a contract February 10, 1938, Davis became a consultant to Consolidated at $200 per month for a minimum of eight days effort monthly for six months. Wind tunnel models of Davis-generated airfoil sections would be tested at Consolidated's expense at the California Institute of Technology.

If tests proved satisfactory and the wing design was used on an experimental airplane, Davis would receive $2500 for the prototype. On production aircraft, Davis would be paid one half of 1 percent of the airframe sales price, not including the cost of engines and government furnished equipment.

Particularly important to Consolidated's competitive position in the industry was the provision that for a year Davis would not disclose his method of generating airfoil sections to other aircraft companies or government agencies. Too, Davis would press forward in getting full patent protection on his pending application. Should Davis' patent position be judged invalid, royalty payments would cease.

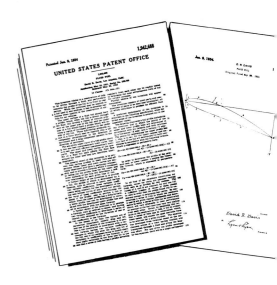

Consolidated had recently flown its four-engine Navy XPB2Y-1 for the first time and already had some rough plans in mind for a twin-engine flying boat that would be a considerable advancement over it and the PBY design. Perhaps the new Model 31 might offer an opportunity for David R. Davis to apply his method of generating the wing airfoil design.

Retiring to his Los Angeles apartment, Davis constructed an eight-foot wing section for the new flying boat incorporating his formula-derived airfoil. Caltech put it into its Guggenheim wind tunnel and began a series of tests. Davis waited for the results but nothing was immediately forthcoming. After several weeks, an inquiry developed the information that the wind tunnel was not performing properly and some equipment had to be reworked. More delays followed.

Dr. Clark Millikan and other scientists at Caltech were perplexed. The results just could not be correct. The efficiency of the airfoil was 102%, exceeding the theoretical maximum, so something must be wrong. No one was sure, although Dr. Theodore von Karman chuckled with glee. Ninety percent efficiency had always been considered about the best one could get. Perhaps it was just some unexplained phenomenon.

The final report was bewildering. The results were there all right but the explanation left much to be desired.

RETURNING BY PASSENGER steamer from Hawaii where they had conferred with Navy officials on PBY operations, Reuben Fleet and Mac Laddon had time to contemplate the future of their flying boat business.

The technical state of the art of aircraft design was advancing rapidly; more powerful reciprocating engines were being designed and produced. The Navy would have need for new and better patrol planes and the market for commercial airliners capable of trans-oceanic flight was just over the horizon. Perhaps, without having the Navy look over their shoulder, the new design they had approved in concept just before leaving San Diego on the Hawaiian trip would meet both commercial and Navy requirements.

Fleet and Laddon had earlier sketched out their ideas; by the time their ship docked they were pretty well determined to go forward on a company-sponsored project. Meantime David Davis was seeing if his wing design could be used.

The new Model 31 would be a deep-hulled twin-engine flying boat, powered by 2000 h.p. twin-row 18-cylinder Wright engines, the most powerful radials available. It would combine high cruising speed with long operating range and the ability to carry large loads.

A commercial version with a crew of five would be capable of carrying 52 passengers in a double-deck interior arrangement. The plane would carry its own fully-retractable tricycle beaching gear.

Engineering drawings for the new flying boat were fairly well along when results of wind tunnel tests of the Davis-designed wing airfoil became available from the California Institute of Technology.

After some serious soul searching following his discussion with Mac Laddon on the merits of the Davis wing, Reuben Fleet made his decision. Consolidated would gamble the $1 million development cost of the Model 31 to determine whether or not the theoretical advantages of the Davis wing could be achieved in a full scale airplane. They would go ahead without waiting through the delays of a formal Navy design competition.

Construction began in July 1938; ten months later the Model 31 was towed outside its assembly building at San Diego's Lindbergh Field. Probably never before had such a large craft been built in such a short time—but then there was no bureaucratic interference from Washington. It revealed the huge mass of a hull 22 feet deep; little wonder that it was promptly dubbed the 'Pregnant Guppy.'

The rear of the hull swept up to the dual fin and rudder similiar in design to the one Reuben Fleet had worked out for the XPB2Y-1. Even more incongruous, the clumsy bulk was expected to be sustained aloft by

'PREGNANT GUPPY' aptly described Consolidated's Model 31 twin-engine flying boat when the thick-hulled craft was first seen by the public in Spring of 1939.

William Wagner

SUSTAINED IN FLIGHT by the mere wisp of a wing, its designer conceded the Model 31 'was, by long odds, the queerest looking of the Consolidated family' but should be its best performing flying boat.

a wisp of a wing. Though 110 feet long it was so narrow in chord it surely must have been intended to be installed on the body of some smaller plane. It was what engineers call a 'high-aspect-ratio' wing, one whose span is long compared with its chord, or width.

Mac Laddon sounded almost apologetic about the plane's appearance. "This airplane is proof that a shape need be streamlined in one view only to slip through the air without too much drag. By long odds it is the queerest looking of the Consolidated family, but should be the best performing of our flying boats. And it will make into a good-looking plane.

"At Major Fleet's request, we relinquished our retractable wing tip floats so that the wing would be suitable for landplane as well as flying boat use.

"In our desire for maximum range and high cruising speed we have reached new limits in aspect ratio (ratio between wing length and chord) and wing loading.

"The Consolidated-Davis airfoil was selected because of greater efficiency at cruising speed and the Consolidated-Fowler wing flaps are employed to reduce take-off and landing speed."

At the end of April, 14 months after he had signed a contract with Consolidated keeping secret his new wing design, David Davis announced in Los Angeles that he and Walter Brookins had perfected a formula

to plot near-perfect curves for wing sections. It was also revealed that Consolidated had spent $40,000 testing the wing at Caltech's Guggenheim Laboratory and that the company had contracted for its use on a royalty basis.

May 4, 1939 the Model 31 was rolled out for the first time. Next day it was towed to the seaplane ramp and moved out into the waters of San Diego Bay.

As with the four-engined XPB2Y-1, Bill Wheatley was at the controls as chief test pilot. Again, in the right co-pilot's seat was young George Newman, son of one of Reuben Fleet's earliest associates.

To everyone's surprise, Wheatley's included, the Model 31 in its first flight rose from the bay in a take-off run as short as that of a landplane. On landing, Wheatley is reported to have compared its performance to that of a pursuit plane. Clearly Consolidated had something remarkable in the Davis Wing design.

In subsequent test flights, the so-called 'secret-wing sensation' bettered by nearly 20 percent the performance of comparable aircraft. Top speed was reported at 250 m.p.h. and range was expected to exceed 3500 miles. By comparison the widely-used PBY's had a top speed of approximately 170 m.p.h. and range of 2500 miles. Armament was carried inside the hull while on the PBY external blisters had to be used.

THE DARK CLOUDS forecasting World War II in Europe began gathering in 1935 when Adolph Hitler boasted that the German Luftwaffe was already as powerful as Britain's Royal Air Force. From that point on England and France began to prepare for what appeared to be the inevitable.

In the United States the role of air power had been traditionally defensive. Bombers would protect the American coastline from enemy surface fleets. The Army Air Corps, however, offended its rival services in 1938 by demonstrating an off-shore capability when it sent a flight of newly-developed B-17 Flying Fortress bombers over seven hundred miles to sea to 'intercept' the Italian steamship 'Rex.' Its wrists slapped, the Army was ordered to restrict the operational range of its planes and to taper off bomber production.

Then, at the end of September, England's Prime Minister, Neville Chamberlain, journeyed to Munich and by appeasing Hitler sought to avoid war and obtain 'peace in our time.' Criticized as it was, the agreement did give England an extra year to prepare for war. Hitler had said at Munich that Germany, which occupied Austria in March, had no further territorial claims in Europe but, of course, immediately took over the Sudeten lands from Czechoslovakia.

The United States was quick to react. To impress Hitler, President Roosevelt spoke out emphatically for an expansion of American air power with an annual production rate of 10,000 planes. To further emphasize his point he promoted Henry H. Arnold to Major General and named him Chief of the Army Air Corps, replacing Maj. Gen. Oscar Westover, who had been killed in an accident just a week earlier, even as Neville Chamberlain was returning from Munich to London. (Contenders with Arnold for the top Air Corps post were understood to be General Delos Emmons, another old friend of Fleet's, and General Frank M. Andrews.)

General Arnold promptly pointed out that the nation with the greatest Navy in the world (England), in alliance with the country having the most powerful Army (France), had virtually capitulated to Germany's newly created air power. Now, with the President's backing, he had a go-ahead on further development of a long-range bombardment capability.

Boeing's Model 299, prototype of the B-17, had caught everyone's attention with its August 20, 1935 non-stop flight from Seattle to Dayton in nine hours. At Wright Field the new four-engine bomber would participate in a fly-off against the Martin B-12 and Douglas B-18 twin-engine planes. Then disaster struck the Boeing entry.

In an October test flight, someone neglected to release the newly developed gust lock of the control system and the 299 was destroyed on take-off. The

bomber production contract went to the Douglas B-18. But since the potential of the Boeing plane had already been demonstrated, the Army awarded the company a service test order for 13 aircraft, to be designated B-17.

General Arnold, the new Chief of the Air Corps, was enthusiastic about the B-17 but concerned that should war come, Boeing's Seattle plant would not be able to build planes in the quantities needed. At that time, the Fall of 1938, only the first 13 B-17s had been delivered. Though a high-altitude super-charged version—the B-17B—was on order, none of the updated model had yet been produced. Arnold thought that perhaps Consolidated could work out a license agreement with Boeing to build the B-17 as a second source.

In December Major Fleet dispatched two trusted aides—Mac Laddon and C. A. Van Dusen—to Seattle

U. S. Army Air Corps

MAJ. GEN. H. H. ARNOLD, longtime friend of Reuben Fleet, who was one of his strongest advocates, poses for official photo on day in September 1934 when President Roosevelt named him Chief of the Army Air Corps.

General Dynamics/Convair

to confer with Boeing executives, but it was clear there was not enough work on Boeing's books to divide the orders. In any case, Fleet saw little reason to produce more planes of a design already four years old.

The Army had just issued Type Specification C-212 spelling out details of a new bomber requirement—3000 mile range, 35,000 foot ceiling, maximum speed of 300 m.p.h. and the ability to carry four tons of bombs.

With what Consolidated had already demonstrated with the efficient Davis Wing airfoil in the Model 31 flying boat, Laddon's engineers could design a new four-engine bomber which could carry the same load as the B-17 but at greater speeds and far longer range. The latter was considered the most important requirement.

When Congress reconvened in January 1939 one of the first messages President Roosevelt sent up to the Hill outlined the need for more planes: "Our existing forces are so utterly inadequate that they must be im-

mediately strengthened." General Arnold backed up his Commander-in-Chief's request with issuance of a policy statement pointing out the need to develop additional sources of supply of heavy bombardment airplanes.

Having studied multi-engine bomber design for some time, it was clear to Major Fleet that the Army at last was ready to commit the required funding. By the end of the month, Mac Laddon and David Fleet, the Major's 28-year-old son, were at Wright Field with specifications and preliminary data for Consolidated's proposed Model 32 bomber.

Consolidated was moving so fast with its proposed heavy bombardment airplane, trying to keep ahead of the competition, that its subsequent contract came close to looking like a directed procurement. Two days after Laddon and young Fleet arrived in Dayton, the Air Corps sent letters to Martin and Sikorsky asking whether they had designs which would meet the new C-212 Type Specification. Both replied that they did not have, at that time, designs which met the specification.

The key design feature of Consolidated's Model 32 was use of the extremely narrow, highly efficient Davis Wing which assured meeting the long cruising range required by Air Corps specifications. The 110-foot wing and hydraulic flaps were lifted virtually intact from the Model 31 flying boat.

For maximum bomb stowage and ease of handling, the fuselage was unusually deep and employed roller-type panels which slid up along the slab-sided fuselage. Bombs—a total of 8000 pounds—could be stowed vertically. The wing was mounted shoulder high on the fuselage.

Four 1200 h.p. Pratt and Whitney Twin Wasp engines powered the Model 32 (later B-24) in its initial 41,000 lb. gross weight configuration. Unlike the B-17, the B-24 had a tricycle gear with the main wheels folding outward to be retracted into the thin 110-foot wing between the inboard and outboard engines.

Borrowing again from features proven in the Model 31 seaplane—and earlier in the XPB2Y-1 four engine boat—the tail featured the same twin fin and rudder. To assure good low speed and landing characteristics, Laddon's design incorporated Fowler area-increasing flaps which slid back and down from the trailing edge of the wing.

By February a mock-up was well along, tests of a wind tunnel model had been completed and fabrication began. Nearly 30 changes in specifications were agreed upon at an Air Corps conference in Dayton February 21, presided over by Lieut. Donald L. Putt

THIN, GRACEFUL WING of B-24 has seldom been more beautifully displayed than in the striking photo on opposite page.

who fortunately had survived the October 1935 crash of the Boeing 299.

The Air Corps, in late March, forwarded to the Assistant Secretary of War a proposed contract in which it pointed out that "Consolidated is the designer and sole manufacturer of this particular Prototype Heavy Bombardment Airplane which is required for experimental purposes as a means of bringing in additional sources of supply.

"Seven airplanes, in addition to the prototype, will be sufficient to obtain a tactical service test. With spare parts, total cost of the seven YB-24 (Consolidated Model 32) airplanes will be $2,880,000."

March 30, 1939 the contract for the XB-24 prototype was approved by the Assistant Secretary of War. Now the United States would have a running mate for the B-17, then the only proven heavy bomber on which it could rely.

Congressional approval of the expansion of the Air Corps to 6,000 planes came in April and with it the order for the seven YB-24s. By then Consolidated had begun negotiating a contract for an additional 38 bombers of the B-24A type.

The urgency for all-out preparedness stepped up. France had begun to order American warplanes. Charles A. Lindbergh, recently living in England and France, had been invited to see the German aircraft industry and observe the capability of the Luftwaffe. On returning to the United States he reported his findings to General Arnold; that German air power was nearly invincible.

Additional inputs came from Jimmy Doolittle, head of Shell Oil Company's aviation department who had left the Air Corps in 1930. Among his friends was the World War I German ace, Ernst Udet. "Each year I went to Europe," Jimmy said, "to tie in American aviation activities with Shell's world-wide aviation programs.

"In 1937, I was in Berlin and had an evening and several days with Udet. He did me the great courtesy of sending me through some of the German factories. They were then tooled up, building military aircraft. Then in 1939, one month before the war started in Europe, I was again in Germany and met Udet at Frankfurt. He invited me down to Munich, where he was going to have a two weeks' holiday. My conscience didn't let me go, because I knew I would be acting as a spy; that it would be a violation of personal confidence.

"Udet had always been very open, telling me very frankly what was going on. It was obvious from things I had already seen that Germany was preparing for war, that in all likelihood we would become involved in a war which was imminent.

"Though I didn't go to Munich with Udet, I did give a comprehensive report to Hap Arnold, as had

Lindbergh, on what was going on in Germany, and in England, too. It was then that I again offered my services to the Air Corps."

General Arnold continued to press for long range bombers "which can hit the enemy before he hits us." On August 10 orders were placed for 461 bombers. Arnold's plan was clear; develop pairs of four-engine heavy and twin-engine medium bombers. The B-24 and B-17 would be teamed. So too would be the new twin-engine bombers—North American's B-25 and Martin's B-26, both still under development.

The August 10 contracts called for 38 Boeing B-17Cs and the 38 Consolidated B-24As which had previously been in negotiation. It was the eve of World War II.

Within three weeks—September 1—the Luftwaffe's Stuka dive bombers attacked the Polish air force, destroying most of it on the ground. September 3, Great Britain declared War on Germany, as did France.

War on the ground was slow and indecisive as both sides probed the enemy across the Maginot Line. It was, some said, a 'phony war.'

Then, from April to May 1940, countries began to topple like dominoes. Denmark, Norway, Holland, Luxembourg, Belgium. The French government under Daladier fell, Winston Churchill replaced Neville Chamberlain. Hitler hit hard at France, which collapsed June 20. A fascist-oriented government for unoccupied France was set up at Vichy under Marshal Petain.

August saw the start of the all-out blitz, the aerial Battle of Britain. That brought retaliation bombing raids by the British against Berlin. Europe was literally aflame.

WORK HAD GONE FORWARD on the B-24 at a feverish pace in the San Diego plant. The March 30 contract called for first flight in nine months—before the end of 1939. The wing and fuselage were mated the end of October; Twin Wasp engines were flown to the plant from the east coast by Army transport plane; the complete airplane was rolled out of the factory the third week of December.

Two days short of the nine months deadline—December 29, 1939—the XB-24, with Bill Wheatley at the controls, roared down the runway at Lindbergh Field and lifted smoothly off on its first flight—a short 17-minute test.

How was it that Reuben Fleet and Consolidated were so successful in designing and building the B-24 in record time and, then having the plane manufactured in greater quantities than any other American aircraft?

"Our whole company," Fleet said, "embraced the best brains of the Engineering Division from McCook Field. I knew the capabilities of men like Mac Laddon,

FIRST OFFICIAL TEST FLIGHT of XB-24 flying Army markings was made in February 1940. Reuben Fleet disliked stubby nose, ordered 3-foot 'plug' inserted ahead of cockpit.

Bernie Sheahan, George Hallett, Roy Miller, Harry Sutton, Ginny Clark, Bill Ring—had worked with them for four years—and brought them with me when I formed my own company. And we knew how to work with the technical people who succeeded them at Wright Field.

"We didn't ignore the Engineering Division, because you can't do that, but we obtained deviations from their handbook for airplane designers where experience showed it was advisable. I had started the handbook at McCook Field as a beneficent guide for aeronautical engineers to tell them what we had discovered was safe, good practice and what was unworkable. However, through the passing of time, the Handbook for Airplane Designers had become a bible as immutable as the laws of the Medes and Persians.

"The words 'small' and 'must' appeared much too often. The handbook had become inflexible. So I went back to Wright Field, arranged a conference and told them they were doing more to hold back aviation than all the rest of the world put together. For instance, the handbook was interpreted as prohibiting electrical welding. Now, the game was too young to have prohibitions of that character which stopped all kinds of innovation.

"As a result a lot of restrictive thinking was set aside. Then, too, we told the Air Corps that we couldn't tolerate a lot of bureaucratic supervision and get the job done on time. They responded by sending Major E. R. McReynolds to San Diego as their resident representative. We made a lot of decisions on the spot that normally would have been referred to Wright Field."

Two design features stood out in Major Fleet's recollection as being particularly significant.

"With our tricycle landing gear—the first on a large bomber—we didn't have to run several hundred yards on takeoff to get the tail off the ground as did Boeing with the B-17. The B-24 was already in flying attitude.

"Secondly, we figured that with a wing made out of duralium sheet it didn't make sense to put a fuel tank of dural inside an already enclosed metal wing section. That made unnecessary extra weight. We'd just let the gasoline swish around among the ribs. So we used duprene (too new to even be mentioned in the designer's handbook) to seal all joints where the wing might leak and thereby had integral wing fuel tanks.

"On these two points alone we were able to leave our competitors behind."

A third point—graceful design—had also caught Reuben's attention. When the prototype B-24 had been

BRITISH early showed interest in B-24 bomber design. Air Ministry representative, left, poses with Major Fleet in front of first plane for RAF.

rolled out for inspection, the Major strode purposefully around the new plane, commenting favorably upon the workmanship, Then, quoting a company photographer taking photos of the roll-out, Reuben stopped near the plane's nose and blurted out, "Doesn't look right. Too stubby! Have them add a steady section—a three-foot long 'plug'—just forward of the windshield. You'll have a better looking plane."

By the time production began to roll, the 63'9" fuselage had been extended to 66'4".

Early in 1940, an Army crew headed by cigar-chomping Major Stanley Umstead flew the XB-24 for the first time. A month later, March 18, the Air Corps made its first official test flight of the long-range, high-altitude bomber.

The 'arsenal of democracy' began to make available to friendly countries the latest American warplanes, providing they supplied the United States with information on operational use and service improvements.

The hard pressed French government placed rush orders for 60 B-24s with options for 120 more and the British contracted for 164 of the bombers, but when France fell in June their order was transferred to the British. Planes under these foreign orders were designated Model LB-30s.

As Western Europe began to collapse, President Roosevelt issued his urgent appeal for 50,000 airplanes, and for the production capacity to build that number yearly. From that point on, though it would be eighteen months before the tragedy of Pearl Harbor, production of the B-24 was assured as long as the war might last. And Consolidated would loom as large in landbased bombers as it long had in flying boats.

Reuben Fleet was prepared to give his best to the defense production effort and he expected as much of all his fellow workers.

"We have a most profound duty to our country," he said, "and for its national defense. We must buckle down to it with fervor and our best patriotic effort.

"We have no place for foreigners or fifth columnists. Most of our employees are of draft age; if a workman can serve his country better with us than as a soldier, we want him, otherwise he should go wherever his country calls.

"We in America must catch up. We cannot do it by working on small piecemeal orders totaling a few hundred bombers or flying boats, each order with changes in the craft, and all done under the strictest profit-limitation, where pennies must be watched lest we go broke.

"But these days are past, and we must not stand, like Lot's wife, paralyzed in the act of looking backward. The future is our Bible.

"So we must visualize the task ahead, for the Good Book says, 'Where there is no vision, the people perish.' It was a quotation the Major frequently used.

General Dynamics/Convair

LB-30 'LIBERATOR' was British designation for their export version of Army's B-24 bomber. British also took over French orders when Paris fell to Germans.

THE NATURE OF THE AIRCRAFT business was such, particularly in time of national emergency, that Reuben Fleet—with the new B-24, PBYs, four-engine boats and Model 31 on his mind—was as likely to be in Dayton or Washington as in San Diego.

Early September 1939 found him in Washington just as Hitler launched his attack on Poland, igniting World War II. Two days later, as England declared war against Germany, Reuben ran into Admiral John Towers, an old friend.

"Come on, Jack, let's have lunch together."

"Fine, Reuben, but afterward come on down to the Bureau. We'd like to talk to you."

At the Bureau of Aeronautics, of which he was Chief, Towers got right down to business.

"What would you propose that the Navy buy from you in case we get into this war? How long would it take you to build 500 patrol bombers?"

"Well, Jack, the twin-engine PBY has been flying long enough now so that it has most of our ideas in it, and it's a damn good ship. You ought to buy it. But I don't think the four-engine PB2Y is worth a damn."

"Why?"

"Because it's a conglomeration of ideas of your engineers and ours. Therefore, it doesn't suit anybody. That's the curse of this business. But before you buy more PBYs I'd suggest you wire out to the fleet and see whether those 'Mae West' gun blisters on the new PBY-4 model are a success or not."

"Okay. But how much would it cost us and how much time would it take to get 500 PBYs?"

"Well, I'll have to figure that out very carefully. I'll get back to you later this afternoon."

Reuben retired to his hotel room and called the factory a couple of times, meantime pricing out a bid. When he returned to Admiral Towers' office he had a proposal.

"If we double the size of our factory, I can give you 500 PBYs in two years. But I don't want to double our factory, and I won't, because it is only half full now. If we had a firm order for 200 planes we could build them for you for $20 million—$100,000 apiece. But the Navy would have to pay for the new factory buildings."

"All right. We'll do it. And I'll give you the order."

"No, I can't take it Jack. The government has never awarded a $20 million order for aircraft without calling for bids. I don't think either you or I should be parties to such a thing."

"But, who else is going to bid, Reuben?"

"How do I know. Probably the whole damn industry. Look at what happened to us in 1930 on that first flying boat production order the Navy awarded to Martin on our design."

"Yes, but now the Navy just can't afford the time delay."

National Air and Space Museum

'MAE WEST' gun blisters on PBY-4 model of *'Catalina' flying boat are emphasized in this unique angle shot.*

"All right, Jack, I'll make a gentlemen's agreement with you. I'll start in right now on PBY-5s just as if we'd won the bid, providing you'll double the factory. In the meantime you call for bids and if anybody underbids us and you prefer to do business with them, you'll hold us harmless—pay us for the work we've already done, but with no profit to Consolidated."

BECAUSE THE PBY-5 ORDER was of such magnitude—the largest single contract for military aircraft yet awarded—there were important tax considerations for Consolidated.

In December Major Fleet was again in Washington, this time to meet with Internal Revenue officials of the Treasury Department and work out in advance an unusual, and perhaps first, closing agreement as to tax matters. When the agreement had been drafted, Admiral Moffett, General Arnold, the Commissioner of Internal Revenue and members of their staffs joined the meeting. Someone began to read the agreement, droning on page after page.

Exasperated, Major Fleet finally drew himself up to gain attention. "Wait a minute, gentlemen! Isn't that a period? If so, its the first one in nine printed pages.

213

How in the name of goodness do you expect me to understand what that says? Let my attorney write it, and if he can't do it in one page, I'll get another attorney."

The chief accountant of the IRS spoke up. "There is only one man in the United States who can write one word into the Code and that man is Herman Reiling who is now reading the text."

"Is that so? Is that the way you feel about it, Mr. Reiling?"

"Yes, there is not one word written into the Internal Revenue Code unless I write it."

"No wonder it is such a conglomeration, if you will excuse me for saying so. If we threw the whole damn tax act in the wastebasket and started over again it would be a great deal better. Tell me, Mr. Reiling, what does it mean?"

"You're a tough hombre, Major Fleet. It means that the minute you say the job is done, you get your money."

On that assurance Major Fleet signed the document, which was approved two days later, December 18, 1939 by Henry Morgenthau, Jr., Secretary of the Treasury.

On December 20 the Navy announced award of the $20 million contract to Consolidated for PBY-5 flying boats, one version of which became the first amphibian type.

Construction of the new 441,000 square foot plant addition, doubling plant capacity, got promptly under way. Including new machinery and other equipment required for expanded PBY construction, the cost was estimated at $2.2 million.

When President Roosevelt, in May 1940, called for a defense production capability of 50,000 planes, Consolidated authorized a further $3 million plant expansion at its own expense. This added another 650,000 square feet of production area, bringing the company's total building area to 1.5 million square feet. This was supplemented by 1.2 million square feet of outside paved area suitable for assembly and final fitting out.

In a memo to his key associates, Reuben noted that May 29th marked the company's 17th birthday. "In counting our blessings," he wrote, "let us consider that we have a factory of our own, tailored for our business, in the city of our choice, with plenty of work on hand and in sight, and no mortgage on our premises or our future. In one sense I regret that we are too busy to celebrate."

"The war in Europe," General Arnold wrote, "is in reality a full scale laboratory in which planes are being tested under actual war conditions. Already we know we must have leak-proof fuel tanks and that our bombers must have more range because if they cannot reach the theatre of war they are of no value.

"With the Army and Navy procurement programs, plus the purchases by foreign governments, American capacity to produce 50,000 planes per annum in the not too distant future, is entirely within the realm of possibility."

As the position of the Allies in Europe worsened, the National Defense Council began to consider the role which the automotive industry should have in warplane production. William S. Knudsen, recently resigned from the presidency of General Motors, chaired the September 1940 meeting at the Pan American Building in Washington with chief executives of ten major aircraft manufacturers.

"The question there," Major Fleet recalls, "was, in case we got into the war, would we let the automobile industry help. They took us one by one as we sat around that huge round conference table, the biggest in Washington.

"When it came to me, Knudsen said, 'Well, Fleet, they tell me you've been on both sides of the fence. You were on the government side for the Army four years at McCook Field, Now you're out in industry. What do you say?'

"My reply was that 'whether we want to let the automobile industry in on our business or not has got nothing to do with it. With all the help we can possibly get in America, we will never be able to get airplanes as fast as the government will want them. Therefore, we've got to let them in. A bigger question is whether you can bank on Uncle Sam's word anymore, gentlemen. If I weren't compelled to use dollar bills bearing Henry Morganthau's signature, I'd certainly look upon them as being worthless.'

"I've got men to be paid the minute they have earned their money."

"At that point James V. Forrestal, Undersecretary of the Navy, who had accompanied Admiral Towers to the meeting, spoke up.

" 'Don't blame Morgenthau, Fleet, because you haven't got your money to repay the cost of doubling the size of your plant. Blame the Navy Department.'

"Well, you're the head man, Jim. Nine and a half months have passed and I haven't gotten a dime of it back.

" 'That's because the Navy hasn't worked out a procedure to pay you. Every single invoice of yours is on the table in my office.'

"For twenty years, " Reuben went on, "I have known every man in this room who's in the airplane business. Although they're competitors of mine, none would be here if they weren't all straight shooters. If there was one crooked hair in any of their heads they wouldn't be here, nor would I. The fault lies with the government!

LARGEST PRODUCTION of PBY 'Catalinas' was of U. S. and export versions of the basic PBY-5 design. Export model, above, is British aircraft with serial 9706 in test flight out of San Diego.

"Gathered here are the best aircraft brains in America and here is a man supposed to be the best business man in the whole damn government and he says that the Navy doesn't have a procedure to pay its bills.

"I'll tell you something, Jim. If you don't have my money tonight, then when we reconvene tomorrow morning every man in this room is going to know it."

" 'All right, Fleet. When we adjourn, you come over to my office and we'll talk it over.'

"I'll be honored to do that, Jim!"

Conversation between the two resumed during their ride together in a Navy car.

"What would you do, Fleet, if you were me?"

"I would call up Supplies and Accounts and tell them to bring over a check for the two and a half million dollars showing on that statement summary. I'd tell them to take those invoices and submit them to any kind of an audit they want. If they ever find anything wrong with any of them, put a stop order against Consolidated. But just for the amount of the wrongness. In the meantime, give us the check.

"We have to spend our money first before we can get it back from you, and we are making every dime go as far as we can. But I've got men to be paid the minute they have earned their money. We have got to pay them and we're running mightly close on money."

As soon as they arrived at the office Forrestal had his secretary call up Supplies and Accounts. "Admiral, I want you to be over here in five minutes. Bring three colored boys with you."

When the Admiral arrived, his jaw dropped as he saw Major Fleet with Forrestal, for the visitor had been after him time and again.

"Admiral, those invoices on the table are Consolidated's. We had them double their factory, at our expense, and it was covered by a closing agreement. You can submit those invoices to any kind of an audit you want. Have those boys take them down to your office. I'll give you five minutes to bring a check up here made out to Consolidated Aircraft Corporation for the full amount of this tape."

That's how Reuben Fleet got his check for $2,470,-000 before the meeting between aircraft industry executives and the National Defense Council resumed the next morning.

As WAR CAME TO EUROPE in the Fall of 1939, Consolidated was deluged with a flood of orders for PBYs. Newer, more advanced patrol plane designs were under development by Major Fleet's competitors, and Consolidated itself had two new designs in test—the four engine XPB2Y-1 and the high-performance Model 31 flying boat with its 2000 h.p. engines and radical Davis wing. But the urgent need of the U.S. Navy and the Allies was for a proven long-range patrol bomber, and this was available only in the PBY as Fleet had pointed out to Admiral Towers.

There had been a two-year gap in orders but on December 20, 1939 the Navy ordered the 200 PBY-5s. To meet their own requirement Allied governments also ordered quantities of the Model 28-5 'commercial' PBY already flight tested by the British. It became the 28-5M (military). For the Coastal Command, the Royal Air Force ordered 50 and, at Fleet's suggestion (after a PBY flight to Catalina Island, off Southern California), christened the new plane 'Catalina,' a name later adopted by the U.S.

France ordered 30 PBYs for its Navy. Australia 18, the Netherlands East Indies 48 and Canada 50. All were basically PBY-5 type aircraft and like the U.S. Navy planes were powered with 1200 h.p. Twin Wasp engines.

Reuben Fleet had long contended that PBYs should be amphibious—able to operate from airports as well as from bays, lakes, rivers or the open ocean, if necessary. "I insisted," he said, "that some of the PBYs carry their own beaching gear so they could climb a ramp under their own power after a water landing, or use it as a retractable tricycle gear for normal airport landings.

"The engineering department hated to do this because it used a whole bay in the hull, but since the wheel retracted into an empty space the only real loss was in the added weight for the gear and mechanism.

"In April 1939 we obtained a contract to modify the last PBY-4 to incorporate the amphibian features and the plane, redesignated XPBY-5A, was first flown November 22. A month later we had the order for 200 PBY-5s and the last 33 planes of this order were converted to the -5A amphibian version.

"The Navy found the versatility of the PBY-5A land- or sea-plane a great convenience because they didn't have to bother with the beaching gear. It more than doubled our production and that was what I was after."

Slightly over half of all PBY-5s—the largest production model patrol bomber—were the -5A version in amphibian configuration.

The French PBY order of early 1940 was taken over by the British since no aircraft could be delivered before the fall of France that June. Britain also shared part of the R.C.A.F. order which was for amphibian versions. Many of the R.A.F. planes were ferried into Bermuda by civilian pilots of American Export Airlines. All but 12 of the Netherlands East Indies 'Catalinas' had been delivered by pilots of Consolidated's own ferry delivery service before the Japanese struck in the South Pacific in December 1941.

The British Purchasing Commission had a hand in setting up production of 'Catalinas' by Boeing of Canada at Vancouver and by Canadian Vickers at Montreal. Boeing built 55 PBY-5A 'Canso' amphibians for the R.C.A.F. and 307 PBY-5 and -6 'Catalinas' under the designations PB2B-1 and PB2B-2 for the U.S. Navy and the British. Canadian Vickers built 369 amphibian 'Catalinas,' of which 139 were Canso-As for the

AMPHIBIAN version of 'Catalina' was the PBY-5A, shown here in squadron strength. In air-sea rescue role, Army designation was OA-10A.

National Air and Space Museum

RETRACTABLE *landing gear of amphibian model of 'Catalina' tucks into hull beneath wing of PBY-5A series aircraft.*

General Dynamics/Convair

R.C.A.F. and the balance OA-10As for the U.S. Army. Also producing a PBY version known as the PBN-1 'Nomad' was the U.S. Naval Aircraft factory at Philadelphia. Of 156 Nomads built, 137 went to the USSR.

The United States used its greatly expanded flying boat capability to establish a Neutrality Patrol for the protection of shipping convoys in the Atlantic. But it was the Coastal Command of the Royal Air Force which got world attention in May 1941.

Germany had sent the pride of its Navy, the great new battleship 'Bismarck,' into the North Atlantic to attack Allied shipping. The British responded with a large task force and in the engagement which followed off Greenland HMS 'Hood' was sunk and the 'Bismarck' damaged. Overnight the 'Bismarck' disappeared, limping away in an effort to reach her base on the coast of France.

'Catalinas' from the Coastal Command based on Northern Ireland were sent to locate the wounded but still powerful 'Bismarck.' On the 26th a PBY from No. 209 squadron, with an American officer as co-pilot, located the German capital ship and began stalking her. Dodging in and out of cloud cover for ten hours the 'Catalina' was hit by gunfire from the 'Bismarck' on several occasions. Holes in the hull were patched in flight by crew members. Finally another 'Catalina,' from No. 240 squadron, took over the tracking until the 'Bismarck' was caught and destroyed next day by carrier-based torpedo planes and surface ships of the British Navy. After loss of HMS 'Hood,' sinking of the 'Bismarck' restored Britain's supremacy of the North Atlantic.

Praise was heaped on Consolidated and its thousands of workers for the important part PBYs were already playing in the war in Europe. Among Fleet's treasured mementos is a large papier-mache admiral's 'cocked hat' that Harry Chandler, publisher of the Los Angeles Times, sent him after the 'Bismarck' was sunk. On the brim were clippings of the sinking and a congratulatory note which read, "Knowing that no San Diego store would be likely to have a hat big enough to fit you now, I have taken the liberty of getting one here."

Reuben was more than equal to Chandler's joking sarcasm.

"My first thought," he wrote "was that you had wildly exaggerated my head size. But, upon trying it on, I was astounded to discover that it fits perfectly!"

Consolidator

Soon after the 'Bismarck' sinking, Admiral Husband E. Kimmel, commander-in-chief, U.S. Fleet, was in San Diego to accept delivery of a PBY and to talk to thousands of assembled workers about the vital task that lay before them.

Somewhat prophetically Admiral Kimmel told his June 23 audience that "America is in a state of emergency that may shortly become a state of war.

"You have read over and over again how the British in the war have done 'too little and too late.' We

'LIBERATOR' TAIL serves as billboard as Ambassador Lord Halifax sends a 'Dear Mr. Churchill' message to Sir Winston, the British Prime Minister, assuring him 'hundreds more like this are on their way to help finish the job.'

Americans must do our utmost to avoid such errors."

In six months the United States would be at war in the Pacific and Admiral Kimmel was to be relieved of his command immediately after the Japanese attack on Pearl Harbor.

As if building up to the climax which was to come, the morale and motivation of workers on production lines was a major concern of the Administration. A month after Admiral Kimmel's visit, General William S. Knudsen, recently named co-director of the Office of Production Management, visited the Consolidated plant, followed a week later by Lord and Lady Halifax.

The British Ambassador came to see production progress on LB-30 Liberator bombers for the R.A.F. On the tail surfaces of one just coming off the production line, Lord Halifax wrote a personal message to Sir Winston Churchill assuring him there were hundreds of 'Liberators' to follow to help finish the job.

While checking progress on Britain's LB-30 Liberators, Lord Halifax saw another Consolidated design which attracted his attention—the Model 31 high-speed, long range flying boat on which the Davis wing was being tested.

"The Model 31 prototype," Major Fleet recalled, "cost us a million dollars to engineer and build, and Lord Halifax offered us a million dollars, Lend-Lease, for it. Well, that meant Uncle Sam was digging up the money for the plane and it made me good and sore to even think of it.

"I was too damn patriotic an American to accept the million dollars and just turned Lord Halifax down on his proposition. Of course I made a mistake in doing so because we were having trouble selling it to the U.S. Navy. They wouldn't have anything to do with the Model 31 because they hadn't had their finger in the pie in developing it. They climbed all over the plane, went through it and admired it but that was about all. I never saw such reasoning as Admiral Cook and his assistants showed on that ship. However, I later recouped the million dollars, which wasn't the only million I lost, or made."

IF PRESIDENT ROOSEVELT was to get his annual production rate of 50,000 airplanes, the aircraft industry could not do the task alone. Automobile manufacturers, with their mass production capability, would have to become additional sources of supply.

One dollar-a-year man from the industry trying to help organize the national production effort was Dr. George J. Mead, recently resigned from United Aircraft to serve as aircraft production chairman of the National Defense Council.

Consolidated was running into problems on early B-24 and PBY-5 flying boat deliveries. Writing to George Mead, Reuben explained:

"The delays in B-24 shipments are the direct result of design changes and, in the case of the PBY-5, poor performance by Brewster, the sub-contractor. I feel certain that a San Diego parts plant, subject to our sole control, is the answer to the delivery commitments we have made.

"I am a firm believer in direct action and while we may suffer a certain amount of inefficiency for not having a more rigidly defined organization structure, it is my considered opinion that we can consummate a job while the 'well-organized' plant makes up its collective mind.

"What we have here, George, is not a one-man show, it is a three-ring circus and when the Washington troupers stop clowning we will begin delivering real quantities of airplanes from the plant. Anything you can do toward elimination of dual inspection and the interminable petty arguments incident thereto will speed up deliveries."

Congress was also looking into aircraft production, adding to industry's apprehension about government interference. However, one guest, surprisingly, turned out to be a delightful exception.

Senator Harry S. Truman of Missouri, chairman of the Senate committee investigating the defense program, showed up in San Diego with staff people to look at Consolidated's efforts.

"Major Fleet," the Senator explained, "I'm going to be with you for the next six hours. Consolidated is too important to our country not to inspect it. Senator James M. Mead of New York tells me he knows you well from Buffalo days and that as a fine American you helped put him in the United States Senate. So he asked me to give you his best regards and to please excuse his not coming with me."

"Well, Senator, we're delighted to have you and suggest you take my chair and run the company from my desk while you're here. Start right in."

Just then the phone rang and Fleet beckoned the Senator to answer.

"This is Senator Truman speaking and I'll be running the company for the next few hours. If whatever you need can't wait that long maybe I can get Major Fleet to handle the matter."

Recalling the visit, Reuben went on to explain, "Evidently this answer sufficed, so the stylishly-dressed U.S. Senator settled back comfortably and we began to talk and enjoy his visit, with him answering all the phone calls. Finally, I suggested we walk through the factory while I explained the operations.

"I never enjoyed a visit more, of course never dreaming that a few years later Senator Truman would be chosen the Democratic nominee for Vice President and on the death of my friend Franklin D. Roosevelt in 1945 become President of the United States. He made an excellent President although I disliked his firing General Douglas MacArthur during the Korean War."

A slightly different version of at least one portion of the Truman visit gained some currency around San Diego. The Major had a habit of dominating most conversations and reportedly talked at length about his personal business success on this occasion. Senator Truman, they say, interrupted the Major: "God damn! I want to see your books, Fleet. I'm not interested in your rise from rags to riches!"

PRODUCTION CAPABILITY of Consolidated is pointed out to William S. Knudsen, chairman of the National Defense Council, and to Gen. Hap Arnold, far right, by Major Fleet. Officer second from right is Major E. R. McReynolds, Air Corps plant representative.

THE DAY BEFORE CHRISTMAS 1940, George Mead was on the phone to Fleet. "The situation abroad is so serious," Mead said, "that we must go forward rapidly in setting up the best possible secondary sources of supply of bomber parts. The safety of our country may well depend upon doing so because the aircraft industry cannot expand any more at present without seriously interfering with the deliveries required by our present program."

Dr. Mead went on to advise Reuben that the big three automobile companies had tentatively been assigned to work on bomber production and had agreed to take educational contracts. Ford would be teamed with Consolidated on the B-24; General Motors with North American on the B-25; Chrysler with Martin on the B-26. In two weeks Mead and Charles E. Sorensen, Ford's production chief, would be in San Diego to size up the situation.

The government's concept was to have the auto companies build parts and subassemblies which would then be assembled in new government-owned factories—'depots'—supervised by prime contractors.

To speed production of Navy flying boats, Consolidated had doubled its plant facilities early in 1940 and followed with another 650,000 square feet of factory space in anticipation of further defense orders.

That explosive expansion was merely a start of what was to follow, but when the newest additions were dedicated on September 2, Fleet sounded a word of warning and a plea for free enterprise.

"We had planned announcement today of further extensive plant expansion," he told an audience of five thousand, "but the Bill recently passed by the Senate authorizing peacetime commandeering of industrial plants which may fail in any respect to please a high official of our government, makes us hesitate, much as we have been striving with all our might as a private enterprise to do our bit."

At the lectern the Major paused to gather his thoughts before resuming on another tack. "Nationalization of her aircraft industry by France was so disastrous that that country's production fell down terribly; even though she frantically resorted to foreign help at exorbitant expense, she collapsed as a nation. We hope our government will not make this mistake, which would be the beginning of labor regimentation, the emasculation of labor unions, which our President has stated cannot strike against the government, and the end in this country of free enterprise."

Although no announcement of additional plant expansion was made during the dedication, Fleet went ahead with his planning despite government insistence that any new facilities be in the Zone of the Interior, away from possible attack on coastal cities. The Navy, too, wanted an inland plant for flying boat production.

Title Insurance and Trust Company

DR. GEORGE J. MEAD, chief advisor on aircraft production for the National Defense Council, left, confers in San Diego with Reuben Fleet.

220

While this discussion was going on, plans for participation of the big three automobile companies in aircraft production were being negotiated. Political considerations played a role in plans for new B-24 plants as related by Major Fleet:

"President Roosevelt had promised Governor William H. (Alfalfa Bill) Murray of Oklahoma that they would have a defense plant. A similar commitment was made to Governor W. Lee O'Daniel of Texas. The President wanted me to pick out the sites for both of these B-24 plants, to help lay out the production facilities and to run them.

"I told the President that I didn't have the personnel to man the eastern plants, but if he felt that I needed to expand to let me do it in San Diego. That way I could develop additional personnel that could later be sent to help out at Fort Worth and other locations. Out of that conversation we received approval to go forward on yet another expansion of our San Diego facilities."

Construction began in November on a huge government-financed parts plant a mile north of the main factory and connected to it by a private road and overpass above busy Pacific Highway, the main route from the north into San Diego. The 1.6 million square feet of the new facility again doubled in size the original plant and all subsequent additions.

The government's plan for expanded B-24 production required an eastern factory site survey. Perhaps to protect him from aggressive Chamber of Commerce promoters, the Major asked Tom Bomar, who had helped bring about Consolidated's move from Buffalo to San Diego, to accompany him.

"Amon G. Carter, Fort Worth newspaper publisher, took us in tow at Ft. Worth and showed us Lake Worth," recalls Bomar, "and at Dallas it was the Chamber of Commerce. Then we took the train down to Houston where we were guests of Jesse Jones, Secretary of Commerce. They showed us where an artificial lake and plant site could be built.

"Next day at luncheon at the Country Club, Reub Fleet got up and said he appreciated everything but that he hadn't seen a damn thing that looked as good as Chula Vista on San Diego Bay. If anyone else had made a statement like that in Texas, they'd have hung him!

"Bill Wheatley was there with a 'Fleetster' and flew Reuben and other company executives to New Orleans to look over Lake Pontchartrain. From there Fleet went on to Washington, and meantime dispatched Van Dusen to Oklahoma to look over plant sites there."

The pattern for greatly expanded war production of B-24s began to take final shape.

Consolidated would operate a new Fort Worth government-built plant for the assembly and production of four-engine bombers and transports. The $45 million plant adjoining Lake Worth would have over three million square feet of production area.

Another government decision in May, 1941 was to build an 800,000 square foot facility at Tulsa, Oklahoma to be operated by Douglas Aircraft Company.

1940-41 SAW MAJOR EXPANSION of San Diego plant facilities as Consolidated doubled and redoubled production capability to meet growing defense requirements.

General Dynamics/Convair

The third component of the plan was the $85 million Willow Run bomber plant of the Ford Motor Company near Ypsilanti, Michigan. Initially the Willow Run plant was conceived as a parts factory to supply assemblies for the Douglas-Tulsa and Consolidated-Fort Worth plants; later it would build complete B-24s as well.

THE TELEPHONE RANG in Reuben Fleet's outer office. After a minute his private secretary, Eva Wiseman, pressed the buzzer. "Major, it's Donald Douglas."

"Okay, put him on." Fleet later related the conversation which followed:

"Reuben, this is Don Douglas. Hap Arnold tells me that I'm going to have to build B-24s. I'll do it, of course, but with great reluctance."

"I don't like it either, Don. You can't build our B-24 without learning our heat-treatment methods and our other secrets. But why the reluctance?"

"Because I am a better designer than you are."

"I guess there is no question about that, Don. You are a better designer. But somehow you never hear about the DC-5 any more. You badly missed it on the DC-5 design didn't you?"

"Yes, I certainly did. We just didn't produce any more of them."

"Well, Harry Wetzel [of Douglas] says you use a regular shotgun method of riveting. You know what a shotgun pattern looks like at 40 yards, whereas we put the rivets where they belong."

"Oh, Reuben! What the hell are rivets anyway?"

"You know there are a quarter of a million of them in a B-24."

"A quarter of a million! How do you know?"

"Because I had them counted. That means at least half a million holes with high speed drills."

"I didn't know rivets were as important as that!"

"They're so important we are putting in a machine here to build 5,000,000 rivets a day. I can't afford to have a whole factory waiting for some kind of new rivet the engineers have specified while I wait for them from some supplier. That's no good. We'll do it ourselves."

Having dismissed the Douglas DC-5 as an inferior design, Reuben went on to recall another story about his 'rivet factory.'

"Incidentally," he began, "Lockheed started buying rivets from us. They ordered quantities of about a dozen different types. On one order the drawing was confusing and we read it the way we thought was right and delivered the rivets. They wouldn't pay us for them. I called up Bob Gross, Lockheed president.

" 'Listen, Bob, don't ask us to make any more rivets for you unless you pay us for these. How in the hell could anybody tell the right way to read that print? You've got to teach your engineers to make it plainer.'

"Lockheed paid up. Well, that's good business. Bob was a fine fellow."

Along with the great potential of the B-24 came an admonition from Hap Arnold to his old friend Reuben Fleet. "He told me," Reuben said, "that he wouldn't stand for us to manufacture any commercial aircraft as that would be cutting into Don Douglas' domain upon which he was principally dependent for transports. We were thus restricted by Hap's wish that we not produce commercial aircraft.

"You see, Hap's son, Bruce Arnold, had married Don's daughter, Barbara Douglas. Kinship exceeded friendship in this case. Naturally we agreed to this restriction."

General Arnold also had a daughter, Lois, whom he had sent to San Diego where Reuben Fleet saw to it that she received a clerical job at Consolidated. Hap knew, too, that his old friend would keep a fatherly eye on his daughter.

"She was worrying me terribly," Fleet recalls, "staying out far too late at night. Next day she'd get to the office late, but that wasn't what concerned me. One day she asked to see me.

" 'Major Fleet, I want you to call my dad and tell him I am going to marry a Navy fighter pilot.'

"Well, Lois, who is he?"

" 'Lieut. Ernest M. Snowden.'

"When do you want me to call your father?"

" 'Right now.'

"I'll call him tonight and he'll ask me if I've met your Lieutenant Snowden. I haven't. So you better get hold of him and the two of you call on Mrs. Fleet and me at our home about five o'clock for cocktails.

"So they came to the house. I saw that he handled his liquor all right. So did Lois. Before the evening was over she wanted me to call her father.

"There was a three hour difference in time and I got Hap out of bed to answer the phone.

"Hap, Lois insists that I call you and tell you she is going to marry a Naval officer."

"Why in the hell are you letting her marry a Naval officer? Is he a graduate of Annapolis?"

"Yes, Class of 1932 at the Naval Academy. And, Hap, if you didn't hold the Navy in high regard you wouldn't have sent her here to San Diego, a Navy town, would you?"

"Yes, of course you're right Reuben. Have you met him?"

"Yes, I have. This fellow is all right. He's flying off the 'Ranger' with Fighting Squadron 5. I judge him to be a pretty good man. They want to get married before Christmas. If you want you can have her married right here in our home. We'll help you arrange it."

"No, you're a contractor to the government. That

PLANT 2, government-financed parts plant, was *connected to Main Plant by overpass and private road through Marine Corps Base.*

wouldn't look good. We will have the marriage there in San Diego, but not at your home."

And so they were married December 20, 1937 at Coronado.

Reuben had been right about Lieut. Snowden. As the Commander of carrier-based aircraft squadrons during the War he lead air attacks on Guadalcanal, Wake Island, Tarawa, the Marshall Islands and other Japanese bases in the South Pacific and received numerous decorations, including the Distinguished Flying Cross.

THE TREMENDOUS EXPANSION of Consolidated facilities and employment brought parallel growth and problems to the entire San Diego area. Reuben Fleet had developed a genuine fondness for the city and its people and was in a position to rally national support behind needed civic projects. Sensing some of the problems which lay ahead, he had a behind-the-scenes role in convening a government commission in October 1940 which unanimously adopted a report that federal aid was necessary. But aid was slow in coming.

The Works Progress Administration (WPA) had abondoned the San Diego sewer collection project, arousing Fleet's ire. San Diego was a Navy town; Consolidated was a Navy plant. The Navy had better take notice.

Reuben fired off a telegram to Navy Secretary Frank Knox demanding action on three fronts: $1 million to complete the sewer collection system. $10 million for a federal aqueduct to bring additional Colorado River water to San Diego when needed. $1.5 million to finish Harbor Drive along Lindbergh Field's southern perimeter to connect government activities along the waterfront from Ft. Rosecrans to the Destroyer Base.

"There are now 100,000 more persons here," Fleet explained, "than when we discussed the necessity of these programs last September. The situation is now impossible without federal aid. Nowhere else is the government more heavily interested than in San Diego.

"We face a possible epidemic due to pollution of our harbor into which 14 sewerage outfalls now pour. The harbor is also full of Navy destroyers, cruisers and aircraft carriers and they are discharging into the harbor. The San Diego River was diverted over into False Bay (Mission Bay) in 1854 so there has been nothing since then to clean out the harbor. Whatever is there stays there except as the tide takes it out, and that's a long process. Something must be done to clear up the harbor."

Impatient with delay, the Major was soon explaining to President Roosevelt that as contractors to both the Army and Navy he felt it would be better to place coordination of San Diego's multiplicity of civic needs related to Consolidated expansion under a single head. Why not, he suggested place it under Treasury Secretary Morgenthau?

"The President," Fleet recalls, "said that I should go over and see Morgenthau and tell the Secretary just what I had told him. Then he phoned Morgenthau.

" 'I think you had better have a member of your staff also listen to Major Fleet, a man to whom you can delegate the work and let him do nothing but handle the San Diego situation.'

"Secretary Morgenthau appointed Edward H. Foley, Jr., General Counsel of the Treasury Department, as coordinator and he came out to San Diego with a large staff from the various departments of government that I told them were necessary if we were to receive the attention we needed."

Reuben was a man of action as well as words as his wife, Dorothy, related. "We had recently bought a yacht, the 'New Moon' from Jimmy Roosevelt. Reuben had decided that an afternoon of cruising on the bay would be both relaxing and educational for our distinguished guests, a small group of dignified Congressmen.

"Then he led our guests to the rail of the yacht. 'Lean over,' he instructed, 'Now sniff! Smell it? It's sewage. Evil, disease-breeding sewage, dumped in this beautiful bay because the City of San Diego has no

EMISSARY and versatile Washington handyman, Patrick Jay Hurley, right, visits the Fleets, Dorothy and Reuben (on either side of Mrs. Hurley).

DEDICATION of new Parts Plant in October 1941 brings out the brass. From left, Adm. A. L. Lyster, Royal Navy; Adm. John H. Towers, USN; Asst. Navy Secy. Artemus L. Gates; Reuben Fleet.

funds for a proper disposal plant!'

"Several days later he came home, beaming. 'The city will get the money for the sewage plant,' he told me. 'Surprised?' "

Housing was another part of the problem which Reuben Fleet tackled head on. By Fall of 1941 Consolidated employment was up to 25,000 workers and would rise another 20,000 in the next nine months. With workers migrating from all over the country to take defense production jobs in San Diego, accommodations simply were not available.

Two make-shift plans filled part of the need—a 'trailer city' near the Destroyer Base and permanent dormitories in a 17-building complex for 750 single men.

But the greater need was for family housing. Reuben Fleet helped ram through a plan which he saw was also placed under the direct control of Treasury Secretary Morgenthau. It was Linda Vista, a new self-sufficient city providing homes for 3000 families. Laid out on a brush-covered mesa north of San Diego, California's first planned community was a city within a city, having its own schools, stores and churches. Built in just six months, Linda Vista was dedicated in 1941 by Mrs. Eleanor Roosevelt, wife of the President.

The new parts factory—known as Plant 2, and as large as the main plant—was completed in the Fall of 1941 and dedicated October 20 by Artemus L. Gates, Assistant Secretary of the Navy for Air, and Admiral John Towers. It was exactly six years to the day since dedication of the first unit of the Consolidated San Diego plant.

It had taken someone like Reuben Fleet to recognize the extent and diversity of the problems created by such vast expansion of war production in San Diego. He was able to get the necessary cooperation at the top levels of the federal government so that within a few years all the civic projects were completed.

Robert P. Patterson
Reuben H. Fleet

FLEET-FORD FRICTION grew out of Ford Motor Company's role as a second source on B-24 production. From left, Charles E. Sorensen, Fleet, and Edsel Ford.

CALLED UPON BY THE GOVERNMENT to get into aircraft production, Ford Motor Company officials set out for San Diego right after New Years Day, 1941 to look over B-24 manufacturing facilities at Consolidated. Edsel Ford, president, brought with him his production manager, Charles E. Sorensen, and his sons, Benson and Henry Ford II. Accompanying them was Dr. George J. Mead of the National Defense Council.

Reuben Fleet recalls Consolidated's relationship with the giant auto company and its executives.

"The Ford people stayed with us for a week, and we made arrangements to lease space downtown where engineers of the two companies could work together converting our aircraft industry drawings to needs of the automobile industry.

"Anyway, I laid out the Willow Run plant at Ypsilanti for Edsel Ford. I told Sorensen that if they built their jigs out of steel (we used duralumin) as he planned, the coefficient of expansion of steel was different from that of aluminum alloy and he would have to hold the factory temperature within six degrees. Otherwise, I explained, the weaker metal, namely the aluminum wing he was going to build, could not retain its seal and would leak fuel.

"Sorensen was confident he could hold the factory temperature within six degrees, 'very easily.' That was typical of Sorensen who once claimed that he could pick up the Washington Monument and move it to another site without destroying a single block in that huge structure. There was nothing, he thought, that he couldn't do.

"Despite my warnings he built his jigs out of steel. Some months later I got a telephone call from Robert P. Patterson, Undersecretary of War, telling me he had a report that Ford had spent $87 million on Willow

BY NOVEMBER 1940, hard-pressed British were beginning to receive LB-30 'Liberators' like this one leaving runway at San Diego's Lindbergh Field.

Run. Would I go up there, look things over and then come to Washington and tell him when the Army was going to get some airplanes out of there.

"I said I would do that, of course, but I could do a much better job if he would have Edsel Ford and Charlie Sorensen there at Willow Run to meet me. It's hard, I explained, for me to look at a bunch of machinery and tell what is in their minds. I needed them there. So he arranged my visit.

"At the Ypsilanti factory we went on a tour down the main assembly line in battery-powered carts. Edsel was on one side of the aisle with a driver, I in the middle with my driver, and Sorensen on the left with his driver, all abreast.

"We came to the end of the aisle and I noticed that the assembly line turned right to continue for another 600 feet. I asked, 'How come this right angle turn in the main assembly line? It wasn't in my layout.'

" 'Well,' replied Edsel, 'we forgot to allow for the offices. You see, if we'd run the assembly line straight we would have run it into Wayne County. You knew the factory was in Washtenaw County, didn't you, Major?'

" 'No, I didn't know that. So what?'

" 'We put it in Washtenaw County because taxes are only one-fifth of what they are in Wayne County.'

" 'What difference does that make? The plant is owned by the government and it pays no taxes.'

" 'Yes, but after the war is over the Ford Motor Company hopes to own it and operate it as an airplane plant.'

"I said to myself quietly, 'That's another reason, Reuben, why you should consider selling the company. Ford's been out of the airplane business for 13 years; since the day of the trimotor. Here you are holding his hand and teaching hundreds of his people the modern aircraft manufacturing business. You are even giving him your secret heat-treat methods which are not even

on the engineering drawings. You are doing everything you can to aid him and he's already telling you he is going to buck you when the war is over. You had better sell.'

"Anyway, Sorensen failed to hold plant temperatures within a range of six degrees. In summer the plant was like a boiler house and the employees wouldn't work without opening the factory doors. As a consequence, the airplanes they built leaked fuel because of minute cracks in the aluminum skin. The Army was forced to put fuel cells inside the wings of Ford-built B-24s, and this extra weight greatly reduced the operating range. When some pilots familiar with the gas-tight Consolidated B-24s had to switch to those built by Ford, they no longer liked the plane because of the reduced range."

Mac Laddon shared Reuben's poor opinion of the automobile industry's capability. "Charlie Sorensen was a real beaut! The quantities they were used to dealing with were so far different from what we build that they screwed everything up from hell to breakfast. They just don't know what the devil it's all about!"

A post-war Air Force study of B-24 production also commented upon the automotive industry's participation in warplane manufacture. "A considerable amount of trouble," the report read, "was experienced by Ford in the early part of the B-24 program as might have been expected. It seemed rather difficult for Ford to adhere exactly to Consolidated drawings and not incorporate ideas of their own, but it was imperative that Ford follow instructions, otherwise interchangeability would have been non-existent.

"Ford at first was reluctant to make the number of changes required to keep the airplane up-to-date from a military standpoint, largely because the company policy was to operate the production lines with a minimum of changes when once started in operation."

TO HELP THE HARD-PRESSED British, the first 26 B-24s were made available to the Royal Air Force as Model LB-30As. This also permitted the Air Corps to install turbo-supercharged Twin Wasp engines instead of the earlier mechanical-supercharged versions in their B-24s, which followed the LB-30s. The first RAF bomber was accepted January 17, 1941. On February 15 George Newman and a British crew flew the camouflaged LB-30, the first 'Liberator,' non-stop San Diego to New York in nine hours, 57 minutes.

The first B-24 model to go into large quantity production was the '-D' version with turbo-supercharged engines and an increase in gross weight to 56,000 lbs. compared with the original 41,000 lbs. Orders were placed for 56 planes in 1940; then increased by 352 D's before the year was out. Some 2728 of the 'D' version were eventually built, most of them at San Diego.

Demanding high standards in any aircraft he produced was almost a fetish with Reuben Fleet. When the first five unarmed LB-30s went to England for the Trans-Atlantic Return Ferry Service between Montreal and Prestwick, Scotland, the Major planted his feet in concrete.

"They took the planes," he recalls, "before we had a chance to complete our static tests. We tested No. 6 and found it failed at 92% in high incidence. Both the British engineers and our own people thought it was strong enough.

"My standard was 100%. I didn't like the idea of having a standard and then not meeting it. I insisted the British return the five planes for rework. They protested they couldn't spare them. I told them to return them one at a time; that the day they returned each one we would give them a new one also, taking cognizance of all problems which had shown up. They would lose just the time in flying from eastern Canada to San Diego and back, and I wouldn't have five airplanes flying around, goodness knows where, underfactored as to safety.

"It cost us a quarter of a million dollars, but after all we had our standards—as near perfection as possible. We simply wouldn't condone having them flying our airplanes with any basic deficiency.

"Our philosophy was 'Nothing Short of Right is Right.' That was our motto and in May 1941 we painted it in letters nine feet high across the longest building we had to force our people to think about their responsibility for quality workmanship. We tried to set an example with the rework done on those first LB-30s; that you can't cut corners and get by with it."

As with all his other aircraft, Major Fleet wanted to get in some actual flight time himself in the prototype XB-24 which the company had retained for additional testing.

Reuben related that "we were flying the original B-24 around as often as possible to see how good, or how poor, it was and how it might be improved. On a

'MY STANDARD WAS 100%,' declared Fleet, whose slogan appeared in 9-foot letters on San Diego plant. 'You can't cut corners and get away with it.' Huge sign was 480 feet long.

San Diego Aero-Space Museum

227

number of these flights with company executives aboard young George Newman was the pilot and I the co-pilot, but a good deal of the time I had the controls. Unfortunately I didn't fly often; didn't have time.

"Howard Hughes was one of the most respected test pilots around and, eccentric though he was, I was anxious to have his evaluation of the B-24. He wanted to see the plane and fly with me, so we took the prototype over to Tucson. While playing golf on the municipal course there I stepped in a gopher hole and twisted my ankle [injured in the 1929 'Fleet' biplane crash] so badly I was laid up for weeks at a mountain resort near there.

"Hughes was a sponger of information and he took advantage of our friendship to fly the B-24 ten or 12 hours a day all the time I was recuperating—though he did pay for the gas. It was typical of his way of doing things. But he was a responsible citizen, the plane was there and I was anxious to get any dope on it that I could especially from such a fine pilot. He was anxious to dope it out, too, and gave me all the information he could from his flights.

"He talked about buying some commercial versions providing we would give him a larger wing but at no extra cost. All airplanes are alike. None had been invented yet that someone doesn't want more range, more load and the same speed, too—if you add more wing—and of course the same price."

During the tremendous pressure to speed deliveries of B-24s some errors in workmanship were bound to creep in with tragic results. One such incident came close to home for Reuben as it involved a personal friend and long time associate. In a June 2, 1941 test flight of the first longer-nosed 'Liberator II' to come off the production line, Bill Wheatley was at the controls with Alan Austen in the right seat as co-pilot. Austen was a close friend of the writer, having been trained as a transport pilot at the Ryan School of Aeronautics across Lindbergh Field from Consolidated.

As we watched the B-24 lift off and start to climb out over San Diego Bay, the plane reared up in a near vertical position, engines wide open, then as Wheatley and Austen fought for control and cut power, it appeared they would be able to flatten out and pancake into the water. But the speed of the B-24 was too great and the plane climbed steeply again, then fell off with one wing low and dove into the bay. The pilots and all but one crew member were killed.

What had gone wrong? The only likely cause was the report widely circulated that there were some loose rivets or bolts left in the fuselage and that one wedged into the sprocket of the control column making it impossible to move the controls.

After the original six LB-30s for the Ferry Service, the next group of 20 'Liberators' went to the RAF Coastal Command and were the first of the B-24 family to see operational service.

By June 1941, No. 120 Squadron of the Coastal Command was operating long range reconnaissance and anti-submarine flight over the North Atlantic out of Ireland.

One of the earliest LB-30s became Sir Winston Churchill's personal transport. Christened 'Commando,' it carried the British leader to conferences with Stalin in Moscow and to others in Casablanca (January 1943) and Cairo (November 1943). Deliveries of B-24s to the U.S. Army Air Forces had also started and the first role for the new bombers was as transports across the Atlantic for the Ferrying Command.

On July 1, 1941, Lieut. Col. Caleb V. Haynes opened the Air Force overseas route to England flying to Prestwick, Scotland via Montreal and Newfoundland. August 31, Haynes and Maj. Curtis E. Lemay pioneered the route over the South Atlantic in a B-24 carrying Maj. Gen. George H. Brett on a special mission to Cairo.

In September, two B-24As were used to carry W. Averell Harriman, President Roosevelt's Lend-Lease coordinator, and members of his mission to Moscow. The final leg from Prestwick to Moscow was 3150 miles non-stop, indicative of the plane's long-range potential. One B-24 continued on around the world via India, Singapore, Australia, Wake Island and Hawaii. The other via Africa, the South Atlantic and Brazil.

THE PUSH FOR BIG LAND-BASED bombers had actually begun in 1934. An Army design contract had been awarded to Boeing to study the feasibility of aircraft larger than anything then flying or planned for production. The plane was identified as XBLR-1 (experimental bomber, long range, first model) and the 150-foot wing giant first flew in October 1937 as the XB-15. Its role was strictly that of research.

Study of a second, still larger flying laboratory, XBLR-2, was initiated in July 1935 and a prototype, the Douglas XB-19, with a wing 212 feet from tip to tip was ordered September 1936.

Meantime, the Army requested bids and competitive flight demonstrations of a more practical, state-of-the-art bomber which could be produced in quantity while research continued on larger aircraft. From this realistic approach came the 104-foot wing Boeing B-17 'Flying Fortress' of 1933 and, in turn, the more advanced 110-foot wing B-24 of 1940 as companion four-engine bombers.

Yet, General Arnold, within two months of the outbreak of war in Europe and before the B-24 had even flown, initiated study of a 5000-mile-range four-engine bomber superior in all respects to the B-17 and B-24. Within the year, September 1940, Boeing and Consolidated had new developmental contracts for the very heavy XB-29 and XB-32 bombers.

Wing spans were 142 feet for the B-29 and 135 feet for the B-32. The Boeing B-29 had a thin wing, similar to that of the Consolidated B-24. Principal designer of the B-29 was George Schairer, formerly of Consolidated, who had assisted David R. Davis in laying out the Davis Wing for the B-24 'Liberator.' Later Boeing had hired Schairer.

The huge XB-19 was delayed in development. Douglas suggested that because of the expense involved and rapid advancement in technology before the plane could be completed, the project be dropped.

The Army, however, wanted data which only a flying laboratory could provide. But it was not until June 27, 1941 that the XB-19 flew.

Enough had been learned, however, that on November 15, 1941—three weeks before Pearl Harbor—Consolidated was awarded a contract to proceed with development of the six-engine XB-36. Later the giant bomber would have four jet engines added to its 230-foot wing.

Thus, in the short span of two and a half years, Major Fleet and his Consolidated associates won contracts for three giant bomber types—the B-24 'Liberator,' the B-32 'Dominator,' and the B-36 'Intercontinental Bomber'—and had the first of these in large scale production.

Because of his penchant to personally keep abreast of design trends and to apply his piloting experience to aerodynamic problems, the Major had a scale model of the B-36 made for his office.

"I had the B-36 model mounted on a pedestal," Fleet recalls, "so I could sit there at my desk, see it constantly and study its finely configured proportions in the thought that perhaps I could get some ideas which would be helpful to R. C. (Sparky) Seabold, our B-36 project engineer. He had come with us from Buffalo and later went to Fort Worth as chief engineer where the huge Intercontinental bombers were built.

"The B-36 was an awfully good airplane."

Forecasting by a quarter century the kind of situation in which there would be an atomic bomb stand-off between major powers, Reuben Fleet in pre-Pearl Harbor days wrote that "Until the temperament of mankind changes, world peace cannot be enjoyed in the absence of power capable of enforcing it.

"Such power is air power, augmented by naval power, and by an army where occupation and policing of territory is necessary. Nothing within its range can stop aircraft; their range is now a continent or an ocean.

"Let us hope that when this war ends, possession of such aircraft, without their employment, will guarantee 'peace on earth, good-will to men.' " It was Reuben Fleet's message to employees on Christmas 1940.

EVER INCREASING PRODUCTION of bombers and flying boats required vast expansion of factory facilities. These were the main tasks in the years immediately preceding America's direct participation in World War II but many other vexing problems faced Reuben Fleet and his management team at Consolidated.

If there was anything that the Major prided himself in, it was his cordial relations with the company's employees—his employees. In the best sense, he had a paternalistic interest in their welfare.

From the earliest days in East Greenwich, Rhode Island, Reuben had always known most of his employees as personal friends; members of his corporate family. Felix Rossoll, already employed by Gallaudet Aircraft for nine years when Fleet became vice president in 1923, vividly recalls the Major's concern.

"Every day he'd look in on what was doing out in the factory. If he saw somebody new he'd go over, introduce himself and make the new worker feel at home from his very first day on the job. He knew all about everyone's family; their children, their successes, their problems. When my wife was in the hospital in Buffalo bearing our first daughter, he sent a baby's bonnet from Macy's in New York City. He was tremendously interested in and concerned about every employee.

"For a long period I worked until ten o'clock every night. Finally I went to the Major and asked for a raise. 'You're a little late, my boy,' he said, 'It's already been put through.' That was more effective in employee good-will than if the raise had come through in a routine, impersonal way."

The spirit of concern for his people had gone with Fleet when he moved the embyro Consolidated company to Buffalo in 1924. It remained a close-knit group of loyal employees with the single exception of a 57-day strike by the Aeronautical Workers Federal Union ten years later, in March, 1934.

PATERNAL CONCERN for long-time employees like Bert Bowling is evident in Major Fleet's expression and friendly pat on the shoulder.

General Dynamics/Convair

Fleet didn't like anyone interfering with his employees, least of all a labor union which would try to supplant him as a father figure by attempting to show they had more interest than did the Major in Consolidated workers and their families.

Eastern industrial cities had notoriously tougher unions and greater leverage in contract negotiations than did those on the west coast, but Fleet moved to San Diego at a time when industrial unions were becoming more aggressive.

The company had been in San Diego little more than a year when the 3600 employees were first subjected to what Fleet called "propaganda tending to give them a biased point of view." The only employee group, loosely organized, was the Consolidators Association, claimed by the expanding International Association of Machinists to be a "company union, dominated by management."

In the plant magazine, Major Fleet tried to explain some of the facts of industrial life to his workers:

> "Practically all of the work we do is for the Navy and, under the Vinson Act, we are barred by law from profiting more than 10% on Navy business. This doesn't mean we are guaranteed 10%; on the contrary it says that is the most we are permitted to make. But we can lose any amount. Any amount, that is, within the size of our corporate purse. Beyond that we would 'go broke,'

> "The lowest responsible bidder receives the government's business, at a fixed price. If his cost estimate is too low, he loses money and is in no way reimbursed. If he is too high, any excess over 10% must be returned to the government.

> "We now have sufficient work ahead for a year and a half and expect to get more. Most of our employees should have steady work for years to come.

> "Our stockholders haven't received a dividend on their common stock in more than eight years. Our recent plant expansion was financed by the sale of preferred stock, which is in the same class as money borrowed, and the holders of such stock must be paid for the use of their money.

> "There are just so many dollars in each fixed-price contract jackpot. It has to cover all costs for labor, material, overhead and—we hope—the permitted profit. In this, labor comes first; it must be paid promptly and its average rate must increase in times like these.

> "Challenge propaganda unless you know it to be a fact! Our products, our business, are founded upon truth!"

Major Fleet's appeal did not stem the rising tide of union organizing effort. In April 1937 the National Labor Relations Board ordered an election to determine which labor organization the employees wanted in collective bargaining. IAM Local 1125 of the AFL or the Consolidators Association.

The vote was 1823 to 531 in favor of the AFL Machinists Union. Their demands were presented and pay rates, including 10% wage increases, agreed to before the month was out. It was the first aircraft agreement since the Supreme Court ruled the Wagner

WITH GREAT RELUCTANCE a dour-faced Reuben Fleet signs contract with labor union.

Labor Relations Act was constitutional.

"All my life," the Major said, "I've tried to abide by the rules and now that the Government has laid down certain rules, I want to play according to them."

Industrial peace at Consolidated was short-lived.

In a crude attempt to embarrass the company, IAM Local 1125 sent off a letter to Rear Admiral Ernest J. King of the Bureau of Aeronautics complaining that shoddy workmanship on PBYs was tolerated by company inspectors and reminding the Admiral that "Navy inspectors need to be disaplined (sic) very urgently." In closing, the Union's recording secretary admitted that "I am not much of a writer but I am sure you will allow for mistakes."

Because of strikes in the east which affected receipt of production materials, Consolidated had to lay off 200 workers less than three months after the IAM contract had been signed. Soon members of the IAM Union were voting on whether to affiliate with the AFL's rival, the CIO, which was then gaining strength in San Diego.

Seeking to oust each other, the rival AFL and CIO factions were called to testify before an NLRB hearing in San Diego. So too, was Major Fleet.

He explained that "When Consolidated signed with the IAM last year we promised to consider a second 10% wage increase effective in June, 1938. When we bid on 64 PBY-4 flying boats for the Navy we assumed our bid would be accepted, and at the price we established further wage raises would have been possible.

"The Navy, however, couldn't afford to buy from us even though we were the lowest bidder. Six months later new estimates were called for by the Navy. We submitted a substantially lower figure and received a contract but for only 33 PBY-4s. Our lower price got us the business this time, but another wage increase now is out of the question

"Managers and owners have their problems, too! Constant concessions to labor eventually will kill the goose that laid the golden egg."

The NLRB ordered new elections in July. Again the IAM won, by a vote of 1098 to 487 for the United Automobile Workers, CIO.

'FINCH' BIPLANE TRAINER, Canadian version of 'Fleet,' was widely used during WW II in Commonwealth Joint Air Training Plan.

GROWING CONCENTRATION on multi-engine flying boats and bombers left management with little time to give attention to the market for single-engine planes, principally those manufactured in small volume by Fleet Aircraft, Ltd. of Canada, in which Consolidated still held a substantial stock interest.

Aircraft manufacturers and training schools had approached Consolidated with the idea of placing the sturdy 'Fleet' and other of their biplane training and observation planes back into production.

For eight years Gordon E. Mounce had been the principal demonstration pilot and European sales representative for 'Fleet' biplane sales. Against stiff competition by English, French and Italian planes and pilots, Mounce had held his own. But in July 1938, as he finished 24 loops in a demonstration at Belgrade, Yugoslavia his plane plunged to earth and Mounce was killed. That personal loss also took its toll with management.

Major Fleet and the board of directors decided that present and future owners of their small single-engine planes could best be served by selling the manufacturing rights. From a long line of candidates, Brewster Aeronautical Corporation of Long Island, New York, was selected in April 1939 to continue the product line

COMPANY-OWNED 'Fleet' was used in San Diego to test various installations for prospective customers. Same month this photo was taken, Fleet Aircraft subsidiary was sold to Canadian interests.

and sales in the United States. Fleet Aircraft, Ltd. of Canada, however, retained foreign rights.

Included in the Brewster arrangement were four basic aircraft types:

- 'Fleet' Model 14 sport and training biplanes
- Model 21 series, including the PT-11 primary and BT-7 basic trainers
- O-19 observation planes originally developed by Thomas-Morse
- PT and NY series trainers, the first Consolidated military aircraft for the Army and Navy

With World War II on the horizon, Brewster found itself involved in war production and never got the commercial 'Fleet' biplane into production.

Fleet Aircraft, Ltd., of Canada fared better. There was an immediate requirement for training planes for Royal Canadian Air Force use under the Commonwealth Joint Air Training Plan. This was met by production between 1939 and 1941 of some 606 'Fleet' trainers (Models 16A and 16B) under the popular Canadian designation of 'Finch I' and 'Finch II.'

One irritation Reuben Fleet had to endure in Buffalo was his next door neighbor, Hall-Aluminum Aircraft Corporation, which was organized there in 1927.

"We were customers of the Aluminum Company of America," Reuben explained, "and spent a good deal of money with them. We objected to their owning an aluminum aircraft manufacturing company and engaging in the metal flying boat business against us. They recognized the validity of the complaint when we suggested they get out of the airplane business or sell it to us.

SPECIAL 'FLEET' TRAINER was entered in 1939 competition for new Army primary trainer. Pilot was George Newman, Jr. Competition was won by Ryan with new S-T low-wing design.

Consolidator

"It was not until 1940 that we were able to buy them out. By then they were located in Bristol, Pennsylvania, having moved there about the time Consolidated moved to San Diego. We simply absorbed Hall-Aluminum and closed it up."

Charles Ward Hall was the head of Hall-Aluminum. He was the son of Charles Martin Hall, inventor of the process for making aluminum and a vice president of the Aluminum Company. When Charles W. Hall was killed in 1936 in a plane crash, his son Archibald M. Hall was named president and later became an executive of Consolidated. A number of Hall-Aluminum engineers and technical people were added to the Consolidated staff then rapidly expanding to meet defense production needs.

Charles W. Hall had gotten his start in aviation in 1920 when his construction engineering firm designed and built duralumin-framed wings for Navy seaplanes. Later they built metal biplane boats for the Navy. Their final product was a twin-engine boat for Coast Guard patrol and research work.

FRED H. ROHR, for five years Factory Manager at Ryan Aeronautical Company, was looking for a new connection and had gone across Lindbergh Field to Consolidated to discuss job opportunities with Reuben Fleet.

"Claude Ryan agreed to release me from my contract," Rohr explained, "and I'm looking for a job."

"Well, Fred," Fleet replied, "you're a wonderful man but I couldn't put you over Jim Kelley, our factory manager, although you're certainly the equal of anybody I've got here. I'd be pleased to make you Jim's assistant but first I'd like to discuss it with Claude."

The Major's secretary got Ryan on the phone.

"Claude, Fred's over here looking for a job. I know he's a very experienced and competent man. How was it he left your company?"

"Well," Ryan said, "Fred asked me to let him leave and I agreed to do so. I know how good a production man he is. If you hire him, you're going to get an awfully competent man."

"I know that, Claude."

Then the conversation between Rohr and Fleet took a new tack. "Why," asked Fred, "couldn't you start me out in business, Major?"

There was no immediate response. Fleet pondered the question as his memory turned back a dozen years to Consolidated's early success in forming Tonawanda Products as a sub-contractor in Buffalo. In the expanding defense program there would again be a place for such an operation.

The Major sent for C. A. Van Dusen, Vice President and coordinator of Consolidated plants. "Van," he directed, "you and Fred put your heads together and see if you can cook up some way under which we can start Fred in business."

An hour later Van Dusen and Rohr were back to report. "We can start Fred in business," Van Dusen said, "but we feel it's essential he should have control of the business but he hasn't got any money."

"So," explained the Major later, "we helped Rohr Aircraft Corporation get out its first stock issue. Out of the authorized 150,000 shares we took 25,000 shares and Fred took 37,500 bonus shares placed in escrow for him as compensation for starting the company." Other friends and business acquaintances subscribed for 74,000 shares, 12,500 were reserved for purchase by key employees and 1,000 went to attorneys in lieu of fees for legal services. (The balance sheet in Consolidated's 1940 and 1941 Annual Reports listed the $25,000 investment in Rohr shares.)

"I haven't the strength or the time to debate the question . . "

For a period in fall 1940 the embryo Rohr company operated from a small brick factory in downtown San Diego, then Fleet, Van Dusen and Rohr sat down to discuss a permanent factory location.

"Van," Reuben began, "you've been anxious for me to take that site in Chula Vista down at the south end of the harbor for a new plant. I had to take the bull by the horns and tell you to quit arguing about it and go home until you could get over your soreheadedness.

"I haven't got the strength or the time to debate the question any longer with you. I just don't care to go that far down the harbor. I've already decided where we're going to put our second San Diego factory and I'm buying the land a half-mile up Pacific Highway from here now. I went right to the president of the Santa Fe Railroad and all we're going to have to pay is $500 an acre to get rid of the mortgage which is on their property. So, let's help Rohr get that Chula Vista property we were considering."

Fred Rohr and his associates did build their new plant in February 1941 at the Chula Vista site. The nucleus of Rohr's organization—men like Joe E. Rheim and Burt F. Raynes, later chief executives of the company—left Ryan to join their former boss in the new company.

Consolidated depended heavily on Rohr as a subcontractor and as Fleet explained, "Fred was a crackerjack of a man. We gave him $18 million worth of work right off the reel, principally for development of the ready-to-install 'power packages' which included installation of all the plumbing, electrical harness, motor mounts, and cowlings around the bare engine for flying boats and later the B-24s."

RUSS ROGERS, pilot of Richard Archbold's 'Guba II' was still in New Guinea when Major Fleet sensed an approaching problem. Consolidated was going to have to provide its foreign customers with delivery service not only of 'commercial' versions of the PBY but possibly also of four-engine landplane bombers, the first of which was then under construction.

The Major wanted Rogers to head the new ferrying service and urged him to return from New Guinea as expeditiously as possible. After a record setting flight, which included the first crossing of the Indian Ocean and the longest hop ever made by a flying boat, Rogers returned to San Diego in July 1939. Four days later he and his veteran crew were flying the first Royal Air Force PBY across the North Atlantic.

Soon Rogers had teams of crews trained and ready to deliver both seaplanes and landplanes across the Atlantic and Pacific. In summer 1941 there were 14 such crews involved in delivery of 36 PBYs to the Netherlands East Indies. The task was then expanded to provide not only ferry service but also the operation of air transports for the Army Air Corps.

Joining the Consolidated flight service group in 1941 was Richard A. McMakin, former transport pilot for United Air Lines, KLM of the Netherlands, and American Export Airlines. McMakin had succeeded Rogers and became manager of recently organized Consairways, by then under contract to the Air Transport Command to operate, at $1 a year, a regular transport service between California and Australia. Such an arrangement had its advantages as related by Major Fleet:

"Flying our own planes with our own crews we had an opportunity to learn first hand the deficiencies of our craft. It seems that all airplanes have bugs in them and it was worth a good deal to us to learn about them the minute the pilots landed from a trip to Australia and back in a B-24.

"The crew could show us exactly what happened. To avoid a repetition we could correct it and make the change on the production line very quickly. For example, we had all kinds of trouble on the Pacific run with a wobble in the nose wheel; even carried an extra wheel along.

"Eventually we got to flying 40 schedules a month to Australia carrying material to Gen. George Kenney and Gen. MacArthur. At our production peak we were also flying the Atlantic every hour of the day and night, not only with PBYs but also with B-24s.

"Pilots preferred the B-24s in flying the Atlantic because, with their greater speed they were over the water a much shorter time. The same pertained to the Pacific.

"Although Consairways was under contract to the Air Transport Command, its head, Major General Harold L. George, wanted to take over the routes, equipment and the five hundred members of our flight crews. That would have eliminated the feed-back we got on our own planes from our own pilots.

"I had to go to President Roosevelt to prevent that from happening. I explained that it was very embarrassing for us not to be able to build an airplane that was faultless as it first came from the factory but that there were, seemingly, always bugs that had to be eradicated—and as soon as possible.

"I told him if the crew worked for us, and reported the trouble directly to us, we could shorten the time as we didn't want to produce any more planes with that same fault. But if the service was turned over to the Air Transport Command, even though General George was a good operator, they would send the adverse report to Wright Field which would re-engineer it and six months would pass before we could get the change into production.

"By everything that's holy, we wanted to continue to do the job as we were anxious to get our planes faultless as soon as we could. It was better for us and better for the Services.

"President Roosevelt agreed 100 percent with us and wouldn't let them take the Consairways operation away from us."

Then, reflecting on his occasionally poor opinion of engineers in general, Reuben continued.

"It's a sad thing that the engineering profession can never seem to design anything right to start with. They always have to redesign and redesign. At our zenith we had ten thousand men who called themselves engineers and thought they were engineers. Although we couldn't produce aircraft without what they had learned, about 99 percent of them, in my book, never had an original thought in their lives."

While General George made a run at taking over Consairways he had developed a high regard for its competence. "I have nothing but praise and commendation," he wrote, "for the highly efficient manner in which Consairways and its personnel carry out their duties. I experienced a deep feeling of pride that they [Capt. McMakin and his crew who flew General George in a month-long inspection of the South Pacific by B-24] were members of the Air Transport Command."

Five days after General George wrote that tribute, Richard McMakin was killed in a B-32 test flight at San Diego.

LABOR UNION PROBLEMS, and especially the company's strained relations with pro-labor members of the Administration in Washington, contributed as much as did the possible future encroachment of the auto industry into aviation to Major Fleet's growing

feeling that he should consider selling his holdings in Consolidated.

The explosive wartime growth of employment in the aircraft industry created tremendous pressure for scaling up wages and repeated reopening of labor contracts.

A new agreement between Consolidated and the IAM was negotiated in December 1940 providing for automatic increases from the beginning wage rates until a base of 60 cents an hour was reached; thereafter additional raises would depend upon merit.

Reuben Fleet was proud that after three weeks of negotiation agreement was arrived at without any work interruption or financial loss to any employee. In advising Admiral Towers of the contract provisions, the Major wrote:

"I find labor is not satisfied with 'absent treatment,' dislikes being shunted to subordinates, likes to talk itself out with the 'boss,' is pleased with concessions although not ever completely satisfied, and never willingly surrenders a concession once granted.

"The Union here is not dominated by radicals, is extremely patriotic and is aiding us in detecting disloyal acts.

"I believe the offer is fair and will be well received; that we are doing our country a service in taking on greenhorns with at best only five weeks' vocational training, permitting them to earn while they learn to do useful work with precision under our standard that nothing short of right is right.

"Our 50-hour work week, with two shifts, gives the lowest paid daytime beginner a weekly pay of $27.50 (with automatic raises to $33.00.) It is enough to enable him to live in decency and comfort, permits him to have off Saturday and Sunday and recognizes the 40-hour week with a penalty of 50% for the overtime necessitated by the national emergency."

When provisions of the new contract were discussed in the plant publication two items drew special attention.

The Union was disturbed by the announcement that "Foremen have been instructed that employees who do not show aptitude for our work should be discharged."

Management was disturbed by the word that the government planned to appoint a Federal Aircraft Wage Board to establish national wage patterns and that its rules could, in effect, override provisions of the contract just signed with the Union.

Payment on government contracts for the increased direct labor cost was slow in coming. Reuben knew how to put on the pressure.

"President Roosevelt," Fleet recounted, "had said that if the defense industries put in raises in their factories he would go to Congress and get permission to pay it. They held back on me.

"One night about 12:30, in my suite on the top floor of the Washington Hotel, I was writing an ad that I proposed to take to the publishers of the newspapers in Washington, D.C. next day telling that we had had our money withheld.

"My door was open and all of a sudden three people appeared—Governor Frank Murphy of Michigan with Chip Roberts, Assistant Secretary of the Treasury and Mrs. Roberts. Governor Murphy lived there as did John Nance Garner, the Vice President. The men were dressed in white tie and tails and Mrs. Roberts, between them, in an evening gown.

"They came in to join me in a little libation and I couldn't help but be complimentary about how well groomed and beautifully dressed they were, absolutely to perfection and exactly according to the Army officer's 'Table of Occasions.' They must have just come from a White House reception. 'You're all tailored like a million dollars,' I told them. They swallowed that, you know.

"Roberts saw the ad on which I was working. 'Now Reuben,' he said, 'If you're writing that article to publish in the morning paper, you just come across the street to the Treasury Building tomorrow morning instead. I'll see that you get your money.' "

The ad did not appear.

A new two-year contract with the A.F.L. Machinists' Union was signed in June 1941. It gave immediate increases to 14,500 hourly-paid workers and provided that there would be no strike or work stoppage, for any cause, on defense production.

For the contract signing, Major Fleet, who had personally carried on all negotiations with labor since moving the plant to San Diego five years earlier, went to the union hall. He was accompanied by Mrs. Fleet, by factory manager Jim Kelley and his wife, and by J. H. Waterbury, personnel director, and the latter's assistant, Herman Wiseman.

Even while signing the new two-year contract, new problems were facing Consolidated. Labor leader Sidney Hillman, recently named co-director of the Office of Production Management and a favorite of President Roosevelt ('Clear it with Sidney'), called the first Aircraft Stabilization meeting of management and labor representatives in Washington.

Hillman's basic strategy to secure labor peace and uninterrupted defense production was to choose the strongest union in the field and give it exclusive right to represent the workers in return for setting up wage and work standards and waiving the Union's right to strike.

The labor picture continued to heat up. Wages and the union shop vs. the open shop were the issues. North American Aviation at Los Angeles had just gone through a brief but rough strike before it was broken by an Army take-over and employees returned to the

FACE-TO-FACE CONFRONTATION over labor matters reached the boiling point as Reuben Fleet, left, and Roosevelt's Sidney Hillman have at each other in discussion of government wage policy. Title Insurance and Trust Company

production line.

The situation reached the boiling point in late September. Lockheed Aircraft at Burbank, California had granted its workers a blanket 10-cents per hour wage increase. The AFL Machinists' Union contended that Consolidated should follow that precedent under terms of its latest contract, signed in June. It backed up its demand by a membership vote authorizing a strike.

To focus attention on the problem, Fleet stubbornly refused to negotiate and forced the matter before the National Defense Mediation Board, whose chairman was William H. Davis. A New York patent lawyer, Davis had tangled with Fleet years before when Consolidated's patent problems with General Motors' old Dayton-Wright company were in controversy.

Reuben Fleet hurried to Washington to represent the company before the Board. Even now as he recalls the incident, the Major shows some remainder of the bitterness of that meeting 33 years ago.

"Davis was so damn anxious to get the matter settled that he kept telling me, 'Give 'em what they want; give 'em what they want.' What they wanted was going to cost somebody, in my opinion, $82 million, and we didn't have $82 million. Provision for pay raises and for increased warplane costs weren't in the contracts we had negotiated with the union and with the government. I wouldn't agree to it.

"I made it clear to my people and to the Board that I wasn't going to sign any agreement unless the government held us harmless—agreed to absorb the increased costs not only of direct labor but also of overhead charges.

"Government hold harmless provisions are like an escalator that goes only to the fourth floor in a 12-story building. The indirect payroll is on top of that because you can't raise pay of just the production workers. Foremen, inspectors, engineers have to be raised at the same time. Unless the government holds us harmless all the way up to the twelfth story we won't sign a formal agreement."

The Major stopped for breath, subsided a bit, then forcefully resumed to describe the 'kill.'

"So the three board members," he said, "were sitting up there at the front of the room urging us to go ahead. I jumped up. 'You board members get the hell out of here and give me a chance to talk to my own men; not in your presence.'

"You ought to have seen them turn tail and get out of there!"

After the hearings, the Mediation Board came up with its recommendation. Accept the pattern that settled the North American Aviation strike—wage increases of 13 cents per hour across the board but not retroactive to July 5 as requested by the machinists. Influenced by workers in the higher wage brackets,

the Union, now representing 24,000 Consolidated employees, voted not to accept the Mediation Board's suggestion. In a compromise, the Board recommended retroactivity to August 5. The Union approved the suggestion but the company said it was unacceptable without government guarantees to cover the increases.

Meanwhile, Fleet had met in Washington with his key executives. "I'll tell you what we'll do, boys," he said in his usual fraternal manner. "We'll get the Mediation Board to send either Bill Knudsen or Hillman, co-directors of OPM, out to San Diego. We'll wire the Chamber of Commerce to get the business and civic leaders of the community there at a noon luncheon in Balboa Park day after tomorrow.

"I will preside at the meeting and we'll have the government's emissary make a speech and see what he has to say; whether or not he recommends that the government hold us harmless all the way through like they should."

Sidney Hillman drew the assignment and flew west with Fleet. Mac Laddon who was there describes the scene. "Reuben had a way of being pretty abrasive if he though the occasion called for it . . . sometimes even if it didn't. I can see him there now, towering over this little guy, sticking his big thumb out at him like this and shouting, 'I'll have you know that I'm not going to have the business I've spent my whole life building up ruined by one branch of the government not knowing what the other branch is doing.' "

The Major continued to tear into Hillman in front of an audience which couldn't help but be on Consolidated's side.

". . . TOWERING OVER THIS LITTLE GUY, sticking his big thumb out at him . . . " From left, Hillman, Fleet, and Maj. Gen. W. P. Upshur, USMC.

Consolidator

WARTIME PRODUCTION EXPERTS, left to right: *T. P. Wright, War Production Board; Brig. Gen. Oliver P. Echols, Air Corps procurement chief; Robert Lovett, Under-Secretary of War; Reuben Fleet.*

"It is high time we were getting some encouragement for the hard work we are doing in preparing for the battle against Hitler. Aviation as an industry is being kicked around. We are being forced to expand more than any other industry, yet we are constantly being subjected to investigations and limitations by congressional committees and the like.

"The military should be getting down to brass tacks. The only way to lick Hitler is by aircraft, but we won't have the planes to do the job in short of five years. We mustn't get into a thing of this kind with the valor of ignorance. We must realize first of all that we are already in it. The question is how far we should go.

"The government should call in the heads of all the big plane companies and ask our advice instead of brow-beating us with Vinson committees trying to figure out how every dollar we ever earned was gotten, and with constant labor trouble.

"This new labor agreement the board proposes is going to cost $82 million. That would break Consolidated. I will never sign the document unless I am assured by the government they will stand by their end of the bargain. Whenever the government says they will take care of it we will be able to give our men a labor life of decency and comfort."

The Major sat down. It had been a long and tiring tirade. He had exhausted himself almost as much as he had the audience. Hillman got up. His reply was brief. "We must have the work done as quickly as possible. You will get the proper cooperation from the government."

The Major had won the first skirmish in his battle with Washington bureaucracy. Another was to follow.

Hillman relayed the message to Washington that Fleet would not sign until he had received telegrams from the Army, Navy and Office of Production Management—all three—that they would hold Consolidated harmless "clear on through."

Reuben picked up the skein of his yarn and continued, "The next day we received telegrams from the War and Navy Departments but nothing from the Office of Production Management.

"I told Washington that we wanted the OPM also.

They asked if we really felt that necessary. I said 'How do I know whether we need OPM or not? I've been dealing with the government a long, long time and wouldn't I be a fool to agree and later find I can't collect for lack of OPM approval? Therefore I want to cover myself absolutely.'

"The Army and Navy got me on the phone. Robert A. Lovett, Assistant Secretary of War for Air, did the talking. 'Why are you the only contractor we're having trouble with?'

"Because all the other companies are holding their breath to see how we're going to handle it. They're going to be up against the same thing we are.

" 'I want you to know who's at this end. I, Bob Lovett, am representing OPM. Jim Forrestal is here for the Navy and Judge Robert P. Patterson, undersecretary, is speaking for the War Department. Hap Arnold's with Patterson and Jack Towers for the Navy Bureau of Aeronautics. We want to know what the situation is out there.'

" 'I'm sitting on a keg of dynamite.'

" 'Supposing we take you over?'

" 'That would be a Godsend. If you think you can run the company better than I can, it would be a wonderful thing. But it's a cinch you'd have to keep it alive, wouldn't you, Bob? So it would be great for us if you'd take it over.

" 'It's at the point where the integrity of the company is at stake. We haven't got the $82 million to pay out. It's not included in the price we quoted the government for airplanes. Now, if you took the company over and ran it, you'd have to put up the money anyway to keep the company going.'

" 'Now, Reuben,' Lovett continued, 'We don't want to do it.'

" 'All right,' I said, 'you don't have to do it. I'll continue to set on the keg of dynamite for you. But I need that wire from the OPM with the government's guarantee to pay the increased costs."

Several hours later the wire from OPM arrived. Reuben had not backed down; he had won his point. Only then did Consolidated sign a new one-year contract with the Union.

BOOK VI

"A TIME TO BUY AND A TIME TO SELL"

1941-1975

Justin C. Gruelle 1958

THREE DECADES of Reuben Fleet's contributions to aviation, from start of Air Mail Service in 1918 to postwar B-36 Intercontinental Bomber, are caught in Justin Gruelle's portrait of Con-

"A TIME TO BUY AND
A TIME TO SELL"

IT WOULD BE ALMOST IMPOSSIBLE for one man to be busier than Reuben Fleet was in 1941. For years he had known every minute detail about the company's business, had made every major decision and most of the smaller ones, too. As late as 1940 the Major had personally passed on every pay raise. Now, the 14,000 employees had swollen to nearly 35,000 and more were being added at the rate of 500 a week.

Business could hardly be better. It had been skyrocketing for 22 months, ever since the Navy's order for 200 PBYs. Following that came the avalanche of B-24 contracts, culminating in a 700-plane order in April 1941 which added $226 million to the huge backlog. Plant facilities had doubled and redoubled and doubled again. It was the greatest one-year growth in the history of American business.

Sales of only $3.6 million in 1939 exploded 26-fold to $95.5 million for the first 11 months of 1941. The backlog of $755.5 million in unfilled orders was then 18 times what it had been just two years earlier.

Reuben Fleet had always known the importance of timing. If you acted at the right time, you were a hero; if your timing was bad you could end up looking like a fool. The Major was no fool.

He had created one of the great industrial successes of the century—one essential to the preservation of democracy. But there were clouds on the horizon which troubled this astute and knowledgeable man.

Necessary though it was, the excess profits tax designed to take the profit out of war had made business less attractive. Too, the bureaucratic domination of employee relations by Washington and the expanding influence of labor unions was a far cry from the days when every worker was virtually a member of Fleet's own family. Lastly, the automobile industry was beginning to impinge on the pioneers of the aircraft industry.

There was, as Bible-reading Reuben Fleet often said, "A time to buy and a time to sell," and as his authority he referred friends to chapter and verse in the Good Book. ("A time to get, and a time to lose; a time to keep, and a time to cast away." Ecclesiastes 3:6)

AFTER HIS EARLY SWIM and unhurried breakfast, the Major joined us one sunny morning in 1974 in the huge living room of the Spanish castle on Point Loma to tell the story of the sale of his interest in Consolidated.

"President Roosevelt," he began, "wanted to fix it so that no one made any undue profit out of the war, so in 1941 a new Tax Act, to become effective in 1942, was enacted and became the law of the land.

"I studied the Act very carefully and decided it was no good from my standpoint and, therefore, I'd sell my personal holdings in Consolidated. There were three buyers ready to purchase my interest.

"As a young man of 23 in Montesano, Washington, I had made $27,400 that year and here I was 54 years old and was making $9,340 clear on a $60,000 salary and had practically all my wealth invested in the company. My investment income amounted to about $1.7 million in 1941 but the federal government would take 93% of it and the State of California 6%, leaving me $17,000. So I went to Washington to discuss the problem with the President, whom I had known since 1931.

34% ownership gave the new buyer working control

" 'Mr. President,' I said, 'you have taken the profit out of war; with a vengeance. To use an old timber expression, it's made a 'load of poles' of my efforts in aviation for the last 25 years. I've made my living that way and have been doing an honest business, but now I've decided the time has come to sell it.'

" 'No, Reuben, you are not going to sell. Consolidated Aircraft is too important to the war effort to let it get into adverse hands.'

" 'We won't let it get into adverse hands, Mr. President. I've got three buyers. You can pick the buyer. They are just as good Americans as I am. I've got it figured that holding the percentage of the business I do I can keep only enough profit after taxes to meet the payroll for just seven minutes.'

" 'You knew damn well, Mr. President, that I would play ball with you in taking the profit out of war irrespective of what it did to me; that I've played ball with you ever since that Air Mail cancellation incident.'

" 'Yes, I certainly do know that, Reuben. Now I'll tell you. I've never moved on aviation from that day to this but what I've first consulted you and I don't propose to ever do it, because you know the business and I don't. I want you to continue to serve us for the same money you will be getting from Consolidated as a consultant. That means serve me, serve Morgenthau, serve the Secretaries of War and Navy, serve the company—and your rival companies—for the same salary you are now getting. I'll help you unload what you say is your 'load of poles,' and I'll let the Army and Navy select the buyer.'

" 'Okay, Mr. President, that's a deal.'

"Not long after that President Roosevelt made me put in a private phone line right here by my desk at the house, so nobody else could use it. Whenever he consulted me it was only on the telephone. I continued my consulting arrangement with him and we followed it out until his death in April, 1945."

All his life the Major held his personal cards pretty close to the vest. He was not inclined to identify the two unsuccessful prospective buyers, but Ford Motor Company most certainly was one of them. Rumor had it that another was Howard Hughes.

By mid-November 1944, when Fleet was the subject of the cover story in TIME magazine, rumors of a pending sale began to be widely circulated. A new name entered the speculation; that of Vultee Aircraft, a comparatively small Los Angeles builder of fighter and training planes. How would it be able to swallow the huge Consolidated complex?

A daily aviation newsletter published a report that the War Department was seeking "to effect a change in management" at Consolidated, a story which was vehemently denied by Edgar N. Gott, Consair vice president.

Major Fleet's son David, also a Consolidated executive, said the reported sale "must be a mistake," adding that his father "does not own the controlling interest," and that reports he would be receiving $10 million for his holding were "ridiculous."

It was finally confirmed November 25 that Fleet had reached an agreement with Victor Emanuel, head of The Aviation Corporation (AVCO holding company) which controlled, among other companies, Vultee Aircraft, Inc. Emanuel, a World War I Navy pilot and graduate of Cornell University, also served on the boards of Republic Steel and Vultee.

The agreement with Major Fleet called for Vultee to purchase from him and from family members 440,000 of the 1,293,444 shares outstanding after a recent 2-for-1 stock split. Their 34% ownership of Consolidated, of course, gave the new buyer working control of the company.

Ten days later the Japanese struck at Pearl Harbor and the United States became a combatant.

Major Fleet never disclosed the exact details of the sale of his interests but elsewhere it was reported that his personal holding was 348,882 shares, with the balance of 440,000 shares owned by various family members, including Dorothy Mitchell Fleet, his wife; William K. Mitchell, her father; Edward K. Bishop, his brother-in-law; Barbara and Edward F. Bishop, his neice and nephew; and Elizabeth G. Fleet, his first wife.

With Consolidated stock then quoted at 22-7/8, the Fleet family received $10,065,000 for its shares, plus a $2 per share cash dividend which had been declared on November 27, bringing the total transaction to $10,-945,000.

By selling when he did, Major Fleet says, "I paid a capital gains tax of 15% instead of the 25% which would have become effective on January 1st. That saved me a million and two-thirds. So you see, I unloaded at the right time and didn't let the glamour of aviation get the better of my judgment.

"But I didn't quit, and had to work hard in doing the other assignments I had agreed to undertake. But at least I got my money out."

IN A CHRISTMAS MESSAGE to employees, which proved to be his last communication as head of the company he had founded 18 years earlier, Reuben Fleet talked of the war the country had just entered and of what lay ahead.

"Sacrifices made during 1941 will seem insignificant indeed compared with those we will make before this battle is won.

"We were getting soft. We were taking it easy, resting upon the smugness of our geographic location and delusions of grandeur."

Then, in an oblique reference to his own English heritage, he noted that "gradually it came to us that our closest international kin was actually endangered. Above the roar of coastal guns along the English Channel, above the din of Stukas diving upon Britain's ancient cathedrals and her populace, it came to us that no longer were we safe."

Reuben Fleet had been Chairman and President of Consolidated, but in a rare display of humility usually chose to identify himself within the company as its General Manager. Succeeding him as Chairman was Tom M. Girdler, Republic Steel board chairman, and as President, Harry Woodhead, board chairman of Vultee and previously president of Aviation Manufacturing Corp.

Mac Laddon remained as Executive Vice President and General Manager. Also staying with Consolidated at San Diego were Chuck Leigh and David G. Fleet, while at the new Fort Worth plant, George J. Newman retained his post as Vice President of that Division. Later Dave Fleet, a director of the company since its move to San Diego and assistant to his father, went to Vultee as Executive Vice President and General Manager.

"Things have been quieter since Reuben Fleet left."

Having sold his holdings, Reuben did not discontinue his affiliation with the company but signed an agreement December 19 with Harry Woodhead under which he would render advisory and consulting service to Consolidated for a period of five years at an annual fee of $60,000, plus $6000 per year for two secretaries of his selection.

The consulting arrangement permitted the Major, as had been suggested to him by Franklin D. Roosevelt, to serve the President, the military services, Treasury Secretary Morganthau and defense contractors as an advisor on aviation matters.

With Fleet out of the top management post, Consolidated would never be the same again. As his friend, Neil Morgan, San Diego's leading newspaper columnist, was to write: "Things have been quieter around San Diego since Reuben Fleet left the aircraft business. He made noises like a tycoon, one of the last of that great breed of roaring, fist-pounding individualists who were proud to make millions and serve their nation and felt they could do both as well as any man alive."

WHY DID REUBEN FLEET sell out? Was it only because of the near-confiscatory taxes? Or the labor situation, coupled with unreasonable government regulations? Or competition from the auto makers?

All three factors entered into his decision, as did his immense self-confidence that he could correctly judge when was the best time to consolidate his personal financial situation.

There was little question but what the government was convinced that operation of the company had gotten too big to be practical for Fleet's autocratic form of one-man rule. Dr. George Mead of the National Defense Council, for one, had written critically to Fleet about his organizational structure. Even his associates conceded that no one person—even Reub Fleet— should make every decision big or small. Probably the report got around that Bob Lovett had rhetorically suggested, "suppose we take you over." This in turn led to the story widely circulated in the aircraft industry and repeated by the press that the Army and Navy had forced Fleet out.

Mrs. Dorothy Fleet, his wife at the time, was certain that Reuben made up his mind to sell because of government interference in labor matters. "When the time had come," she said, "that he couldn't tell his employees what to do, he was through. He had always taken a genuine interest in his employees and their families. It was not anything put on.

"When the company got so big that he could no longer get to know all his family, so to speak, he must have realized that the time was not far off when he would sell.

"It all came to a peak when a union negotiator told Reuben, 'can't you get it through your thick head that the time is past when a company can tell an employee what to do.' "

Reuben's own view was that "I sold because federal taxes were so high that what I had left after paying them made the risk too great for the possibility of gain. After all, business is not a plaything. Defined briefly, it is risk-for-gain. Whenever the possibility of gain is so remote that it exists only to an infinitesimal degree, better cash it in as 'the lesser of two evils' and follow some other vocation."

SPANISH CASTLE on Point Loma overlooking San Diego Bay and North Island where he learned to fly in 1917 was Reuben Fleet's home for 40 years.

SOON AFTER REUBEN FLEET MOVED Consolidated Aircraft to San Diego, his second wife Dorothy, and their two-year-old son Preston (Sandy) followed. David, the Major's oldest son—by Elizabeth, his first wife—was already living in San Diego with his bride. Before long David's mother and his sister, Phyllis, also moved to San Diego from Buffalo.

Initially, Reuben and Dorothy (with son Sandy) leased a big home in Mission Hills which had been closed for nearly ten years. There, in an upstairs bedroom, their daughter, Dorothy Lillian, was born. Mrs. Fleet and her parents, then living at the house, soon discovered that the mansion had an unsavory reputation as a 'haunted house,' and she was more than pleased when a year later Reuben showed an interest in buying a home of their own.

The property that most attracted the Fleets was Dias Felices (Happy Days), a huge Spanish baronial mansion atop Point Loma.

The owners were Dr. and Mrs. Ernst Ulrich von Buelow. She had built the show-place home eight years earlier when she was Mrs. John Smiley. Reportedly the wealthy Mrs. Smiley's family had owned the Thomas automobile company.

After traveling the world over looking for the ideal location, Mrs. Smiley bought the Point Loma property, then employed an architect and sent him to Spain to study Mediterranean architecture before designing her three-story dream home of 20 rooms, each of which had a magnificent view of San Diego and its world famous harbor.

During the depression Mrs. Smiley suffered financial reverses. In addition, it was reported that as Hitler came to power in Germany and reoccupied the Rhineland in March 1936, her new husband, a German national, member of a prominent titled family and distinguished geophysical engineer, wanted to return to his fatherland.

A sound investor and knowledgeable in real estate values, the Major purchased the rambling Spanish villa and three acres of terraced gardens in November 1936 for a bargain-basement $70,000.

Perhaps to stimulate the real estate market, the story got out with local realtors and was published that the purchase price had been $100,000, "the largest single residence sale in San Diego's history."

That unwanted publicity on the inflated price of the estate bode ill for the Fleet family.

"No sooner had we moved in," the Major recalls, "than I received a letter signed with a black hand dipped in ink. 'If you can pay 100 grand for your house,' it read, 'you can pay 100 grand for one of those children of yours. We mean business, and we'll show it by exploding a bomb in your gateway tonight.'

"They did.

"The next morning I told Mrs. Fleet to take the children to Palm Springs—that I'd arrange for them to be flown over by Bill Wheatley in the company's 'Fleetster.' My sister Lillian and her husband, Ned Bishop, had spent some time there during the winters and I thought Dorothy and the children should move over to Palm Springs and rent or buy a home.

244

"She phoned to say she'd found two places in the $20,000 range and I told her to take her pick. Of course I had to stay in San Diego nearly all the time to run the business but she and the children continued to live in Palm Springs that winter and spring until the kidnapping scare blew over. Since then I've maintained a second family home in Palm Springs where we continued to spend the winters."

Mrs. Fleet—Dorothy Mitchell—knew her man and his eccentricities intimately, as secretary, then wife and later as homemaker.

"During our early years in San Diego," she recalls, "my role was that of Reuben's wife, mother of our two infant children and, fundamentally important to him, his hostess.

"He always brought people home from the office. As I prided myself on my gourmet dinners, I used to keep a staff of at least four in the kitchen for we never knew far in advance how many were coming to dinner. Perhaps six or eight or a dozen guests.

"Often they were the famous—men and women of national stature. Or perhaps aviation pioneers, or key military and naval officers, or foreign dignitaries.

"Many names come to mind. James H. Rand of Remington-Rand, Reuben's partner in the NYRBA airline to South America. Richard Archbold, Standard Oil heir and purchaser of the 'Guba' flying boat. Patrick J. Hurley, President Herbert Hoover's Secretary of War. Jimmy Doolittle. Larry Bell, with whom Reuben had re-established diplomatic relations. James Roosevelt, the President's eldest son. Sir Hubert Wilkins, the Australian polar explorer. Admiral Ernest J. King. Jacqueline Cochran, who returned our hospitality at her desert ranch near Palm Springs.

"Some visits to the plant were so brief that we didn't have an opportunity to welcome Reuben's guests to our home. I recall a visit in 1939 by Crown Prince Olav and Crown Princess Martha of Norway, and later Senator Harry S. Truman of Missouri.

"Then, too, there were the inscrutable Russians and their interpreters here to buy flying boats for the USSR. But there were times the interpreters were unnecessary—when Reuben quoted a price. The Russians would look at one another, shake their shaggy heads in unison and chorus, 'Too much money.'

"Of particular interest and pleasure as a houseguest in 1939 was Charles A. Lindbergh while he was in San Diego doing a survey of American aircraft manufacturing capability for General Arnold.

"Little did I imagine when I stood in the crowd in New York in June 1927 that a dozen years later the hero being paraded down Fifth Avenue to the cheers of millions would be a guest in my home. When I did meet him, I was charmed. Quiet and unassuming, he seemed untouched by the fame and publicity that accompanied his every move."

Because of his business-social evening engagements, Reuben often did not go to the office until noon. Time meant nothing to him. He would do what he could when he could in the 24 hours each day even if others had to accommodate their schedule to his. It was particularly grating to Mac Laddon who recalls that "The rest of us had been at the office since eight o'clock in the morning. Reuben had an inter-com squawk-box and about six o'clock in the evening he'd press down all the keys and find out who the hell was still there. Usually everybody was. He'd say, 'Come on over to the office, boys, I want to talk to you.'

"And we'd come over. And he would talk. And talk, and talk. Reuben just loved to talk. He'd go on and on with this repetitious monologue until he'd worn us all out."

Dorothy Fleet also recalls that "Reuben would get an idea in the middle of the night and he didn't care who he called at some ungodly hour; the President of the United States if he had it in mind. What he wanted to do, he did, as he didn't really care about other people's opinions or feelings."

Dorothy Fleet paused long enough to make it clear that some other recollection of the past had broken through. "During the hectic years of almost constant and lavish entertaining, one of my problems was keeping Sandy and Dot under control.

"We were proud of our children and never passed up an opportunity to show them off to good advantage. When guests arrived we allowed them to make a brief appearance, but they did not have the run of the house while Reuben was entertaining important guests.

"Sometimes I grew weary of the strain of constant entertaining, of playing the gracious hostess at any and all hours. On one such occasion, not only tired but pregnant, I had gone to bed early, completely exhausted.

"Through the haze of light slumber I heard the doorbell. Soon Reuben was beside my bed. 'Jimmy Roosevelt and Rommie (Rommelle Schneider) are here. They want to show you her new engagement ring from Jimmy!'

"Please apologize for me," I told Reuben, "I simply can't dress and go down stairs."

" 'Do you mean to lie there and tell me,' he said, 'that you refuse to get out of bed and say hello to the son of the President of the United States?'

"Reuben left in obvious disgust, reappearing minutes later with the word that 'Jimmy and Rommie are on their way up.'

"A year or so later I was to run into considerably more formality when I was their guest at the White House."

Others may have looked on with envy at the life style

Dorothy Fleet was able to maintain, but even under the most favorable of conditions problems have a way of closing in on people regardless of their station in life.

Raising three small children—Nancy had also arrived on the scene, August 28, 1940—was a full-time job in itself. For one thing it left Dorothy Fleet little time for travel with Reuben, certainly not abroad. Too, being his hostess, nearly always with business guests, was also time and energy consuming.

Then, as the pace of defense production rose ever higher, business matters in San Diego and extensive travel east took more and more of the Major's time and interest. Dorothy had been warned in advance that with Reuben business came first. And she knew from personal experience, and that of her Aunt Lauretta Golem, what an important and personal role his secretary always played in his life.

It was as if Reuben had two wives—a homemaker to be his hostess and care for the children, and the 'office wife' of novels to be part and parcel of his all-consuming business activity.

"There were times," Dorothy recalls, "when Reuben had to go out of town, perhaps for a week, and he always took his secretary along just as he had taken me on business trips when I was his secretary. Because he had so much on his mind he had to have someone with him to look after details, so to him taking a secretary was far more business convenience then it was personal consideration. But if his secretary could fill a social as well as business role there was bound to be a real conflict with the wife and homemaker."

The Major's efficient and devoted secretary was Eva May Wiseman, and her husband had been employed as Consolidated's assistant personnel manager. Reports in the inner executive circle at the plant were that several of the Major's associates had made a play for Mrs. Wiseman's attention and that there had been fisticuffs.

In 1940, at the peak of plant expansion and preparation for all-out military plane production, Reuben Fleet purchased a home in Beverly Hills. Mrs. Fleet, attracted by the potential of social life among the luminaries of filmland, moved there with the three children.

The extensive entertaining of business guests shifted from the Spanish castle on Point Loma to the La Jolla Beach and Tennis Club where Consolidated maintained an apartment for the use of important customers and friends.

After a period there was a reconciliation. Dorothy Fleet returned to San Diego and to the mansion atop Point Loma, but the arrangement did not last and the separation resumed.

U. S. Navy/National Archives

JAPANESE PLANE over Pearl Harbor is caught by alert photographer as first attack is struck on December 7, 1941.

JUST AS ADMIRAL ERNEST J. KING had predicted three years earlier, the Japanese struck at Hawaii within a 90 degree sector from the north. Not by submarine or surface ship but by air. The 183 Japanese aircraft in the first wave had flown the 200 miles that Sunday morning from a carrier force which had left Japan November 28 and then bore down on Hawaii from the Aleutian Islands almost due north. It was 7:55 a.m., December 7, 1941 when the bombs began raining down on Pearl Harbor.

JAP'S-EYE VIEW of Battleship Row and Ford Island air field. Note speck-size Japanese plane on far side of island pulling up after bombing run.

As a consequence of the Fall of France in June 1940, the weak Vichy French government a year later permitted the Japanese to get control of French Indochina. That takeover and the two-year undeclared war on China led to economic sanctions against Japan by the United States, Britain and the Netherlands, including a threat to water-borne commerce and continued oil supplies for the Japanese fleet.

The diplomatic pot boiled throughout the fall of 1941 as Secretary of State Cordell Hull attempted to get Japan to back down in Indochina and on the Chinese mainland as well. On November 26 Secretary Hull gave Japan a final statement of the American position.

Japan's special envoy, former Ambassador to Germany Saburo Kurusu, was dispatched to Washington to join Ambassador Kichisaburo Nomura in 'peace' negotiations seeking a settlement of the controversy. On Saturday, December 6, Kurusu passed through Honolulu on his way to Washington. Next day Japan struck—"a date which," President Roosevelt said, "will live in infamy." In a single stroke Japan had gained air and naval supremacy in the Western Pacific.

How was it possible for the Japanese to have struck at Hawaii without being detected? Where were the 'eyes of the fleet,' the PBY patrol bombers that were supposed to protect the approaches to Hawaii? Hadn't there been warnings enough of a pending attack?

American pilots ferrying PBYs for the Netherlands East Indies government from the Philippines to Surabaja, Java reported receiving orders the day before the Pearl Harbor attack to get all available planes out of there and on their way to the Indies. An old friend, Fox Movietone News cameraman Al Brick, based in Hollywood, played a hunch and left after Thanksgiving Day for Honolulu to be on hand for the news he felt sure was coming. His was the motion picture coverage of the attack most frequently screened.

Reuben Fleet, too, was shocked when he first heard, on his car radio, of the surprise attack. He couldn't imagine how the daily PBY patrols had missed sighting the Japanese carrier force steaming down from the north.

"Although it was Sunday," Fleet recalls, "I was planning to go to the office but when I heard the news on my car radio I hurried straight there. I hadn't been at my office five minutes when a call came through from the Chief of Naval Operations.

" 'We're going to send Secretary Knox to Hawaii to assess the damage and we want you to deliver him there with the best craft you've got.'

"I said, 'That's a four-engine PB2Y-3 like the Secretary flew in last year from Honolulu to San Diego. We'll have one waiting for him. When is he going to leave Washington?'

" 'He leaves here in 20 minutes.' Then they told me when he was expected to arrive at North Island. I was there to meet him, and see him on his way."

Three days after Secretary Knox's departure from San Diego, Major Fleet received another message from the Chief of Naval Operations: SECRETARY LANDS NAS [Naval Air Station] SAN DIEGO THIS

DESTROYER SHAW explodes in a devastating fireball as ships in harbor and drydock are struck.

EVENING, SPENDING NIGHT CORONADO
HOTEL. WANTS YOU TO STAY WITH HIM. BRING
YOUR PAJAMAS.

"Secretary Knox and I spent the night together
reviewing the tragedy of Pearl Harbor," Fleet went
on. "He showed me some photographs of what had
happened, then went on to tell me that 69 of our PBYs
were lined up in a row like sitting ducks at Ford
Island, Pearl Harbor, and at Kaneohe. They were
there just as if on dress parade when the Japanese
came in like this [gesturing] strafing and bombing and
burned the PBYs up in their own gasoline.

"Neither Secretary Knox nor anyone in Washington
had any idea of Japanese airpower when they hit us. I
know the nation didn't appreciate the capability of airpower or they never would have had everything sitting
on the ground like they did.

"The next morning a rather odd thing occurred as I
was coming down the ancient cage elevator and walked out into the main lobby of the Hotel del Coronado.

"Who was sitting there waiting for me but Lieut.
Colonel Jimmy Roosevelt from the Marine Corps Base
at nearby Camp Pendleton. 'Reuben,' he said, 'I hear
you spent the night with Secretary Knox. Tell me, is he
loyal to my father?'

" 'Jimmy,' I said, 'you know the country is at war
now. I honestly don't believe your father's name was
mentioned all evening but I never saw a more able or
patriotic American than Secretary Knox.'

"That seemed to satisfy Jimmy. He said 'so long'
and left. But it was a strange question, the significance
of which I've often thought about since the attack on
Pearl Harbor and the investigations which followed."

After the initial shock of the attack, inquiries in-

itiated following Secretary Knox's visit brought out
more specific information about the PBY squadrons.

All 45 planes of Patrol Wing 2 at Ford Island, Pearl
Harbor, were destroyed or knocked out of commission. Twenty-seven of Patrol Wing 1's PBY-5s at
Kaneohe, on the windward side of Oahu, were
destroyed and six were damaged. Three planes,
however, had been on a dawn patrol early that Sunday
morning.

Ensign Fred Meyer, plane captain of 14-P-2, and his
crew of seven, had taken off from Kaneohe at dawn
for an anticipated four-hour patrol.

VP-14's skipper, Comdr. Thurston Clark, had brief-
ed the plane captains on Saturday. "This," he told
Meyer, "is to be the most critical week-end in the
history of the Islands. While on patrol, if you see any
submarine in the Fleet operating area, drop your
depth charges on it and don't even ask for recognition.
No U.S. or friendly subs are to be in that area. If it's
one of ours, he's not supposed to be there; he's got a
problem!"

Meyer explained: "I was a very junior officer and
didn't completely comprehend the implications of the
explosive international situation. What I thought was
of prime concern . . . what the Navy was expecting . . .
was that there might be an attempt by Japanese sub-
marines to sink some of the ships of our fleet. In the
Navy's concern about subs, there was no mention of
possible attack by hostile aircraft."

There had been routine daily anti-sub patrols to insure that there were no hostile forces in the normal
U.S. Fleet operating areas south of Oahu. 14-P-2 and
two other PBY-5s were on just such a patrol
December 7th.

"LINED UP IN A ROW like sitting ducks, PBYs [and dive bombers]
at Ford Island burned up in their own gasoline."

Plane captains had already received the usual assignment of sectors to search in the northern quadrants off Oahu in case they were advised of any enemy submarine action during their patrols. It was a routine precaution.

"While flying south of Oahu," Meyer recalls, "I was ordered by radio to execute the emergency aerial search of my sector and had proceeded some 40 miles north of the island when I sighted eight or ten aircraft ahead of us. As a precaution I took the 'Catalina' right down to the deck—25 feet off the water—so if they were enemy aircraft they couldn't fly in under us.

"The approaching aircraft circled around behind us so I called my aft gunners on the intercom and told them to man their stations and keep a sharp lookout because the planes were so far away they couldn't be identified and I didn't know whether they were friendly or not.

"In a few seconds I looked down on the water and saw a pattern of white splashes. 'What's going on now?' I asked on the intercom.

"Over my earphones came the reply, 'Mister Meyer, I think they're shootin' at us.' Then I knew what the white spots were and made a turn back toward Oahu expecting to pick up fighter cover, little knowing there weren't any fighters left.

"We opened up with our guns, meanwhile taking repeated heavy fire, particularly in the aft part of the fuselage. One Jap plane spiraled down, apparently smoking pretty good, but whether we had hit him I couldn't say for sure.

"I had my co-pilot man the bow gun, but despite my orders he was terrible slow responding. It was a week later before I learned he hadn't plugged in his headset."

Meyer got on the radio.

"We are under enemy attack."

Silence. Then in a minute or so came a response.

"14-P-2. Is this a drill?"

"Drill, hell. This is god-damn realistic. It's the real thing!"

"Having failed to pick up any of our fighters, I resumed patrol in my assigned sector, ranging some 300 miles northwest after our unscheduled 100 mile detour. By then we were near our maximum outbound range and I requested permission to return to Kaneohe. After our scuffle with the Japs we saw no more enemy aircraft or ships, the enemy carrier force having apparently exited the area on a northeast course.

"When we reached Kaneohe everything was dark except for the hangars still burning on the beach. No trouble in landing. We had often done that at night. But we had to beach the plane in total darkness, except for the beachmaster's small hooded flashlight. The other two PBYs had already returned from patrol

U. S. Navy/National Archives

78 OF 81 PBYs at Kaneohe and Ford Island were destroyed or damaged in initial attack on Hawaiian installations.

of their sectors."

Ensign Meyer's PBY was the first American plane to draw enemy aircraft fire in the war in the Pacific.

Meantime Ensign William P. Tanner, at the controls of 14-P-1, sighted the periscope of a Japanese midget sub at 6:33 a.m. off the entrance to Pearl Harbor. Tanner dropped his depth charges. A few minutes later the destroyer 'Ward' attacked and sank the sub. It was the war's first Naval engagement. Like Meyer, Tanner then resumed the patrol of his assigned sector.

For years Reuben continued to think about Pearl Harbor. When Reader's Digest, in November 1963, carried an article titled 'Tora, Tora, Tora" he discussed the matter extensively on the telephone with the author, Dr. Gordon W. Prange, Professor of History at the University of Maryland.

But what finally galvanized Fleet into further inquiry was the motion picture of the same name which he saw in 1970. "I can understand Admiral Kimmel's keeping our fleet in Pearl Harbor," he said, "but why the patrol aircraft were not operating to protect the fleet, Honolulu and our air bases there, I cannot comprehend. After all, the Navy bought the PBYs specifically for that purpose.

"These patrol aircraft were under command of my lifelong friend, Rear Admiral Patrick N. L. Bellinger, Naval Aviator No. 4, who first reached national fame as commander of the NC-1 trans-Atlantic seaplane in 1919.

"Because Pat Bellinger had passed on I decided to try and unravel the mystery by getting hold of Vice Admiral Charles F. Coe who, as a Lieutenant Commander, was his war plans officer. His letter, which follows, is an interesting footnote to history:"

V ADM. CHARLES F. COE, USN, RET.
2210 Belle Haven Road
Alexandria, Virginia 22307

12-06-70

Dear Major Fleet,

I remember you as "Major" Reuben Fleet, is that incorrect? I met you in Pensacola in 1930 when you introduced the prototype 'Fleet' trainer, in fact I took up the girl whom I was later to marry in that airplane.

And I also remember you as manufacturer of the PBY series, and as President of Consolidated Aircraft for I was Engineer Officer on the staff of Admiral E. J. King when the PBYs were being placed in commission. Admiral King was then ComAirBaseFor. He later moved up to ComAirBatFor and I with him briefly, but requesting a flying job, was sent to VP-11 as Exec. VP-11 was equipped with PBY-2s with Curtiss Electric props.

But to reply to your letter of 11 Nov. 1970 enclosing a copy of your draft of 20 Nov. 1963 to Dr. Gordon W. Prange—

Dr. Prange interviewed me in Washington before writing "Tora, Tora, Tora" and my recollections helped in his description of the events of that terrible day, 29 years ago tomorrow as I write.

Your question was why patrol aircraft under Rear Admiral Patrick N. L. Bellinger were not screening Pearl Harbor on 7 Dec. 1941. You may remember that the Japanese Special Envoy, Ambassador Extraordinary Kurusu, was enroute to Washington that weekend, ostensibly to see President Roosevelt in response to the President's personal appeal to the Emperor. Kurusu's mission was expected to soothe U.S-Japanese friction. His message was to be WAR not PEACE, but this our President and his cabinet could not know. For they sent messages to Hawaii to the effect that our armed forces in Hawaii were to present a peaceful and unworried aspect to Kurusu as he passed thru.

Admiral Kimmel and General [Walter C.] Short accepted this. The general opinion was that Japan would not stick her neck out so far as to attack Pearl Harbor; in case of hostilities it was felt that the Philippines, not Hawaii, would be an initial objective of the Japanese. The Japanese could then sit back and defend the Greater East Asia Co-prosperity area from a defensive enclave of great strength, with short communication lines, against enemies who could attack only at great disadvantage at the end of exceedingly long communication lines. (Such was the logical Japanese military strategy. In my opinion Japan threw away a major advantage by not following it. They over-reached themselves and inadvertently showed us that naval strength then lay in aircraft carriers, not battleships. We naval aviators knew this, but Pearl Harbor convinced everybody.)

And so to present a peaceful aspect to Kurusu, all Hawaiian commanders received direct orders to observe strict peacetime routine that week-end. Admiral Bellinger's Patrol Wings were placed on beaching gears and at moorings, and the usual early morning security patrols were specifically stopped for Kurusu's benefit. Maj. Gen. Indian Joe Tinker's Bomber Command (B-18's) were lined up for inspection at Hickam Field. Brig. Gen. Davidson's fighters (P-12s) were similarly lined up at Wheeler Field, and early morning pursuit aircraft exercises were cancelled. We were blissfully peaceful. Kurusu passed thru on Saturday, 6 December but I doubt if he even noticed! But you may be sure that Yamamoto was told and exulted. It was either the most stupendous coincidence of event or one of the most astute politico-military coups of history.

But Pearl Harbor was not all loss. It aroused and united the American people. It showed us the way to victory over Japan. It was Japan's major mistake of the war.

Sincerely,

Charles F. Cox
Lt. Comdr. (in 1941)

In a post-war assessment of U.S. Naval Aviation in the Pacific, issued in 1947 over the signature of Vice Admiral Forrest Sherman, Deputy Chief of Naval Operations, appears this comment:

"Pearl Harbor showed the need for air patrols. The Japanese Fleet whose planes did such damage on the morning of 7 December 1941, were within range the evening before. Had enough 'Catalinas' been out, the fleet might have been discovered, but . . . more than planes in the air were needed to conduct an adequate search. Above all it required special radar equipment . . ."

PEARL HARBOR MAY HAVE BEEN a military disaster but no event in the twentieth century so united the American people in preparation for what was recognized as a life-and-death struggle.

Reuben Fleet was well aware of the background about which historians continue to speculate. "Soon after Britain got into the war," he said, "President Roosevelt began to prepare for our possible participation. He was wise enough, however, to wait for an overt act that unified our people."

That unity made itself highly visible on defense production lines and nowhere more effectively than at Consolidated, which had become America's largest integrated aircraft manufacturer.

One of the many stories, perhaps apocryphal, told about Reuben Fleet illustrated his concentration on production. Immediately after the attack on Pearl Harbor, the liaison officer at the Eleventh Naval District, responsible for coordination with Mexico, received a call from his counterpart across the border advising that the lights in Tijuana were being switched off as a safety precaution to protect San Diego.

What was the Navy doing about the lights in San Diego? They advised Mexico that steps had already been taken for a blackout there, too. But when nightfall came the lights at the huge Consolidated plant continued to burn.

The Commandant of the Naval District phoned Major Fleet, who barked out his reply: "All right, Admiral. Make up your mind. What do you want us to do?—make planes, or play games!" The plant lights stayed on, but blackout curtains went up.

The year 1942 brought the expanded plants into full production and saw completion of such new B-24 facilities as Consolidated at Fort Worth and Ford at Willow Run.

After formal merger of Consolidated and Vultee (Convair) in March 1943, the complex consisted of 13 manufacturing, modification and operating divisions in ten states with a combined payroll of one hundred thousand workers.

Among all Convair plants, the home factory at San Diego was the largest producer, turning out 8.2 percent by weight of the entire U.S. warplane production. San Diego employment reached a peak of 45,000 workers during 1942-43. Parts were being built by a hundred subcontractors and a dozen feeder plants.

"Rosie, the Riveter" made her appearance, joining men on the war production line at the main factories where by war's end nearly 40 percent of the workers were women, but in the "feeder plants" the figure rose to 90 percent of the 1700 employees.

Along with Ford and Douglas, North American Aviation was also brought into the B-24 production complex in 1942 with construction of a $28 million government-owned plant at Grand Prairie, Texas, near Dallas.

To incorporate design changes dictated by combat experience, and to do so without slowing assembly line production, a B-24 modification center was established at Tucson, Arizona in May 1941. Two other "mod" centers were later established for work on B-24s and PBYs.

Consairways operations were moved to Hamilton Field near San Francisco and that Division continued to operate a private airline service to Hawaii, the South Pacific and Australia for the Air Transport Command. Most of the runs were flown with C-87 Liberator Express transport versions of the B-24.

The huge Fort Worth plant—windowless, air conditioned, 4000 feet long and 320 feet wide—swung into B-24 production in March 1942 with two parallel, fully powered assembly lines, the world's longest. Its initial task was assembly of 600 B-24D bombers that Ford was to ship knocked-down from Willow Run. Ford production ran behind schedule so the San Diego plant sent components for the first 150 planes.

One thousand men had been hired at Fort Worth and sent to San Diego for on-the-job training. When the U.S. was drawn into the war in December 1941 these workers and a group of executive and engineering personnel moved from San Diego to Fort Worth as the nucleus of the Texas production plant.

From May 1942 on, over three thousand B-24s and the C-87 transport version came from the Fort Worth

WORLD'S LONGEST ASSEMBLY LINE, at Fort Worth plant, featured parallel, powered production lines, built 3034 Consolidated B-24 'Liberator' bombers.

Liberator Club

assembly lines, which were staffed by over 30,000 workers.

By war's end, 18,481 B-24s had been built, by far the largest production of any bomber or of any American aircraft. They operated on more war fronts for a considerably longer period and in a greater number of combat versions than any other bombers. Though their role in Europe was a major one, the B-24s' greatest contributions to victory were in the Pacific.

Final production figures for the B-24 were:

Convair San Diego	6,724
Convair Fort Worth	3,034
Total—Convair	9,759
Ford Willow Run	6,792
Douglas Tulsa	964
North American Dallas	966
Total	18,481

During the peak year of wartime production, 1944, Convair outproduced every other aircraft manufacturer in the world. Between Pearl Harbor and VE Day, the company and associated manufacturers produced 33,000 planes, almost 13 percent of the nation's total aircraft output during World War II.

In addition to building half the 18,481 'Liberator' bombers, including nearly 900 PB4Y-1s for the Navy, Convair produced 739 of the single-tail Navy 'Privateer (PB4Y-2) version, 27 'Privateer Express' transports, 2393 seaplane patrol bomber and other versions of the PBY 'Catalina,' and 216 four-engine PB2Y 'Coronado' flying boats.

In a change in its production planning, the government in January 1943 assigned to Consolidated a plant at Lake Ponchartrain, New Orleans, then nearing completion for assembly of Vought-Sikorsky flying boats. Instead, the twin-engine Consolidated Model 31 flying boat—which pioneered the radical, narrow-chord Davis wing—would be put into production at New Orleans.

'V GRAND,' the 5000th B-24 built at San Diego, bore names of hundreds of workers who assembled plane. Employees of Mexican descent inscribed "Viva Los Estados Unidos."

General Dynamics/Convair

General Dynamics/Convair

HUGE BUILDING and sign made Consolidated plant easily-identified target, but camouflage netting, right, made production area blend with near-by streets and houses if Jap planes overflew San Diego.

During testing, the Model 31 prototype had undergone modifications to the bow of the hull, and the tail surfaces had been raised. In April 1942 it emerged as the XP4Y-1 'Corregidor' with a capability to carry mines and torpedos as well as bombs.

The Model 31 had been the first plane to use the Wright R-3350 twin-row Cyclone engine rated at 2000 h.p. When the decision was made to push production of the new Boeing-designed B-29, priority in delivery of the powerful new Wright engines had to be given the 'Superfortress' and production of the P4Y-1 'Corregidor' was cancelled.

The New Orleans plant then took on production of Consolidated PBY-5 amphibians, of which 235 were built at this facility after transfer of the project from San Diego.

Preliminary design and mock-up of the huge six-engine XB-36 had been undertaken at San Diego after the contract award was made in November 1941 but in August 1942 Consolidated's Texas Division at Fort Worth took over responsibility for the detailed design and construction of two experimental intercontinental bombers.

The B-36 project, however, was given low priority because of the production emphasis which had to be placed on current production types. It was not until after the war that the B-36 got into the air.

Meantime development had started on the second-generation of Army four-engine long range bombers—the Boeing B-29 'Superfortress' and the Consolidated B-32, both classified as Very Heavy Bombers since they represented a significant scaling

OUTDOOR ASSEMBLY, possible in mild climate, had first attracted Consolidated to San Diego. Twin-engined PBYs, left; four-engined PB2Y 'Coronado' at right.

General Dynamics/Convair

up in size, speed, range and bomb capacity over the B-17 'Flying Fortress' and the B-24 'Liberator.'

In contrast to its B-17, Boeing's B-29 appeared with tricycle landing gear and long, narrow wing, not unlike features pioneered in the B-24, although the 'Superfortress' did retain the B-17's single tail.

The XB-32 (Consolidated Model 33) when first flown at San Diego on September 7, 1942—exactly nine months after Pearl Harbor—appeared to be a scaled-up version of the B-24, having retained a quite similar basic configuration including the Davis wing and twin-tail design adapted from the Model 31 flying boat. Wing span was 135 feet, gross weight 110,000 lbs., compared with the B-24's 110 foot span and 65,000 lb. gross weight in the J model. Contracts were in hand for the three experimental B-32 aircraft plus 13 additional for service test. Project engineer was Sparky Seabold.

After the XB-32 had made thirty flights, it crashed May 10, 1943 on take-off from Lindbergh Field, killing Richard McMakin, manager of Consairways, who was at the controls on that flight. Spectators indicated that the flaps had not been extended as they should have for the long take-off run. However, work was well along on the second and third airplanes which, when rolled out, showed a stepped-down cockpit. They were flown July 2 and November 9, respectively.

San Diego Aero-Space Museum

P4Y-1 'CORREGIDOR' was Navy version of Consolidated's Model 31 flying boat featuring Davis wing. Plane never got into mass production.

B-32 'DOMINATOR' was near look-alike of B-24 when prototype with twin tail first flew, top. Boeing developed single tail for production version, below.

General Dynamics/Convair

Liberator Club

EXTENDED-FUSELAGE, single-tail Navy versions of B-24 included *RY-3 transport type,* above, *and much-used PB4Y-2 'Privateer,'* below.

General Dynamics/Convair

In a somewhat unusual contract, the Air Force and Convair in November 1942 contracted with Boeing to develop a single-tail empennage for the B-32 much like that on the B-29 'Superfortress' but, at 32 feet, even taller and more angular. Pilots reported it gave the plane greater stability and maneuverability than any bomber of comparable size.

Extensive re-design for the production model was required and the entire B-32 'Dominator' project was then transferred to the Fort Worth plant. The original production contract called for 300 'Dominators'; a year later several hundred additional B-32s were added. A second supplemental contract—also for several hundred planes—was awarded to the San Diego plant, then beginning to phase out B-24 production.

At Fort Worth, 114 'Dominators' were built. Fifteen saw some action in the Pacific before the end of the war. Forty planes were designated TB-32 and used for training. Orders for over 1500 B-32 were then cancelled.

BASED ON COMBAT EXPERIENCE, the B-24 'Liberator' went through a series of major model changes and designations following introduction in 1941 of the mass-produced B-24D and its Navy PB4Y-1 counterpart. The B-24E was the early Ford-built model on which deliveries started in September 1942 and the -G designation covered those built by North American at Dallas starting February 1943.

Thirty one hundred -H models were produced at Fort Worth, Willow Run (Ford) and Tulsa (Douglas).

Most of the model changes involved varying armament installations, including powered gun turrets and their location, up-rated engine performance, new propellers and turbosuperchargers.

The largest of all 'Liberator' production models was the B-24J of which 6678 were built. It was the only model built by all five production facilities—San Diego, Fort Worth, Willow Run, Tulsa and Dallas. At San Diego, unit price of the B-24 had declined from $269,805 in 1941 to $137,000 in 1942. In addition to the large B-24J production there were 4260 of the -L and -M models, basically the same as the J except for details of armament.

A transport version, the C-87 'Liberator Express,' of which 286 were built at Fort Worth, was developed early in the B-24D program for carrying high priority passengers and cargo. Its Navy counterpart was the RY-2. Five examples of the C-87 were equipped for Army flight engineer training and were designated AT-22. There was also a fuel tanker model, C-109, capable of carrying 2900 gallons of gas in addition to its own needs. It was used on the India-China run ferrying supplies in support of early B-29 'Superfortress' flights against Japan. The XF-7 was a photo-reconnaissance version of the B-24D which carried eleven cameras and the F-7A designation described 86 B-24 Js converted to carry three cameras in the nose and three in the bomb bay. They were used on photo missions in the Pacific theatre.

Because of heavy losses on long-range bombing missions in Europe which could not be protected by shorter-range fighter aircraft, a B-24 version was developed as an escort plane for bombing formations. This was the XB-41, tested in February 1943. It was armed with 14 machine guns in seven turrets, but only the one plane was modified from a B-24D. Reportedly the plane had difficulty maintaining formation and was aero-dynamically unstable.

Two variants of the usual twin-finned B-24, one Navy and the other Air Force, seemed radical in appearance only because of their single-tail configuration.

"The Navy," Reuben Fleet recalls, "was anxious to get a third man—a flight engineer—in the cockpit so we extended the fuselage seven additional feet forward of the wing. We also extended it a little aft so we could use a single vertical tail instead of the double vertical tail, and it became a very satisfactory job for the Navy."

The extended-fuselage, single-tail Navy bomber was contracted for in May 1943. Designated PB4Y-2, and called 'Privateer,' 739 of this model were produced. As a transport, its Navy designation was RY-3.

Believing that a single fin-and-rudder arrangement would give greater stability, the Air Force contracted with Ford for the XB-24K, a B-24D modified to carry a single, squarish vertical tail while retaining the box-car fuselage and graceful Davis wing. When the decision was made that all future 'Liberators' would be single-tailed, the production version, with a more rounded tail, was designated B-24N but only seven examples were built before the war's end. The single-tail Navy and Air Force versions were developed independently.

The last B-24 off the assembly line, the 6724th 'Liberator' produced at San Diego, was completed May 31, 1945.

THREE WEEKS after German surrender, but 2½ months before V-J Day, last B-24 built is completed at San Diego plant.

Warren D. Shipp

B-36 INTERCONTINENTAL BOMBER, whose 230-foot wing span made it the world's largest plane, first flew in 1946 and for a decade was America's principal deterrent in cold war. Below. XC-99 transport version which, however, never reached production.

Warren D. Shipp

SIX PISTON ENGINES, four jets at wing tips powered late versions of 384 B-36s built. Here an Air Force fighter is suspended beneath the B-36.

Warren D. Shipp

BOOKS HAVE BEEN WRITTEN, and more will be written, about the legendary exploits of 'Catalinas' and 'Liberators' in World War II. Little more than a kaleidoscopic picture can be given here, for the wartime history of the three thousand PBYs and eighteen thousand B-24s is but one part of the life story of the founder of Consolidated Aircraft.

'Catalinas' of Patrol Wing 10 in the Philippines fared little better than those at Pearl Harbor on December 7th. In the first few weeks of the war in the Pacific, 25 of their 28 PBYs were expended as the group withdrew to the Netherlands East Indies.

As the United States tried to recover from the initial attacks, evacuation of key personnel from the Philippines became a special mission for the 'Catalinas.' On December 24, two PBYs ferried Brig. Gen. Lewis H. Brereton, Commander of the Army Far East Air Force, and his staff to Australia. Many such flights continued in the next few months, including evacuation of members of the staff of General Douglas MacArthur, recently recalled to active duty as Commander of U.S. Forces in the Far East.

After blunting Japanese attacks aimed at Port Moresby, New Guinea and stopping their southward expansion in the all-air Battle of the Coral Sea in May 1942, American forces staged their initial landings three months later on Guadalcanal.

Japan had gone into the Coral Sea engagement with fewer aircraft carriers than anticipated due to vigilance on the part of R.A.F. 'Catalinas.' In an early April attempt to duplicate their success at Pearl Harbor, the Japanese had planned a sneak attack on the British Naval Base at Trincomalee, Ceylon but the approaching task force was sighted several hundred miles off-shore.

When the attack came, the British were ready and won the air battle against the carrier-based Japanese planes. Three carriers had to return to Japan for new aircraft and missed the Battle of the Coral Sea.

At Guadalcanal and in subsequent phases of island-jumping, amphibious warfare—which was to last for the balance of the war in the southwest Pacific—strong support was supplied by U.S. and Australian PBY patrols.

It was mid-1942 before the U.S. had recovered sufficiently to initiate strong counter attacks against the Japanese. On the morning of June 3, a PBY on patrol made the first contact with support ships of the Japanese fleet steaming eastward toward Midway Island, 700 miles distant.

During the night four PBY-5As took off to lead a courageous torpedo attack on elements of the enemy fleet. The main enemy carrier force was discovered next day by a 'Catalina' search plane which gave distance and bearing information to U.S. Naval Forces, then managed to elude planes launched against the patrol planes by four Japanese carriers.

After U.S. victory in the Battle of Midway, which proved to be the turning point of the war, PBYs went out on daily patrols searching for American airmen

U. S. Navy/National Archives

RANGING THE SOUTH PACIFIC, PBY-5
'*Catalinas*' *participated in major engagements against the Japanese.*

downed in the battle. From bobbing life rafts they rescued 27 crewmen.

A diversion to the attack on Midway and possibly a prelude to a full scale attack on Alaska and Canada was a similar Japanese operation aimed at Dutch Harbor, Alaska in connection with occupation of Attu and Kiska in the Aleutian Island chain half way between Japan and Alaska. Capt. Leslie E. Gehres, later the famed captain of the carrier 'Franklin,' had 20 of Patrol Wing 4's PBYs under his Alaskan command out of Kodiak.

Weather conditions in the Aleutians were likely as adverse as anywhere in the world for aircraft operation, becoming progressively worse as the western end of the island chain is approached. There is rain almost every day, replaced by fog rather than clear skies. In succession may come rain, sleet, freezing rain, snow and fog, with zero-zero visibility. "Williwaw" squalls sweep down from the mountain peaks which are usually veiled in fog or clouds, making flying even more hazardous. And, since weather moves from east to west, the Japanese always knew in advance what the weather would be in the Aleutian chain.

'Catalinas' on patrol on June 2 sighted the enemy force south of Kiska and on June 10 discovered the enemy beachhead on Attu. Staging round-the-clock sorties from the seaplane tender Gillis, Gehres and his men, operating under impossible weather conditions, tried for 48 exhausting hours to dislodge the enemy from Kiska, where the Japs had also landed. Some Air Force support was provided by arrival of the first B-24 'Liberators' of the 11th Air Force.

After returning to the Gillis at Atka, 'Catalinas' refueled and rearmed at once and resumed the shuttle bombing. The strain upon pilots and crews was terrific, one pilot flying 19 1/2 hours during a single 24-hour period.

Ground crews faced incredible tasks in servicing the planes. Engines had to be warmed with blowtorches, ice and snow had to be scraped from wings, bombs and torpedos had to be manhandled onto their racks, whaleboats had to service PBYs tossing at anchor off shore.

The operational records of combat aircraft and men were most convincingly told by the naval and military commanders who bore the brunt of responsibility for conduct of the war.

Peter F. Girard

Capt. Leslie E. Gehres

"With few exceptions," Gehres wrote, "the pilots had no experience in Alaskan operations. The Squadrons had no period of preparation. They came with only what they could carry in their planes. Yet, in less than four full days out of California, these squadrons were dropping bombs on the enemy in Kiska in the face of increasingly heavy opposition, and they kept it up for nearly forty continuous hours.

"The squadrons of Patwing Four had been trained for patrol and that's all. A PBY is expensive, and it's hard to replace. All our patrol plane commanders had been indoctrinated with the idea of safety at all costs. To lose a 'Cat' was a cardinal sin.

"Now, that is the right way to operate patrol squadrons; but when you make patrol squadrons serve as bombers and torpedo units, you have to do more than load the planes with bombs and torpedos. You have to change the state of mind of the men. They have to learn that it's part of the job to sacrifice their planes and their lives if it's necessary to accomplish their missions.

"The psychology of the officers and men of Patwing Four changed overnight from that of searchers and reporters to aggressive combat fliers. They did some things that were simply incredible. Some of them got away with it because they hadn't had enough combat experience to know any better.

"In the early weeks of the engagement, we couldn't leave our planes overnight at established bases because the Japs would have caught them on the water and strafed them out of action, so we would always fuel them and disburse them to various obscure little bays in the islands. But Lieut. Comdr. C. J. Jones always had to land at Dutch Harbor, because whenever he came in his planes were so full of holes from enemy anti-aircraft they wouldn't float."

CAMOUFLAGED PBY-5 'CATALINA' of VP-42 on patrol near Seward, Alaska, in August 1941, three months before Pearl Harbor.

'CATALINA' GROUND CREWS faced incredible tasks in servicing the planes such as shown here in Attu in the Aleutians.

OFFICIAL VISIT to Patrol Wing 4 in the Aleutians soon after Pearl Harbor. Far left, Congressman Lyndon B. Johnson of Texas. In center, facing camera, Artemus L. Gates, Asst. Secy of Navy for Air. Between them, almost hidden, is Capt. Leslie E. Gehres. Johnson went on to become President. Gehres, who was promoted to Rear Admiral as heroic skipper of carrier "Franklin," later became key figure in Republican politics in California and close friend of Major Fleet.

Peter F. Girard

'BLACK CAT' PBY squadron based at Guadalcanal made all-night search and bombing runs to hinder enemy movements in Solomon Islands.

Round-the-clock reconnaissance became a reality in December 1942 when newly available radar was combined with the extended cruising range of PBYs. Painted jet black, the 'Catalinas' of VP-12, then based at Guadalcanal, normally took off after 10 p.m. to range up "the Slot" of the Solomon Islands east of New Guinea on all night search and bombing missions.

The Black Cat squadrons were particularly effective in spotting targets for bombardment by surface craft. Their slow speed was an advantage in locating and stopping the night time movement of enemy troops and supplies in small vessels and barges hidden during the day among the many islands.

Early in the war 'Catalinas' had developed a deserved reputation for their efficiency in air-sea rescue work. Throughout the war, downed pilots and airmen were being plucked from hostile waters and shores, often within range of enemy gunfire. Open ocean landings were possible because of the beefed-up hull design which followed the 1939 French Frigate Shoals tests.

In March 1942, Ensign F. E. Pinter spotted a liferaft between San Juan, Puerto Rico and Guantanamo Bay, Cuba. After landing in rough seas, 18 survivors of a torpedoed merchant ship were taken aboard the greatly overloaded 'Catalina,' which Pinter managed to get back into the air only by repeatedly bouncing the plane off the rolling swells.

Then, in June at Midway, the PBY's again did yeoman rescue service in open sea landings and takeoffs. Soon the Air Force had its own "Dumbo" aircraft—56 model OA-10s, the Army version of the Navy's PBY-5A amphibian. Later Canadian Vickers and Convair supplied 305 more rescue craft for the Army.

Individual exploits were illustrative of the many spectacular incidents which have been reported. In "George Kenney Reports," the Fifth Air Force Commanding General describes a raid by 40 B-24s on Kavieng in the Bismarcks north of Rabaul and the rescue which followed:

"Three of the crews were picked up in one of the most striking rescues of the war, when one of the Navy 'Catalina' flying boats assigned to the Fifth Air Force for air-sea rescue service picked up all 15 men in Kavieng Harbor itself, while under fire from the Jap shore batteries.

"The pilot, Lieut. Gordon, landed, picked up three men, saw two more clinging to a piece of debris, landed again, kept seeing more survivors, and kept on landing, until he had gone into that hornet's nest seven times.

"The 'Catalina' pilot had a rough time getting off the water after each landing. As he kept picking up survivors he kept adding weight, and each time he came back into the harbor he collected some bullet holes, and finally more water leaking into the hull added still more weight. It was a masterful exhibition of courage and airmanship."

NAVY PBY-5A AMPHIBIANS, right, *and Army's similar OA-10s were widely used in air-sea rescue.* Above, *PBY-5A lands at Bougainville in the Solomon Islands.*

'Catalinas' often operated far in advance of other Naval units because their seaplane tenders provided floating bases which could constantly be moved. Rear bases were provided out of Perth in western Australia and later Brisbane in the east as U.S. Forces moved steadily northwest back toward the Philippines.

Photo reconnaissance became an additional task for search planes which were camera-equipped starting in Spring 1943 so they would be able to supplement visual sighting with photographic evidence. New radar and camera installations greatly increased the effectiveness of the PBYs. The 'Catalina' patrol planes also operated as bombers against individual enemy merchant and war ships which made logical targets for the lightly-armed PBYs.

Toward the end of the war, longer-ranging landplanes became available for patrol work. Since modification of existing types was costly, the Navy ordered its own version of the B-24 'Liberator' and gave it the nautical name of 'Privateer' (Consolidated PB4Y-2).

When Army 'Liberators' began staging bombing raids from New Guinea bases in 1944 against the oil refineries on Borneo, the air-sea rescue 'Dumbo Catalinas' picked up all crew members of three B-24s and half the crew of the fourth B-24 downed in the September 30 raid on Balikpapan.

SEAPLANE TENDERS provided floating bases from which PBYs could be operated far in advance of other Naval units.

PB4Y-2 "PRIVATEER" Navy version of B-24 had long-range capability which made possible extended over-water patrol missions by landplanes.

General Dynamics/Convair

AMPHIBIAN PBY-5As operated out of Argentia, Newfoundland, as in this March 1943 photo.

U. S. Navy/National Archives

FOUR-ENGINED PB2Y-5 'Coronado,' used late in the war, was equipped with JATO for jet-assisted takeoff.

General Dynamics/Convair

In contrast to operations in the Pacific, PBYs in the Atlantic were used chiefly in anti-submarine warfare missions. Their work began with the Neutrality Patrol organized in September 1939 when war broke out in Europe. Later they operated out of bases ranging in a vast arc from Iceland to Newfoundland to Florida and the Caribbean. After Pearl Harbor additional PBY squadrons patrolled off South America, operating from Natal, Brazil.

While escorting shipping convoys in the Atlantic, PBYs sighted many German U-boats both submerged and on the surface. Some were sunk by the 'Catalinas'; others by the destroyers which came in for the kill. Of 55 subs sunk by U.S. planes, 20 are credited to PBYs.

Big brother of the twin-engine 'Catalina' was the four-engine Consolidated PB2Y-3 'Coronado,' of which 210 had been produced through October 1943. In its combat role, such as the bombing of the Marshall Islands, the PB2Y-3 carried six tons of bombs or various combinations of depth charges, torpedos and mines. It was manned by a crew of ten.

Ten flying boats of the -3B version were delivered to the British for the R.A.F. Coastal Command which used them as cargo transports across the North Atlantic and between the Caribbean and Africa.

For a similar role in U.S. Navy service, transporting key personnel across the Atlantic and Pacific oceans, 31 of the model PB2Y-3R were modified by Rohr Aircraft to carry 44 passengers and a crew of five. Two other versions were designated PB2Y-4 and -5, indicating different engine installations.

The PB2Y-5H variant was equipped as an ambulance plane; others served in air-sea rescue work. On Iwo Jima, during the first fierce assault on the beaches, the sea-borne plane was used to evacuate wounded before a landing strip could be built. All -5 models were equipped with JATO (jet assisted takeoff) so advantage could be taken of the additional thrust under heavy overload conditions.

General Dynamics/Convair

Of ALL WORLD WAR II aircraft, none was produced in larger numbers than the B-24 'Liberator,' nor flown on combat and transport missions on more operational fronts over a longer time span. Because it was a versatile work horse, it appeared in the many versions dictated by operational requirements which were vastly different in different war theaters.

In Europe, Air Force bombing missions had to be closely integrated with those of the British, who took on responsibility for night area raids while U.S. aircraft conducted the daylight precision raids. In the South Pacific, under entirely different operational conditions on long overwater flights, Air Force missions were flown in close coordination with the U.S. Navy.

Finally, in the latter portion of the war, the longer range of the B-24 brought the decision to concentrate B-24 'Liberator' operations in the South Pacific, replacing all B-17s.

Anticipating Japan's entry into the war, two of the first B-24s were equipped for photo reconnaissance and scheduled to try and obtain sneak photos of Japanese military installations in the Marshall Islands and at Truk while on a flight from Hawaii to the Philippines. The first arrived in Hawaii December 5, 1941. Two days later it was blown to bits on the ground

at Hickham Field in the attack on Pearl Harbor and other military installations. It was the first American B-24 in "combat."

Fifteen British LB-30 'Liberators' still in the U.S. were taken over by the Air Force and dispatched to the Philippines to bolster America's dwindling strength, but were diverted to the Dutch East Indies, arriving there in mid-December, where four took part in the first 'Liberator' bombing missions of the war.

In the Battle of the Atlantic, the 'Liberator's' endurance made it a favorite of all anti-submarine forces. With additional fuel capability and newly acquired search radar, long-ranging B-24s based on the Atlantic seaboard could fly a thousand miles to sea and remain on station four hours before returning to base. Other ASW B-24 squadrons were sent to England to operate with the R.A.F. Coastal Command. The U.S. Navy also began to operate their PB4Y-1 version of the B-24 with the British on maritime reconnaissance, replacing the AAF groups.

A detachment of two dozen B-24Ds, under command of Col. Harry Halverson, had been organized in the spring of 1942 to make a Doolittle-type raid on Tokyo from some base in China. Crossing the south Atlantic and Africa, the detachment was held up in Egypt for a single special mission. The B-24's long-range capability would be put to maximum test in staging a raid on the Ploesti oil fields and refineries in Rumania which were believed to supply one-third of Germany's needs.

On June 11, thirteen of Halverson's 'Liberators' took off from an R.A.F. Base near the Suez Canal for an all-night flight, dropping their bomb loads on the refineries before flying on to landings in Iraq, Syria and Turkey. Bomb damage was not extensive, but this first American raid against 'Festung Europa' demonstrated a long range strike potential which was the precursor of massive assults to come.

In October 1942 initial B-24 strategic bombing missions against Western Europe were begun out of England when 'Liberators' joined Flying Fortresses of the 8th Air Force under Brig. General Ira C. Eaker in raids on the steel and locomotive works at Lille, France. In the months and years to follow came the massive daylight raids which moved inexorably eastward into the heart of industrial Germany as the range of fighter escorts was progressively extended when the P-51 'Mustangs' came into use.

The targets for the 8th Air Force—and later the 15th from Italy—are a catalog of destruction: U-Boat pens, the Ruhr steel complex, Hamburg, Kiel, Schweinfurt ballbearing plants, Wilhelmshaven, Antwerp, fighter plane production plants, oil refineries in Poland, Czechoslovakia, Hungary and Austria, Berlin, V-bomb launching sites, Regensburg, rail centers, airdromes and coastal defenses. The offensive directed by Lieut. Gen. Carl (Toohy) Spaatz, Commander U.S. Strategic Air Forces, Europe, culminated in the March 18, 1945 daylight assult on Berlin by 1250 four-engine bombers and Spaatz's April 16 announcement that the strategic air war in Europe was at an end.

Operating from North Africa, B-24s pounded shipping and ports in the Mediterranean, German Army ground targets in the Western Desert and then began to strike at the "soft underbelly" of Europe.

From headquarters of the Middle East Air Force, later the 9th Air Force, its commanding officer, Maj. Gen. Lewis H. Brereton, got off a July 22, 1943 report to Washington:

EIGHTH AIR FORCE B-24 Allied bomber group flying out of England drops its bombs on Nazi ground installations. Rear plane in formation has apparently been hit by enemy fire.

U. S. Air Force

"Dear General Arnold:

"I was very much interested in your recent report on the B-24H production and its armament equipment. With the added guns it should offer a formidable defense. We have so far had fortunate results from enemy fighter opposition. I make this statement with reserve however, as our formations have never been attacked by the large numbers encountered in Western Europe. We have been attacked repeatedly, by forces of from twenty to forty fighters but the majority of our losses are due to flak. The B-24 will take a phenomenal amount of punishment from both ack ack and enemy fighter attacks. They return so badly shot up at times that their return is due only to the courage and skill of our pilots. Malta has been a life saver as a port of refuge for our cripples, many of whom could never return to the Benghazi bases.

"As a strategic weapon the 'Liberators' have flown more than fifty combat missions that have ranged the Mediterranean in attacking targets in Africa, Southern Europe, Sicily, the Balkans and Rumania. I think more publicity should be awarded the B-24. It is a magnificent hunk of bomber, and I am going to write to Reuben Fleet and tell him so.

"Tidal wave training is well underway. I am thoroughly pleased with the attitude of all commanders—and the planning has been excellent. We will have a plane for every combat crew available which will be 185.

Sincerely yours,

Brereton"

Air Force Museum

SUN GLISTENS off 'Liberator' which has just hit Porto Marghera oil storage tanks. Photo taken by combat photographer from bomb bay of accompanying B-24.

THROUGH FLAK-FILLED SKIES, waves of B-24 'Liberators' of the 15th Air Force leave the burning ruins of the Concordia Vega oil refinery at Ploesti.

"Tidal wave" became one of the most publicized raids of the war, the low level attack on Rumanian oil refineries, as Ploesti was revisited. Until after the invasion of Italy, this prime target could be reached only by B-24s flying from Africa.

Three bomber groups, two from England and one en route overseas from the United States, joined two from General Brereton's Ninth Air Force. Flying north over the Mediterranean, 177 B-24s left Benghazi, Libya early August 1, 1943 for the 2700-mile round trip.

The mission navigator was lost enroute as the heavily loaded lead B-24 banked steeply and plunged into the Mediterranean. Another 'Liberator,' with the deputy route navigator aboard, dropped out of formation and spiraled down to search for possible survivors but could not then catch up with the main formation. Two groups arrived late over the target. These mishaps seriously downgraded mission effectiveness.

When the remainder of the main formations of B-24s did arrive they ran into intense flak and dense black smoke which had been generated to screen not only the targets but also the cables of defensive balloons. Later waves of B-24s had to fly through fires and the explosions of delayed action bombs of earlier 'Liberators.' The targets were hit hard but at great expense. More B-24s were lost as Me-109s and other enemy fighters attacked the homeward bound 'Liberators.'

Thirty percent of the men and planes which had left Benghazi that morning did not return, but 40 percent of Ploesti's refining capability had been wiped out. It was a costly but effective operation.

Despite the Ploesti attrition the remnants of the five groups were able two weeks later to stage the first strike launched from North Africa against targets inside Germany.

DRAMATIC PHOTO at Astra Romana Refinery is vivid evidence of how low B-24 squadrons flew in bombing the important Ploesti installations.

269

NOT THE A-BOMB but a B-24 attack by 15th Air Force 'Liberators'
in August 1944 on the Xenia oil refinery at Ploesti, Rumania.

From the Southwest Pacific, General Brereton had been transferred soon after the outbreak of hostilities to head the 10th Air Force in the new China-Burma-India theater. Attacks on enemy forces over-running Burma continued until June 1942 when Brereton and his bombers were hastily transferred to the Middle East where the German offensive under Rommel threatened Cairo.

Subsequently, the 10th and 14th Air Forces under Brig. Gen. Claire L. Chennault ranged widely for several years throughout China and Southeast Asia—Burma, Thailand and the Malay peninsula—making excellent use of the long-range of their fleet of 'Liberator' bombers.

In the Southwest Pacific, the first all B-24 units began to arrive in Australia in October 1942 as part of the recently created Fifth Air Force under Maj. Gen. George C. Kenney, who also served as General MacArthur's air commander. Later B-24s of the 7th and 13th Air Forces joined the fray, with the former staging December raids on Wake Island, the first at any Japanese-held base in the Central Pacific.

'Liberators' continued to play key roles in the twin-pronged offensive under which MacArthur moved from Australia through New Guinea into the Philippines, while forces under Admiral Chester W. Nimitz, hero of the Battle of Midway, swept northwest toward Japan through the Gilbert, Marshall, Mariana and

AMID SERPENTINE SMOKE MARKERS, *four B-24s of 8th Air Force* hit
*Tours, France. Photo catches the -J model B-24s at the instant all release
their bombs.*

BIGGEST COORDINATED BOMBING attack in the Pacific is how 13th AAF described B-24 raid on Japanese oil supply at Balikpapan, Borneo, in the Netherlands East Indies.

Ryukyus Islands.

It was General Kenney who introduced the imperious MacArthur to the potential of air power. In a July 21, 1970 letter he wrote in response to Reuben Fleet's compliment on an article Kenney had written:

"Dear Reuben:

"Thanks for the kind words about Billy Mitchell article. In reference to General MacArthur, you are right. He didn't know much about air power, but he was big enough to buy it lock, stock and barrel. I am proud to have made the sale, and to have become a real friend and admirer of his in the process.

Best regards,

George Kenney"

October 1943 brought sustained raids staged from Port Moresby against the great Japanese air base at Rabaul, followed in the spring of 1944 by those against Truk. In September and October the oil refineries at

Balikpapan on Borneo became the target for B-24s of the 5th and 13th Air Forces in a raid reminiscent of Ploesti. Mine-sowing 'Catalinas' of the Royal Australian Air Force helped neutralize Balikpapan by crippling shipborne oil deliveries.

'Catalinas' also came in for their full share of credit in support of B-24 raids in their role as effective air-sea rescue planes picking up downed crews.

After Borneo came attacks on the Philippines and Iwo Jima and finally fire-bomb raids against the Japanese home islands as U.S. forces gained a foothold on Okinawa in the Ryukyus, bringing American's new B-29 'Superfortress' bombers within range.

Counterpart of the B-29 was the new Consolidated B-32 'Dominator,' similarly classified as a Very Heavy Bomber. It too began to be delivered, from the Fort Worth plant, for operations in the Pacific.

"George Kenney," Fleet recalls, "had directed bombing for three years in the Southwest Pacific using B-24 'Liberators' and in Spring 1945 was anxious to

TRAGEDY AND VICTORY *often flew side by side in aerial warfare. Hit by flak, wing of B-24 explodes and crumples on mission over Italy. Only radar bombardier survived.*

DESPITE FLAK BURST which exploded inside *'Liberator' over Yugoslavia, severing rudder cables, this B-24 made it home with loss of only one crew member.*

CAUGHT IN HEAVY FLAK BELT *over Blechhammer, Germany, this 15th AAF B-24 explodes and disintegrates as bombs tumble from overturned 'Liberator.'*

DURABLE 'LIBERATOR', (above), of the 392nd Bombardment Group has already flown 77 missions as evidenced by decals on nose.

HIGH-TAILED B-32 'DOMINATORS', (below), saw service in final weeks of war in the Pacific, flying from base in Okinawa.

replace them with the newer Very Heavy Bombers because of their longer range and more-than-doubled bomb capacity.

"In March 1945 General Kenney was in Washington seeking all the B-32s we could give him. Hap Arnold agreed to give him, starting in June, enough for two bomb groups and had one B-32 flown to Washington so George could test fly it himself. As it could fly ten tons of bombs from the Philippines to Kyushu, the main Japanese island, Kenney was anxious to have the planes assigned to him.

"We had done about all we could with the B-24 and what we had learned was put into the improved design for the B-32. The 'Dominator' was a fine airplane."

The first group of B-32As, fifteen in number, was assigned to Kenney's Fifth Air Force and flown into Clark Field in the Philippines. After a month of shakedown flights, the 'Dominators' were assigned to the 386th Bombardment Squadron and based on Okinawa.

Initial raids with the B-32 were against Formosa where an alcohol production plant was the main target. In late July and early August the 'Dominators' were equipped with low-altitude bombsights for night missions and used for "snooper" flights over Tokyo, in one of which four B-32s were attacked by 15 enemy fighters but escaped after knocking down three Jap planes.

Only a week before the atom bomb fell on August 6, 'Liberators' were bombing the rail terminals at Nagasaki. On September 2, General MacArthur accepted the Japanese surrender, bringing World War II to an end.

In August, 1970, three weeks after receipt of the Kenney letter, Reuben Fleet, General Jimmy Doolittle and Mac Laddon met with Air Force historian Dr. Murray Green to research important phases of the air war.

"Just seven days before the war was over," Reuben related, "the Chief of Intelligence of the Navy was my house guest. 'Admiral,' I said, 'how long does the Navy think the war is going to last?'

" 'Two and a half years,' he replied.

" 'What does the Navy figure is necessary to be done?'

" 'We'll have to land two and a half million soldiers and Marines on Japan. But, Major Fleet, what do you think about it?'

" 'I think it will be over in two weeks.'

" 'You do?'

" 'Yes, sir."

" 'Why do you think that?'

" 'Because Japan can't continue to take what they are getting now, and they haven't any airpower left to resist. What can they do to stop us? Nothing.' "

Reflecting on the air war in the Pacific, Doolittle recalled that "MacArthur gave George Kenney his head, and from then on with his full support Kenney did a tremendous job of running the Air Force."

"And," added Fleet, "we never had to land a foot soldier in Japan to whip them. We needn't even have dropped those two atomic bombs, because we had the war won anyway."

It was the first time in history that victory had been won without an invasion of the enemy's territory.

AFTER BOMB STRIKE on Japanese-held Nauru in the Gilbert Islands, above, B-24 heads for base. FORCED LANDING on partially completed fighter strip, below, is made by photo reconnaissance version of B-24.

U. S. Air Force

500-POUNDERS from the 'Bird of Paradise'

TAKEOFF FROM KWAJALEIN

PICTORIAL SOUTH PACIFIC was as much documented in these heretofore unpublished Air Force photos as was the heat of battle.

As the 27th Bombardment Squadron of the 30th Bombardment Group, Seventh Air Force, moved northwestward from Abemama Atoll in the Gilbert Islands, through Kwajalein in the Marshalls, Saipan in the Marianas and finally Iwo Jima, photographer Al Saiget recorded these breath-taking scenes of B-24s in action.

JUNGLE MAINTENANCE on Abemama, Gilbert Islands

KWAJALEIN, above and below

IWO JIMA; Mt. Surabachi at tip

277

IN HIS POST-PEARL HARBOR role as consultant to the new management of his old company, Major Fleet continued to have an office—and Eva Wiseman as his secretary—but did not easily fit into his changed circumstance. For one thing he was moved from his old office in the main plant to similar facilities in Plant 2, the parts plant; no doubt to isolate him from the company's day to day activities.

Nor was Mac Laddon, as Executive Vice President and General Manager, completely comfortable with Reuben still around for he was torn between responsibility to his new bosses and respect for his long-time associate and leader.

By long-hand note to Laddon in August 1942, Fleet complained that his reserved parking places were being used by others and asked that three convenient stalls be painted with his name. Laddon's written reply must have sparked a furious outburst:

> ". . . we have always refused to personalize parking stalls within the plant and I can not make an exception in your case."

As if that memo was not enough burden to bear, another even more pointed one arrived the same day:

CONSOLIDATED AIRCRAFT CORPORATION

August 6, 1942

Major R. H. Fleet
Mr. I. M. Laddon
Speeches, Radio Broadcasts and Published Articles

Reference the above, although you may preface your remarks with the specific statement that the opinions expressed are your own and not those of this Corporation, your long association and past position with Consolidated precludes your remarks being so interpreted. It does not appear to be practicable or possible to keep you fully informed and in agreement with present management policies and such of your statements as are at variance with same will prove embarrassing and damaging to the Corporation. Therefore, in the interest of the Corporation, you are requested to refrain from further broadcasts, speeches and published articles.

I. M. Laddon

Reuben Fleet was not about to be intimidated nor take direction from former subordinates much as he may have respected their abilities. And, of course, there wasn't the man living who could silence him when the Major felt compelled to speak his mind on national issues.

Other unpleasantries arose in connection with his capacity as a consultant. Cost inspectors disallowed that portion of salaries for Fleet and his secretarial staff which company accountants had charged to Navy contracts.

In many ways it was a difficult period for the Major. He maintained an office at Consolidated Vultee, the name adopted in 1943, but as a consultant had no responsibility or authority for the company's operation. At the same time his family situation was unstable with Mrs. Fleet and the children living in the Los Angeles area. He hoped the marriage might be saved.

Reuben's long-time financial assistant, Russ Stanberry, former Consolidated corporate secretary, had gone to Los Angeles the year after the Major sold out his interest. There Fleet and Stanberry set up an office to handle the Major's personal business. It also provided a weekend base while trying to work out a reconciliation with his wife.

Fleet had come to know and greatly respect Charles A. Lindbergh. Here, he felt, was the ideal individual to follow in his footsteps. With guidance from the Major, the Lone Eagle could well be groomed for the top spot in Consolidated Vultee. It was a refreshing idea but a great disappointment when Tom Girdler rejected the idea. The steel executive simply felt that the company could not afford to take on a man who was then so controversial because of his "America First" view that the United States should not get involved in the war in Europe.

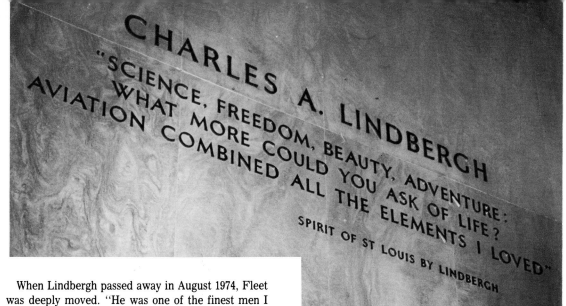

CHARLES A. LINDBERGH
"SCIENCE, FREEDOM, BEAUTY, ADVENTURE: WHAT MORE COULD YOU ASK OF LIFE? AVIATION COMBINED ALL THE ELEMENTS I LOVED"

SPIRIT OF ST LOUIS BY LINDBERGH

When Lindbergh passed away in August 1974, Fleet was deeply moved. "He was one of the finest men I ever knew," the Major said. "If I'd kept my company back there in 1941, I'd have had him as my assistant—at my right hand. He was a grand man; an able, talented, hard working man." *

Giving substance to his high regard for Lindbergh, Reuben got in touch with his widow, Anne Morrow Lindbergh, and obtained her approval for a memorial bust to be erected in his honor by Fleet's fellow Air Mail Pioneers. As so often was the case, the Major quietly funded the project—a bust by sculptor Paul Fjelde for which Lindbergh had posed a dozen years after his New York-Paris flight.

Today the memorial bust at Rockefeller Center in New York—thanks to Reuben Fleet—serves as a reminder of Lindbergh's great achievements and as "a continuing inspiration to all mankind and to posterity."

Rockefeller Center

LINDBERGH BUST AND TRIBUTE sponsored by Reuben Fleet and Air Mail Pioneers is dedicated in New York's Rockefeller Center by Laurance S. Rockefeller, who shared environmental concerns with his friend Charles A. Lindbergh.

Rockefeller Center

AIR MAIL PIONEERS at August, 1975 dedication. From left, Louis Krentz; R. C. (Tex) Marshall, president; and E. M. Allison.

*In his wartime journals, Lindbergh noted three separate offers in 1941 and 1942 from Fleet, first at $25,000 annually, then $50,000 and finally $100,000. Instead Lindbergh became a consultant to Ford Motor Company on production of the B-24 bomber. Later he went to the South Pacific as a technical representative to help develop fighter plane combat tactics.

Before Fleet shed his role as a consultant, an old matter cropped up on which the Major took a strong stand. The highly efficient Davis wing had been a primary factor in success of the company's big bombers and Fleet did not begrudge David Davis and Walter Brookins the royalties which were being paid for use of their patent.

However, when the Navy began to contract separately for the single-tail PB4Y-2 Privateer version of the B-24 they began looking into the patent situation because of the royalty payments involved.

"Consolidated," Fleet recalls, "had paid Davis-Brookins several hundred thousand dollars in royalties on the B-24 before the Navy looked into the patent. They went through the ordinates, discovered that they didn't check out and, therefore, considered the patent invalid.

"The Navy notified us to put a stop-order on further royalty payments and also to have Davis return whatever money we had paid him. We took decided exception to that and explained to the Navy that the wing was carrying more weight than any comparable wing has ever carried in the history of aviation. Therefore, Davis had earned his money."

Fleet called Davis in to talk about the matter. "Major," he replied, "I would have been a damn fool to file the correct ordinates with the patent application because anyone can buy a copy from Uncle Sam for five cents. A public disclosure like that would reveal it to the whole world. I, naturally, didn't expect anyone to check the ordinates and used false data just so no one could steal the information in case of my death."

Major Fleet explained the situation to the Navy. "Gentlemen," he said, "I urge you not to go so far for you're making a horrible mistake. Davis simply was trying to protect his own interest. His wing is doing everything claimed for it. At the very least don't take away the payments he's already received; besides he's already paid the government taxes on what he's gotten so far. Don't forget, nearly all the B-24 contracts have been with the Army; and anyway what business is that of yours?"

The outcome was that the Navy let the prior royalty payments stand, but wouldn't approve payment of any more.

For the year ended November 30, 1942 royalties paid to the Davis-Brookins Aircraft Co. totaled $92,665 according to company records. Subsequently some modification of the original royalty schedule was worked out and a new license agreement signed June 29, 1943. Payments totaling $44,005 were made between October 1943 and February 1946 and involved a royalty of $5.00 per plane on 8801 planes, including Army B-24s, Navy PB4Y-2 Privateers and Army B-32 'Dominators.'

With the coming of V-E Day (victory in Europe) in May 1945, Reuben felt it was time to step aside and bring to an end the somewhat unsatisfactory relationship with Consolidated Vultee (Convair) management.

"I stayed on as a consultant," he then explained, "at the insistence of the Army and Navy. But my obligation is over now and I want to become a free agent once more."

Mac Laddon packed up Reuben's personal office furniture—a gift from a Buffalo furniture manufacturer—and sent it out to the Spanish mansion on Point Loma.

Fleet's contract with Convair still had a year and a half to go but as the Major explained, "I didn't hold them to it."

FLEET'S ROLE AS CONSULTANT on aviation matters to President Roosevelt had not only continued without interruption but in one respect increased. At White House request a private phone line, No. 5039, was installed right into the Fleet home as well as to his office so that the Major was immediately and privately available to President Roosevelt.

As a private citizen—but still a very public figure—Fleet continued to speak out vigorously and to appear before congressional committees on the need to preserve free enterprise, on air power, on the evils of excessive taxation. In addition, his voluminous correspondence gave unsolicited advice to many a Congressman and Senator.

As conditions on the war fronts in Europe and the Pacific began to go better as the result of American air power, Fleet began to give attention to the industry's post-war problems. In a December 10, 1943 letter to James Forrestal, Undersecretary of the Navy he wrote:

"Aircraft manufacturers are driving full blast to a precipitous abyss—the war's end. They fear the postwar holiday for their wares that will force them to discharge employees, and maybe break them [financially] before they can design and get into production of commercial products.

"They have been, and will continue to be, indispensable to our Nation; therefore, they should have fair treatment from a grateful country, whose postwar policy toward them should be decided upon and announced soon."

The Major then went on to make specific recommendations about termination of war contracts, recovery of some profits taken in the process of renegotiation of contracts, rework of combat aircraft by their original manufacturers, contracts for development of new aircraft, loans of equipment to aeronautical schools, lease of government aircraft to airlines extending routes abroad, and the use of war plants by private industry.

Pointing out the need for prompt action, Fleet wrote that ". . . the Government is likely to be small in its dealings, penurious and exacting, dilatory in action, and fearful of criticism. It should be exactly the contrary."

Ever the advocate of air power, Major Fleet later appeared before the Fort Worth Chamber of Commerce speaking on "Aviation; Savior of Civilization."

"In 1935 when we moved to San Diego we were in the valley of the world's worst depression; military aviation was a neglected luxury and remained such until the outbreak of war in 1939 when England declared war on Germany. At that time, Consolidated had orders for only five airplanes from the United States Government. Our little factory was like a graveyard and had been forced to trim our organization from nearly 4000 trained employees to less than 1200.

"Then in 1941 Consolidated's forced growth was the greatest of any private enterprise in any line of endeavor in the history of the world. But we must not stand like Lot's wife, who crystallized in the act of looking backward. (Genesis 19:26). Let us look forward to the future.

"Now we have a war and a peace to win. The time for apathy is past; the time for thinkers has come—for clear thinking, and hard-headed action.

"Out of this war will come to humanity a particularly great blessing—namely, an instrumentality capable of enforcing world peace while peacefully spreading good will among men. That instrumentality is aircraft, which saved England from Nazi subjugation, and which is lessening the task of our soldiers and sailors immeasurably in the war and bringing the conflict to a conclusion much sooner than would otherwise be the case.

"Airpower does not involve policing—its possession in preponderance is sufficient. Aircraft are helpless on the ground, but their mobility and potentiality are so great that an aggressor would court serious trouble in ignoring them.

"I shudder to think of what would happen to civilization if another world war is repeated in this century. We must not be soft-hearted or impractical in this; I repeat, we must win the peace as well as the war. Solomon said, 'Where there is no vision, the people perish.' "

A month after his Fort Worth speech, in a February 1944 appearance as President of the Institute of Aeronautical Sciences before a postwar planning committee of the House of Representatives, Fleet urged a tax plan conducive to free enterprise.

"During the war," he said, "it is all right to tax profits the same as manpower is drafted," but "the minute the war is over, you stop drafting men, so you must stop at that time—instantly—drafting the profits from industry; otherwise you will not have any private enterprise to carry on. Reverse the New Deal, and refertilize the soil of America by giving business a chance!"

In a strong, authoritative tone the Major addressed the chair:

"Mr. Chairman, I believe in business. Business is risk for gain. It looses attractiveness when the possibility of gain disappears or fails to warrant the risk involved. Business must be permitted to have a run for its money if it is to give post-war employment. Otherwise, new capital will refuse to invest and private enterprise, the very thing we're fighting to preserve, will have been killed by taxation. Adventure money must have fertile soil to come out from hiding. Socialism is the alternative. America must not embrace it!"

In closing he again emphasized that the Government should not be put in competition with private industry and recommended that after the war Government-owned aircraft plants be offered for "low prices" and "on easy terms" to industry.

"I place air power first, sea strength second, land forces third."

Decisive and strongly opinionated in all things, Reuben Fleet spoke out forcefully on behalf of air power as a deterrent to war.

"Since air power is the key to our ability to carry out a commitment to insure world peace, it is the nearest thing to the heartthrob of our Nation. Which would you rather we be—mistress of the seas, or master of the air? I place air power first, sea strength second, land forces third.

"Aviation, through the fear it can instill, may well be a great instrument for peace. Along with peace through fear must run the thread of brotherly love that alone can make for enduring peace. We must turn from hate to love if we ever hope to solve the world's multitude of problems.

"Like truth, love is God-given, and we need never fear that there won't be enough of it to go around. When another child comes into a family, the father loves both equally. This isn't achieved by halving the love for his first child, but rather by finding new capacities for affection."

Still, if in this imperfect world, war should come, Fleet knew there was no substitute for victory. As the lesser of two evils, he strongly advocated all-out bombing to bring any conflict to a swift though necessarily destructive end.

Although Convair had earlier looked with disfavor on Fleet's public appearances, he was asked to be the principal speaker at the company's 30th anniversary celebration in 1953.

Speaking with emotion, in sentences punctuated by frequent pounding of his fist on the lectern, the Major struck out against what he called a "retreat from victory" in Korea, arguing that America should use every resource at its command, including the atomic bomb, before it was too late.

"When the B-36 bomber was conceived," he said, "we believed we were creating an instrumentality to give us airpower supremacy, the mere possession of which in preponderance, as a threat without its employment, would stop aggressors and assure world peace. Of course, we assumed we would have the will to use it if necessary.

"Meanwhile we fought and won World War II. Devastating airpower, coupled with magnificent Navy and Marine action, and two dosages of atom bombs, gave Japan all she could stand. Horrible, inhuman, diabolical—thousands of our boys' lives were saved, together with years of war and billions of dollars; it was unnecessary to land a foot-soldier!"

U.S. strength, he concluded, should be used if necessary "to help end war decisively and make acts of aggression too fearful for comtemplation by any country that might desire to impose its will upon another nation."

In similar vein, more than a decade later, on his 80th birthday, the Major again pleaded with the country's leaders to bring another war to a speedy conclusion.

"I think that in Vietnam," he said, "we should endeavor to win immediately. Go in and use whatever it takes to polish this thing off. Pick your targets and announce that you're going to annihilate that target tomorrow. And do it!

"The next day, do the same thing and keep it up until they yell uncle. We can't pussyfoot forever. We whipped the Japanese with aviation. We can do it here."

It was five and a half years later before President Nixon made the hard decision to bomb Hanoi at Christmas-time, 1972. Finally, with decisive use of airpower, the U.S. extricated itself from the morass of Vietnam.

ⒺDSEL FORD HAD DIED in 1943 and his son, Henry II, had been named President of Ford Motor Company while his grandfather was still alive. After the war, Reuben Fleet recalls, young Ford phoned him in San Diego.

" 'Have you got any plans to come east, Major Fleet?'

"No, but if you want to see me, of course I'll come."

" 'I wonder if you would meet me at Willow Run; I want to talk to you about the plant there.'

"When I arrived I was met by young Ford and his friend Cyrus McCormick of International Harvester Company. His question was 'What will I do with Willow Run?'

"Henry, your father is gone; so is your grandfather. They have left you hundreds of millions of dollars worth of factories all over the world. Factories are no good without a product in them. They are, in fact, a liability. I am told that your product is dwindling down to about 18% of the automobile business.

"If I were you, I wouldn't let the glamour of aviation attract me. I would never in the world keep this plant unless I could use it in the aviation business. I would work hard to get my automobile products up to snuff.

" 'Well, what do you think of our organization? You've seen and helped train some of our best brains.'

"You have some wonderful men, but I believe other companies here in Detroit have better ones."

" 'Who, for example?'

"I don't know because I don't live here in Detroit. But I'd get somebody with General Motors experience; somebody on the second level because the top people are too well paid. The company has their nests too well feathered.

"If you hire the right man on the second level, he'll be able to advise you on who else to get.

" 'That's fine, Major. But don't you have some recommendation?'

"Well, I think Ernie Breech is the best man you could get. He came up through the Accounting branch, and that is very important because he'll be concerned with how much things cost. He came from a small town in Missouri and is not spoiled by having been around a big city all his life. He is an honest fellow and a damn good man. And I'd take his judgment as to recruiting other men from the other companies here."

Young Ford took Fleet's advice. From top executive at North American Aviation in the mid-thirties, Ernest R. Breech had gone to General Motors, then to Bendix Aviation. In 1946 he accepted Henry Ford II's offer to become executive vice-president of Ford Motor Company.

Ⓘ T IS PERHAPS PURE MYTH that successful business executives, if they don't keep busy, literally die of boredom within 18 months after retirement because they've lost the zest for living through lack of challenge. Reuben Fleet did not fit that stereotype because he never really retired. Though not aware of it himself, he felt a compulsion after retirement to keep sufficiently busy at productive work to justify his continued presence on this earth.

The Major's interest in civic work in his adopted city, San Diego, and in national military, political and

SAN DIEGO CIVIC GROUP includes, from left, Chamber of Commerce executive William A. Van Dusen, pioneer aircraft builder T. Claude Ryan, and Fleet. Van Dusen, a Reserve Air Corps pilot, became wartime inspector at Convair.

economic matters occupied much of his time. In 1943 he accepted chairmanship of the San Diego Chamber of Commerce Industrial Committee; in 1949 he became a member of the California State Highway Commission. Additionally, there was the matter of stewardship of something over $10 million . . . in 1941 dollars . . . received from sale of his controlling interest in Consolidated. Not only should the assets be conserved; they should be wisely invested and given an opportunity to grow in the expanding American economy.

Although Reuben and his second wife, Dorothy Mitchell, had separated he was very conscious of his responsibility to her, to his children by both marriages and to his grandchildren. He would provide wisely and amply for their benefit.

As his marriage to Dorothy faltered, Reuben came to depend more and more on Eva Wiseman, his secretary since his earliest days in San Diego. Eva had worked as a secretary for the Army at Rockwell Field on North Island. Army officers recently assigned to the new Consolidated plant got in their required flying time at Rockwell, and Eva came to know them well. In October 1935 the Army gave up its facilities at North Island, which then became exclusively a Naval Air Station. Eva decided to retire but Major Leland Hurd insisted she go to Consolidated for an interview as he knew there was an opening as secretary to Gordon Mounce, sales manager for the 'Fleet' biplane.

When Eva showed up for the interview Mounce asked Major Fleet if he would check out the new applicant himself. As a test of the girl's stenographic ability he dictated the text of the speech he had given only a few weeks before at the plant dedication. Except for the strange French word "empennage," Eva did a workmanlike job and was congratulated by the Major as a "bright girl." She got the job as Mounce's secretary.

Her new boss traveled a great deal so that when the Major had an overload of dictation it was Eva Wiseman who was able to help out. During this period Fleet had a male secretary whose work was not entirely up to his expectation. The day it was necessary to make a replacement, Eva Wiseman became his private secretary.

When the Fleet family sold its 34% interest in the company in December 1941 the Major's agreement to continue as a consultant contained provision for office help so that Eva continued in her role as the Major's secretary.

In May 1944, Mrs. Dorothy M. Fleet filed a petition for divorce from Reuben H. Fleet charging him, according to newspaper reports, with "inflicting great mental suffering and bodily injury." Later she dropped those charges. It was July the next year before the uncontested divorce was final. Mrs. Fleet retained custody of the three minor children, Preston, 11; Dorothy, 9 and Nancy, 4.

The wire service story out of Los Angeles stated that "Mrs. Fleet told Judge Thurmond Clarke that the former aircraft executive had a violent temper and that he insulted her friends and business people with violent and abusive language."

Press stories also indicated that Mrs. Fleet received a $1-1/4 million trust fund as part of a $1,550,000 settlement. Subsequently the Guiness Book of World Records erroneously and embarrassingly claimed the divorce settlement to be "the greatest alimony ever paid—$11,550,000." The error stemmed no doubt, from combining the original divorce petition claim for $10 million in community property with the actual settlement.

In time, Dorothy Fleet remarried but both her husbands passed away. She moved from home to ranch to home throughout Southern California, finally settling in the San Diego area, first in Point Loma, then Coronado and La Jolla but later on the bayfront just below Reuben's stately Spanish house high on the hill above.

On his way back from Palm Springs one day in March 1947, Reub must have been daydreaming—perhaps thinking about Eva Wiseman who he was planning to marry. In any case he dozed at the wheel of his large sedan as he drove through San Jacinto. It swerved out of control and jumped the curb. Crashing straight into a large tree, the car's engine was pushed back almost into the front seat as the Major's chest crushed against the steering wheel.

Once again, badly hurt, Reuben was rushed to the hospital, in not much better condition than had been the case with the 1929 crash in the 'Fleet' biplane. Fortunately, this time, there were no other occupants. Again his son David rushed to the Major's bedside. "Only his strong constitution," said Dave, "pulled him out of danger quickly this time."

Two years after his divorce from Dorothy—two months after his car accident—Reuben Fleet and Eva May Denburgh Wiseman were married May 20, 1947 in Point Loma Community Presbyterian Church. Some months earlier Eva, then living in Escondido, a rural community north of San Diego, had divorced her husband, Herman, who had been a junior executive at Consolidated and later at Rohr.

In applying for the marriage license, Fleet had listed his occupation as farmer but when Eva protested that the name "Reub" did make him sound like a farmer, it was changed to the more genteel "rancher." [Reuben had reservations about Eva's name, too. To him she was always EVE, not Eva.]

Eve brought to the marriage three daughters—twins Susan and Sandra, aged two, and Sally, four. The Major adopted the girls, not only legally but completely in every sense; they were never "Eve's children," but always "our children."

At the time of his marriage to Eve, Reuben was 60 and, as an old associate later said, "He'd gotten old enough to settle down. Eve has been a good wife for him, and to his credit he has treated his former wives very well, too."

After seven years of marriage, the Fleets and their three daughters made their most extended foreign trip. For three months in 1954 they toured Mexico, the Caribbean and South America. Always an inquisitive and astute observer, the Major took advantage of the opportunity to meet with leaders throughout South America to discuss world affairs.

In addition to his own business affairs, Reuben also took on the responsibility of financial advisor for the trust he had set up for his former wife, Dorothy. Certainly he was in a position to hire the best financial brains or trust company available to handle his investments, but to do so would be abrogating his own responsibility.

"In selling my company," Fleet explained, "I could hardly have done so at a more advantageous time so far as being able to pick up bargains among listed stocks is concerned. The market was way down.

"My policy has been to invest in companies that I feel have good prospects and to manage those investments myself; to add to them, and to sell them if they don't pan out.

"I chose my investments very carefully. Ned Bishop, my brother-in-law, operated on the general policy that America was going ahead and that anything you bought was bound to come out alright. He invested in, say 150 companies. I told him, 'Ned, you can't ever watch the progress of 150 companies. You need only twenty or fewer companies, and then you can watch them.' "

NED BISHOP

Reuben and I had been talking in the office of his Palm Springs home. He reached across the desk to one of the many charts prepared for him. As he did so I couldn't help but reflect on the fact that the Dow Jones industrial stock average which was around 125 in 1941 had advanced to 1973's figure of over 1,000. Nor could I resist speculating how this effected his present net worth.

"I've watched my investments closely," he continued, "I haven't changed them often, and I carry the investments of my whole family on this one sheet. It has just 16 stocks on it, and the changes since the first of the year show that I'm alert to any developments.

"It would be terrible to let someone else do the research and make the decisions for me. I know these companies . . . blue chip firms like Exxon, General Motors, DuPont, IBM. I've followed them for 33 years. Fotomat is a rank speculation which I carry just for fun."

Reuben went on to explain the changes in share ownership in the various companies like SafeCo, of which he was a director for 15 years. Usually 'sales' represented appreciated securities he had donated to charitable and educational institutions, often as memorials to business associates, nearly all of whom he has now outlived by a decade.

As shrewd an investor as he was an aircraft executive, the Major often relied upon the Biblical admonition that "there is a time to buy and a time to sell." Early in life he learned that to be successful you must pay as much attention to selling as to buying, and that the decision to sell, especially in a rising bull market, is more difficult than buying. "Most talent in the investment profession," he pointed out, "is devoted to the art of buying, but little to the art of selling."

The Major liked to quote Will Rogers on the subject: "Buy a good stock and hold it for a rise, and when it has risen, sell it. Of course if it don't rise, don't buy it."

When one visits Fleet's "office" in the Spanish mansion on San Diego's Point Loma, it is not difficult to imagine that you are in the trust department of some bank.

Three incoming phone lines ring constantly as the Major, secretary Martha Green and accountant Russ Stanberry, share the various tasks. Often the call may be from one of his daughters or a grandchild asking help on an income tax return or seeking some information on a bank account opened years ago, and regularly added to by the Major.

Through it all nothing distracts Reuben; his power of concentration at 88 is as good as it ever was. And, perhaps somewhat remarkably, all his children, all family members appear to be treated equally without favoritism regardless of which of three families they are from.

What distinction there is between children is a matter solely of male responsibility. In an earlier, more traditional family setting, sons David G. Fleet and Preston M. (Sandy) Fleet, were expected to make it on their own.

"Dad was more than happy to provide us with a good education and medical care," Sandy recalls, "but beyond that we were expected to make it ourselves."

"Both the boys," Fleet explained, "were graduates of Culver Military Academy. That was a fine education and training for them as it was for me, and as it has also been for my grandsons. David, of course, worked his way up in the Consolidated company for nearly ten years before making a success on his own in real estate. Preston was too young to work for us but from childhood on he took a decided interest in photography and organized the Fotomat company and has done quite well with it."

Considerate of his employees as he is loving of his family, the Major will go out of his way to pay compliment to others. Recently his secretary, Martha Green, wanted to resume her career as a lead singer in light opera. Known professionally as Martha Gene she had appeared often with the San Diego Starlight Opera in years past. An opportunity to play the wife of Tevye, the leading character in "Fiddler on the Roof" could not be passed up. Despite nightly rehearsals to well past midnight, Martha never let it interfere with her work for the Major.

The afternoon of opening night, Martha was still at her desk late in the afternoon. The Major's last instruction for the day was to "get us four good tickets right down front for tonight."

Backstage after the glow of opening night, no one was prouder of Martha than Reuben and Eve Fleet.

THE FOUR YEARS REUBEN Fleet spent from 1902 to 1906 as a cadet at Culver Military Academy had a profound effect upon his life. The strict discipline, the military atmosphere, the devotion to scholarship helped mold his character and sharpen his intellect. Cadet life may have been austere but with the passing of the years Reuben's appreciation of what it had contributed to his own life continued to increase.

A sound education was in the family tradition. Reuben's father had attended Virginia Military Institute; his Confederate officer uncle, Col. Alexander F. Fleet, had founded Missouri Military Academy, then became superintendent of Culver Military Academy in Indiana. And, at nineteen and just out of Culver, Reuben had taught school in his native Montesano, Washington for a year before going into the real estate business.

With such a background, one of the first commitments Reuben made after sale of his interest in Consolidated was to establish, in 1942, the Fleet Foundation to assist outstanding high school students in completing their college education. Serving with the Major as trustees were his oldest son, David G. Fleet, also a Culver graduate, and his long-time friend and associate, Chuck Leigh. President of the Foundation was Walter Ames, a San Diego attorney.

Over a quarter-century period, some two hundred young men, principally from the San Diego area ("and a few in Riverside County where my wintering in Palm Springs enabled me to come across worthy youngsters"), received assistance in the form of grants and loans to train at Stanford, Harvard, Yale, Caltech, Cornell, M.I.T., Notre Dame, Columbia, the London School of Economics and other leading colleges and universities.

On his father's eightieth birthday, David Fleet came up with a suitable tribute—hosting nearly 200 guests made up of recipients of Fleet Foundation scholarships and their families. Those who could not attend sent letters to the Major explaining how their own careers had been helped.

Typical was Paul L. Dawson who wrote "There is no

way I can adequately thank you other than to contribute as much as possible to the industry and country you have served and loved so well, and to help other young people when my time comes.

"As you can see I have maintained my interest in aviation for I am currently the general manager of military production engine programs for General Electric at the Evendale plant. The J93 engine, for which I was engineering and project manager, is used to power the B-70 trisonic bomber. The photo with test pilot Al White was taken just after the first Mach 3 flight at Edwards Air Force Base."

Recalling the founding of the Fleet Foundation, Walter Ames said that "Reuben was not interested in providing funds for brick and mortar but wanted to do what he could in improving people. Originally the Foundation's emphasis was on assisting students from families which had suffered casualties as a result of World War II or in flying and testing aircraft."

Fleet provided an ingredient almost as important as money—personal interest in the students. While recommendations of worthy students came from a number of sources, no scholarships or loans were granted until there had been an interview with the Major or other of the Foundation's directors. Scholarships were regularly reviewed and if the recipient failed to demonstrate continued competence, his grant was withdrawn.

Although Fleet knew and had a high regard for Dr. Charles W. Eliot, noted educator and father of the modern Harvard University, the Major had little respect for its liberal policies in later years.

"There was a young chap in Palm Springs," Fleet explained, "who stood at the head of his high school class and who went on to Pomona College where he graduated as president of the student body. His marks were so excellent that I talked it over with Jimmy Doolittle, Dr. Thomas J. Killian of M.I.T. and with General Eisenhower. There was a critical need at that time for bright young men to take up engineering. The four of us wanted him to follow that line but he wanted a law career instead. He explained he hoped eventually to get into the State Department and bring it more to the right than in recent left-leaning years.

"We told him to pick any college he wanted in California, we would send him through law school, but he insisted on Harvard which was outstanding but too much to the left for our patronage. However, to my surprise I later found we already had a boy from San Diego county attending Harvard."

Eventually, after a long phone call from Fleet, the student's brother paid for his education at Harvard. "I told the brother," Reuben recalls, "that Harvard had alienated itself from us by being so leftish and spend-thrifty too. Harvard advocated huge government spending for foreign aid and many other such things."

In recent years there has been a further disenchantment with scholarships because of the involved reporting procedures "and so many things," Reuben says, "that it becomes too burdensome. Instead we are looking at doing something through an Air Force Association project for sons and daughters of servicemen. Among other advantages, it gets away from the responsibility for selection of participants, so we may depend on this program instead of doing it ourselves."

Though deeply interested in the work of the Fleet Foundation, the Major was even more devoted to Culver Military Academy, of which he wrote, "I cannot give enough praise for the educational foundation it gave me. My 'formal' education ended there, but I contribute a great deal of my business success to the fact that I have never stopped studying and learning."

For eighteen years Reuben served on the Board of Culver, resigning only after reaching his eightieth birthday. Graduation from Culver has been a Fleet family tradition, David, the oldest son, graduated in 1929; Preston (Sandy) in 1952; grandson David F. Fleet in 1954 and Preston's son, Allen (Mitch) Fleet, in 1974.

FIRST OF FIVE FLEETS to graduate from Culver was Reuben, '06, shown here at 40th Reunion. Others, sons Dave, '29, Sandy, '52; grandsons, David F., '54 and Mitchell, '74. Culver Military Academy

"When my Uncle was Superintendent," Reuben said, "he apparently gave me my education—which amounted to a lot—because I don't think my father had the money to pay. Therefore, I have been very generous with Culver, which has been very near and dear to my heart these many years. I have 14 boys there now on scholarships, and have given the school over half a million dollars."

Nondenominational religious services at Culver had long been held in the recreation building. While Preston was a student and his father a Board member, the decision was made to build a suitable chapel as a memorial to cadets who had given their lives in World War II. Again, Major Fleet was asked to lend his leadership to the $1 million fund raising program.

"As he always does," Sandy says, "my father did a fantastic job. He raised the full amount from alumni and friends of the school.

"The last two gifts needed to reach the million dollar goal were the largest. One would pay for the pipe organ; the other for the carillon, a fantastically beautiful set of full bells—51 in all—coming from Croydon, England. Each gift would require a $50,000 contribution.

"My father, of course, was figuring on one for himself; the other for Amon G. Carter, owner of the Fort Worth Star-Telegram, himself a Culver graduate. As with my father, Carter's son was also then in school.

"Dad called him up, told him about the organ and the carillon and politely gave him the choice as to which one would he like.

"Amon Carter, so the story goes, said, 'Well, Major, I'll take the carillon; you take the organ. By the way. What the hell's a carillon?' "

Culver got its first taste of aviation in 1919, thirteen years after Reuben had graduated. The Superintendent, Gen. Leigh R. Gignilliat (married to Fleet's cousin), had written Reuben, "I sincerely hope you will land on us sometime in your airplane."

And land Reuben did at a class reunion that June—on the Culver polo field. As a result of the interest Fleet's visit created, the Culver School of Aviation opened the next year with five N9 seaplanes. Later a landing strip was opened for the use of school patrons and friends. A half century later son Preston represented the family at the 1971 dedication of Fleet Field, and a new hangar and aviation education center.

Although the Major could not be present, Sandy read a message from him: "As a young cadet, I felt in my heart a drive to develop and utilize my God-given talents for the betterment of mankind and, while I have always thought I had vision, my wildest dreams would not have envisioned my return to Culver 65 years later for the dedication of Fleet Field."

GOLD CEREMONIAL SABRE, Culver's Distinguished Service Award, was presented to Major Fleet in December 1974 by Col. Ben A. Barone, superintendent.

Culver Military Academy

Along with his interests in education through Culver and the Fleet Foundation, Reuben had a special concern for providing means for "scientists, engineers and technicians to meet and interchange ideas with a view to advancing the aeronautical science, avoiding needless duplication of effort, and assuming leadership in this important field."

Fleet found just such a vehicle in the Institute of Aeronautical Sciences, the country's most prestigious organization of aircraft professional men. In 1944 he became national president of the organization which had been established in 1933 largely through the efforts of his friend Major Lester D. Gardner, former editor of Aviation Magazine. It was Gardner, accompanied by Col. Virginius Clark, who had gone on a five months trip sponsored by Fleet to survey European aviation in 1927. Gardner, too, had been President Calvin Coolidge's appointee as U.S. representative to various international aviation conferences.

In 1944, when Fleet took over direction of IAS, it maintained offices in Rockefeller Center, New York City. One of his first efforts was to obtain for the IAS its own buildings not only in New York City but also in Los Angeles and San Diego.

Title Insurance and Trust Company

The Rockefellers offered the family mansion on Fifth Avenue as a possible location, but Major Gardner was fearful the Institute might take on too big a task and might jeopardize the Institute's tax-exempt status. Ford Motor Company and Aluminum Company of America offered to donate sites and buildings in Detroit and in Pittsburgh, but nothing came of the offers since it was impractical to locate IAS Headquarters other than in New York City.

A past master at fund raising, Fleet put the arm on his fellow San Diego aircraft manufacturers to help finance construction of an IAS building on Lindbergh Field. After preliminary architectural plans were approved in 1945, the Major got together with Consolidated Vultee and the Harbor Commission, the company's landlord. Convair agreed to relinquish its lease of 2.7 acres on the waterfront as the location of the new IAS building.

Culminating four years effort by the Major, the new facility, including the Fleet Aeronautical Library, was dedicated in March 1949. A similar project for an IAS building in Los Angeles was also completed that year. Generous personal gifts by Fleet to IAS helped bring the three building projects to fruition.

ARCHITECT'S SKETCH of new building for *Institute of Aeronautical Sciences is displayed by the Major.*

General Dynamics/Convair

STORY-TELLING PAINTING of Fleet career by *artist Justin C. Gruelle is admired by proud Reuben and Eve Fleet when unveiled for display in new IAS building.*

Education—and cultural activity in Fleet's native state of Washington got a helpful boost after the death in 1968 of his 95-year-old brother-in-law, Ned Bishop. As a tribute to her husband, Lillian Fleet Bishop provided funds which made possible the Bishop Center for the Performing Arts at Grays Harbor College in Aberdeen.

Then, on his sister Lillian's death December 11, 1971, Reuben contributed a substantial amount of IBM stock with the request that the theater add her name so that it be known as the E. K. and Lillian Fleet Bishop Center "in fond recollection of the many happy years they walked hand-in-hand . . . in the county in which our gentle parents met, married, lived and died, and where Lillian and I, and her two children and my two eldest, were born."

LILLIAN FLEET BISHOP

IT WAS CHRISTMAS 1949. Reuben and his next door neighbor, Roscoe (Pappy) Hazard, one of the San Diego area's great pioneers, were in the downstairs rumpus room decorating the tree. The butler announced a visitor, James Forward, head of the local title and insurance company.

"Environment" had not yet become a catchword, but Reub and Pappy were alert to any condition that might spoil their beloved, scenic Point Loma and its magnificent panoramic views of one of the world's great harbors. Jim Forward was the bearer of bad news.

"Jim told us" Reuben recalls, "that banker Joseph Sefton, another Point Loma resident and large landowner, had instructed him to go into escrow to sell his 186 vacant acres, and that the buyers were going to build 792 little box houses all over that beautiful property and spoil the whole district.

"Forward came out to see if I wouldn't buy the property from Joe and prevent that catastrophe by subdividing it properly, preserving the views and selling it for quality homes that fit the area. I asked Jim if he thought Joe would sell it to me instead for the same price—$240,000. His answer was, 'That's what I'm hoping.' I told him to tell Joe I would pay cash.

"Roscoe said he'd take 15% of the proposition and that a lawyer friend, Ruel Liggett, would take the same amount. So we called Joe up and he agreed to sell to us instead of to the box-house builders who ought to find some other piece of property for that kind of development."

Later Reuben sold 50% of the project to his son David who had only recently resigned from his long-held position with Convair as assistant to the president. It would be a good opportunity for his oldest son to strike out on his own.

Though working with his father, David had been raised by his mother; after reaching his teens he had spent only the one year in Rhode Island under the same roof with his father. Dave had known his father's second and third wives in their roles as Reuben's secretaries but never as stepmothers because he had never lived in the same households with them.

At this juncture, David had a son who was 13 years old. Dave's half-brother, Sandy, was only 15 and just entering Culver Military Academy, consequently he seemed more nephew than brother to Dave. In any case, Sandy was too young to take into partnership on the real estate project.

David took full charge of what was appropriately named Fleetridge. He employed the best subdivision planners to lay out the property in curving streets which followed natural contours and preserved unobstructed the scenic vistas for all properties facing the bay.

Fleetridge today stands as one of San Diego's choicest residential districts. And, if the writer may be permitted a personal aside, he purchased from Dave Fleet the first lot and built the first home in Fleetridge. The architect and builder was Robert Maw, son of a friend of Reuben's from Washington state.

SAN DIEGO'S SEWAGE problems seemed to have a way of bringing out the best in Reuben Fleet. Where necessary during the years of war production build-up he tilted successfully with the verbal windmills of official Washington to get action on San Diego's urgent problems.

It was not until 1943 that the first sewage plant went into full operation but even then the remaining effluent and industrial waste, along with raw sewage of Navy ships, was still discharged into San Diego Bay.

Because of increasing pollution and hazards to public health that facility was enlarged again and again but it was 1954 before a bond issue for a master sewerage plan was presented to the voters. They turned it down.

Two years later clorination of effluent was begun but there were sewage overflow problems and areas of the bay had to be quarantined. Not until November 1960 were bonds approved for the Metropolitan Sewerage System. Meantime technical arguments had been going on and on about the location of the treatment plant and the outfall into the Pacific Ocean.

If located at Imperial Beach in the south bay near the Mexican border, the treatment plant would be surrounded by subdivisions then planned, and the water offshore was so shallow there might be serious contamination of the beach. Off Point Loma the proposed treatment plant could be virtually hidden on the Army's Fort Rosecrans but residents of that exclusive area could hardly be expected to take kindly to the idea of a sewerage plant nearby. However, one advantage of the location was that the effluent could be discharged in deep water two and a half miles offshore.

The Major felt it was time to take a stand, as he later explained:

"I figured I had too much money invested in San Diego to stand by and let the city make a bad mistake with its sewerage system, so in May 1960 I employed the best man I could get from the California Institute of Technology to make a study. If was done by Dr. Jack E. McKee, professor of sanitary engineering, and cost me personally $42,000.

"It was about this time that Anderson Borthwick, head of the First National Bank and a Point Loma neighbor came to see me, asking that I sign a petition to change the proposed outfall of the sewerage system to have it empty just off the Mexican border. I gave Borthwick the two inch-thick volumes prepared by Dr. McKee, which confirmed that the outfall should be off Point Loma at a depth of several hundred feet where there was an ideal current to carry the effluent away.

" 'Andy,' I said, 'take these home and study them carefully and if they convince you this is the best plan you just abandon your petition and get busy helping out on the Point Loma outfall.' "

Not only was Borthwick convinced, he soon was taking a hand in getting Reuben Fleet even more involved. Dr. Richard Worthington, a Point Loma psychologist, had filed a taxpayers lawsuit to stop sale of bonds for the $60 million project until an investigation could be make of the feasibility of water reclamation for irrigation of parks, golf courses, agriculture and in heavy industrial uses.

Many others were equally concerned because San Diego, being semi-arid, had to consider the reclamation of water as a valuable resource.

The San Diego City Council worked out a compromise with the warring factions. Dr. Worthington would withdraw his suit if the Council would appoint a citizens Water Reclamation Commission. Unanimously selected as Chairman was the venerable 74-year-old Major Fleet, with Dr. Worthington as vice chairman. "I favor reclamation," Reuben said on his appointment, "because it is terrible to just swill the effluent into the ocean."

"The Commission's major role," Fleet later recalled, "was to listen to the dissident elements from all over the county. Our public hearings were not held at City Hall, which was seething with politics, but in the small auditorium of the San Diego Water System.

"I told people we were not going to accomplish any wonderful things, that we had to listen to and iron out the various arguments. Some didn't want the sewerage system at all; some wanted it divided into several systems. So we listened and learned and heard the arguments of each man completely. We never choked anyone off, just let him talk; let him bring out every argument and every proponent that he wanted to present in support of his position.

"Finally, after two years of work we got the sewer system in and all law suits settled. Today it's one of the finest sewer systems in the country."

The Point Loma treatment plant was dedicated in September 1963. It was little more than two miles from Reuben's castle and other expensive property on the Point. Rather than being a stumbling block and objecting on aesthetic grounds, Fleet had been a major factor in bringing about the best sewerage system for his beloved city.

AN INTEREST IN PHOTOGRAPHY, which is Preston (Sandy) Fleet's forte, was the motivating force behind the Reuben H. Fleet Space Theater and Science Center, San Diego's new, world-acclaimed planetarium.

Separated by a generation from David, his older half-brother, Sandy was too young to become involved in Consolidated Aircraft except for the boyhood thrill of being more or less free to wander through the giant war production plant.

When his mother and father separated, his sisters Dorothy and Nancy remained with their mother but Sandy shunted back and forth between Beverly Hills, Santa Barbara and the Spanish mansion on Point Loma. He lived with his father during junior high school in San Diego and because of an interest in photography was showing movies at home for schoolmates every Friday night. Then, at thirteen, the always independent Sandy was put on the train and sent off alone to Culver Military Academy in the family tradition.

Even when his father, a director of Culver, visited

HAPPY MOMENT at Space Theater opening is enjoyed by father Reuben Fleet and son 'Sandy,' whose long interest in photography is continued in his role as producer of featured films shown there.

PRIME LOCATION in San Diego's world-famed Balboa Park is enjoyed by the Reuben H. Fleet Space Theater and Science Center.

the Academy he saw little of his son lest Sandy be the victim of charges of nepotism, and the Major wanted the boys to make it on their own. It was the same problem Reuben himself had faced in 1902 when his uncle was superintendent.

At Culver, Sandy was the school photographer, photo editor of the yearbook and did photography and wrote a column of movie reviews for the school newspaper which he edited. Although interested in aviation, Sandy had promised his father he would not take flying lessons while at Culver. Flying was hard to resist because one of his classmates had his own 'Fleet' biplane near the school.

Returning to San Diego he built a projection room and small theater at home to screen motion pictures for his father and his business friends.

In time, Sandy's interest in photography and aerospace began to merge. During the peacetime conversion after World War II, a group of San Diego engineers had formed an organization to arrange science and industry shows as a means of interesting youth in scientific careers. Out of that came a proposal to build a museum of science and industry with a planetarium as a major attraction.

Meantime Sandy Fleet and Charles Brown, Jr., a Convair engineer, helped organize the San Diego Aero-Space Museum in 1961. Young Fleet was its first president and Brown its director.

AN ENTHRALLED AUDIENCE finds itself surrounded by the universe during a 'Voyage to the Outer Planets,' as projected by planetarium's unique system.

Then, in 1968, after years of frustrating disappointments, the City and County of San Diego finally established the Planetarium Authority to provide facilities for the San Diego Hall of Science.

"I had studied the project over a period of about a dozen years," Reuben recalls, "and became very much interested. We decided to go for it. The City and County built the building at a cost of about $2.6 million, and we agreed to provide the planetarium's sophisticated interior equipment.

"The Fleet family put in $800,000, just twice the $400,000 we had originally intended. The family wanted to come in and help too and those who could afford it did. I upped my ante so it cost me $525,000 personally, and the balance of the $800,000 was made up by the children under Sandy's and David's leadership. The boys were in on all of the design and engineering and had gotten more and more enthused over it. We got the finest people in the country to work on the planetarium equipment."

The most advanced planetarium design in the country, the Fleet Space Theater features eye-popping, three-dimensional projection through a 180-degree fish-eye lens which displays a single image across the 76-foot spherical tilted dome. Its first showing—"Voyage to the Outer Planets"—was under Sandy Fleet's direction and leaves the traditional planetarium and movie theater far behind. The sensation of flying through space is incredibly realistic.

On March 10, 1973—just four days after Reuben's 86th birthday—the Space Theater and Hall of Science Center was dedicated.

Although the children of Reuben's second marriage were usually at public functions honoring the Major, Mrs. Dorothy Fleet kept discreetly in the background. But, because of the key role played by their son, Sandy, Dorothy was present for the Space Theater dedication.

On such occasions the Major was apt to recognize and introduce all the members of his three families. This time he left that to others and to Neil Morgan, master of ceremonies.

Reuben had promised himself—and others—that he'd make no speech; nor would he serve on the Theater's board of directors. "I just supply the money and let them worry about it," he said with a chuckle.

But when it came time, the Major indulged himself in just six emotion-choked words—"This is a gift of love." Tears slowly trickled down his cheeks, and of the cheeks of many of the hundreds of friends who surrounded him.

Sandy Fleet's photographic interests took another, less altruistic form when he founded Fotomat Corporation in 1967 to provide a chain of franchised drive-through photo developing and merchandising kiosks located in shopping center parking lots. Its first San Diego location was a shopping center on the site of Dutch Flats Airport where Ryan Aeronautical Company got its start.

Although Major Fleet could readily have supplied some of the initial capital, Sandy preferred to make a go of it on his own. Early in the program the New York investment firm of Hayden, Stone Inc. paid $1 million cash for an approximate 3% stock interest in Fotomat.

Sandy's enterprise caught the Major somewhat by surprise. Reuben decided that he'd like a bit of the action too and asked for an opportunity to invest half a million dollars on the same basis Hayden, Stone had done. Quite obviously, both son and father prospered from their transactions in Fotomat shares. Today Fotomat does a $50 million annual business.

BUOYANT EVE AND REUBEN FLEET shared with hundreds of guests the thrill of opening night at the Space Theater.

Les Herling

FOUR GENERATIONS of Fleets—sons, daughters, grandchildren, great grandchildren turn out to honor Reuben at Space Theater premier.

APOCRYPHA

LONG BEFORE REACHING 88 years of age, Reuben Fleet was a legendary figure and the subject of countless stories which, in their way, were comments upon his unique personality. To record only the highly complimentary ones would be to deny history some amusing, though often exaggerated, stories about a rugged, self-energized individualist who was frequently the butt of behind-his-back yarns perpetrated, or at least embellished, by his contemporaries.

Not exactly shrinking violets themselves, his fellow aircraft executives were inclined to tell their inflated yarns about Fleet in his absence because in his presence he usually outshown and certainly outtalked them. Thus, many stories about the Major are apt to be apocryphal. We cannot, of course, vouch for these.

BUREAUCRATS AND RED TAPE—at least paperwork Reuben felt unnecessary—really got under his skin. During the war the bureaucrats deluged Consolidated and other warplane builders with requests for information. The questionnaires and forms to be filled out were seemingly endless.

On one occasion Washington wired the Major that a response was needed immediately to their latest questionnaire. His response: "Do you want airplanes, or questionnaires answered? You can't have both."

ONE PROMINENT AIRCRAFT EXECUTIVE— let's call him Watson—often described Major Fleet as an overpowering salesman who not only was tenacious in presenting his case but on occasion extremely rude, particularly if he was, for some perhaps understandable reason, in a bad mood.

On one occasion Watson had an appointment at the Major's office in San Diego but found that an Air Force Colonel was already there talking with Reuben. Nonetheless, Fleet had his secretary bring Watson in anyway with a blunt "Sit down Watson. What do you want?" Watson had prepared a memo covering the points of their intended discussion and laid the paper in front of Fleet, then using his own copy began reading aloud, to which the Major responded, "I can read!" and showed his contempt in front of the Colonel by shoving the memo aside.

As Watson recalled later, "Rube never mentioned the matter again but I feel has been trying to make up for his rudeness to me ever since that occasion."

THE MAJOR'S CONTEMPORARIES in the aviation business and in the military were both amused and irritated by his nerve and super salesmanship. One industry executive passed along the following example:

The executive had just gone in to see Admiral John Towers, head of Naval aviation during World War II at his office in Washington. Jack Towers related that Major Fleet had been in the office just ahead of him and that he had tried a scheme on him in the hopes that the Major wouldn't take up as much time as he had in previous visits.

Towers said he simply couldn't spare the time and that it was hard to get rid of the Major, so he had all chairs in his office removed before the Major showed up for his appointment. That didn't bother the Major one bit. He plopped down on the edge of Jack Towers' desk and managed to consume two hours of the Admiral's busy day. As Towers later said, "at times he's ruthless and rude but he's a loveable old son-of-a-bitch."

KNOWING YOUR MANUFACTURING costs, and pricing the end product accordingly, is the key to profitable operation in the aircraft industry as it is in all business. Unfortunately many executives dealing with the government have a tendency to underprice an initial order—buy their way in—in the expectation of making a profit on subsequent orders once they "get a foot in the door."

Not so poetry-loving Reuben Fleet. When one such price quotation was submitted for his approval he reportedly responded with this quatrain:

> Count that day as lost
> Whose low descending sun
> Has seen quotations made at cost
> And business done as fun

FORMAL AND RIGID in many ways from his military career, the Major was also occasionally so casual that others found him rude. One friend reports on a visit by a Congressional committee.

"The Major," he said, "wasn't at all enthused about the honor being bestowed on him by a group of inquiring Congressmen. When the Air Force plane flying them to San Diego landed at Lindbergh Field, the Major dispatched an assistant to greet them instead of doing so himself.

"As the assistant escorted them to Fleet's office, the Major was just leaving and met them in the hall. It was no time for introductions or a word of greeting. 'I'm going to the men's room! You go to Room 216 and I'll be along in a few minutes.' "

IT WAS JUNE 1973 when the Federal Aviation Administration dedicated its new control tower at San Diego's Lindbergh Field. Reuben Fleet was invited to participate. At the conclusion of the ceremonies in which the Major, tears in his eyes, talked movingly in an emotion choked voice of General Lindbergh, guests were invited to inspect the new facilities.

When it was learned there was no elevator in the 50-foot tower, there were virtually no takers willing to climb the six flights of stairs. An exception, of course, was the spry 86-year-old Reuben Fleet, fresh from 36 laps of his swimming pool, who virtually alone took the climb in stride.

REUBEN CLIMBED to the top.

FLEET'S LONG-TIME FRIEND and associate, Mac Laddon, recalls "a lot of scurrilous talk about when he came back from having made the deal to sell to Vultee.

"In Los Angeles, Reuben got into a B-24 which was being piloted back to San Diego by Colonel Don Putt. He is alleged to have shaken the check in front of others and to have said, 'Well, I got mine!' Of course he never said anything like that, but that's the way it was interpreted.

"There is no doubt he irritated a lot of people over the years, and bored them almost to death. Long winded and repetitious, he used to bore me to tears."

PERHAPS THE UNKINDEST cut of all may have come from Sir Arthur Harris, Marshal of the Royal Air Force and member of the 1938 British war mission to the U.S.

Sir Arthur thoughtfully omitted the name of the American aircraft executive to whom he referred in "Bomber Offensive." Nor do we know. No one has said it concerned Reuben Fleet; neither has it been denied that it could have been him.

Like so many stories, it may be of doubtful authenticity and, too, we may be doing the Major an injustice by implying that he might be the subject of this quotation:*

"I met one very efficient aircraft manufacturer who was afflicted with verbal diarrhea to an extent I had never known before or since. He talked me into a coma and, when I was just about to pass out, invited us to lunch with him at his home. The prospect appalled me, but there was no polite way of getting out of it. When we got to his very pleasant house outside the city and were introduced to his very charming wife, I could not help thinking, while I was still in a daze and the continuous babble went on, that it was astonishing that any woman could possible live with a man like that. Some time later I learned the explanation. She was very deaf but an expert lip reader; she did not have to listen unless she looked, so she didn't look. Afterwards I expressed to General Arnold my astonishment at this gentleman's capacity for talking. 'Talk,' he replied, 'you have never heard him talk. You ought to see him on his knees in my office, with the tears running down his face at the prospect of gaining or losing aircraft orders, and still talking.' "

IT NEVER WAS EXACTLY EASY to get a word in edgewise when the Major was around and disposed to talk, as he usually was. Perhaps this tendency is what led someone to express the hope that Fleet's Bible reading had included the 3rd chapter of James. ". . . the tongue is a little member, and boasteth great things . . . the tongue can no man tame . . ."

CHARLES A. LINDBERGH made occasional note of the garrulous nature of his friend Reuben Fleet, citing a 40-minute long distance phone call; a non-stop 'sales' talk on why he should join Consolidated, during a plane trip between Los Angeles and San Francisco; and breakfast in Fleet's room at the Waldorf-Astoria in New York which lasted from 9 a.m. to 4:20 p.m.

Lindbergh, on an earlier visit to San Diego, had gone through the plant with Fleet and talked with him—("listened to him talk, to be more exact").

Despite his dislike for politics, Fleet—according to Lindbergh—said in 1942 that he might run for governor of California. "He has," wrote Lindbergh, "vision and judgment."

WHEN "OUR FLIGHT TO DESTINY" came off the press in 1964 it did not set the publishing world ablaze. Dorothy Fleet, the second Mrs. Fleet, felt that the career of her former husband should be suitably chronicled and set out to do so. The Major was less enthusiastic, feeling that his life story was his property and that only he should write it, or arrange to have it written. That may be the reason why, ten years later, the Major has not yet deigned to read it.

Despite his understandable apprehension about Dorothy's book, she always spoke with restraint and with great respect for her former husband.

PEOPLE ARE OFTEN CRITICIZED for excessive use of the first person singular. Reuben was no exception, though he consistently made an effort to correct himself when the matter became obvious.

Although his percentage of ownership in Consolidated Aircraft gradually declined during two decades, the "I" of the founding years and the corporate "we" of later years remained interchangeable in conversation as is usual with the founders of large corporations. Such firms are indeed the shadow of a single man whose attention so focused on the success of the enterprise that he and the corporation were indeed one.

ALWAYS STANDING ON HIS OWN two feet, Major Fleet was not disposed to have someone else speak for him. It's a moot question whether other Southern California aircraft manufacturers—Don Douglas, Bob Gross of Lockheed, J. H. (Dutch) Kindelberger of North American and others—asked Fleet to join their informal pre-Pearl Harbor industry group or whether Reuben, if asked, played his usual independent role and insisted on going it alone. In any case, such gatherings were apt to bring out each executive's pet story about his own encounter with the irrepressible, domineering and frequently ill-tempered Major.

FOR ONE OUTDOOR PARTY at the Spanish mansion, the world-famed San Diego Zoo sent several seals and a trainer to put on a show in the Major's swimming pool. Only problem was that one seal so enjoyed his new surroundings that even the trainer could not get him out of the pool when the guests had left.

Next day, the Major's stockbroker, Phil Neary, who had been a guest the previous night, called to give Reuben a status report on the market and to ask the current status of the seal. Fleet reported, "They're draining my pool now to get him out!"

LIKE MANY WHO TRAVEL a great deal on business, the Major reportedly had trouble getting to sleep at night in strange hotels. With a Gideon Bible on the nightstand of most hotels, Reuben found it convenient to further a lifetime habit of reading the Good Book.

One night in 1941 while considering the possibility of selling out—or, as rumor had it, being prodded by Washington to do so—Reuben decided to open the Bible at random, place his finger upon a passage and be guided by the text he read. Reportedly it was Ecclesiastes 3:6 (". . . a time to keep, and a time to cast away.") which he interpreted as an omen to sell. In the light of subsequent events, the Major rightly felt that he acted wisely in selling.

AT ANY PUBLIC MEETING where protocol indicated that Major Fleet should be introduced, he would frequently grasp the opportunity to take over the podium for impromptu remarks—which had a tendency to become "extended remarks." On one such occasion he went on and on, becoming repetitious to the point of boredom. One unwilling listener leaned over and whispered to his neighbor, "That's the fifth or sixth place at which Reuben could have stopped. Can't someone shut him off?"

DURING A VACATION TRIP abroad in 1949, the Fleets were in Spain when Reuben got the idea that he'd like to go to Russia since relations between the two countries had improved. Reuben decided to go to Paris and see the French agent who had represented Consolidated during the war about making arrangements.

"All the way to Paris," Reuben recalls, "Eve kept saying, 'I don't want to go to Russia, and I don't want you to go. They might impound you.'

"I knew we enjoyed the confidence of the Russians because everything we had told them about the PBY 'Catalina' flying boats had come true. So I went around to see David K. E. Bruce, our Ambassador to France, and told him if I could be of value to the country I would be glad to make the trip to Russia.

"Dean Acheson, the new Secretary of State, was due in Paris the next day so Ambassador Bruce arranged a reception at the Embassy the following afternoon to which he invited Mrs. Fleet and me. He suggested that Secretary Acheson and I could get off together and discuss the matter.

"Robert Lehman, a New York investment banker friend of mine, was also at the reception and introduced me to Dean Acheson.

"The Secretary and I got off in a corner and talked about it, but he said he didn't need me, so I didn't go to Russia."

GOOD FELLOWSHIP ABOUNDS on Fleet's 80th birthday as the American Institute of Aeronautics and Astronautics honors the aviation pioneer. At right, Convair pilot test and sales executive Phil Prophett. In center, AIAA national president Harold T. Luskin.

As REUBEN FLEET APPROACHED his 80th year it began to dawn on a grateful community and industry that the unique contributions of an uncommon man had done much to shape the city's growth and should be recognized during his lifetime.

First to pay tribute to the iron-willed curmudgeon was the International Aerospace Hall of Fame, San Diego, which enshrined him in 1965 to join such contemporaries as his friends Hap Arnold, Jimmy Doolittle, Donald Douglas, Charles A. Lindbergh, T. Claude Ryan, Igor Sikorsky and the Wright Brothers, Orville and Wilbur.

On the Major's 80th birthday in March 1967, the American Institute of Aeronautics and Astronautics (the former Institute of Aeronautical Sciences) joined with the San Diego Chamber of Commerce in honoring the city's leading industrialist. In the presence of 500 guests, including key city, county and national figures, the laudatory salutes went on for two hours.

In acknowledging the tributes, Fleet recalled many anecdotes about Consolidated's early years and, as he talked, pointed out many in the audience associated with him in those pioneering days. Always sentimental about those who had earned a fond place in his memory, Reuben's voice was frequently choked with emotion. Nor was he ever ashamed of the tears which flowed on such occasions.

In closing, he recalled his lifelong motto, "Nothing short of right is right." "Trying to live up to that motto has brought me this night." he said. "I thank you for your gracious and generous recognition."

For the Golden Anniversary of the U.S. Air Mail service, Reuben Fleet, air mail pilot No. 1, flew to Washington as a principal participant in ceremonies May 15, 1968 at the Smithsonian Institution.

Not only did Fleet present the detailed story of the start of the mail service fifty years earlier, (told elsewhere in this book) but also assisted in the donation of a rebuilt de Havilland mail plane to the Smithsonian Institution.

"MR. SAN DIEGO" for 1969 is congratulated by Mayor Frank Curran as a beaming Eve Fleet looks on.

San Diego Fire Department

In December 1922 that particular DH-4 had crashed in the mountains east of Salt Lake City, although pilot Henry G. Boonstra was able to walk out with the mail. Forty-two years later the Air Mail Pioneers, under leadership of J. W. (Bill) Hackbarth, trucked the bits and pieces back to Santa Paula, California. There, almost rebuilt, "Old No. 249" was nearly destroyed in a brush fire. Five days later, work was started on rebuilding the rebuilt plane. By May 1968 the plane was completed and 67-year-old Bill Hackbarth flew the sturdy old craft cross-country to Washington, D.C., to be met there by Henry Boonstra.

"We present," Fleet said, "Old 249, the last of the Mail Airplanes of the United States Postal Service, to the National Museum here in Washington to inspire faith in God in whom we trust, courage to strive, and again courage to act, with hope and love for all mankind."

For 1969, the Grant Club chose Reuben Fleet as "Mr. San Diego," its annual selection of the area's top citizen, to be the year-long spokesman for what the Major considered to be "the most beautiful city in all the world."

In recognizing Fleet's contribution, Mayor Frank Curran pointed out that Consolidated's move to San Diego in the midst of the Depression was what "turned the tide for San Diego . . . from a sleepy little town to an industrial complex."

Mayor Curran also reminded the audience of 400 that "after investigating 186 cities in search of a per-manent home for his company, Fleet picked San Diego where he began his aviation career half a century ago."

Accepting the honor, Reuben said: "In contemplating what to do to be worthy of representing our fine city for 1969, I am humbly, deeply appreciative of the honor, inspired by the opportunity, thankful for health, faculties and energy, mindful of the few years here remaining, thoughtful of others' needs and careful of my conduct."

ALL HIS LIFE REUBEN Fleet liked a challenge, be it in school, the legislature, military service, business or sports. He didn't just like challenge; he thrived on competition of any kind. He wanted to test himself against others; prove that he could hold his own with anyone and surpass most of his fellows.

Whether the sport was cerebral like chess and bridge, called for stamina like swimming, or skill like trap shooting and golf, Reuben's combative nature made him a stiff competitor.

At age six, Reuben learned to swim in an eddy of the Wynooche River in Montesano and has been at it ever since. Long before a dozen laps of his pool attracted national attention to President Gerald Ford during the first few days of his administration, the Major had been following the same kind of regimen for eight decades.

"Every morning before breakfast," Fleet says, "I'm in the pool. At 87, I swim a third of a mile a day. To be precise, that's 36 lengths of the 50-foot pool here in San Diego, and 51 lengths of the 36-foot pool at Palm Springs.

"In places where I didn't have a pool, I generally belonged to the athletic club and swam there."

One morning recently after his daily swim we were congratulating the Major on his tenacity and mentioned how much pleasure it must have given him over the years. "William," he said, "it's a lot of work. But the exercise is the only thing at my age that keeps me alive."

Always interested in golf, and a better than average player, the Major took the game very seriously once he convinced himself—along about 1950—that he had really retired.

Purchasing 5 acres of prime residential property adjacent to the Spanish villa, the always ingenious Fleet laid out a private 18-hole course—longest in the world for its size—by using only six tees and six greens. Each tee and each green was used in three different combinations to make the 18 holes.

"Not only is it a practical sized private golf course," Fleet said, "the tract is a thing of beauty. As an added attraction we planted 100 orange trees. Our eastern guests, I'm sure, have never played golf and picked oranges at the same time."

At Palm Springs, the Fleets' winter home, golf became especially important. Long a member of the resort's first club, the "downtown" O'Donnell Golf Club, the Major helped it over more than one financial hurdle. When a strip of land and residence adjacent to the sixth fairway became available, Reuben led the campaign to raise $2000 each from 25 members to buy the property. Today the "Committee of 25" have their own special club within a club.

On those occasions when more members were needed, Reuben carried out a hard-selling one man campaign, inviting prospects to the club to join him in a game. One member, when asked by another where "Maj" could be located, replied "I just saw him on the seventh green. He's got a prospect down there, and he's sitting on him!"

When the newly-formed, very exclusive Thunderbird Country Club first opened it was inadequately

36 LENGTHS OF THE POOL is 'a lot of work . . . but the only thing at my age that keeps me alive.' Reuben enjoys his daily swim among beautiful surroundings of his Spanish-style estate.

Ted Lau

financed and facing tough times. Reuben took out a membership and then quietly set out to get the club organized on a more realistic financial basis which assured its survival.

At his second home, Fleet took as much interest in the city of Palm Springs as he had always done in San Diego. A skilled fund raiser, the Major not only hustled others to support good causes but usually started the ball rolling with a pace-setting gift. He had early learned that once you give your own money you find it twice as easy to convince others that they should do likewise and carry their share of the load.

Beneficiaries of Fleet's concern have been such Palm Springs facilities as the Eisenhower Hospital, the Desert Hospital, Presbyterian Church and the Desert Museum and Cultural Center.

Reuben's own golf scores were never as good as he would have liked. Still, as Fleet pointed out on his 80th birthday, "I have played golf for more than 50 years. Just this week I shot 91 in a tournament. Subtract my 22 handicap—well, that's a pretty good score."

One golfing crony pointed out that Fleet's stance and a somewhat stiff swing, both carry-overs from the 1929 airplane accident which broke a score of bones, somewhat restricted his ability to get into the low eighties. Nonetheless he was so highly competitive that he could figure out some type of bet on every hole.

Nor was "Maj" above psyching out his opponent. Lining up a putt, his opponent was likely to have his concentration interrupted by "I'll bet you two-bits you don't make it." That generally blew the stroke.

Fred Ingram, the desert's leading banker and a long-time friend, said that "Reuben was the backbone of the O'Donnell club for many years. In addition to all he did by way of financial help and sound management, Maj was a star at signing up new members. He'd wear them out until, to get out from under the pressure, they'd join."

Many who knew Fleet well learned how best to use his talents. They'd plant an idea with him. He'd ask time to think it over. If it had merit he'd be back in two weeks. By then he had convinced himself the idea must have been his in the first place, and as such he'd put every bit of his charm and salesmanship behind making it a success.

At the golf club as elsewhere, Fleet never was stumped for words. Occasionally some in Palm Springs ducked an encounter with him but even those who did admitted that "what Reuben had to say was always interesting and worth hearing. But not over and over again."

Braven Dyer, one of the country's great sports editors, wrote about his Palm Springs neighbor. "Just being around Reuben Fleet is a treat. You can tell immediately that he loves life. He must. He's enjoyed 85

years of it and is still going strong.

"His clear eyes send forth a special sparkle which seems to say, 'I'm fine, thank you, and hope you are the same.' His voice is strong and you never have to guess which side he's on.

"Some people might say that Major Fleet is stubborn. Most of his close friends put it another way. They say he's generally right.

"If the Major sometimes sounds corny, so be it. With him it's the United States of America first, last and always."

1956 - FELLOW SAN DIEGANS join the Major for golf in Palm Springs. From left, Fleet; real estate investor Donald Burnham; Convair engineering chief Mac Laddon; retired banker Armistead Carter.

1972 - STILL GOING STRONG 16 years later at 85. Fleet, second from left, with golfing cronies at Whitewater Country Club.

Photos—O'Donnell G

One of the most sought after brokerage accounts in San Diego was, of course, Major Fleet's. When Philip E. Neary was appointed San Diego manager of one of the country's largest investment banking firms he went after the account.

Reuben and Eve had just been married—it was 1947—and the house was being remodeled. He didn't want any unnecessary interruption. With Russ Stanberry in Los Angeles handling his investments, Reuben was not in the market for a broker. Fleet brushed Neary off with a "Call me in six months," hoping by that time Neary would forget the matter.

Six months to the day, Neary phoned. "Major Fleet, this is Phil Neary. You told me to call today. When may I have an appointment to see you?"

Fleet picks up the story.

"I had more important matters on my mind just then. We had three for golf at 11:30 and needed a fourth. I asked Phil if he played golf, and if so did he belong to the San Diego Golf Club. The answer was 'yes' to both questions. We met, and ever since—it's more than a quarter century now—Phil has handled most of my security trades. Incidentally, our caddy that day in 1947 was Billy Casper, who became a big name in professional golf."

ONE VINTAGE AIRCRAFT the San Diego Aero-Space Museum lacked was a Consolidated PT-3 trainer. Col. Owen Clarke, museum director, set out to correct that deficiency. After following all kinds of leads, Clarke finally heard of a plane which had been restored in Texas and subsequently sold to a former Marine Corps pilot in Arkansas.

After considerable persuasion the owner agreed to sell it to a museum for just what he had paid for it—$15,000. The catch was that Clarke did not have the $15,000, so he phoned Reuben Fleet.

"Major, I've located a PT-3 'Husky' trainer," Clarke said, "which apparently is in excellent condition. The owner will sell it to the museum for what it cost him."

" 'How much is that?'

"Fifteen thousand."

For a moment or two there was silence, then Fleet put the whole matter in perspective.

"Why that's nearly three times what I sold it to the government for 40 years ago! But I'll tell you what—you go down to Arkansas and take a look at it and if it looks real good I'll give the museum the money to buy it."

At Little Rock, Clarke found the ancient trainer in mint condition. He decided to fly it back to San Diego. "After all," he reasoned "it would be cheaper than trucking the plane back and we didn't want to rob the grand old plane of its proud heritage and dignity."

Preston M. Fleet

"YOU NEVER FORGET THE FUNDAMENTALS once you learn to fly." At 82 Reuben Fleet spotted a technical flaw, and skillfully handled the controls as of yore.

Thus, on a cloudy, windy and rainy April 9, 1969, Clarke lifted the last of the legendary PT-3s from the grass runway and headed west. The four day trip to San Diego was low, slow and windy, but the 'Husky' made the 1700 miles in 25 flying hours.

On hand to greet the PT-3 and Col. Clarke when the plane landed in an unpaved area of Lindbergh Field was Reuben Fleet. "Major," Clarke called out, "how about a ride?" The Major was enthusiastic but Mrs. Fleet and other members of the family managed to keep Reuben on the ground—that day.

Seven weeks later the plane had been refurbished before being sent to the Museum. Reuben's son Preston (Sandy), a pilot himself, had arranged with Col. Clarke for a flight for himself and his son, Mitch, in the ancient trainer. Clarke recalls the occasion:

"On the appointed Saturday morning—a beautiful day—I was preflighting the airplane when who should show up but Major Fleet. 'Let's go,' he said.

"We outfitted him with helmet and goggles. It was hard to believe that he was 82 years old as he swung into the rear cockpit and began his own pre-flighting. He called me over. 'Go get that mech over there.' he said, 'and have him bring a grease gun.'

"What's the trouble?"

"Fleet wiggled the stick back and forth. 'There's a fitting down there—a ball and socket joint—at the bottom of the stick. Have the mech give it a couple of squirts of grease so it will limber up the way it's supposed to be.'

"How he could remember details like that after forty years I'll never know.

IN 40-YEAR OLD PT-3 'HUSKY' training plane he built, Reuben 'banked it up steeply in a perfectly coordinated turn and made a beeline for his home on Point Loma' to surprise Eve with his skill.

"That done, the Major and I worked out a few hand signals for the flight since we didn't have a Gosport tube through which we could talk back and forth. I told him that soon after takeoff I'd give him a thumbs up signal and he could take control of the plane and do anything he wanted.

"As we reached the coastline, and while we were still climbing after takeoff, I shook the stick and signaled for him to take over. He leveled the plane off in professional style and then banked it up steeply to the left with his nose right on the horizon—a perfectly coordinated turn—and made a beeline for his home on Point Loma.

"Reuben did two steep 360-degree pylon turns over the Spanish villa (I can imagine what Mrs. Fleet was thinking), and headed back to the shoreline where he shook the stick for me to take over again and land the plane. His ability to fly the airplane was uncanny. He hadn't forgotten a thing. Later he told me that you never forget the fundamentals once you have learned them."

After the landing Clarke made another flight, this time with Sandy and his son Mitch as passengers—possibly one of the few times two passengers occupied the single rear cockpit.

REUBEN FLEET was not only the stormy petrel of the aviation industry; he was an outspoken advocate on behalf of all who shared his defiance of government interference with private enterprise.

Although his father was a Democrat and his association with Franklin D. Roosevelt was intimate and one of mutual respect, the crusty Major was a lifelong Republican given to offering free advice to elected officials whose thinking on critical public issues he often felt needed to be straightened out.

His appearances before Congressional Committees had often been the forum for blistering rhetoric critical of New Deal thinking. On one occasion he was asked by a committee member to comment about "the economic theory of plenty rather than scarcity."

"Of all the asinine things I every heard of," Reuben exploded, "the worst is to plow under cotton, kill off pigs, pay people for not raising things, and all that!"

And of the ivory-towered planners he told the committee: "We do not need any of these super-intelligent, wonderful, brainy people, who have never themselves made a success of business, tell us how business should be run. Let us get somebody who has ordinary, common horse sense, somebody who has earned his living and knows the value of a dollar."

A few months after he had sold his interest in Consolidated Aircraft in 1941, Reuben appeared before the Vinson Committee on Capitol Hill where he was questioned sharply about the profit he had made on the transaction.

Frank Watson, a veteran lawyer who attended the hearing thought Reuben's son David would enjoy his comments:

"In ten years of seeing the best of them in operation," he wrote, "I've never seen a performance such as your father put on.

"The whole thing turned into a regular Horatio Alger story in which he was the hero and not the villian. Instead of being a bad conspirator he was the lone citizen trying to save the country—and still trying.

"Neither the printed testimony in the Congressional Record nor this letter can describe the show with the actual flavor it had—the perfect gesture, the walking over to the Committee Counsel's table to reverse the position of prosecutor and accused, the joke at the right time. It was a master's touch; better than I've ever seen and that includes both the New Deal's [Thomas G.] Corcoran and [Henry A.] Wallace, and every other master in between.

"At the end of the hearings, the committee members, the counsel, the committee's auditor witness and the press were all fighting for a chance to tell what a fine company Consolidated was and what a tremendous contribution R. H. Fleet had made to American aviation and the present war effort. It was a clean sweep, Democrats and Republicans alike, and 'Rube' could have been elected committee chairman.

"There's no use talking, the old boy [only 55 at the time] has something and it was a privilege and a rare experience to see him perform."

As an active campaigner and fund-raiser for Republican candidates, Fleet had come to know and to develop a high regard for General Dwight D. Eisenhower's Vice President, Richard M. Nixon. Perhaps, if Nixon should not be available for a second term, he would be willing to assume a senior statesman role. The thought was worth a try. From his Palm Springs winter home, the Major sent the Vice President a warm "Dear Dick" letter in March 1956:

If you decide not to run for the Vice Presidential nomination (which I hope will not be the case) you may wish to remain aloof from public office for a while at least.

In such event I offer you a job that may be to your liking, which would give you freedom of action and residence, that would appeal to you and your family. Your job would be educationally to explain in articles and speeches the action of our Washington Government as they are intended to and do affect our people and their future happiness and prosperity.

Your remuneration from me would be a salary of $50,000 per year. You could keep any proceeds from speeches and articles for yourself and for travel expense. The job would begin after you retire from public office and last as long as you are so retired and wish, up to four years, whereupon, if we're both alive, we could continue or stop as we mutually decide.

I've been a life-long Republican but never a public office-holder, except one distasteful term in my State Legislature. I have no political aspirations or axe to grind but I've not had repose of mind for our country's future. Above all, I'm a patriotic American and love my country and its Constitution. I have eight children and three grandchildren and hope America will be a land of opportunity for them, as it has been for me.

R. H. Fleet

P.S. I think your actions during the unfortunate illness of our President have been most admirable in every respect and you have handled a most difficult situation with great tact and talent and have earned the country's lasting gratitude.

R.H.F.

Nixon's "Dear Reuben" reply was noncommittal; his political aspirations were not to be sidetracked. But he did pay tribute to "the man I know you to be—straightforward, frank and a great American. Your words . . . have reinforced my sincere admiration and respect for your own integrity and love of country. Your generous offer . . . springs from deep and selfless interest."

Taxes were a subject that particularly irritated Fleet. So as not to get soft on the subject with the passing of the years, the Major kept several reminders on his desk—"If Patrick Henry thinks taxation without representation is bad, he ought to see it with representation." and "You may not know when you're well off but the Internal Revenue Service does."

Because of taxes, Reuben sold his company. Thirty-three years later he was still complaining; this time to Senator Lloyd M. Bentsen, Jr. (D.-Tex.) of the Joint Senate-House Economic Committee:

"Will a man work himself or his money, for . . . an insignificant net return? Wouldn't he be a fool to venture in business (risk for gain) with such tax penalties. Excessive taxation forces the death of capitalism in America. In 1848 the Communist Manifesto prescribed what was necessary to destroy capitalism in 13 words: 'a heavy progressive or graduated income tax' 'abolition of all right of inheritance.' On 17 January 1961 Khrushchev restated this when he said, 'We don't need war to win.'

"Punitive tax rates are steadily, inexorably killing the competitive enterprise system that has made America great. Business needs billions annually in new investment which can come only from men with money. If we would preserve and stimulate our enterprise system, federal income taxation should be limited constitutionally to 50%—inoperative automatically upon declaration of war or armed attack on our country.

"This study comes from one who in 20 years created the largest business of its kind in the world and sold it at the height of its prosperity because federal taxes left him a net earning of enough to meet his payroll for only 7 minutes. He asks no sympathy; but he warns America against continuing the prescription of Karl Marx for destroying the competitive enterprise system that must have confidence, courage and capital."

In the political arena—in the world of ideas—Fleet was as committed and hard-hitting as he was in business. Ever the salesman, Reuben became a major fund-raiser and behind-the-scenes power in Republican politics, partly because of his ability to make pace-setting gifts which brought others into the fold.

A lifelong Republican with impeccable credentials with FDR, Reuben successfully spurned his friend's efforts to get him to switch political allegiance. "Although the President put terrific pressure on me," Fleet recalls, "I never left the Republican party and joined him. I wouldn't even pay $500 for the book he and the Democrats used as a fund-raising vehicle!"

In the fall 1962 elections, Fleet wrote for the 'San Diego Union' that "I have concluded that it is normal for us to have to select between 'the lesser of two evils.' My own conclusion is that the Constitution which our forefathers adopted, and under which we are still living, will be preserved better by Republicans than by Democrats, wherefore I have decided to vote the straight Republican ticket, and I hope others will similarly do."

The Major never gave up on trying to influence top government leaders. He didn't just complain; he always had a creative idea to offer. While Jerry Ford was enjoying a skiing holiday at Vail, Colorado, during Christmas 1974 a dispatch reached him through mutual friends.

"Printing notes running into hundreds of billions,"

he wrote the President, "without provision to repay is absurdity. Careful study of capital gains has convinced me that part of the gains which our people make through investment and reinvestment of their capital should be used solely to reduce our Federal debt. Each quarter of the year, every taxpayer should be required to pay the Treasury 50% of the net of whatever capital gains he has been able to make.

"The President who inaugurates this policy," he concluded, "will go down in history as a man of great vision."

Reuben could be unrelentingly persuasive in soliciting financial support for a worthy community cause—or for a candidate for public office. "No" was never an acceptable answer to a request for help. It was always implicit that your answer to an appeal would be "yes;" why else would he call you? After all, the Major was giving you the benefit of his careful analysis and you were expected to show your appreciation by acting affirmatively on his recommendation.

Fleet knew only too well that once a man commits his money to a candidate or principle he also commits himself to continued interest in the success of that individual or project.

The choice was not whether you would give; only how much. He had committed his money and expected you to do likewise. Reuben applied the power of positive thinking with a vengeance, and turning him down was one of the most difficult chores you could ask of anyone in the San Diego "establishment."

THIRTY-SIX LENGTHS of the Fleet pool before breakfast have a way of building up a terrific appetite. The August 1974 morning Gerald Ford assumed the Presidency we arrived at the Spanish mansion just as Reuben, dripping wet, was emerging from the pool.

Wrapped in a turkish towel, the Major entered the hall just as Mrs. Fleet came down the stair from her bedroom. Oblivious of his visitors, a radiant Reuben called out a spontaneous, cheery greeting: "Eve, I love you!" in a manner that would have done romantic credit to a man 60 years younger. What a way to start the day!

Fifteen minutes later we joined the Major in the breakfast room. Waiting for him was half a grapefruit; then the butler appeared with a bowl of oatmeal which the Major sprinkled generously with a heaping tablespoon of sugar before consuming. This was followed by two fried eggs, three strips of bacon and plenty of buttered toast. Then came the other half of the grapefruit.

Minutes later the butler reappeared with a plate of cookies and a fresh pot of coffee. Properly dunked in coffee, the cookies disappeared in short order. A second plate of cookies arrived and disappeared. More coffee. With arrival of the third plate of cookies, Raymond Buchtel, the butler, announced, "Major, that's your ration!"

Daughter Sally arrived with granddaughter Sheri and joined us in the breakfast room; later Susan, one of the twins, appeared briefly. All got an affectionate hug and kiss which, as well as the endearing words spoken to each, conveyed the beaming Major's genuine, outgoing love for every member of his large family.

Only then did we begin to talk of the tragedy of Richard M. Nixon. How it was all so unnecessary if the President had only openly laid all the cards on the table two years earlier. "The truth," Reuben said, reaching into his store of Biblical lore, "shall make you free." (John 8:32)

Though the Major had seen a friend he had long admired go down in disgrace, the prospect of a new beginning, an era of consultation, cooperation and openness under Jerry Ford brought forth a glow of anticipation on the face of the rugged Republican patriarch.

For Reuben Hollis Fleet there were few 'new beginnings' in life. His 88 years had been one headlong, untiring plunge forward. There was so much to accomplish and so little time to achieve all the goals he set for himself.

Purposeful activity was at the very heart of his dynamic career. Still there were, and are, reflective moments.

William Wagner

THE CONTEMPLATIVE Reuben Fleet
Palm Springs, March 1974

From his winter home at Palm Springs, the Major—after his daily third-of-a-mile swim—recently wrote us that "I now study the Bible and other religious works as is proper for a man whom God has spared and guided within 16 days of his 88th birthday."

Being around the tall, erect octogenarian—especially seeing him in profile, head thrust forward, keen eyes glinting—is to be reminded of the proud American eagle. It is a fitting description, for Reuben gave his country wings needed to win the war, and throughout his useful life the kind of resolute determination that made his beloved America great.

. . . IN PROFILE, HEAD THRUST FORWARD, keen eyes glinting—is to be reminded of the proud American eagle.

On the terrace of his Point Loma home, Reuben Hollis Fleet surveys the world against a background of runways on North Island where he had learned to fly six decades earlier.

HOMEWARD BOUND ON THE LAST FLIGHT   Al Saiget

AVIATION HALL OF FAME

No honor that came Reuben Fleet's way was more deserved or more appreciated by the honoree than election by his contemporaries to the Aviation Hall of Fame.

With rare anticipation the Major looked forward to the recognition he was to receive on November 22, 1975 at Dayton, Ohio where he had served the then Army Air Service from 1919 to 1922. And it pleased him greatly that the presentation was to be made by an old and valued friend, General George C. Kenney.

This final honor eluded the rugged individualist and aviation pioneer by a mere 24 days. In his place, sons David Girton Fleet and Preston Mitchell Fleet accepted the award posthumously for their father.

Major Reuben Hollis Fleet, vigorous and alert to the end, passed away at San Diego at age 88 on October 29, 1975.

APPRECIATION

As a youngster breaking into the newspaper game 50 years ago we soon learned the difference between research and plagiarism. "Research," we were told, "is plagiarizing from several sources."

While others—to whom we are indeed indebted—have compiled useful background information on Reuben Fleet and on Consolidated Aircraft, most of our material came from the Major himself.

For months, each Tuesday and Thursday at 11 a.m. we tape-recorded in-depth interviews with 'Major' (as we always called him) since we wanted this book to be, as much as possible, his own story.

Still, we have benefited greatly from library reference material and from the work of others, although space permits mention of only a small percentage of them. These we particularly thank —

Members of the Fleet family—and the Major's secretary, Martha Green, and financial assistant, Russ Stanberry.

Many friends at General Dynamics/Convair including Nelson Fuller and Howard Welty who compiled an excellent historical reference, based in large measure on original company records which Gordon Jackson thoughtfully saw were saved from the corporate trash barrel. For access to these records we are indebted to Dean McCoy, Jack Love, Angie Holmes and Betty Jones.

Mention should also be made of the helpful executives and staffs of the organizations we visited in the course of our research. Among these are Louis S. Casey of the National Air and Space Museum, Smithsonian Institution; the Air Force Audio-Visual Service; the National Archives; Col. Bernie Bass and Royal Frey of the Air Force Museum; and Brewster Reynolds of the San Diego Aero-Space Museum.

Tape-recorded interviews were also helpful; especially those provided by Fleet's longest and closest associate, I. M. (Mac) Laddon. Dr. Murray Green, Air Force historian, generously made available a significant 1970 interview with Gen. Jimmy Doolittle, Mac Laddon and Reuben Fleet. Another recorded interview with Fleet, by E. W. Robischon of the Smithsonian, proved helpful as did the personal recollections of Gen. Leigh Wade, Col. Ralph O'Neill, Tom Bomar, Felix Rossoll, Col. Owen S. Clarke and others who are mentioned throughout the text.

Supplementary material and photos came from many sources—Capt. Ed Betts of TWA; Bob McGuire of the Liberator Club; Larry Booth of the Title Insurance and Trust Company, San Diego; Warren S. Shipp; and Samuel S. Kloda of the Canadian Aviation Historical Society.

In the physical production of the book we are indebted to those who typed their hearts out preparing the manuscript—Lora, Kathy, Jan, Audrey—and to those who helped in other ways—Terry and Peggy. Special mention, too, goes to Robert J. Stewart for the fine quality of the photographs.

For our turn-of-the-century research on Washington Territory we are indebted to Mrs. Rosalie Spellman of the Public Library at Aberdeen and to Jane Goldberg of the Aberdeen Daily World; also V. I. Whitney of Montesano and Bud Pritchard of the Montesano Vidette. William D. Jones made available his Grays Harbor, Washington, historical photo collection for our use.

For material on Culver Military Academy we acknowledge the help of David Gaskill, and for that on the World War I Gosport Flying School in England, the interested assistance of John W. R. Taylor, editor of Jane's 'All the World's Aircraft.'

Lastly, we acknowledge with appreciation the editorial guidance of Keith Monroe, an old 'student' of ours in the field of aviation public relations.

William Wagner

December 1975
San Diego, California

CONSOLIDATED AIRCRAFT
INDEX

The Story of
CONSOLIDATED PLANES

PT-6		see Page **135** and 150
N2Y-1		see Page **136**
PT-11 ⎫		
PT-12 ⎬	(Model 21)	**167, 168**; also 170, 232
BT-7 ⎭		
N4Y-1		see Page **168**

OBSERVATION/TRAINING

O-17	Courier	**36, 37**; also 131
O-19	(Thomas-Morse)	**148**; also 130, 167, 169, 232
Y10-41 ⎫	(Thomas-Morse) ⎫	
(XO-932) ⎭	(Model 23) ⎭	**169, 170**

PERSONAL/TRANSPORT (Single Engine)

	(Model 10)	**131-132**
Y1C-11 ⎫	Fleetster ⎫	**153-157**; also 126-129, 140, 161,
Y1C-22 ⎭	(Models 17, 20) ⎭	167, 178, 179, 221, 244

PURSUIT/ATTACK/BOMBER (Single Engine)

XP-13	Thomas-Morse ⎫ Viper ⎭	**168-170**
XBY-1	Fleetster ⎫ (Model 18) ⎭	**168-170**; also 155
XB2Y-1	Thomas-Morse ⎫ (Model 24) ⎭	**169-170**
Y1P-25 ⎫		
P-30 ⎬		**170, 171, 184, 185**; also 180
PB-2A ⎬		
A-11 ⎭		

SEAPLANES

	Admiral	**112-117**; also 120, 121, 129, 158, 162, 164
XPY-1	Commodore ⎫ (Model 16) ⎭	**117-129**; also 140, 158, 161, 162, 167
P2Y-1 ⎫		**158-166**; also 117, 185, 186, 170, 178
P2Y-2 ⎬	Ranger	198, 214, 218, 219, 233
P2Y-3 ⎭		
XP3Y-1 ⎫		Design and production - **177-180, 185, 186**;
PBY-1 ⎬	**Catalina**	also 158, 167, 198, 213-219, 241, 252-254
thru ⎬	**(Model 28)**	Mass delivery flights - **187-190**; also 197, 233
PBY-5 ⎭		In combat - **217, 247-251, 259-264**; also 272
PBY-5A ⎫	Catalina	**16-217**; also 254, 262, 263
OA-10 ⎭	Amphibian	

	'Commercial' **PBY Catalinas** **(Model 28)**	**190-196**; also 216, 233, 245
PB2Y-1 thru PB2Y-5	**Coronado** **(Model 29)**	**198-201, 264**; also 185, 204, 208, 213, 216, 247, 253, 254
P4Y-1	**Corregidor** **(Model 31)**	**204-206**; also 208, 213, 216, 218, 253-255

LANDPLANE BOMBERS AND TRANSPORTS (Multi-engine)

XP-496	**Guardian** **(Model 11)**	**109-112**
B-24	**Liberator** (Model 32)	Design and production - **207-213, 218-222,** **225-228, 257**; also 252-255, 241, 279, 280 In combat - **228, 259-263**; also 227, 233, 234, 265-275
LB-30 (British)	Liberator	**212, 218**; also 226, 227, 228, 265
C-87 RY-2	Liberator Express	**252, 257**
PB4Y-1	Navy Liberator	**253, 257**; also 265
PB4Y-2 RY-3	Privateer	**253, 256**, 257, 263, 264, 280

(Other versions of B-24 Liberator included AT-22, C-109, F-7, XB-41 - see page 257)

B-32	Dominator (Model 33)	**254-257, 272-274**, 229, 234, 280
B-36	Intercontinental Bomber (Model 36)	229, 240, 254, 258, 282
XC-99	(Model 37)	**258**

GENERAL INDEX

For all references to Consolidated corporation, Consolidated planes, the company's subsidiaries and predecessor companies including Gallaudet, Dayton-Wright and Thomas-Morse, see 'CONSOLIDATED INDEX' immediately preceding this General Index.

A

B

C

H

I

J

M

N

S

T

X

Y

*Printed by Aero Publishers, Inc., Fallbrook, California, on
80 lb. Quintessence paper produced by Northwest Paper
Division of Potlatch Corporation and distributed by Ingram
Paper Company.*